modern

FORTRAN 77

for Scientists and Engineers

modern FORTRAN 77

for Scientists and Engineers

PETER B. WORLAND
University of Wisconsin, Oshkosh

HARCOURT BRACE JOVANOVICH, PUBLISHERS
and its subsidiary, Academic Press

San Diego   New York   Chicago   Austin   Washington, D.C.
London   Sydney   Tokyo   Toronto

Published in Association with Ablex Publishing
Corporation, Norwood, New Jersey

Cyber 205 is a registered trademark of Control Data Corp.
IBM is a registered trademark of International Business Machines Corp.
VAX is a registered trademark of Digital Equipment Corp.
CRAY-2 and CFT are registered trademarks of Cray Research, Inc.
RM/FORTRAN, RMFORT and PLINK86 are registered trademarks of
Austec, Inc.
IMSL is a registered trademark of IMSL, Inc.
UNIX is a registered trademark of AT&T

Throughout this book and in Appendix C, syntax charts are reproduced
with permission from American National Standards Institute
publication ANSI X3.9-1978 (Appendix F), Copyright 1978 by the
American National Standards Institute. Copies of this standard may be
purchased from the American National Standards Institute at 1430
Broadway, New York, NY 10018.

ISBN: 0-15-561156-9
Library of Congress Catalog Card Number 88-81837

Printed in the United States of America

To the programmers in my life
Development: Mary, Harry, Kate, and Helen
Maintenance: Nancy, Todd, and Dana

FORTRAN is an evolving language. In 1958, it became the first high-level computer language generally available. The 1966 ANSI Standard FORTRAN (FORTRAN 66 or FORTRAN IV) was a significant improvement over the first version, and the 1977 standard corrected many of the deficiencies of FORTRAN 66. The block IF structure and CHARACTER variables are examples of two such improvements. The 1977 version encompassed some of the more powerful features of Pascal (the block IF) and surpassed Pascal in others (CHARACTER string manipulation). The next version in the evolution of the FORTRAN language, the ANSI-proposed standard 8X, is due for release soon as a new standard (FORTRAN 88?). It is expected to include array-processing statements, recursion, and machine-independent hardware references (e.g., DIGITS, for the number of significant digits in the computer). One of the aims of this book is to provide for the transition from FORTRAN to the FORTRAN 8X version.

Some academic professionals in computer science see FORTRAN as an outmoded language, unsuitable for the primary teaching of structured programming. They believe Pascal and its variants to be clearly superior for this purpose, and they have a point. However, for a number of important reasons, we must continue to teach FORTRAN. FORTRAN is needed for mathematical computation; it was designed for that purpose, and it remains the best widely available language that provides for easily used representations of powerful mathematical relationships. Furthermore, a large, and ever-growing volume of FORTRAN code requires continuing support. Many subprograms for engineering, scientific, and general computational problems require FORTRAN programs to drive them. A number of scientific and engineering journals accept algorithms written in FORTRAN for publication. Since its general introduction in 1958, a tremendous amount of software has been developed in the language. That software volume continues to grow, and FORTRAN 77 compilers are now available on systems ranging from personal computers to such supercomputers as the Cray 2 and the CDC Cyber 205. FORTRAN continues to be the language of choice for solving engineering, mathematical, or scientific problems on a digital computer. Finally, this and other textbooks attest to the fact that it is easy to do structured programming in FORTRAN. It seems clear that powerful features will continue to be added to FORTRAN and that it will not become outmoded.

Because this textbook is based on two basic premises of the current FORTRAN market, it differs from most textbooks on FORTRAN 77 in two fundamental respects. First, it assumes that the student has some familiarity with another computer language, such as BASIC or Pascal. This is a reasonable assumption because the trend in colleges and universities is toward using a language other than FORTRAN for introductory programming courses; students will, therefore, learn FORTRAN as a second (or third) language. Additionally, most college and university students with technical interests will have had some prior exposure to programming.

Second, this book is written primarily for students of engineering, mathematics, and science (including computer science), and all the examples and exercises are taken from those disciplines. For example, problem topics include trajectories, optics, numerical integration, root finding, systems of linear equations, simulations, and chemistry data bases. This approach follows from a belief that to solve a problem on a computer, one should use the language most appropriate to the problem. FORTRAN remains the principal programming language for computation and the universal programming language of the scientific community.

This book is appropriate for a one-quarter or one-semester course on FORTRAN 77 or as part of a more comprehensive course on computer languages. Because of its emphasis on computation, it is also appropriate as a companion text in a numerical analysis course. This textbook could, for example, be used in a lab in which numerical problems are solved via FORTRAN programs. It is also ideal for self-study or for anyone who wants an overview of FORTRAN. Finally, it can be used as the textbook for a FORTRAN-based introductory programming course, if the instructor provides some supplementary material or if some knowledge of another programming language is a prerequisite.

FEATURES

Computational Approach

The main objective of this textbook is to prepare students to use FORTRAN 77 to solve computational problems. The following features support this objective:

1. *Emphasis on subprograms.* Solving most real-world computational problems is likely to involve the use of existing packages of high-quality software such as IMSL and LINPACK. Since these packages are used in the form of subprograms, the use of subprograms has been emphasized; they are introduced very early in the text (Chapter 4), and Chapter 7 describes subprograms completely, along with the use of some of these packages.

2. *Elementary numerical analysis.* Some numerical analysis has been included in order to make the student aware of some of the basic problems inherent in the use of finite-precision arithmetic.

3. *Debugging.* One full chapter (Chapter 6) is devoted to the topics of error avoidance, detection, and correction. These very important topics for the scientific programmer are usually glossed over or omitted in introductory programming textbooks.

4. *Efficiency.* Since efficiency is often a major concern in solving computational problems, this book includes a section (Chapter 11, Section 2) that describes techniques for writing efficient programs in FORTRAN.

5. *Supercomputers.* Because of both recent and potential growth of vector supercomputers, this book includes a section (Chapter 11, Section 3) on the use of FORTRAN techniques for these machines.

6. *Simplified I/O.* List-directed I/O is used through Chapter 8 to allow the student to concentrate on the use of FORTRAN for solving problems. Formatting details are deferred to Chapter 9, when the student should have a good understanding of the language as a whole.

Prerequisite Assumptions

Because a prerequisite language is assumed, the presentation can be concise without any loss of clarity. And questions such as "What is a computer program?" and "What is a variable?" are avoided. At the same time, the book's presentation is such that only a very modest overview of programming is needed to learn FORTRAN.

Pedagogy

Several unique approaches are used to teach the language.

1. *Early presentation.* Complete programs are presented early in the text, along with corresponding explanations. Such programs can be very helpful models for writing new programs. Although the examples require no more than high school algebra for understanding, a number of the exercises require calculus to be fully appreciated.

2. *Introduction by examples.* Each language element is introduced by a set of examples and followed by its syntactic definition. Teaching by example is always effective for programming languages.

3. *Syntax charts.* The syntax is defined by means of compactly represented syntax charts. Commonly used to define the syntax of Pascal, such charts significantly reduce the volume of explanation that would otherwise be required to define clearly the language elements. In this case, a "chart" is indeed worth a thousand words.

4. *Batch and interactive mode.* Since FORTRAN programs are used in both batch and interactive modes, the book tries to preserve a balance between these approaches. Therefore, some examples are written as batch programs while others are written for interactive use.

5. *Modern presentation.* References to card decks, flowcharts, and other outmoded tools have been avoided in favor of terminals, pseudocode, and the like.

6. *Example programs.* Some textbooks use many complete but trivial examples to introduce a simple concept or a single statement type. Others provide lengthy, complex examples that tend to overwhelm the student. The numbered examples in this textbook are moderate in length and appropriate to the material being studied and to the intended audience.

Modern Structured Programming

The book uses a modern approach to teaching FORTRAN programming.

1. *Structured programming.* Example programs are well structured, with complete documentation. Structured programming and modularity concepts—given the early introduction of subprograms—are emphasized throughout the book. For example, loops are implemented as either DO loops, WHILE loops, or REPEAT loops. GOTO statements are used only to implement the latter two types of structures, but the often-accepted practice of using a GOTO as a "break" statement to exit from a DO loop is also described. All variables are declared and explicitly typed, even though this is not required in FORTRAN. Where it is instructive to present program development, it has been presented in a top-down, modular fashion using a simple pseudocode. These examples should help to instill, or reinforce, good programming habits in the attentive student.

2. *Transportability.* A strong emphasis is placed on transportability issues. It is important for students to be aware of these issues early in their education.

3. *Style guides.* Most sections conclude with a style guide that summarizes suggested programming techniques described earlier. These guides promote good programming style and avoid potential errors.

Complete FORTRAN 77 Coverage

Unlike most textbooks on FORTRAN, this one presents the FORTRAN 77 language in complete detail. Except where noted, the book adheres strictly to the *full* ANSI FORTRAN 77 Standard (ANSI X3.9—1978). This insures that the examples will run on virtually any system with a full standard FORTRAN 77 compiler. It also promotes good programming habits in that it encourages students to write programs with portability in mind. WHILE and REPEAT loops are discussed, but the student is warned that they are not part of the standard; to maintain portability the loops must be constructed using GOTO statements. Each of the examples in the text was compiled and executed using the F77 compiler on a DEC VAX 11/750 computer, and again using Ryan-McFarland's FORTRAN 77 compiler, RM/FORTRAN, on an IBM PC. Both compilers encompass the full FORTRAN 77 language.

FORTRAN 8X

This textbook is written to provide a smooth transition from FORTRAN 77 to the next ANSI standard, which will be based on FORTRAN 8X. The 8X version will keep FORTRAN 77 in its entirety as a subset. However, it will refer to some elements, such as PAUSE and EQUIVALENCE, as *deprecated* features, targeted for omission from the 9X version. Although this book avoids the use of these features where possible, they are still presented late in the book (Chapter 11, Section 1) because students may be required to read *existing* code at some point, and because FORTRAN 77 will be the version used for some years to come. Furthermore, 8X is still not in its final form, and it must still be accepted by a large segment of the computing community (IBM for one).

Student Aids

Several features are to be noted that will assist the student in learning the language:

1. *Abundant exercises.* There are approximately 250 exercises for review and practice at the ends of the chapters. They vary in difficulty, some requiring a short answer and others requiring programs of varying length. They are also grouped according to the corresponding section within each chapter. And a number of exercises require the students to modify or improve an example in some way.

2. *Reference textbook.* Each of the language elements is highlighted in the margin, making the element easy to find. This feature, together with the complete presentation of the language and the numerous examples given with each of the language element definitions, makes the textbook suitable as a reference.

3. *Appendixes.* Appendix A contains tables of the ASCII, EBCDIC, and CDC Scientific character sets. Appendix B contains a complete table of the intrinsic functions for the full ANSI FORTRAN 77 language, including the generic and specific function names (a table of the most common functions is introduced in Chapter 2). For ease of reference, Appendix C contains a complete listing of the syntax charts that appear in the body of the textbook, in alphabetical order by language element. Appendix D contains the answers to the starred (*) exercises.

Instructor Aids   Two aids are available to assist the instructor in teaching the course.

1. *Instructor's manual.* An instructor's manual is available from the publisher. It includes transparancy masters of most of the examples and language element definitions, answers to all of the unstarred exercises, and chapter tests with solutions.

2. *Software.* An IBM PC–compatible diskette contains the source code and executable module for each of the numbered examples in the textbook. These examples were compiled and linked using Ryan-McFarland's FORTRAN 77 compiler RMFORT and linkage editor PLINK86. The instructor could use the diskette to provide in-class demonstrations or to provide students with copies of the examples that could subsequently be modified or improved according to a given exercise.

ACKNOWLEDGMENTS

I would like to thank the following outstanding reviewers who evaluated the manuscript at various stages of development and who provided many helpful suggestions:

Jacquelyn Jarboe, University of Wisconsin—Milwaukee; John B. Lane, Edinboro University of Pennsylvania; Paul W. Ross, Millersville University of Pennsylvania; and Dale Shaffer, Lander College.

I would also like to thank Professor Karl Knight, Gustavus Adolphus College, for the idea for Example 4.3; Richard J. Bonacci, Computer Science Editor at Harcourt Brace Jovanovich, for his continued guidance and helpful suggestions; and Walter Johnson, President of Ablex Corporation, for his help in making the HBJ connection. Finally, I would like to thank my wife Nancy, and my children, Todd and Dana, for their great patience, understanding, and support when my free time became writing time for the book. Thanks too, Nancy and Dana, for typing the manuscript.

New programming languages continue to be introduced, others die out for lack of use, while still others, such as FORTRAN, evolve. Someone has said that "FORTRAN will be around until the last engineer dies." I believe that it will be around until the last computer stops running.

Peter B. Worland

Contents

modern
FORTRAN 77

for Scientists and Engineers

In this chapter you will get an overview of the features of this book and the entire FORTRAN programming process. Depending on your background, you may be able to skip some of this material. For example, you could omit the overview of job control if you are already familiar with the computer system you will be using. However, to prepare yourself for the rest of the text, be sure to study the most important parts of this chapter: the material on syntax diagrams and the extensive explanation of the FORTRAN program in Example 1.1.

1.1 SOME FACTS YOU SHOULD KNOW ABOUT THIS BOOK

This book is designed to help you write FORTRAN programs and to use programs that others have written in order to solve problems on a digital computer. A quick survey of the book will give you a reading knowledge of the language and the ability to understand algorithms written in FORTRAN. However, to write effective FORTRAN programs on your own, you must practice with the language. Even experienced BASIC and Pascal programmers will have to write dozens of FORTRAN programs before they are proficient in FORTRAN.

The book assumes that you already have some experience with a programming language. Consequently we can get into FORTRAN early, and you will not have to sift through material that you already know. Furthermore, since FORTRAN is best suited for solving computational problems, all of the examples and exercises have that orientation.

Like BASIC and Pascal, FORTRAN has many versions, or *dialects*. Computer manufacturers often include so-called enhancements to these languages that make them more powerful: fewer statements may be required to solve a problem, or the program may run faster. However, employing such enhancements may mean that you will not be able to run that program on another manufacturer's computer. A FORTRAN program written for a VAX 11/780 computer may not produce the same results under Microsoft's FORTRAN running on an IBM PC. In fact, it may not even begin to execute; a valid statement on one system may produce a syntax error on another. What would you do if your employer or school changed computers, or if you changed jobs or schools? The work involved in converting a program from one computer to another may be staggering. Imagine a program that requires modifications to 5%

of its statements. Perhaps that doesn't seem too bad, until you learn that the program comprises 20,000 lines of FORTRAN code. Finding and changing all of the lines in error and testing the program to be sure that it works correctly could take you weeks or more.

To avoid these problems, you should try to write programs that are *transportable*, meaning that once they work correctly on one system, they will require few changes to work correctly on another.

In this book we use the full standard version of the language referred to as FORTRAN 77. FORTRAN spawned many dialects in the first 10 years of its existence. As transportability issues became critical, the American National Standards Institute (ANSI) formed a committee that eventually published the first FORTRAN standard, known then as FORTRAN IV and now as FORTRAN 66, after the year that the standard was accepted. Since then the strengths and weaknesses of the language have been debated, and the latest standard, FORTRAN 77, has emerged, encompassing a number of features lacking in the earlier version. In fact the groundwork has already been laid for the next standard, currently referred to as *FORTRAN 8X*, to be published in the late 1980s. The language is evolving. From this point on we will refer to FORTRAN 77 simply as FORTRAN, or as the Standard.

Writing your programs in strict conformity to the FORTRAN standard will not guarantee that they will be transportable. There are other issues, such as the word size of the computer, that can affect the program solutions and must therefore be accounted for. However, FORTRAN is available on most personal computers and every minicomputer and mainframe today, and transportability is a more likely possibility with FORTRAN than with other languages. However, be careful to note whether your version includes the full ANSI standard. ANSI also published a FORTRAN subset that omits a number of features in the full version. Transportability issues will be discussed in detail in chapter 5.

In this text we define each language *item*, or structure (the IF statement, for example), by presenting some concrete examples and a *syntax chart*, which is a compact graphic structure that describes the syntax of the item. These charts will help you understand the general rules for building FORTRAN statements. We use the variation specified by the ANSI standard publication.

For example, we can define a *digit* as

digit

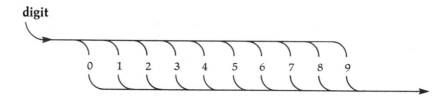

To see how this works, start in the direction of the arrow in the upper left of the chart and exit at the bottom right. It works as a kind of railroad track that you can traverse in the direction of the arrows. Forks in the path specify alternatives. As you follow a path, you will pass through one or more items written in lowercase letters, which represent items that have been defined previously, or items in uppercase or special characters, which must appear as written. In the above example as we move from left to right, we will pick up exactly one of the digits 0 through 9. Thus, a digit is defined as any one of these values. Note that each path is a "one-way street": you are not permitted to back up or to traverse a sharp corner. For example, in the following chart,

a legal traversal could produce one of the sequences AD, BD, or CD, but not ABCD, which would require the traversal of two sharp corners.

A path may loop back on itself, as in the following example:

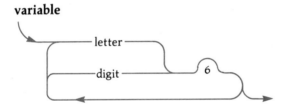

In words, a *variable* must start with a letter, followed by one or more letters or digits. The value 6 in the half-circle indicates that the path can be traversed a *maximum* of six times. This means that a variable can have at most 6 characters. Similarly, a number in a full circle indicates that the path must be traversed *exactly* that many times. Restrictions that cannot be included as part of the chart will be specified in remarks immediately following the chart.

1.2 AN OVERVIEW OF FORTRAN

FORTRAN is an acronym for FORmula TRANslation. That name is very appropriate since the language was designed for solving numerical computational problems, which arise primarily in science and engineering applications. After its introduction in the mid-fifties, it quickly became, and still is, the most widely used programming language for such applications.

It succeeded partly because "it got there first," and a very large volume of software has been developed that requires on-going support.

However, its success is also due to several nice language characteristics. First, it fits its design objective well by allowing users to express complicated mathematical formulas conveniently. Second, it is compact; one may solve complex problems with reasonably short programs. Third, the standardization of the language makes possible programs that are transportable, an advantage we have already explained. BASIC and Pascal programs, by comparison, are generally not transportable. Fourth, FORTRAN is sufficiently powerful to be used for problems other than numerical computation. For example, there are some large data processing systems written in FORTRAN, although languages exist that may be more suitable for these applications. Finally, to your benefit, you will discover that FORTRAN is easy to learn and use.

Before we look at specifics of the language, you should first have an understanding of the process involved in running, or executing, FORTRAN programs. It is likely that your first experience with programming was with an *interpreter*, especially if you used BASIC.

Any program written in FORTRAN, BASIC, Pascal, or other high-level language, which is referred to as the *source program*, must be translated in some manner into the machine language of the computer being used. An interpreter, which is also a program, in essence translates, or interprets, one source statement at a time and then executes it before retrieving the next statement to be processed. Figure 1.1 shows the overall operation of an interpreter.

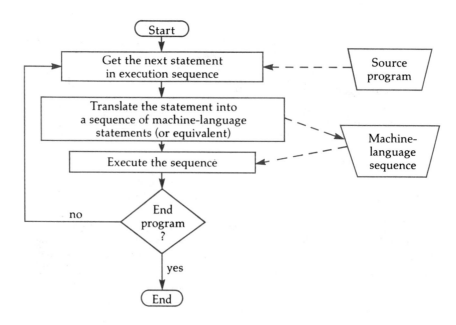

Figure 1.1
Operation of an interpreter.

The dashed arrows indicate input and output of the data for the interpreter (program statements), and the solid arrows show the flow of control. Note that retrieving the statements in execution sequence implies that statements inside loops must be interpreted over and over again as the interpreter cycles through the loops. For that reason interpreted programs tend to run slowly. Interpreters are widely used because they are relatively easy to write and because they generally produce excellent error diagnostics, making them valuable for teaching programming concepts.

FORTRAN programs, in contrast, like most versions of Pascal, are usually translated into machine language by a *compiler program*. Compilers operate basically as shown in Figure 1.2.

Note that the compiler is not involved at all in executing the program. It translates the *entire* program into an equivalent machine-language sequence called the *object program*. Then, if there are no errors, one or more additional steps take place before execution begins. Compiled programs tend to run much faster than interpreted programs because the translation process is not involved repetitively—each source statement is not retranslated as the program cycles through a loop. For a program that simulates the behavior of an aircraft for pilot training, execution speed is critical: the program must react almost instantaneously to the pilot's actions. Once a program has been tested and determined to be correct, it is stored and used in object form. The compiler is no longer needed, except to make required changes at a later time.

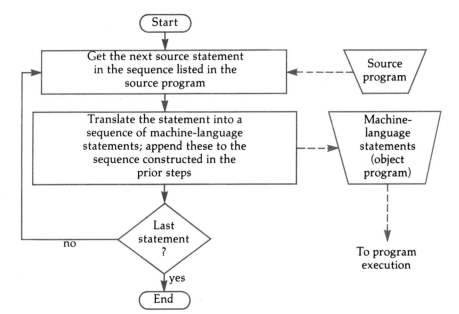

Figure 1.2
Operation of a compiler.

Keep in mind the separation of the compile step from the execution step. It will help you to understand the function of some of the FORTRAN statements and the behavior of programs that use these statements. FORTRAN statements are often classified as either *executable* or *nonexecutable*. An executable statement *does something* when it (that is, the equivalent machine-language code) is encountered during execution. An assignment statement, an IF statement, and a GOTO statement are examples of executable statements.

Nonexecutable statements (also called *specification statements*), on the other hand, provide information to the compiler for constructing the object program. For example, they tell the compiler how much memory space to allow for arrays, or what *type* a variable should be, such as a character or an integer. It is important for you to remember that whatever is specified by a nonexecutable statement is *fixed at compile time*. It *cannot* be changed during execution time. Just because a statement appears in the middle of a sequence of statements in the source program, it does not necessarily cause some action during execution.

To get a quick overview of FORTRAN before you get into the details, it will be helpful to study an example program. The following program computes the mean, maximum, minimum, and range of the positive values in a collection of numbers. It first reads the numbers, placing the positive values into an array, and then computes the statistics. Sample output follows the program, but the input is not shown. The numbers in the column to the far left are not part of the program; they are used only for reference by the accompanying explanation. The term *line n* will mean the line in the program with reference number *n*, whereas the FORTRAN statements themselves will be referred to as *statements*. Thus, for example, we may refer to the IF statement in line 35, or to statement number 20 (part of the FORTRAN statement) in line 44.

This example and all programs in this book are written in uppercase letters. Some versions of FORTRAN allow the use of lowercase but this is not Standard, and some printers and terminals support only uppercase.

The *PROGRAM* statement in line 1 identifies the program by naming it (BSTATS in this case). This is a nonexecutable statement.

Lines 2 to 23 are *comments*, identified by the asterisk in the first position of each line. This first block of comments, called the *prologue*, is a convention that is used to name the author(s), describe the purpose and limitations of the program, define each of the variables, and provide other information.

Lines 24, 25, and 27 declare all of the variables used in the program. These statements serve the same purpose as the *type* statement in Pascal. Their use is optional in FORTRAN for scalar (nonarray) variables, but we strongly recommend this convention.

EXAMPLE 1.1

```
1         PROGRAM BSTATS
2    ************************************************************
3    * AUTHOR: J. BOGGS     3/86
4    * REVISED: P. CHEN     8/86
5    *
6    * THIS PROGRAM COMPUTES THE MEAN, MAXIMUM, MINIMUM, AND
7    * RANGE OF SELECTED REAL NUMBERS FROM A LIST OF VALUES PRO-
8    * VIDED ON THE DEFAULT INPUT UNIT.  THE INPUT VALUES MUST BE
9    * ENTERED ONE NUMBER PER LINE. POSITIVE VALUES ARE SELECTED.
10   *
11   * PARAMETERS AND VARIABLES:
12   * NMAX - MAXIMUM NO. OF SELECTED VALUES ALLOWED
13   * MAXST - MAXIMUM VALUE NOT COMPUTED (ZERO HERE)
14   * PVALS - ARRAY OF SELECTED VALUES
15   * MEAN - THE MEAN
16   * MAX - THE MAXIMUM
17   * MIN - THE MINIMUM
18   * RANGE - THE RANGE
19   * SUM - THE SUM OF THE SELECTED VALUES
20   * COUNT - THE TOTAL NUMBER OF SELECTED VALUES
21   * VALUE - THE INPUT VALUE
22   * N, I - LOOP AND ARRAY INDICES
23   ************************************************************
24         REAL MEAN, MAX, MIN, RANGE, SUM, COUNT, VALUE, MAXST
25         INTEGER N, I, NMAX
26         PARAMETER (NMAX = 500, MAXST = 0.0)
27         REAL PVALS(NMAX)
28
29         N = 0
30   *
31   * READ THE DATA AND STORE THE SELECTED VALUES IN PVALS
32   *
33   10    CONTINUE
34         READ (*,*,END = 20) VALUE
35         IF (VALUE .GT. MAXST) THEN
36            N = N + 1
37            IF (N .GT. NMAX) THEN
38               PRINT *, 'MAXIMUM NO. OF VALUES EXCEEDED'
39               STOP
40            END IF
41            PVALS(N) = VALUE
42         END IF
43         GOTO 10
44   20    CONTINUE
45   *
46   * COMPUTE SUM, MAX, MIN OF STORED VALUES
47   *
```

```
48              IF (N .EQ. 0) THEN
49                  PRINT *, 'NO SELECTED VALUES'
50                  STOP
51              END IF
52              MIN = PVALS(1)
53              MAX = PVALS(1)
54              SUM = PVALS(1)
55              DO 30 I = 2, N
56                  SUM = SUM + PVALS(I)
57                  IF (PVALS(I) .GT. MAX) MAX = PVALS(I)
58                  IF (PVALS(I) .LT. MIN) MIN = PVALS(I)
59      30      CONTINUE
60      *
61      * COMPUTE MEAN, RANGE AND PRINT RESULTS
62      *
63              COUNT = REAL(N)
64              MEAN = SUM / COUNT
65              RANGE = MAX - MIN
66              PRINT *, 'THE TOTAL NUMBER OF VALUES IS ', N
67              PRINT *, 'THE MEAN IS ', MEAN
68              PRINT *, 'THE MAX, MIN, RANGE ARE ', MAX, MIN, RANGE
69              END
```

Sample output:

```
THE TOTAL NUMBER OF VALUES IS 150
THE MEAN IS 72.5600
THE MAX, MIN, RANGE ARE 97.5000 41.0000 56.5000
```

The *REAL* statement in line 27 defines the size, or dimension, of the real array PVALS to have NMAX elements; in that sense it is performing the same function as a DIM statement in BASIC. N, I, and NMAX are *typed* as INTEGER variables and the others as REAL. Variables that store whole numbers (−5, 0, 7, etc.) are generally of type INTEGER. For you BASIC programmers, specifying the type of the variable is akin to denoting string variables by using names that end with a dollar sign.

Line 26 defines *parameters*: symbolic names for constants that are used in the program. NMAX, for example, represents the maximum number of positive values that can be processed by this program. The use of parameters simplifies some program revisions. Change the value of NMAX in line 26 and you change the number of values that the program can handle. This is equivalent to the *const* declaration in Pascal.

Line 29 is a simple assignment statement used to initialize the variable N to its starting value.

Lines 30 to 32 are comments to describe briefly the procedure that follows.

Line 33 marks the beginning of a loop. The number 10, called a *statement number*, is used as a reference point for the program to jump to. Statement numbers are similar to labels in Pascal and line numbers in BASIC, except they do not appear on every line, and they have nothing to do with statement ordering. The end of this loop is line 43, GOTO 10. The CONTINUE statement actually doesn't do anything during execution but acts essentially as a place marker to start the loop.

Line 34 is a FORTRAN READ statement. The number being read is assigned to the variable VALUE. This form of the READ accepts the data as *format-free*, which means, for example, that the input numbers may appear anywhere on the input line. The END = 20 clause forces a jump to statement number 20 (to line 44) when the program runs out of input data and acts, in effect, as an exit from the loop.

Lines 35 to 42 represent a *block IF* statement. If the condition specified inside the parentheses is true, then all of the statements between the IF and the END IF (line 42) will be executed; otherwise they are skipped. In this case they are executed if VALUE is greater than (.GT.) MAXST (0). What would you expect the test for a VALUE less than 0 to look like? How about less than or equal to 0?

Inside the block IF, the variable N is increased by 1 in line 36. N represents the number of positive numbers stored. The block IF in lines 37 to 40 prints the error message (PRINT) on the standard output device, such as a terminal screen, and terminates the program (STOP) if there are more values than the program was designed to handle. If there is still room for the value, however, the program continues by storing the value in the Nth location in the array PVALS (line 41). Note the use of N as the *subscript* of the array.

The GOTO in line 43 jumps back to statement number 10 (line 33). In summary, lines 33 to 43 form a loop, with the END = option in the READ as the exit to line 44, which immediately follows the loop. If you have Pascal experience, you will be disappointed to learn that standard FORTRAN does not include the WHILE loop or its equivalent.

The block IF in lines 48 to 51 stops the program with an appropriate error message if there are no positive values at all.

In lines 52 to 53 the first value is copied to MIN and MAX, representing the smallest and largest values thus far encountered. It also becomes the initial value of SUM (line 54).

Lines 55 to 59 represent another loop, a so-called DO loop, which is similar to a FOR loop in Pascal or BASIC. In this case the number 30 indicates that the last statement, or *terminal statement*, of the loop is marked by the statement number 30. The loop proceeds with I = 2, then 3, and so forth up to and including N.

Within the DO loop, the sum of the array elements in PVALS is accumulated in SUM in line 56. This use of an assignment statement, in which the variable at the left of the = sign also appears on the right, is an example of *iteration*. The two IF statements in lines 57 and 58 are simpler than the block IF statements in lines 48 to 51. The statement following the parenthetical expression is executed only if the condition inside the parentheses is true. In this way MAX always holds the largest value examined so far in the array. The action of line 58 is similar for MIN.

Note that a CONTINUE statement represents the terminal statement of the DO loop. We will always use a CONTINUE statement this way as a matter of style.

The assignment statements in lines 63 to 65 compute the total number of values, the mean, and the range. Line 63 is not necessary since N also represents the number of values. However, observe that N is an integer variable and COUNT is real. As a convention, we will avoid mixing real and integer quantities in arithmetic expressions for reasons to be made clear later. Thus COUNT, which is assigned the real value corresponding to N by means of the function REAL, rather than N itself, is the divisor in line 64.

The results are printed out by the PRINT statements in lines 66 to 68. Sample output is shown following the program.

Finally, the END statement marks the physical end of the program, which terminates when it encounters the END statement during execution.

As you study this program, take note of its style. What are its desirable features?

1. It is *transportable*. It should compile and run on any computer with a FORTRAN 77 compiler.

2. It is *well documented*. The prologue is a cogent summary of the program, and other comments distributed at appropriate places assist the reader in understanding how it works.

3. It is *well structured*. All the variables are explicitly typed. Loops and IF-THEN blocks of statements are indented and easy to find. There are no GOTOs, except for line 43, which is necessary to implement the loop. You can read the program from top to bottom without jumping back and understand what it is doing. This is a good indicator of a well-structured program.

4. It is *easy to change*. The use of constants is minimized. You need modify only the PARAMETER statement to make the program work for 1000 numbers. How would you modify it to apply to numbers greater than 100?

5. The program *aims for generality*. It is essentially independent of the data—it works on a wide variety of data, not just a specific set. Minimizing the use of constants helps make this possible. This characteristic is particularly important for programs that will be run many times, because it eliminates the need for recompilation to fit the data.

6. The program is *robust*. This means that if it fails because of user error, such as providing an input list with too many values, it will halt under its own control and notify the user. That is the purpose of the IF-THEN blocks in lines 37 to 40 and 48 to 51. What will happen if the user provides only one positive value? No values?

Unless your program is to be a "one-shot" program—one that will be discarded after solving a given problem—you should write it with the above features in mind. Doing so consistently will help you develop the good habits that professional programmers must have. You will also help anyone—including yourself—who will use or modify the program in the future. Without adequate documentation, it is very easy to forget what a particular program does and how it works.

We will discuss style in detail later. For now you should use the program in Example 1.1 as a model for those you write as you study the forthcoming chapters.

1.3 THE FORTRAN LINE FORMAT

Unlike BASIC and Pascal, FORTRAN reserves certain columns, or line positions, of the lines in a source program for particular functions. The line format is basically a carry-over from the days when programs were punched on cards. A FORTRAN line consists of 80 columns, and its format is as follows:

1. *Column 1* is a *comment* indicator. Either an *asterisk* (∗) *or a letter C* in this column marks the line as a comment. FORTRAN does not process the information on a comment line but merely copies the line as is to the source program listing. We will use asterisks in this book.

2. *Columns 1 to 5* are used for *statement numbers*. A statement number, which is an unsigned integer in the range 1 to 99999, can be placed anywhere in this field; in this book all statement numbers start in column 1. Most statements do not need a statement number. They are used to enable the program to jump to the numbered statements by means of a GOTO or other branch statement. They also identify the last statement in certain loops (the DO loop) and statements that specify the formats of input and output data (the FORMAT statement). Except for FORMAT statements, no nonexecutable statement may have a statement number. Finally, no 2 statements in a program may have the same statement number.

3. *Columns 7 to 72* contain the FORTRAN statement, which may be

written free-form within these columns. Blanks are almost entirely ignored (except as part of a character string enclosed in quotes), even between characters in a variable name or between digits in a number. Thus, the statement

```
EN ER G Y = EPS + 1.    07 39 5
```

is processed the same as

```
ENERGY = EPS  +  1.07395
```

However, we strongly recommend an appropriate use of blanks. Don't write expressions like the first one above. Instead, precede and follow each keyword variable, operator, constant, and so forth with a blank. Doing so makes the statement much more readable, and some versions of FORTRAN actually require blanks around keywords, even though this is not part of the Standard. Second, indent statements to identify structure in the program, such as statements within loops or IF-THEN blocks (between the IF and END IF). Notice how the indentation used in Example 1.1 makes the program much easier to follow. You may be used to this if you have experience with a structured language like Pascal. In this text we indent 3 columns whenever we enter a structure, and we return to the original column when we exit. Some FORTRAN versions automatically indent for you on the source output listing, but this will not improve the clarity of source code that may require editing.

4. *Column 6* is a *continuation line* indicator. Sometimes we cannot fit a complete statement within columns 7 to 72. In that case simply place a character other than 0 in column 6 in the next and, if needed, successive lines, and the code that appears in columns 7 to 72 of these lines will be treated as part of the first line of the statement. Note that the first line of the statement must have a blank in column 6.
   For example,

```
X = Y + Z * (1. - RHO)
```

represents the same statement as

```
X = y + Z *
$    (1. - RHO)
↑
└── column 6
```

The Standard limits the number of continuation lines to 19. Although some programmers like to number consecutive continuation lines, we will use a dollar sign ($) for our continuation character to minimize confusion with the rest of the statement.

5. *Columns 73 to 80* are *not processed* by FORTRAN; if used, they are usually for program identification. They were originally used for sequence numbers of program cards in case someone dropped the deck.

Some versions of FORTRAN allow *free-format* representation of statements, but you should avoid this flexibility in order to comply with the Standard.

Style Guide:
1. Use blanks around keywords and other items to improve the readability of statements.
2. Indent within structures, such as loops, 3 or more columns.

1.4 RUNNING YOUR PROGRAM

The computer is a general-purpose machine. It is used by many people —often at the same time—for a great variety of tasks. A general-purpose language is required to tell it what to do.

In order to run a program you will need to know some computing procedures outside the realm of FORTRAN, such as how to enter your program into the computer or how to get a listing of the output. These procedures require the use of *Job Control Language* (JCL), sometimes called *control language*. JCL enables you to communicate with the *operating system*, which is the collection of software that controls the overall operation of the computer. The operating system and its accompanying JCL may be relatively simple, such as the Disk Operating System (DOS) for the IBM PC, or very complex, such as the Network Operating System (NOS) for CDC mainframe computers. This section gives a brief overview of the procedures you will need to run your programs, but because JCL varies greatly from system to system, you must obtain the necessary details locally.

The first step is to *log on* to the computer, which means getting the computer's attention so that it can provide you with the resources you need, such as computer memory, to do your work. On a personal computer this may involve nothing more than inserting a diskette into the computer and turning on the power. On a large, *time-shared* computer, to which many users have simultaneous access, you will need to enter your *account number* and *password* on a terminal. Your instructor or the computer center will provide you with these.

Next, you may want to create a *file*—a storage area for recording a copy of your program, input data, or other information—and to enter your program into it by means of an *editor*, a program that facilitates the entry and modification of text. Your editor may be language-specific, in that it expects only FORTRAN statements, or generic, which means that it can be used to edit any text file. If the editor is language-specific, it will help you by catching the syntax errors as you enter the statements; otherwise, the compiler will flag those that you miss.

How you run a program depends on the type of system you are using. In an *interactive* system, each JCL statement is executed as soon as you enter it. In a *batch* system a sequence of JCL statements, called the *job stream*, is submitted to the operating system, which executes them when it is ready. On a personal computer, you will probably carry out this process interactively.

To run your program *interactively:*

1. Compile your program. This step will require a JCL statement such as

   ```
   $FORTRAN   NAME
   ```

   where NAME is the name of the file containing the source program. You will need to repeat this process until you have corrected all of the syntax errors with your editor.
2. Load and execute your program using the appropriate JCL statement(s).

This actually involves several steps. Some systems may require separate statements, or the statements may be embedded in the compile statement. First, all of the necessary program components are combined into a single machine-language program, the object program. This includes the output from the compile step and the necessary routines from the *FORTRAN library*—for example, the machine-language code to compute the square root of a number. The library contains commonly used routines, such as input/output and math functions, to relieve the programmer of the burden of writing them. The actual execution of the program takes place after it is loaded into memory.

Input data can be supplied to the program at the keyboard during execution or can be read from a file. Note that if the object program is saved and no changes are required, the compile step is not necessary for repeated execution.

If you will be running your programs interactively, write your compile and load/execute JCL statements in the box at top of p. 15.

To run your program in *batch*, you must use the editor to create a job stream by including the appropriate JCL statements in the file with your program. The skeleton of a sample job stream is the following:

Skeleton of sample job stream	**Write your specific job stream here**
Job statement(s)	
FORTRAN compiler statement	
[FORTRAN program source]	
End-of-program statement	
Load/execute statement	
[Input data]	
End-of-data statement	
End-of-job statement	

The *job statement(s)* identifies the statements between itself and the *end-of-job* statement as the job to be processed. It includes pertinent information such as the job name, an account identifier that the job should be charged to (computer time costs money), the job's priority, and its time limit. An example of a job statement is:

```
$JOB TESTRUN SMITH PRI = 5 SEC = 20
```

In batch mode, JCL statements are also needed to mark the ends of sequences of lines: end-of-program, end-of-data, and end-of-job. These statements will have a simple form such as

```
$EOJ
```

Finally, the input data could be stored in a different file rather than as part of the job stream. Many variations of this sample stream are possible.

Once you have created the batch job stream, you can instruct the computer to execute it with another JCL statement.

This concludes the overview of the minimal steps necessary to run your FORTRAN programs. However, as you work on the computer, you will find it helpful to be able to list your source program, save a copy of the object program, copy all or part of your program, redirect output from the terminal screen to the printer, and erase a copy of a program that you no longer need. To accomplish these and other tasks you will have to further investigate the JCL of your particular computer.

Exercises

All of the exercises in this chapter are based on the material in Section 1.2.

1. What is a compiler? An interpreter?
2. What is a source program? An object program?
3. What does it mean for a program to be transportable?
4. Define an executable statement and give an example. Do the same for a nonexecutable statement.
*5. What characterizes a comment statement in a FORTRAN program?
6. Write FORTRAN statements to:
    *a. Declare that the variables ALPHA and BETA are integers.
    b. Add X to DSUM and store the result in Y.
    *c. Print the values of PROD and QUOT first on the same line, then on different lines.
    d. Store the average of A and B in C.
    *e. Declare DEL to be a real array of 1000 numbers.
    f. Define EPS to be a parameter equal to 10^{-3}.
    *g. Initialize STCNT to 1.
    h. Store the sum of the first 3 elements of the array PIC into SUM.
7. Write FORTRAN IF statements to:
    a. Set DIFF equal to A minus B if A is greater than B.
    b. Add X to SUM if I is equal to 0.
    *c. Set Y equal to the product of EPS times the difference between X1 and X2 if THRESH is greater than or equal to EPS.
    d. Add 1 to I, 2 to J, and 3 to K if XVAL is greater than YVAL.
    *e. Print the value of A divided by B if B is not 0.
    * f. Set X and Y to 0 if the difference between X and Y is less than EPS times 0.01.

*Solution to this exercise is given in Appendix D.

8. Write a loop to:
  *a. Read a sequence of 50 real values and accumulate their sum in XSUM.
  b. Compute the product of the first N positive integers. (Do it two different ways, once with a DO loop and once without.)
  *c. Set the first 100 elements of the array XMT to 0.

*9. State briefly what the following program does.

```
      INTEGER N, A, INT
      N = 0
      A = 0
      DO 10 I = 1, 1000
          READ (*, *, END = 20) INT
          IF (INT .LT. 0) N = N + INT
          A = A + INT
10    CONTINUE
20    CONTINUE
      PRINT *, N, A
      END
```

10. Enter the program in Example 1.1 using whatever editor you have available. Be sure that comments and statement numbers start in the first position, or column, on the line, and that the FORTRAN statements themselves start in column 7. Make intentional errors: modify words, change some of the values, and omit some lines. Observe the results for each change when you run the program. This exercise will help you to familiarize yourself with your editor, the program execution process, and compile-time and run-time FORTRAN error messages. Some particular changes are suggested in the exercises that follow, but you are encouraged to experiment on your own. You will need information from a local source, such as your instructor, on how to supply input data, how to use the editor, and other necessary JCL. The FORTRAN and operating system manuals should provide this information if you are using a personal computer.

11. Enter Example 1.1 exactly as given, run it, and observe the results. Run the (correct) program with
  a. No input values
  b. One positive value
  c. Only negative input values
  d. Ten values of varying sign

*12. Change the parameter NMAX to be equal to 5, and run the programs with more than 5 positive input values. What happens?

13. Remove line 36 from the program, run it, and observe the results. What was the function(s) of the deleted instruction?

14. Same question as Exercise 13 for line 40.

15. Same question as Exercise 13 for line 43.

16. Same question as Exercise 13 for line 65. What value prints for RANGE?

17. Take the END = 20 clause out of the READ statement in line 34. What happens? Why?

18. Remove line 29 from the program and run it. Are the results the same as in Exercise 12? Your answer could be yes or no depending on your system. To be safe you should always initialize all variables before you use them; for example, make sure they have a value before you use them on the right-hand side of an assignment statement.

*19. The text recommends using parameters in place of constants whenever possible. Why then is the initial value of N not parameterized; that is, why not set N = ZERO in line 29, where ZERO is a parameter?

20. Modify Example 1.1 to compute the same statistics for all values greater than −100. Note: don't forget one of the PRINT statements.

*21. Modify Example 1.1 to work for all values greater than 0 and less than 100.

22. Insert the following code after line 51.

```
*
*  SORT THE ARRAY INTO ASCENDING ORDER
*
        DO 26 I = 1, N - 1
          K = I
          DO 24 J = I + 1, N
            IF (PVALS(K) .GT. PVALS(J)) K = J
24        CONTINUE
          TEMP =   PVALS(I)
          PVALS(I) = PVALS(K)
          PVALS(K) = TEMP
26      CONTINUE
```

This procedure, called an *exchange sort*, sorts the array PVALS into ascending order. Given this addition, modify the program to:

a. Compute and print the **median** of the position values. The median is defined as that value in the array that is greater than half of the values and less than the other half. Given that the array of N values has been sorted, the median is defined as:

$$\text{Median} = \begin{cases} \text{PVALS}(N/2 + 1) \text{ if N is odd} \\ [\text{PVALS}(N/2) + \text{PVALS}(N/2 + 1)]/2 \text{ if N is even} \end{cases}$$

  b. Determine the maximum and minimum in a way different than in Example 1.1. You may wish to modify the prologue appropriately.
23. Describe briefly how the exchange sort given in Exercise 22 sorts the array PVALS into ascending order.

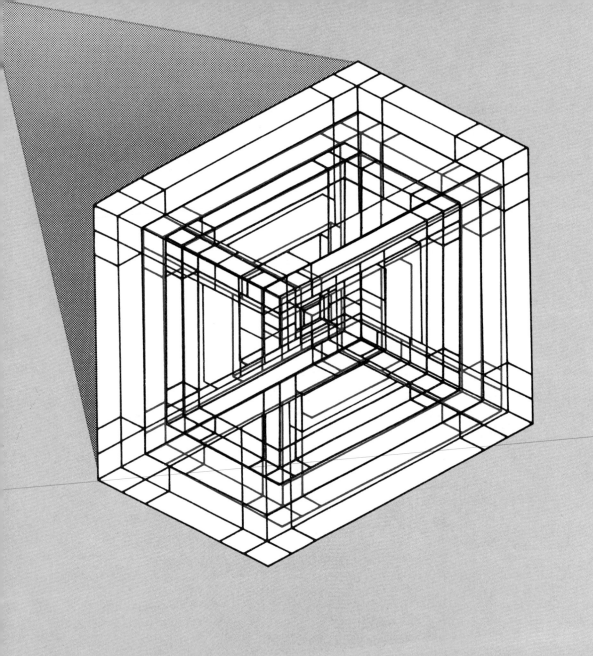

2 *Assignment Statements and List-Directed Input/Output*

This chapter introduces you to the building blocks of FORTRAN (e.g., constants and variables), the INTEGER and REAL type statements, END, PROGRAM, the arithmetic assignment statement, and simplified forms of the PRINT and READ statements. You can use these elements to build the skeletons of FORTRAN programs, albeit very simple ones. The approach here is somewhat formal in its use of syntax charts for definitions. Depending on your experience with another programming language, you may be able to skim over material that looks familiar to you. However, you should be careful to note differences.

Upon completion of this chapter you will be able to write programs to carry out hand-calculator types of computations; that is, to read data, compute a value, and print the result.

2.1 CONSTANTS AND VARIABLES

The set of valid characters in a FORTRAN program, the *character set*, consists of

- The uppercase letters A to Z
- The digits 0 to 9
- The special characters = + − * / ( ) , . $ ' (apostrophe) : and blank.

These are the characters used to write a program, not to be confused with character *data* for the program. This character set is somewhat limited compared to that of Pascal, for example. References are often made to *alphanumeric characters*, which are either letters or digits.

Characters outside of the character set are illegal in FORTRAN programs, except for comment lines and in character strings (see Section 2.8). To be on the safe side, you should stick to the character set in comments as well.

Except where it is noted, blanks have no meaning in a program. Their use in FORTRAN is primarily to separate items in a line to promote readability.

A *symbolic name* is used to represent a variable, an array, and other FORTRAN items. It is constructed according to the syntax chart that follows the examples.

Symbolic Name

Examples:

```
A    EXPT    PVALS    R12345    ROOT    X2A    END
```

symbolic name

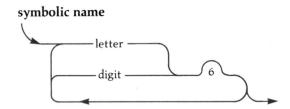

Does this look familiar? It should, since it is the same chart used in Chapter 1 to define a variable. Since a variable is represented by a symbolic name, the charts are the same, although symbolic names can represent other entities too.

From this chart we see that 23HIKE, FOR.5, and FAHRENHEIT are illegal symbolic names. The Standard limits them to 6 characters, although some compilers will allow more. Note too that the Standard allows symbolic names that are also FORTRAN *keywords*, such as END, but some compilers will not accept them. It is best to avoid them anyway, since their use is confusing. Be sure to use names that are meaningful in order to promote program clarity. The name STDEV is clearly a better name for the standard deviation of a set of numbers than is X or SALLY.

Style Guide:
1. Avoid using FORTRAN keywords as symbolic names.
2. Use meaningful symbolic names.

Before we define constants, we should mention that each constant and variable in a program has a *data type* associated with it, which may affect the interpretation of the operation involving these items. The most usual data types in BASIC are numeric and string; among those in Pascal are char, boolean, and integer. There are six types of data in FORTRAN; you have already encountered two of them, INTEGER and REAL. We will define the others and the corresponding constants and variables in later chapters. Assigning data types to variables is covered in a later section in this chapter.

Unsigned Integer Constant

We will define constants in terms of an *unsigned integer constant*.

Examples: 23   1   0   78156   054

unsigned integer constant

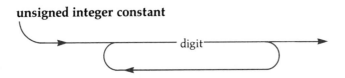

We use the following to define an *integer constant*.

Examples: 17   −123   +4000

integer constant

Remarks: In words, an integer constant is an unsigned integer constant optionally preceded by a sign. No limit is given on the number of digits because that value is computer-dependent. Typical limits are ±32,767 for microcomputers and minicomputers, ±2^{31} − 1 (about 2 × 10^9) for IBM compatible mainframe computers, and ±2^{63} − 1 (about 9 × 10^{18}) for some supercomputer models. Your FORTRAN manual should contain this information.

We can now define a *real constant* in terms of these:

Examples:

```
3.5      −0.712    .000827    0.    +377.
6.2E−8   −27E3     3.14E+15
```

real constant

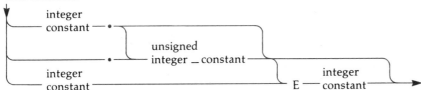

This chart is more complex than the others you've seen so far. Check it out by following the paths to verify that each of the preceding examples is valid.

Observe that there are two basic forms of a real constant, one with an *E* and one without. If *E* is absent, a decimal point must be present for the constant to be real. Constants with an *E* are said to be in *exponential notation*. Thus, 3.7 × 10^5 can be written as 3.7E5 (or .37E6, or 37E4, or

37.E+4, and so forth). Because of this facility for moving the decimal point, reals are also referred to as *floating-point numbers.*

Integers and reals differ in their internal computer representation and in their computation. It is very important to remember that 7 is different than 7. or 7.0. One of the most common errors, for both novice and experienced FORTRAN programmers, is to use an integer where a real should have been specified, and vice versa. Generally, you should use integers for counting and subscripting, for dealing with integer data such as test scores, or for algorithms that require integer arithmetic (i.e., computing the greatest common divisor of two positive integers).

2.2 ARRAYS

We have already defined variables. For convenience, we now define a restricted form of an array. This will enable us to use some arrays early in the text without the details of the full definition. Recall that an array is a collection of variables with the same name, and that each member of the array, or *array element*, is distinguished by its subscript(s).

**Array
Declarator**

An array is defined by means of an *array declarator*, which specifies, in a type statement, the name of the array and the range of its subscript(s).

> **Examples:** MEASR(50)   X(1000)   VOLTS(220)

array declarator (restricted)

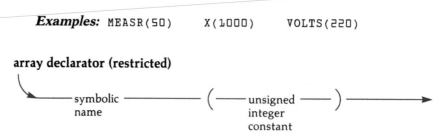

This defines a one-dimensional array in which valid subscripts range from 1 to the integer constant in the parentheses. The array X, for example, can store up to 1,000 values: X(1), X(2), . . . , X(1000). Some readers may not be familiar with more general representations of arrays; we will cover them fully in a later chapter.

2.3 PARAMETERS

You may not be familiar with the next building block, the *parameter*, sometimes referred to as a *symbolic constant*. It is equivalent to a symbolic constant in Pascal and should not be confused with Pascal's subprogram parameters. Like variables and constants, a parameter has a type associated with it. A parameter looks like a variable but behaves like a constant. Once defined, it *cannot* be redefined during execution of the program; its value is set during compilation.

A parameter is assigned a value by means of the nonexecutable *PARAMETER* statement.

PARAMETER Statement

> *Examples:*
> ```
> PARAMETER (PI = 3.1416)
> PARAMETER (MAX = 5000, MIN = 1000, AVG = 2124.5)
> PARAMETER (AREA = 625.0 * 625.0)
> PARAMETER (TWOPI = PI + PI)
> ```

PARAMETER statement

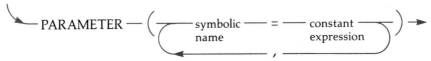

Remark: The symbolic name represents the parameter. Here the term *constant expression* means an arithmetic expression consisting only of constants or *other parameters that have been previously defined*, as in the fourth example, or of both. TWOPI will have the value 6.2832. No variables, array elements, or function references (to be defined later) are allowed in the defining expression. The parameter being defined and all the constants and parameters in its defining expression should be of the same type.

Note that the Standard does not impose a limit on the number of parameters per statement, but a particular compiler may have one.

Parameters can simplify program modifications. Suppose the same constant occurred dozens of times throughout a program. We would have to locate and modify each occurrence if a change were necessary. With a parameter, only a single PARAMETER statement need be changed. It is also easy to change the precision of a parameter. For example, we may easily modify PI to be 3.1415926.

Parameters can also enhance the legibility of a program by providing constants with meaningful names. We will point out examples of appropriate parameter usage throughout the book. Note also Exercise 20 in Chapter 1.

Style Guide: Use a parameter in place of a constant:
   1. For array sizes (dimensions) in array declarators
   2. If the constant is used frequently in a program
   3. If the constant might be changed when the program is modified
   4. To improve the readability of the program

Array Element

In a like manner we can define an *array element* for this restricted array. Array elements refer to the individual elements in the array.

Examples: `MEASR(1)`   `X(5)`   `VOLTS(N)`   `DEV(I + 1)`

array element (restricted)

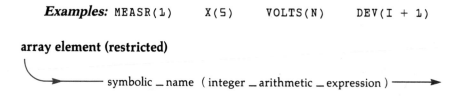

symbolic _ name (integer _ arithmetic _ expression)

Remark: The item enclosed in parentheses must be of type INTEGER. (See below on how to specify a data type). This item is the *subscript*, which must evaluate to a value less than or equal to the subscript in the corresponding array declarator.

If N has the value 100 in the above example, then VOLTS (N) represents the 100th element in the array VOLTS. In the last example, the subscript is an *arithmetic expression*, I + 1, where it is assumed that I is of type INTEGER. We assume here that you have an intuitive concept of arithmetic expressions, which will be defined formally later in this chapter, from your prior experience.

The following program segment illustrates the definition and use of arrays, although some of the details have yet to be covered.

```
INTEGER LEVELS(50)
REAL VOLTGE(1000),  AMPS(1000), R
.
.
LEVELS(I) = LEVELS(I) + 1
.
.
VOLTGE(I+1) = AMPS(I) * R
.
.
```

The arrays VOLTGE and AMPS are defined as REAL arrays of 1000 elements each, and LEVELS is an integer array of 50 elements (see the next section). In the body of the program, the value 1 is added to the Ith element of LEVELS, and the I+1st element of VOLTGE is set equal to the product of the Ith element in the array AMPS times the real variable R.

Like constants, variables, arrays, and parameters have a type associated with them. We will review how to specify their type next.

2.4 SPECIFYING THE DATA TYPE

The type associated with a given constant is determined by the form of the constant; for example, 27 is an integer and 27.0 is real. How do you specify the type for variables, arrays, and parameters?

It turns out that you can do this either explicitly or implicitly. To declare variables, arrays, and parameters explicitly as integers, we use the *INTEGER statement*.

Examples:
```
INTEGER X
INTEGER COUNT, MAX, MIN
INTEGER MEASR(50), TREEHT(1000)
INTEGER SCORES(CLMAX), LIMIT
```

INTEGER statement

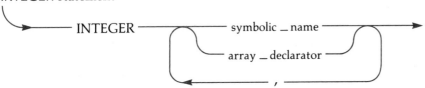

Remark: Nonexecutable. The Standard sets no limit on the number of elements in the list.

Observe that explicit type statements such as INTEGER serve a dual purpose: they specify both the data types of elements in the list and the size of the specified arrays.

Also note that variables and parameters usually cannot be distinguished in the INTEGER statement alone. We must specify the type of a parameter before we assign it a value, and we must specify its value before using it. The fourth example above assumes that CLMAX is a parameter of type **INTEGER** whose value has been defined previously. Thus, a proper sequence would be

```
INTEGER CLMAX
PARAMETER (CLMAX = 500)
INTEGER SCORES(CLMAX), LIMIT
```

To type elements explicitly as real, use the *REAL statement* in a similar fashion.

Examples:
```
REAL Y
REAL AMPS, VOLTS, OHMS
REAL SAMPLE(15000), REFDAT(1000)
REAL DPOP(MAXPOP), CAR1
```

REAL statement

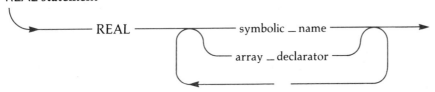

Remark: Nonexecutable.

We will cover the other type statements in a later chapter.

If you omit a name from a type statement, whether intentionally or by accident, the type is determined implicitly, that is, by a simple default rule unique to FORTRAN: the *first letter* of the symbolic name determines the type. If the name begins with *I, J, K, L, M,* or *N,* then the name represents an integer; otherwise it is real. An easy way to remember the rule is to associate the first and last letters of this range, *I* and *N,* with the word *INTEGER.* Thus, in this case, VOLT, X, and Y(6) would be reals, and N, MAX, and ISCORE(50) would be integers. (Of course, array dimensions, and therefore their types,* must still be specified.)

The implicit approach was emphasized in FORTRAN programs in the past, but the trend now is toward explicit typing. We strongly recommend that you explicitly type all of the symbolic names in your programs. You will be less likely to mistype a name, which can create serious errors whose source may be difficult to find. Pascal guards against this possibility by requiring all symbolic names to be explicitly typed. With FORTRAN you will have to be more careful.

Actually, there is another way to assign types implicitly to names: the *IMPLICIT statement.* We recommend, however, that you avoid using it, in general, although there are special circumstances where it may be useful. We postpone its discussion to a later chapter.

Style Guide: Use explicit type statements to assign types to variables, arrays, and parameters and to specify the sizes or dimensions of arrays.

2.5 THE BEGINNING AND THE END

PROGRAM Statement

We use the convention of starting each program with a *PROGRAM statement.*

Examples: `PROGRAM CRVFIT`

PROGRAM **statement**

———— PROGRAM ———————— symbolic _ name ————————➤

*Unless the DIMENSION statement is used—see Chapter 11.

Remark: Nonexecutable.

The PROGRAM statement is optional in most—*but not all*—compilers. It provides documentation of the program, by naming it, and a common beginning, which is easily found. It is similar to the program statement in Pascal. Some versions of FORTRAN extend the PROGRAM statement to include other information, such as the data files used by the program.

The last statement in a program must be an *END statement*. The form is simply

```
END
```

END is an executable statement that terminates the execution of the program.

2.6 ARITHMETIC EXPRESSIONS AND ASSIGNMENT

Much of the computational work in a program, especially in engineering and scientific applications, involves the evaluation of formulas and functions. FORTRAN was designed to facilitate the representation of these computations.

Arithmetic expressions are similar to those in BASIC, Pascal, PL/I, and other languages, and the evaluation rules are pretty much the same. The FORTRAN operators are listed in Box 2.1.

Note that there is only one division operator, which is used for both reals and integers.

We can formally define the syntax, or form, of an arithmetic expression as follows. The examples are given with the mathematical expressions they represent.

BOX 2.1   FORTRAN Arithmetic Operators

+	Addition
−	Subtraction
*	Multiplication
/	Division
**	Exponentiation

Examples:	Representing:
`-X`	$- x$
`N + 1`	$n + 1$
`A + B * (C - D)`	$a + b \cdot (c - d)$
`4.0/3.0 * PI * RAD ** 3`	$\dfrac{4}{3}\pi r^3$
`(ALPHA + 2.5) ** (N - 1)`	$(\alpha + 2.5)^{n-1}$
`-1.0 / (1.0 + X / (1.0 + X ** 2))`	$\dfrac{-1}{1 + [x / (1 + x^2)]}$
`X(I) * (R - 0.5)`	$x_i \cdot (r - 0.5)$
`2. * SIN(X) + 1.`	$2 \sin x + 1$

arithmetic expression

Remark: *Function reference* means the mathematical function references such as SIN(X)—sin x in the last example). We will discuss functions in the next section. Note that this definition is *recursive*; that is, it is defined in terms of itself. An expression may contain a parenthetical expression.

The definition implies that an expression can begin with a plus or minus sign, as in the first and last examples. It also indicates that it is illegal to place two operators next to each other, as in X * − Y, which should be written instead as either X * (−Y) or −X * Y. You will not be able to produce the illegal expression using the syntax chart. Try it!

The syntax chart does not tell us how an arithmetic expression will be evaluated, which you need to know in order to convert mathematical expressions to FORTRAN. This is determined by the *precedence rules* for arithmetic expressions in FORTRAN, which are given in Box 2.2.

BOX 2.2   Precedence Rules of Arithmetic Expressions

1. Evaluate a parenthetical expression before evaluating a (sub)expression containing it.
2. Unless the sequence of operations is completely specified by parentheses, perform the operations in the following order:
   a. Exponentiations
   b. Multiplications and divisions
   c. Additions, subtractions, and negations
3. Perform consecutive exponentiations right to left.
4. Subject to rules 1 to 3, perform operations left to right.

Thus, for	X − Y + Z	subtraction is first,	(rules 2,4)
and for	X − (Y + Z)	addition is first.	(rule 1)
Similarly			
	X / Y * Z	means $\frac{X}{Y} \cdot Z$	(rule 2)
and	X / (Y * Z)	means $\frac{X}{Y \cdot Z}$	(rule 1)
Also,	−X ** 2	means −(X ** 2)	(rule 2)
From rule 3,			
	X ** Y ** Z	is the same as X ** (Y ** Z)	

Regarding rule 4, you should note that the *effect* is as if an expression were evaluated left to right. If the order does not seem to be important, the compiler may choose a different order. For example, in A + B + C either addition could be performed first, depending on the context.

In addition to rules regarding the order in which expressions are evaluated, there are also rules based on the *modes* of the operands: the operation may perform differently according to whether the operands are integer or real. There are three cases.

Case 1. Consider an operation between two integers (constants, variables, and so forth). The result is an integer. If one integer divides another, the result is *truncated* to an integer value. In other words, throw away everything to the right of the decimal point and keep the sign.

Examples:

3 / 2	equals 1
1 / 2	equals 0
−7 / 2	equals −3

The other operators perform as expected on integers, although you should be careful of integer expressions with negative integer exponents. For example, 2 ** (−3) is equal to 1 / (2 ** 3) which is 1 / 8, which is 0.

Case 2. Consider an operation on two reals, which yields a real result. The operations perform consistently with real arithmetic in Pascal, BASIC, and other such languages. However, it is illegal to raise a negative value to a real power (e.g., (−3.0) ** 5.0) or to raise 0 to the 0 power.

From the standpoint of efficiency, it is better to raise a real to an integer power, if possible. For example, 3.14 ** 3 is better than 3.14 ** 3.0. This is because the compiler may use exponential and logarithmic functions to compute the value for a real exponent, but uses chained multiplication for an integer exponent. That is, the former expression would be computed as

$$3.14 * 3.14 * 3.14$$

where as the latter would likely be evaluated as

$$e^{(3.0 * \ln 3.14)}$$

This approach allows FORTRAN to deal effectively with nonintegral exponents.

Case 3. Consider an operation between an integer and a real. The result is always real. Except in the case of a real with an integer exponent, the integer operand is converted to a real before the operation takes place. It is illegal to raise an integer to a real power.

Examples:

1 + 4.0	equals	5.0	
3.0 ** 2	equals	9.0	
3 ** 2.	is illegal		
1 / 2. * 2.	equals	1.0	
1 / 2 * 2.	equals	0.0	(Why?)
1. / 2 * 2	equals	1.0	(Why?)

It is proper to raise a real to an integer exponent. However, you should avoid all other cases of mixing integer and real operands in expressions, except where necessary, in order to avoid results like the last example, which is called *mixed-mode*, or *mixed-type*. Unintended mixing of reals and integers like this is one of the most frequent and frustrating bugs in FORTRAN programs. There are also efficiency considerations. Type conversions take time, and if they are repeated unnecessarily in a loop, they can be costly.

Style Guide:
1. Use integer exponents wherever possible.
2. Make sure that all operands in a real (an integer) expression are real (integer).

Of course, an expression is only part of a statement—most often an *arithmetic assignment statement*—in which the value of an expression is assigned to a variable or array element.

Arithmetic Assignment Statement

Examples:

```
Y = X ** N - 1.0
```

```
VOL = 4. / 3. * PI * RAD ** 3
```

```
THETA = -1. / (3. * X ** 2) + Y ** (1. / 3.)
```

```
LEN(I + 1) = R(I) * SIN(THETA)
```

Representing:

$$y = x^n - 1$$

$$v = \frac{4}{3}\pi r^3$$

$$\theta = -\frac{1}{3x^2} + \sqrt[3]{y}$$

$$l_{i+1} = r_i \cdot \sin\theta$$

arithmetic assignment statement

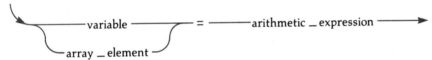

During execution the expression on the right of the = is evaluated, and the result is stored in the item on the left. This is similar to assignment in other languages.

If the types differ between the expression and the item being assigned the value, the value of the expression is automatically converted to that of the item before it is assigned. Thus truncation may take place. For example, let the variable X be real and I be an integer. The following examples illustrate the results of various assignments.

Statement	Result
X = 3.5	X equals 3.5
X = 3	X equals 3.0
I = 3	I equals 3
I = 3.0	I equals 3
I = 3.5	I equals 3
X = 7/2	X equals 3.0

The last example shows that all of the operations on the right side take place before conversion and assignment of the resulting value.

It is important to note that type conversion using an assignment statement this way is quite acceptable, although we will describe a better way in the next section. For example, if we need a real value corresponding to the current value of the iteger variable I, we can write

```
REALI = I
```

where REALI is a real variable. Thus REALI could be used in place of I to avoid a mixed-type expression: use X + REALI in place of X + I, where X is real.

However, a related potential problem should be mentioned. Because FORTRAN allows real/integer type conversion in this way, it creates a potential for errors. Consider the following sequence of code in which the variables X and Y are to exchange values.

```
REAL X, Y
    :
    :
INTCHG = X
X = Y
Y = INTCHG
    :
    :
```

Because INTCHG was not typed, its type defaults to *integer*. Thus Y will contain the truncated value of X. This illustration suggests that you should be very careful to *specify the type for every symbolic name in your program*.

2.7 INTRINSIC FUNCTIONS

Frequently used mathematical functions, such as square root, absolute value, sine, and cosine are built into most modern programming languages, including FORTRAN. Referred to as *built-in functions* in **BASIC** or as *standard functions* in Pascal, they are called *intrinsic functions* in FORTRAN. Many scientific and engineering problems require these functions for their solution. Their provision and ease of use in FORTRAN is one reason for the language's continuing popularity among those involved in mathematical computation.

These routines compute approximations to the corresponding mathematical function with an accuracy that is usually equal to the computer's precision or the precision supported by the given version of FORTRAN, although you might expect the accuracy to degrade for a function like tan x, where x approaches the value of $\pi/2$.

Computing the value of one of these functions for a given argument is easy. Simply use the function applied to a given argument in an expression just as you would a variable. For example, to compute the value of the mathematical expression

$$\sqrt{b^2 - 4ac} + 1$$

you could write

```
DISC = SQRT(B ** 2 - 4. * A * C) + 1
```

assuming A, B, and C had been assigned values previously.

The subexpression SQRT(B ** 2 − 4. * A * C) is an example of a *function reference*. The expression in parentheses is the *argument*.

Function Reference

Examples:

```
SIN(X)
EXP(APX ** 2 - APX + 1.)
LOG(ABS(SIN(X) - COS(X)))
```

function reference

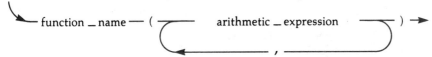

Remarks:

1. Although this definition allows more than one argument, the number is fixed in most cases and depends on the particular function.
2. All functions restrict their argument(s) to certain data types.
3. Where there is a choice, the data type of the argument(s) determines the data type of the function reference.
4. The function reference is undefined for arguments where the corresponding mathematical function is undefined. For example, a reference to SQRT(X) where X equals −1.0 will generate an error.
5. The term *function reference* also applies to functions written by the programmer. We will cover these later.

Note that an argument can be any arithmetic expression, including one with other function references, as in the third example. The most common intrinsic functions are listed in Table 2-1, together with their definitions and types.

Except where noted, all of these functions have only one argument. The complete set of ANSI Standard functions is given in Appendix B.

TABLE 2-1   Common Intrinsic Functions

Function name	Definition	Function type	Argument type
SQRT	Square root	Real	Real
EXP	Exponential (base *e*)	Real	Real
LOG	Logarithm (base *e*)	Real	Real
LOG10	Logarithm (base 10)	Real	Real
SIN	Sine	Real	Real
COS	Cosine	Real	Real
TAN	Tangent	Real	Real
ASIN	Arcsine	Real	Real
ACOS	Arccosine	Real	Real
ATAN	Arctan	Real	Real
SINH	Hyperbolic sine	Real	Real
COSH	Hyperbolic cosine	Real	Real
TANH	Hyperbolic tangent	Real	Real
ABS	Absolute value	Same as argument	Real or integer
MAX	Largest value from arguments (≥ 2)	Same as arguments	Real or integer
MIN	Smallest value from arguments (≥ 2)	Same as arguments	Real or integer
INT	Type conversion of argument to integer	Integer	Real or integer
REAL	Type conversion of argument to real	Real	Real or integer
MOD	Remainder on division of first argument by second	Real	Real or integer

All of the FORTRAN trigonometric functions assume that the argument is in radians. If you want to compute the sine of X where X is in degrees, then you should convert it to radians by writing

```
SIN (PI / 180. * X)
```

where PI = 3.14159 . . . .

All of the above functions are examples of *generic* intrinsic functions: they allow arguments of various types, and the function type may depend on the argument type. For example, SQRT may be applied to arguments of type *double precision* or *complex*, which we have not yet introduced. There are also *specific* intrinsic functions such as IABS, which computes the integer absolute value of an integer argument. There is no need to use the specific name, since the generic name will do the job. See Appendix B for details.

Most of these functions are probably familiar to you. We will clarify the last five functions with examples.

MAX and MIN can have two or more arguments, but all of them must be of the same type.

Examples:

```
MAX (-5., -1., 2.1)     equals 2.1
MAX (27, 10)            equals 27
MIN (4, -15, 2)         equals -15
MIN (3.5, 4, 17.0)      is illegal
```

In the following program fragment,

```
    :
    :
A = 17.5
B = 129.3
C = -2.1
D = 0.0
HIGH = MAX (A, B, C, D)
LOW = MIN (A, B, C, D)
    :
    :
```

HIGH = 129.3, and LOW = −2.1.

The INT and REAL functions provide a way other than simple assignment to do type conversion. For example, suppose that X and Y are reals and that I and J are integers.

Examples:

```
X = REAL(I)                    is equivalent to X = I
J = INT(Y)                     is equivalent to J = Y
Y = REAL(1) / REAL(3) * X      is equivalent to Y = 1. / 3. * X
I = INT(4.9) * J               is equivalent to I = 4 * J
X = REAL(Y)                    is allowed but useless (why?)
Y = REAL(I) / REAL(J) * X      (see below)
```

For clarity it is better to write X = REAL (I) than X = I. The reader will then know exactly what was intended. Also, the INT and REAL functions enable you to avoid mixed-type expressions without the use of extra assignment statements, as in the last example. Without them, if we required the division to precede the multiplication, we would have to do something like this:

```
RI = I
RJ = J
Y = RI / RJ * X
```

where RI and RJ are real.

Style Guide: use the REAL and INT functions for type conversion.

The *mod*, or *modulo*, function, MOD, computes the remainder using real or integer arithmetic depending on the type of the arguments, which must be the same for both. The function reference

$$MOD(M, N)$$

is equivalent to the expression

$$M - INT(M / N) * N$$

Clearly, the second argument must not be 0.

Examples:

```
MOD (7, 2)      equals 1
MOD (15, 5)     equals 0
MOD (-7, 2)     equals -1
MOD (5.2, 2.)   equals 1.2
MOD (5.2, .2)   equals 0.
MOD (3., 2)     is illegal
MOD (7., 0.)    is illegal
```

You should note that most of these functions also allow arguments of types we haven't discussed yet. Extensions to these types, as well as other functions, will be covered later.

2.8 INPUT/OUTPUT

FORTRAN is rich in features for dealing with input and output of data. To enable you to do some basic input/output (I/O) early, we postpone many of the intricate details and present the most simple forms, known as *list-directed* input and output. *List-directed* implies that the format, or presentation, of data is not supplied by the statement and is to be done by default. A list-directed I/O statement is characterized by an asterisk following the keyword.

PRINT Statement

The list-directed form of an output statement is a *PRINT statement*. It is very similar to the PRINT statement in BASIC and to simple forms of the writeln statement in Pascal.

Examples:

```
PRINT *, A, B, C
PRINT *, 'SUM = ', SUM, 'AVERAGE = ', AVG
PRINT *, 'THE VALUE OF PI USED IN THIS PROGRAM IS ', PI
```

```
PRINT *, X ** N - Y + 1.0
PRINT *, PRES(I + 1), TEMP(I + 1), VOL(I + 1)
PRINT *
```

PRINT statement (list-directed)

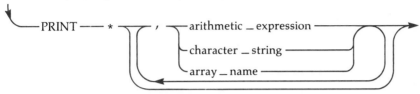

Remark: *Character string* is a string of characters enclosed in apostrophes, such as 'SUM = ' in the second example.

The PRINT statement displays the character strings and the values of each of the expressions in its print list all on the same line, if they fit, or on more than one line if necessary. The output line(s) is referred to as a *record*. Records are single-spaced. The last example prints a blank record.

The format of the printed data is not fully specified by the Standard and is therefore computer-dependent. Numerical items in the list may be separated by one or more blanks, or by commas. A real value may print with a decimal point or in exponential form, depending on its magnitude. The number of digits displayed is also computer-dependent, and it can vary according to the magnitude of the value.
For example,

```
        PRINT *, 'SUM = ', 430000.0, 'COUNT = ', 3500
```

might print as

```
        SUM = 430000.0 COUNT = 3500
```

or as

```
        SUM = .43E+6    COUNT = 3500
```

whereas

```
        PRINT *, 7, 2.5, -123
```

might print as

```
        7    2.5    -123
```

or as

```
        7, 2.5, -123
```

Since

```
        PRINT *, 'SUPER', 'MAN'
```

will print

`SUPERMAN`

you must put the blank at the end of the first character string itself if you require a blank between two successive strings, as in 'SUPER '. (Alternatively, you may put a blank at the start of the second string.)

If two or more successive values in an output record have identical values, they may print as a *repeated constant*; for example,

`PRINT * , 2.5, 2.5, 2.5`

may produce

`3 * 2.5`

The number 3 is called a *repeat factor*.

Finally, you can print *all* of the elements of an array by using the array name without a subscript in the output list. For example, let X be an integer array with 3 elements, 5, 7, and 9. Then both

`PRINT * , X(1), X(2), X(3)`

and

`PRINT * , X`

will print

`5     7     9`   (or equivalent)

List-directed output is displayed on the so-called *standard output unit*, which could be a line printer or a video screen, depending on the type of computer and local site rules. Having tried the exercises in Chapter 1, you should already know what the standard output unit is for your computer. The number of items printed on one line also depends on the compiler and the standard output unit. Thus,

`PRINT *, A, B, C, D, E, F`

could display values on one or two lines, depending on the environment.

**READ
Statement**

Next we examine the list-directed form of the input statement, the *READ statement*. The input values are assigned in their given order to the items in the READ list. It corresponds to readln in Pascal and to READ or INPUT in BASIC, (depending on how the data is provided).

Examples:
```
READ *, X
READ *, A, B, C
READ *, PR(I), PR(I + 1), PR(I + 2)
```

READ statement

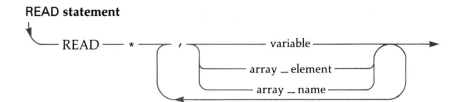

Remarks:

1. Each value in the input line, or record, must be a constant of the same type as the corresponding item in the READ list. (Exception: real values like 7. and 3.0 can be entered as 7 and 3).
2. Successive constants in the input record must be separated by a comma or by one or more blanks.
3. Each READ statement begins reading a new record. It reads as many records as necessary to supply values for *every* item in the READ list.

As in the PRINT statement, an array name in the READ list produces the same result as if *all* of the array elements were in the list, in consecutive order. For example, if X is an array with 3 elements, then

```
READ *, X
```

produces the same result as

```
READ *, X(1), X(2), X(3)
```

Also, rather than entering consecutive identical input values, such as

```
1 1 1 1 1 1
```

you are allowed to use a repeat factor:

```
6 * 1
```

Similar to the PRINT statement, the READ statement expects to find its input data in the *standard input unit*, not as part of the program, as in BASIC DATA statements. Depending on the computer system you are using, this means that you will probably include your data as part of the job stream in the file containing the program or enter it at the keyboard when the program encounters the READ statement during execution, although there are other options. Recall the discussion of JCL in Chapter 1.

2.9 STATEMENT ORDER

Most programming languages restrict the order in which the various classes of statements can appear in a program, and FORTRAN is no exception. For the statements we have encountered in this chapter, the following order should be observed.

1. PROGRAM statement
2. Type (INTEGER, REAL) and PARAMETER statements
3. Executable (Assignment, READ, PRINT) statements
4. END statement

Comments may be placed anywhere between the PROGRAM and END statements.

2.10 AN EXAMPLE

The statements you have studied in this chapter are sufficient for you to write programs to perform a calculation on input data and print the result. In other words, at this point you have the capability of a reasonably powerful hand calculator. The following example is representative of this capability.

You are probably familiar with the well-known sequence of numbers 0, 1, 1, 2, 3, 5, 8, 13, 21, . . . , called the *Fibonacci sequence*. This sequence can be generated by the formula

$$f_n = f_{n-1} + f_{n-2}$$

for $n \geq 2$ and where $f_0 = 0$ and $f_1 = 1$. The nth number in the sequence, f_n, can be computed by first computing all of the numbers that precede it using this formula, or it can be computed *directly* using the formula

$$f_n = \frac{1}{\sqrt{5}}\left[\left(\frac{1 + \sqrt{5}}{2}\right)^n - \left(\frac{1 - \sqrt{5}}{2}\right)^n\right]$$

The following little program computes an approximation to the nth Fibonacci number using the latter formula. The number n is an input value. The result is only an approximation since $\sqrt{5}$ cannot be represented exactly.

It should be noted that this program and all of the formal examples in this book have been tested on a DEC VAX 11/7XX series computer using DEC's FORTRAN compiler, and on an IBM PC using Ryan-McFarland's RM/FORTRAN compiler, which supports the full ANSI FORTRAN 77 Standard.

EXAMPLE 2.1

```
      PROGRAM FIBON
*****************************************************************
* AUTHOR:  T. FIBONACCI   4/86
*
* THIS PROGRAM COMPUTES AN APPROXIMATION TO THE NTH FIBONACCI
* NUMBER.  IT WILL ABORT IF N IS TOO LARGE (SYSTEM DEPENDENT)
* OR IF N IS NOT AN INTEGER.  IT IS WRITTEN FOR INTERACTIVE
* USE.
* VARIABLES:
* N     - THE POSITION OF THE NUMBER IN THE SEQUENCE (INPUT)
* FIBNO - THE NTH FIBONACCI NUMBER (APPROXIMATE)
* SQRT5 - EQUAL TO THE SQUARE ROOT OF 5.
*****************************************************************
      INTEGER N
      REAL FIBN, SQRT5
      SQRT5 = SQRT(5.0)
      PRINT *, 'ENTER THE SEQUENCE NUMBER OF THE FIBONACCI'
      PRINT *, 'NUMBER YOU WANT.  IT SHOULD BE NON-NEGATIVE.'
      PRINT *, 'A NEGATIVE IS REPLACED BY ITS ABSOLUTE VALUE.'
      PRINT *
      READ *, N
*
* FORCE N TO BE NON-NEGATIVE
*
      N = ABS(N)
      FIBNO = (((1. + SQRT5) / 2.)**N - ((1. - SQRT5) / 2.)**N) / SQRT5
      PRINT *
      PRINT *, 'FOR N = ', N
      PRINT *, 'THE NTH FIBONACCI NUMBER IS ', FIBNO
      END
```

Sample output:
```
ENTER THE SEQUENCE NUMBER OF THE FIBONACCI
NUMBER YOU WANT.  IT SHOULD BE NON-NEGATIVE.
A NEGATIVE IS REPLACED BY ITS ABSOLUTE VALUE.

FOR N = 8
THE NTH FIBONACCI NUMBER IS 21.0000
```

It is not necessary to include a prologue on a short demonstration program like this one. It is given here for consistency.

Note that this program prints instructions to the user, called a *prompt*, which is appropriate for an interactive program. If the program is to be run in batch mode, the PRINT statement should be deleted and the value of N provided on the standard input unit.

It would be quite appropriate for $\sqrt{5}$ to be defined as a parameter. Unfortunately, however, the PARAMETER statement does not allow function references, such as SQRT, because the parameter values must be available at compile time. Therefore the variable SQRT5 is assigned the value instead.

The answer turns out to be exact in this case because of the way the internal value, which is an approximation resulting from the use of real arithmetic and the approximation to $\sqrt{5}$, is rounded off for printing. On the other hand, the same program, compiled with Ryan-McFarland's RM/FORTRAN compiler, produced a result of 21.0000090. The resulting value for N = 11 printed as 88.9999 (exact answer: 89) on a DEC VAX 750 computer using the F77 compiler. Your computer may give somewhat different results.

Finally, note that the input value, N, is printed along with the answer. Printing the original input data, called *echo printing*, is generally a good idea, unless there is a large volume of data. It allows the user to verify that the data was entered correctly.

2.11 COMPLEX NUMBERS

This section may be omitted if you are not familiar with or interested in complex numbers.

Complex numbers are used in science, engineering, and applied mathematics. Just as real numbers can be thought of as points on the real line, complex numbers can be associated with points in the plane. A complex number is an ordered *pair* of real numbers, *a* and *b*, written (*a*, *b*). The number *a* is called the *real* part, and *b* is called the *imaginary* part. For example, (−1.0, 3.5) is a complex constant. You can associate the value *a* with the abscissa (*x*-axis) and *b* with the ordinate (*y*-axis). The four operations for complex numbers are defined in Box 2.3.

Complex Constant

In FORTRAN a *complex constant* is also a pair of real or integer constants enclosed in parentheses.

Examples:

    (1.5, −1.0)   (10.0, 0.0)   (0.0, −5.0)   (3, 4)

complex constant

BOX 2-3   Complex Arithmetic

Addition/Subtraction:	$(a, b) \pm (c, d) = (a \pm c, b \pm d)$
Example:	$(3.0, 1.0) + (4.0, -3.0) = (7.0, -2.0)$
Multiplication:	$(a, b) (c, d) = (ac - bd, ad + bc)$
Example:	$(2.0, 3.0) (-1.0, 4.0) = (-14.0, 5.0)$
Division:	$(a, b) / (c, d) = \left(\dfrac{a \cdot c + b \cdot d}{c^2 + d^2}, \dfrac{b \cdot c - a \cdot d}{c^2 + d^2} \right)$
Example:	$(4.0, 2.0) / (1.0, -1.0) = (1.0, 3.0)$

Remark: Although the Standard accepts integers as the real and imaginary parts, as in the last example, they are actually stored as reals. Therefore we recommend that you use only reals.

Complex variables are declared by means of the *COMPLEX type statement.*

COMPLEX Statement

Examples:

```
COMPLEX A, B, X
COMPLEX VEC(100)
```

COMPLEX statement

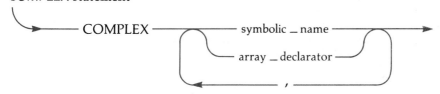

Remarks:

1. Nonexecutable.
2. The COMPLEX statement(s), should be placed at the beginning of the program with the other type statements.

Complex arithmetic is performed according to the rules in Box 2-3. Therefore, given

```
COMPLEX Z
Z = (7.0, 0.5) + (2.1, -1.0)
```

then Z will be equal to $(9.1, -0.5)$.

A complex number may be raised to an *integral* power only. Thus

```
Z = (7.2, 3.5) ** 3
```

is allowed, but

$$Z = (1.0, 2.0) ** (0.5)$$

is not.

Actually, complex arithmetic is a convenience rather than a necessity since it could be simulated using real arithmetic. For the above example, we could write instead:

```
REAL ZR, ZI
ZR = 7.0 + 2.1
ZI = 0.5 - 1.0
```

That is, we would have to compute explicitly both the real and imaginary parts of each complex variable.

Mixed-mode expressions are allowed. For example, if

$$Z = 3 * (4.0, -1.0) - 1.0$$

then Z has the value   (11.0, -3.0)

Note that if X = (5.0, 1.0) and X is real, then X is equal to 5.0. However, we recommend that you use explicit type conversion intrinsic functions to avoid confusion. Some of the intrinsic functions for complex expressions are given in Box 2.4.

BOX 2.4 Intrinsic Functions for Complex Expressions

Assume that Z is complex and that X and Y are real.
REAL(Z) = the real part of Z
AIMAG(Z) = the imaginary part of Z
CMPLX(X, Y) = the complex number (X, Y)
CONJG(X, Y) = (X, −Y), the *complex conjugate* of (X, Y)
ABS((X, Y)) = SQRT(X ** 2 + Y ** 2)

Using these functions, a preferred expression for Z is

$$Z = CMPLX(3) * (4.0, -1.0) - CMPLX(1.0)$$

and X should be defined as

$$X = REAL((5.0, 1.0))$$

Complex numbers can be read or written using list-directed I/O. On input the number should be written as an ordered pair in parentheses, just like a complex constant. A complex number is also printed with the parentheses.

Exercises:

Note that in this and the remaining chapters the exercises are grouped, where appropriate, with the corresponding sections in the chapter.

Section 2.1

1. Which of the following are valid FORTRAN symbolic names?

   *a. X1738Y   **f.** PARI.5

   b. X23   ***g.** READ

   c. 23X   **h.** GRAVITY

   *d. eps   ***i.** B SPACE

   *e. ALP$ **j.** X + Y

2. Write each of the following constants in exponential form.

   *a. .7193   ***d.** -10^{-8}

   b. 1/250   **e.** .0000053

   c. 186,000   ***f.** $3/10^7$

Section 2.3

3. Why does the definition of π in PARAMETER (PI = 3.14159265) represent a better programming practice, in general, than its definition in

$$PI = 3.14159265?$$

Section 2.4

*4. What is wrong with the following sequence?

```
REAL VIN(1000), PART(1000), INDEXF
INTEGER N, I, LIM, MAX
INTEGER CAL(LIM)
PARAMETER (INDEXF = .0632, LIM = 500)
```

Section 2.6

5. What is the difference between the following assignments?

   a. X = 3.27 * 10. ** 12

   b. X = 3.27E12

6. What is the value of X in each of the following expressions, where X is a real? Where X is an integer?

   a. X = 1.5 ** 2   ***h.** X = (-4) ** (-3)

   b.* X = 5 + 3 * 2   **i.** X = 4. ** (3 / 2)

   c. X = 4 ** 3 - 1   **j.** X = 4.** (3. / 2.)

   d.* X = 1 / 2 * (3 - 5 ** 2)   **k.** X = 7. + 9 / 2

   e. X = 4. * 12. / 2. * 3.   ***l.** X = 1. / 3. + 1. / 3. + 1 / 3

   f. X = 50 / 5 / 4   **m.** X = 1 / 2. * 7. / 2

   g.* X = 11 / 3 + 4 / 3   ***n.** X = 1. / 2. * 7 / 2

*Solution to this exercise is given in Appendix D.

7. Suppose that `I` and `J` are integers and that `X` and `Y` are reals. Given the assignment `Y = REAL(I) / REAL(J) * X` for each of the following, determine whether they are equivalent to this assignment. If they are not, give an example that would produce different values.

    a. `Y = I / J * X`
    b.`*Y = REAL(I / J) * X`
    c. `Y = REAL(I) / J * X`
    d.`*Y = I / REAL(J) * X`

8. Verify that the examples preceding the definition of arithmetic expressions are valid according to the syntax chart.

9. Determine whether or not the following expressions are valid or invalid as FORTRAN arithmetic expressions according to the definition.

    a. `X * - Y`
    b. `X * (- Y)`
    c.`*A (B + 1)`
    d. `((((P (U)))))`
    e. `Y2 - X3.1`

    f. `A + B -`
    g. `*A * (B - C * (D - E) / (F + G)`
    h. `(ALPHA - BETA) (GAMMA + RHO)`
    i. `* LAMBDA / (2. * PI * EPSILON) * Y`

10. Modify the syntax chart for arithmetic expressions to allow a plus or minus sign to immediately follow another operator (e.g., X * − Y).

Section 2.7

11. Write an equivalent FORTRAN assignment statement for each of the following equations.

    a. $a = \pi r^2$

    * **b.** $t = 1 / 2\, b \cdot h$

    c. $y = \dfrac{1}{\dfrac{1}{r_1} + \dfrac{1}{r_2} + \dfrac{1}{r_3}}$

    * **d.** $z = \dfrac{x}{a + \dfrac{x}{b}}$

    e. $R_s = \dfrac{I_G R_G}{I_0 - I_G}$

    f. area $= \sqrt{s \cdot (s - a) \cdot (s - b) \cdot (s - c)}$

    * **g.** $a = p\,(1 + r / k)^{k \cdot n}$

    h. $v = (f \cdot q)^{-1/2}$

    i. $l = 1 - \dfrac{x}{2} + \dfrac{x^2}{3} - \dfrac{x^3}{4}$

j. $v = \dfrac{\sigma}{2\varepsilon_0} (\sqrt{a^2 + x^2} - x)$

* k. $T = \dfrac{n}{(n - a)(n - b)}$

l. $y = (2 \cdot \pi)^{1/3} X^{t+1} e^{-x}$

*m. $x^2 + y^2 + z^2 = (ct)^2$

n. $E = \dfrac{P}{2\pi\varepsilon_0} \dfrac{\cos \theta}{r^3} e_r + \dfrac{P}{4\pi\varepsilon_0} \dfrac{\sin \theta}{r^3} e_\theta$

o. $p = \dfrac{h}{\lambda} \cos \phi + \dfrac{m_0 v}{\sqrt{1 - \left(\dfrac{v}{c}\right)^2}} \cos \theta$

p. $r = \sqrt{\dfrac{2mV}{eB^2}}$

q. $v = c\left[\log\left(\dfrac{1 + u}{1 - u}\right)\right]^{t-1}$

* r. $q = \log_{10} |\sec x + \tan x|$

s. $r = m \cdot e^{-\sqrt{v/2y} \cdot n}$

t. $r = n + \dfrac{[\arcsin (2x)]^{p+1}}{p + 1}$

* u. $f = x \cdot \arctan \dfrac{x}{a} + \dfrac{b}{2} \log (x^2 + b^2)$

v. $y = \max \begin{cases} x \\ p^2 \\ \sqrt{|v/p|} \end{cases}$

12. Write an algebraic expression equivalent to each of the following FORTRAN expressions.

*a. `A + B / C + D`
b. `1. / (A + (B / C + D / (E + F))))`
c. `*X ** Y * C ** D + 1.`
d. `P * SQRT(R - THETA / PI)`
e. `SIN(X * 180. / RHO) ** .5`

Section 2.8

13. Write 1 or more statements to accomplish the following:
   a. Declare `SD`, `VAR`, and `SUM` to be reals and `N`, `ULIM`, and `LLIM` to be integers.
   *b. Declare `SCORE` and `DIFF` to be real arrays, each with dimension 300. The value 300 should be a parameter.
   c. Read values into `X`, `Y`, `Z`, and `A(1)`, assuming that the four corresponding data items are on the same input record; on 4 different records.
   *d. Print `A`, `B`, and `C` on the same line, followed by a blank line, followed by `SUM = X(1)` (the value of `X(1)`) on the next line, and `ERROR SUM = X(2)` (the value of `X(2)`) on the last line.

Section 2.10

For the remainder of the exercises write a short, but complete, program to do what is specified. Where input data is involved, run the program for several values. Use parameters where appropriate. Be sure all variables and parameters are assigned a type.

Print the input data and the indicated results with meaningful labels.

14. Read a, b, and c. Compute and print the roots of the quadratic equation $a \cdot x^2 + b \cdot x + c = 0$; that is, print

$$x_1 = \frac{-b + \sqrt{b^2 - 4 \cdot a \cdot c}}{2 \cdot a}$$

and

$$x_2 = \frac{-b - \sqrt{b^2 - 4 \cdot a \cdot c}}{2 \cdot a}$$

Be sure that the discriminant $b^2 - 4 \cdot a \cdot c$ is nonnegative.

15. Verify the double-angle formulas

$$\sin 2\theta = 2 \sin \theta \cos \theta$$
$$\cos 2\theta = 1 - 2 \sin^2 \theta$$

and

$$\tan 2\theta = \frac{2 \tan \theta}{1 - \tan^2 \theta}$$

for several values of θ. That is, compute and print the left and right sides of each equation, and their corresponding difference.

16. Compute and print an approximation of π using the series

$$\pi^6 = 945 \left(1 + \frac{1}{2^6} + \frac{1}{3^6} + \frac{1}{4^6} + \cdots\right)$$

using
   a. Four terms of the series
   b. Eight terms
      Compare your results to 3.14159265.

*17. Given a triangle labeled as follows

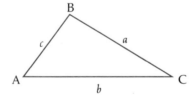

the law of cosines is

$$-a^2 + b^2 + c^2 = 2 \cdot b \cdot c \cdot \cos A$$

and the area is given by

$$area = \frac{1}{2} b \cdot c \cdot \sin A$$

Read A *in degrees*, b, and c, and compute the length of side a and the area.

18. The equation

$$y = y_0 + v_0 t - \frac{1}{2} \cdot g \cdot t^2$$

represents the vertical position of an object, y, at time t, given initial height y_0, initial vertical velocity v_0, and g, the acceleration constant due to gravity (use $g = 32$, where time is in seconds and distance in feet), assuming the object is dropped or thrown downward (v_0 is negative) or upward (v_0 is positive). Read y_0, v_0, and t, and compute and print y.

19. The following figure illustrates light being bent, or *refracted*, as it passes from one medium through another, for example, from air to water.

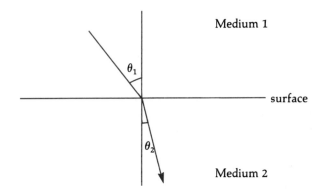

Angle θ_1 is the *angle of incidence* and θ_2 is the *angle of refraction*. *Snell's law* is given by the equation

$$n_1 \sin \theta_1 = n_2 \sin \theta_2$$

where n_1 and n_2 are the corresponding *indices of refraction* for the two media ($n_i = 1$ for air, 1.33 for water, and 1.5 for typical glass). Read n_1, n_2 and θ_1, in degrees. Compute and print θ_2 (in degrees). How would you change your program if media 2 were always water?

20. The equation

$$I = \frac{E}{\sqrt{R^2 + (2\pi f L - 1/(2\pi f C))^2}}$$

yields the current I in an AC circuit, where E is the voltage (volts), R is resistance (ohms), L is the inductance (henrys), C is the capacitance (farads), and f is the AC frequency (hertz). Fix C at $.5 \times 10^{-6}$ and L at $.1$; read f, R, and E, and compute I.

21. A baseball park has an outfield fence that is y feet high and x feet from home plate. It can be shown that to clear the fence, the minimum velocity (in ft/sec) needed by the ball as it leaves the bat is given by

$$v_0 = \left(\frac{gx^2}{(x \tan \theta - y)^2 \cos^2 \theta}\right)^{1/2}$$

where g is 32 ft/sec^2, and θ is the angle with the ground at which the ball is hit. Read x, y, and θ, and compute v_0.

*22. The *Taylor series* for sin x, given by

$$\sin x = x - \frac{x^3}{6} + \frac{x^5}{120} - \frac{x^7}{5040} + \cdots$$

gives an increasingly better approximation for sin x as terms are added. Read x and compute the Taylor series approximation to sin x using the first four terms. Compare it to the intrinsic function value. Compute and print the two values and their difference.

23. Same as Exercise 22, but use the following approximation in place of the Taylor series:

$$\sin x \doteq \frac{\left[1 - \dfrac{325523}{2283996}x^2 + \dfrac{34911}{7613320}x^4 + \dfrac{479249}{11511339840}x^6\right]}{1 + \dfrac{18381}{761332}x^2 + \dfrac{1261}{4567992}x^4 + \dfrac{2623}{1644477120}x^6}$$

where x must be in the range

$$\left[-\frac{\pi}{6}, \frac{\pi}{6}\right]$$

Try to represent the constants as accurately as possible.

Section 2.11

24. Do Exercise 14 using complex arithmetic. Try it on an example for which the discriminant is negative.

3

Control Statements and Looping

Control statements enable programs to execute instructions in nonsequential order. Without them, computer programs are reduced to doing basically calculator functions. Thus the statements introduced in the last chapter are not sufficient for most programs.

We can view all programs logically as groups, or *blocks*, of statements known as *control structures*. It is well known that any algorithm can be programmed exclusively in terms of three classes of control structures: (1) simple sequences, which consist only of noncontrol statements, such as assignment and I/O statements; (2) selection structures, such as the IF-THEN block in lines 35–42 of Example 1.1, and (3) loops, or iteration. Control statements are required to implement the latter two. The disciplined use of these three classes of structures forms the basis of *structured programming*, a methodology that promotes readability and correctness in programs.

In this chapter we discuss the IF and associated statements in detail, the GOTO, CONTINUE, and STOP statements, and the END = clause for READ statements. Using these, we will implement selection and most loop forms in FORTRAN and discuss their use in structured programming. Together with the items from Chapters 1 and 2, this material constitutes a "minimal" FORTRAN from which complex programs may be constructed.

3.1 LOGICAL EXPRESSIONS

Since logical expressions are important components of IF statements, we examine them first. Let us first add another data type—logical—to our collection. Type LOGICAL is equivalent to type Boolean in Pascal.

Symbolic names are declared to be of type LOGICAL by means of the *LOGICAL statement*.

LOGICAL Statement

Examples:
```
LOGICAL L
LOGICAL FLAG, SWITCH, VAL
LOGICAL BOOL(500), EMPTY(1000)
```

LOGICAL statement

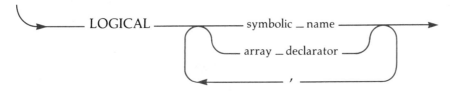

Remark: Nonexecutable.

Logical items—constants, variables, and array elements—can have only one of two possible values:

.TRUE.   and   .FALSE.

This is how we represent the two constant values in FORTRAN. How they are represented internally is computer-dependent. Often logical items take up less memory space than items of other types. It is legal to define a logical parameter, which could be helpful for program documentation.

Relation

Given these logical building blocks we can form *logical expressions* just as we write arithmetic expressions using arithmetic type items. First, we define a *relation*, which is a comparison between two arithmetic expressions and has a logical value: true or false. You should be accustomed to using relations in IF-statements in another language.

Examples:

```
X .LT. 0.0
Y .EQ. ABS(N - 1) + MIN
SUM + X(N) .GE. THRESH * PI
SIN(X) + 1. .LE. EPS
```

relation

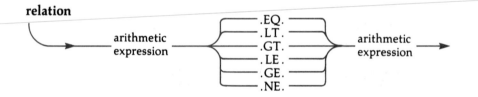

Remark: The elements .EQ., .LT., and so forth, are called *relation operators* and are defined as follows:

Element	Meaning
.EQ.	equal ($=$)
.LT.	less than ($<$)
.GT.	greater than ($>$)
.LE.	less than or equal ($<=$)
.GE.	greater than or equal ($>=$)
.NE.	not equal ($<>$)

Both expressions are evaluated before the comparison is made. It is recommended, but not required, that the types of both arithmetic expressions be the same. Suppose you compare a real expression e_1 with an integer expression e_2. FORTRAN will compare e_1 with REAL (e_2). Depending on the compiler, such an occurrence in a loop could result in needless but costly repeated conversions.

Thus, arithmetic expressions can be combined, using relational operators, to produce a logical type result. Logical items, in turn, can be combined to form another logical result, using the *logical operators*, .AND., .OR., .NOT., .EQV., and .NEQV., which are defined by the *truth table* (Table 3-1). Let A and B be logical items; i.e., they evaluate to true or false.

**Logical
Operators**

TABLE 3.1 The FORTRAN Logical Operators

A	B	A.AND.B	A.OR.B.	NOT.A	A.EQV.B	A.NEQV.B
.TRUE.	.TRUE.	.TRUE.	.TRUE.	.FALSE.	.TRUE.	.FALSE.
.TRUE.	.FALSE.	.FALSE.	.TRUE.	.FALSE.	.FALSE.	.TRUE.
.FALSE.	.TRUE.	.FALSE.	.TRUE.	.TRUE.	.FALSE.	.TRUE.
.FALSE.	.FALSE.	.FALSE.	.FALSE.	.TRUE.	.TRUE.	.FALSE.

For example, if A and B are both true, then so is A .AND .B; otherwise it is false. The operator .NOT. is *unary*, negating the value of the logical operand that immediately follows it. The other operators are *binary*, applying to the two operands that immediately surround them.

The operator .EQV. means *equivalent*; it tests whether the two operands have the same value. Thus A .EQV. B is true if A and B are both true or both false. The operator .NQEV. means *not equivalent*. Thus A .NEQV. B is true if A is true or B is true, but *not both*. This operator is precisely the same as what is called the *exclusive or* operator in other languages.

Finally, remember that the logical operators apply only to logical operands. If X is an integer, it is illegal (and meaningless) to write, for instance,

```
X .AND. 1
```

Now we can define a *logical expression*—analogous to an arithmetic expression—which has a logical value.

**Logical
Expression**

Examples:

```
1. .TRUE.                              (a logical constant)
2. A                                   (A is logical variable)
3. X .LT. 0.0                          (X is arithmetic)
4. X .GE. -5.5 .AND. X .LE. 9.2        (X is arithmetic)
5. (X(N) .LT. X(N - 1) .OR. N .EQ. MAX) .AND. Y .LE. FMAX
6. .NOT. (A .GT. B - 1.)               (A and B are arithmetic)
```

7. `(N .EQ. MAX) .AND. (.NOT. X .LT. 0.1)`   (N and X are arithmetic)

8. `R .EQV. (P .AND. (.NOT. Q))`   (R, P, and Q are logical)

logical expression

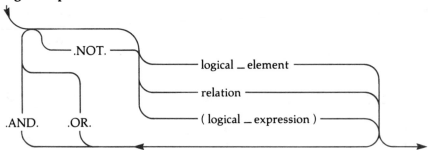

Remarks: *Logical element* means any of the following: logical constant, logical variable, logical array element, or logical function reference (a function reference whose value is true or false). Note that the .NOT. operator may immediately follow an .AND. or .OR., without intervening parentheses. Example 6 means the same as

$$A .LE. B - 1.$$

Relations may therefore be combined in a meaningful way to form a single logical-valued expression, as in the fourth and fifth examples. These expressions may be quite complex, but the complexity is worthwhile if the number of statements and the corresponding overall complexity of the program is reduced. In summary, apply relational operators to arithmetic expressions and logical operators to logical expressions.

Just as with arithmetic expressions, there is a precedence associated with the evaluation of logical expressions, as given in Box 3.1. The precedence rules are similar to BASIC's, but quite different from Pascal's.

Thus,

$$P .OR. Q .AND. R$$

is evaluated as

$$P .OR. (Q .AND. R)$$

and

$$P .AND. .NOT. Q$$

is the same as

$$P .AND. (.NOT. Q)$$

BOX 3.1 Precedence Rules for Logical Expressions

1. Evaluate a parenthetical expression before evaluating a (sub)expression containing it.
2. Evaluate relations before applying logical operators:
   a. Carry out arithmetic operations first, according to the rules in Table 2.2
   b. Apply the relational operation to the values of the corresponding arithmetic expressions.
3. Unless the sequence of logical operations is completely specified by parentheses, perform the operations in the following order:
   a. `.NOT.`
   b. `.AND.`
   c. `.OR.`
   d. `.EQV.` and `.NEQV.`
4. Subject to these rules, perform operations left to right.

From these rules, you may observe that parentheses are not needed in the last three examples in the definition. We strongly recommend, however, that you use parentheses to improve the readability of expressions and to ensure that an expression is evaluated in the order you intend. For example, in this book we prefer

```
(X .GT. A) .AND. (X .LT. B)
```

to

```
X .GT. A .AND. X .LT. B
```

Logical Assignment Statement

We use logical expressions most often for making comparisons, but since they evaluate to .TRUE. or .FALSE., they may be used for convenience whenever their use makes sense. For example, FORTRAN allows the *logical assignment statement*, in which a logical variable is assigned a value.

Examples:
```
1. TEST   =  .FALSE.
2. FLAG   =  X .LT. Y
3. SWITCH =  P .AND. (N .GE. NMAX)
```

logical assignment statement

Example 1 illustrates how you might initialize a logical variable, which is often used to represent a condition as true or false—for example, to determine whether or not to exit from a loop. Logical expressions may also appear as items in PRINT lists.

Finally, it should be obvious that it is illegal to assign a logical expression to an arithmetic variable and vice versa.

3.2 IF STATEMENTS

IF statements are found in some form in virtually every procedure-oriented language. FORTRAN has three versions of IF statements, two of which are covered in this section. The third form is considered obsolete and will be treated briefly in a later chapter.

Logical IF Statement

The *logical IF* statement is similar to the IF-statements found in BASIC. It causes the execution of a *single* statement if the value of its logical expression is true.

Examples:

```
IF (X .GT. Y) COUNT = COUNT + 1
IF ((F(X) .LT. EPS) .OR. (N .GT. NMAX)) ROOT = X
IF (.NOT.(A(I).LE. A(I + 1)) PRINT *, 'LARGER VALUE:', A(I)
IF (FLAG) READ *, X, Y     (FLAG is a logical variable)
```

logical IF statement

```
IF ——— ( logical _ expression ) ———executable (restricted)
                                       statement
```

Remarks: The statement following the logical expression in parentheses is executed if the logical expression is true; otherwise it is skipped. *Executable statement (restricted)* means any executable statement except an END, DO, or another IF statement of any type, including the components of an IF block (see below): ENDIF, ELSE IF, and ELSE. For example,

```
        IF (A .GT. 0.0) IF (A .LT. AMAX) SUM = SUM + A
```

and

```
                IF (N .NE. M) INTEGER X, Y
```

are illegal.

Block IF Statement

There are no statements in FORTRAN like the *begin* and *end* of Pascal for grouping instructions into blocks, or compound statements. Instead, the block structures are either specific to the structure—as in the block IF statement to be described next—or they are the responsibility of the programmer.

The next version of the IF statement has a block structure; it was introduced in the FORTRAN 77 standard to promote structured programming. This version, the *block IF statement*, is used with the ENDIF statement and, optionally, the ELSE and ELSE IF statements to control the sequence of execution. Rather than a single statement, a whole *block* is selected for execution from a set of one or more blocks, depending on the values of the corresponding logical expressions. Thus, the term *selection structure* is often used to describe it. The block IF is similar to the if/then statement in Pascal and other modern languages. Since a block IF involves more than 1 statement, we will refer to it as a *structure*, or as a *block*, and we will depart from our usual use of syntax charts in favor of a kind of "skeleton" for its definition. There are three variations of the block IF.

Examples:

```
1. IF (X .LE. THRESH) THEN
      PRINT *, X, X ** 2
      SUM = SUM + X
   ENDIF

2. IF (ABS(A) .LT. 1.) THEN
      FNA = PI * LOG(1. + A) * A
   ELSE
      FNA = PI * LOG(1. + 1. / A) / A
   ENDIF

3. IF (X .LT. - EPS) THEN
      LIMF = (SIN(PI * X) - COS(PI * X)) / X
   ELSE IF (ABS(X) .LT. EPS) THEN
      LIMF = 0.0
      PRINT *, 'DISCONTINUITY AT X', X
   ELSE
      LIMF = TAN(PI * X) / X
   ENDIF
```

block IF structures

1. IF (logical expression) THEN

   ⌈block of 1 or more statements—   ⌉
   ⌊executed only if logical expression is *true*⌋

   ENDIF

2. IF (logical expression) THEN

$$\begin{bmatrix} \text{block of 0 or more statements—} \\ \text{executed only if logical expression is } \textit{true} \end{bmatrix}$$

ELSE

$$\begin{bmatrix} \text{block of 0 or more statements—} \\ \text{executed only if logical expression is } \textit{false} \end{bmatrix}$$

ENDIF

3. IF (logical expression 1) THEN

$$\begin{bmatrix} \text{block of 0 or more statements—} \\ \text{executed only if logical expression 1 is } \textit{true} \end{bmatrix}$$

$$\left\{ \begin{array}{l} \text{ELSE IF (logical expression 2) THEN} \\ \begin{bmatrix} \text{block of 0 or more statements—} \\ \text{executed only if logical expression 2 is } \textit{true} \\ \text{and logical expression 1 is } \textit{false} \end{bmatrix} \\ \vdots \\ \text{ELSE} \\ \begin{bmatrix} \text{block of 0 or more statements—} \\ \text{executed only if } \textit{all} \text{ of the above logical} \\ \text{expressions are } \textit{false} \end{bmatrix} \end{array} \right\}$$

ENDIF

Remarks:

1. The first two variations are actually special cases of the third, in which the braces contain optional components. They are defined separately because the block IF is used most often in these forms.

2. The phrase *0 or more* in each block means that each block may actually be empty, a practice justified perhaps for documentation purposes only; it would mean "under this condition do nothing." For example,

```
IF ((X .GT. A) .AND. (X .LT. B)) THEN
ELSE
    PRINT *, 'OUTSIDE THE INTERVAL', X
    N = N + 1
ENDIF
```

is legal but equivalent to

```
IF ((X .LE. A) .OR. (X .GE. B)) THEN
    PRINT *, 'OUTSIDE THE INTERVAL', X
    N = N + 1
ENDIF
```

which is more compact and more readable.

3. The ellipsis means that the number of ELSE IF blocks is unlimited (except of course for local limits).

4. The ELSE block is optional; at most one is permitted.

5. Execution is as follows. The block IF executes *at most one* of the IF or ELSE IF blocks—the *first* one whose logical expression is true. If none are true, the ELSE block—if present—is executed. The third variation thus provides the equivalent of the generalized nested if statement in Pascal (see also below).

6. ELSE IF, ELSE, and ENDIF are executable statements. ELSE and END IF are simply place markers; they don't do anything except transfer control to the next statement.

In general, if there is at least one ELSE IF block, place the blocks in decreasing order of likelihood that the corresponding expression is true in order to minimize comparisons.

Observe that the logical IF is just a special (but convenient) case of the block IF. For example, the statement

```
IF (N .GT. MAX)  SUM = SUM + N
```

is equivalent to the sequence

```
IF (N .GT. MAX) THEN
    SUM = SUM + N
ENDIF
```

The remarks do not consider the contents of each of the blocks themselves. Actually, these structures can be somewhat more complicated. The blocks may contain any statements, including other block IFs. Thus one block IF may contain another block IF, which in turn may contain another, and so forth, as in lines 35–42 of Example 1.1. When one block, such as a block IF or a loop, contains another completely, the blocks are said to be *nested*.

The nesting of blocks is akin to placing a box inside another box. It implies that if structure B begins inside structure A, then structure B terminates inside structure A, as in Box 3.2.

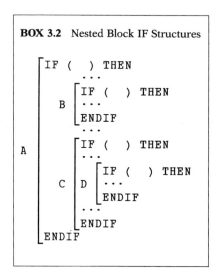

BOX 3.2   Nested Block IF Structures

```
IF (   ) THEN
    . . .
        IF (   ) THEN
   B    . . .
        ENDIF
    . . .
        IF (   ) THEN
A       . . .
            IF (   ) THEN
   C  D     . . .
            ENDIF
        . . .
        ENDIF
ENDIF
```

Associated with nested block IF structures is the idea of *levels*. Each time you encounter a block IF statement as you read a program from top to bottom, you increase the level by 1. When you encounter an ENDIF statement you decrease it by 1. Thus in Box 3.2 the statements in block D are at level 3, those in C but outside D and those in B are at level 2, and the rest are in level 1.

With this in mind, note that the remarks in the above definition apply for blocks *at the same level*. For example, remark 4 means that no more than one ELSE block is allowed at the same level within a block IF structure. Clearly, it would be ambiguous to have more than one at the same level anyway.

As a matter of style, it is best to keep the number of levels of nesting to a minimum. Too many levels overcomplicate the problem and makes the program hard to follow. Consider the following example, which determines the minimum of the three numbers N1, N2, and N3:

```
IF (N1 .GE. N2) THEN
    IF (N2 .GE. N3) THEN
        MIN = N3
    ELSE
        MIN = N2
    ENDIF
ELSE
    IF (N1 .GE. N3) THEN
        MIN = N3
    ELSE
        MIN = N1
    ENDIF
ENDIF
```

Even though there are only two levels, properly indented, the code is still needlessly complicated. The use of logical operators and/or ELSE IF blocks can reduce the complexity and shorten the code. The following sequence accomplishes the same result in only seven statements and is much easier to understand.

```
IF ((N1 .LE. N2) .AND. (N1 .LE. N3 )) THEN
    MIN = N1
ELSE IF ((N2 .LE. N1) .AND. (N2 .LE. N3)) THEN
    MIN = N2
ELSE
    MIN = N3
ENDIF
```

In both cases the comparisons are performed in the given order until one is found to be true. If the order doesn't matter, the tests are mutually exclusive, and the actions are one-line actions, then the code can be further simplified:

```
MIN = N3
IF ((N1 .LE. N2) .AND. (N1 .LE. N3)) MIN = N1
IF ((N2 .LE. N1) .AND. (N2 .LE. N3)) MIN = N2
```

Here we need only three statements. Obviously the first statement (MIN = N3) could have been used to simplify the first two examples too.

Style Guide:
1. Use logical IFs in place of block IFs where they are equivalent.
2. Indent IF, ELSE IF, and ELSE blocks consistently.
3. Avoid the use of empty blocks.
4. Minimize the nesting of block IFs: use ELSE IF, ELSE blocks, and logical operators.
5. Write the logical expressions in an IF–ELSE IF–ELSE structure in decreasing order of likelihood of occurrence.

3.3 THE GOTO, CONTINUE, AND STOP STATEMENTS

A control statement may cause the execution of a block other than the one immediately following the block that contains it. Control statements are classified as *conditional* when the block selection is based on the value of a logical expression, or as *unconditional* if the normal execution sequence is *always* changed.

**GOTO
Statement**

An IF statement is conditional; a *GOTO statement* is unconditional. A GOTO causes execution to continue at the statement labeled by the corresponding statement number.

Example: GOTO 500

GOTO statement

```
         ┌──────────────────────────────────────────────────────────────→
         ↑
  ───────┴──────────GOTO ────────────────statement ─ number ──────────────→
```

Remark: The statement number must label an executable statement, and it must be unique. Thus, IF statements, assignment statements, I/O statements, and even END, ELSE, and ELSE IF statements can have a statement number. However, ELSE and ELSE IF are unusual in that the Standard does not allow a GOTO to jump to them, and so statement numbers are useless in these two instances. Finally, even a GOTO can have a statement number, but that would be a poor programming practice. (Why?)

You are probably aware that the programming community generally looks askance at the GOTO statement and its equivalents in other languages. It has been said that "GOTO is a four-letter word." Overuse of the GOTO statement usually leads to programs with poor structure—sometimes referred to as "spaghetti code"—which makes them difficult to understand and maintain.

Programming languages vary with respect to the number and types of control structures they provide. Most versions of BASIC have very few control structures*; Pascal and PL/I, in contrast, have a rich variety. Given any Pascal program that solves a problem, it is possible—at least in theory—to write an equivalent Pascal program that uses *no* GOTO statements at all.

Unfortunately, standard FORTRAN is not sufficiently powerful to enable you to avoid GOTOs altogether. However, if you *limit your use of the GOTO strictly to the implementation of certain control structures*, your programs will automatically be well structured. However, this text is not dogmatic regarding the GOTO. An occasional use of the GOTO beyond the necessary implementation of control structures is probably acceptable as long as such use is kept to a minimum. A good program design will ensure that this is the case.

**CONTINUE
Statement**

In this book we follow the increasingly popular convention of using statement numbers only on *CONTINUE* statements (and, necessarily, on FORMAT statements, which are used for the layout of data for I/O). A

---

*However, the proposed ANSI BASIC, and TRUE BASIC, for example, have a good selection of control structures.

CONTINUE statement simply passes control to the next statement in sequence. Its purpose is to act as a place for a control statement, such as a GOTO, to jump to. Its form is simply

<u>n</u>   CONTINUE

where *n* is a statement number.

Limiting statement numbers to CONTINUE statements has two advantages. First, it limits the format of loops to a few conventions. Second, it simplifies modifications that require the addition of one or more instructions. For example, suppose that the statement

    10   READ *, X

represents the first statement in a loop. Suppose also that a later modification requires the statement

        N = N + 1

to precede the READ statement in the loop. In that case we must remove the statement number and indent the READ. On the other hand, if the original sequence is

    10   CONTINUE
            READ *, X

then the other statement can be inserted before the READ without any other changes.

Before we examine loop structures in the next section, we present one more control statement, the *STOP statement*, which terminates execution of the program. Its form is simply

STOP Statement

        STOP

Execution will also terminate if there is a transfer to the END statement. The use of STOP instead avoids a needless GOTO. Recall its use in Example 1.1.

The STOP statement can also be written as

        STOP <u>n</u>

where *n* is either an integer no more than five digits long, as in

        STOP 125

or a character constant, as in

        STOP 'RANGE ERROR IN X'

The value of *n* can provide information to the user regarding the reason for program termination. Many systems will display the value of n upon execution of the STOP statement.

Style Guide: Keep the number of GOTOs to a minimum.

3.4 LOOPS

Loops are sequences of statements that may be repeated. You are undoubtedly familiar with them in another programming language. The loops we construct here represent not a standard but a convention that is similar to others proposed by a number of FORTRAN experts. Strict adherence to this convention will promote the writing of well-structured programs. All necessary loop variations are discussed here except the *DO loop*, which is covered in the next chapter.

WHILE Loop

One of the more useful forms of a loop is the *WHILE loop*, (sometimes *DO-WHILE*) which is characterized by a test of a *condition*—a logical expression—*at the beginning of the loop*. If the condition is *true*, execution proceeds with the loop; otherwise execution continues with the statement immediately following the loop. We refer to the statements inside the loop as the *loop body*.

Unlike Pascal and similar languages, standard FORTRAN does *not* have a WHILE statement or its equivalent. To be sure, there are many versions of FORTRAN that do, with a typical loop construct like the following:

```
WHILE (logical expression) DO
      [body of the loop]
ENDWHILE
```

BOX 3.3 WHILE-Loop Simulation

```
*        WHILE (logical_expression) DO
n        CONTINUE
         IF (logical_expression) THEN
             loop body--executed if the
             logical_expression is true
                 :
                 :
             GO TO n
         ENDIF
*        ENDWHILE
```

However, since it is not part of the Standard it should be avoided. Instead, we *simulate* the WHILE loop with the structure given in Box 3.3. Here *n* is a statement number. The loop body is executed if the logical expression is true; otherwise execution continues with the statement immediately following the end of the loop (the ENDIF). Note the use of the GOTO to implement the loop. Since it is part of the loop body, it too is executed when the expression is true. Since the test of the expression occurs at the beginning, the loop behaves exactly like a WHILE loop.

The comments immediately preceding and following the block make it clear that the block IF is a loop, as in the following example:

```
        SUM = 0.0
        X = DECP(1)
        N = 1
*       WHILE (N .LE. NMAX) .AND. (X .GT. 0.0)) DO
100     CONTINUE
        IF ((N .LE. NMAX) .AND. (X .GT. 0.0)) THEN
            SUM = SUM + X
            X = X * DECP(N)
            N = N + 1
            GOTO 100
        ENDIF
*       ENDWHILE
```

In this example it is clear that the IF block is a loop. The loop continues as long as N is greater than or equal to NMAX and X is greater than 0. The two statements preceding the WHILE statement are required to *initialize* the loop. Both N and X must be defined because the exit condition depends on their values. A WHILE loop always requires this initialization process.

Actually, it may be best to let the WHILE comment do double-duty by using a more meaningful phrase than the logical expression, as in

```
*     WHILE (NO. OF VALUES BOUNDED AND POSITIVE POTENTIAL)
```

for the above example.

Another variation on the loop structure is the *REPEAT-UNTIL loop* (also called the *DO-UNTIL loop*). In a REPEAT-UNTIL loop, *the test for exit from the loop is made at the end.** If the condition is *true*, execution continues with the statement immediately following the loop; otherwise execution proceeds with another pass through the loop. Because the test

REPEAT-UNTIL Loop

---

*Actually, some DO-UNTIL structures test at the beginning of the loop (e.g., COBOL's PERFORM-UNTIL).

occurs at the bottom of the loop, the body is always executed at least once. The following sequence is typical of the REPEAT-UNTIL structure:

```
REPEAT
   [body of the loop]
UNTIL  (logical_expression)
```

The DO-UNTIL loops may be simulated in FORTRAN as in Box 3.4.

BOX 3.4 REPEAT-UNTIL Simulation

```
*       REPEAT
n       CONTINUE
           [loop body]
        IF (.NOT. (logical_expression)) GOTO n
*       UNTIL (logical_expression)
```

Here *n* is a statement number. The comment lines clarify the purpose and boundaries of the structure. Because the logical expression causes an exit from the loop when true, the expression is negated in the IF statement to continue the looping progress. Since the program exits the loop when the expression is true, the sequence behaves exactly like a REPEAT-UNTIL loop. Here is a short example:

```
*       REPEAT
100     CONTINUE
           POL = POL + A(N) * XI
           XI = XI * X
           N = N + 1
        IF (.NOT. (N .GT. POLMAX)) GO TO 100
*       UNTIL (POLYNOMIAL EVALUATED)
```

The loop continues until N is greater than POLMAX.

The REPEAT-UNTIL variation does not seem to be as useful as the WHILE loop, but on occasion it is convenient; for example, to ensure a valid selection from a menu in an interactive program (i.e., repeat prompt until choice is valid). If you know that the loop body will *always* be executed at least once, you can use a REPEAT-UNTIL loop. If you use it in a FORTRAN program, be sure that it is restricted to the above form.

END = Clause   Looping often involves I/O. A typical process reads data and then performs some computations, looping until the input data is exhausted. For this we need some way to detect the end-of-data condition and to exit from the loop. FORTRAN provides the *END = clause* for this purpose, which provides the same function as EOF in Pascal and in some versions of BASIC. It eliminates the need for a *sentinel* (sometimes called a *trailer*)—a special value as the last data item—to detect the end.

The list-directed READ statement may be written as in the following example:

```
READ (*,*, END = 300) X, Y, A(1)
```

Execution transfers to the statement labeled with statement number 300 when there is no more data, or insufficient data to assign to the three items in the READ input item list. The asterisks are explained below.

We can now revise our definition of the READ statement as follows:

READ statement (revised)

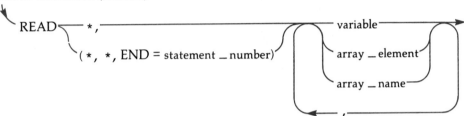

If the END = clause is used, it must be enclosed in parentheses with the two preceding asterisks as shown. The parenthetical expression is called the *control information list* and may contain many other options that we will examine in later chapters. The first asterisk implies that the data will be read from the standard input unit; the second means that the data is format-free, as in a list-directed READ. Note that *no* comma follows the control information list.

If we enter the input data interactively, the end-of-data condition is usually specified by a special character, such as CTRL-Z. Since that is system-dependent, you will have to obtain that information locally.

This form of the READ statement can be used to construct another useful version of a loop, as in Box 3.5.

BOX 3.5   READ-Controlled Loop

```
*     WHILE (NOT END OF DATA) DO
n     CONTINUE
      READ (*,*, END = P) input_item_list
          ⌈loop body
          ⋮
          ⌊GO TO n
P     CONTINUE
*     ENDWHILE
```

The items n and p are statement numbers.

As indicated by the comments, this loop variation is actually a special case of the WHILE loop, since the test for exit—the-end-of-data condition—is made at the beginning. NOTE: it is important that *the loop exit jumps to the statement immediately following the loop, that is, the statement labeled p.* This is a cardinal rule of structured programming. Since FORTRAN does not enforce this convention, it is the programmer's responsibility. The following example reads pairs of numbers into two arrays, A and B, and computes their sums.

```
          N = 0
          SUMA = 0.0
          SUMB = 0.0
*         WHILE (NOT END OF DATA) DO
50        CONTINUE
          READ (*,*, END = 60) A(N), B(N)
              SUMA = SUMA + A(N)
              SUMB = SUMB + B(N)
              N = N + 1
              GOTO 50
60        CONTINUE
*         ENDWHILE
```

Clearly, it would be easy to design a REPEAT-UNTIL variation with the READ taking place at the end of the loop.

A loop that involves incrementing an integer variable and a subsequent exit when that variable surpasses a maximum value is usually written as a DO loop, which is covered in Chapter 5. In summary, all loops should be restricted to DO loops and to the three variations discussed above.

3.5 AN EXAMPLE

We conclude this chapter with a complete program that illustrates the use of these loop constructs. Many applications in science and engineering require the computation of the maximum or minimum value of a real-valued function, $f(x)$, in an interval, $[a, b]$. Certainly calculus can be used for this purpose, but these values can also be approximated in a straightforward manner by means of a computer program. Most computer installations have FORTRAN libraries that contain rigorous programs to solve problems like these, but the algorithms used are outside the scope of this book. The following solution is presented only as a simple application of loops.

To simplify the problem, we assume that the function value $f(x)$ falls in the range of representable numbers, for every x in $[a, b]$.

To find approximations to the minimum and maximum values of f, we first compute the *smallest positive real number, EPS,* that can be represented in the computer. You could look this up in a manual, but then you would probably have to change the value if you were to run the program on another computer. The approach used here promotes transportability. The value *EPS* is defined as

$$EPS = 2^{-n}$$

where n is the smallest positive integer such that

$$1.0 \equiv 1.0 + 2^{-(n+1)}$$

EPS is sometimes called the *unit roundoff* (for that particular computer).

We would like to use *EPS* as the interval size between successive values of x, so that every possible value of f in $[a, b]$ is computed. We can then compare the current value of f with the extrema determined so far, updating them as we step through the interval.

However, if the interval $[a, b]$ is not close to 1 (e.g., $[1000, 2000]$) then the following equality

```
X = X + K * EPS
```

will hold for small integral values of K because of the relative difference in the size of X and EPS. (This concept will be clarified in Chapter 6.)

Therefore, to avoid taking a large number of useless steps, we will first *scale* the interval to the range $[0, 1]$. If y varies between 0 and 1, then x will vary between a and b, where

$$x = (b - a) \cdot y + a$$

The following sequence is a pseudocode representation of the solution for a specific function f.

1. Read the endpoints of the desired interval: a and b.
2. Compute *EPS*
3. set K = 0
4. set $maxf = minf = f(a)$
5. set $y = EPS$
6. While $y < 1$ do
   a. set $x = (b - a) \cdot y + a$
   b. compute $f(x)$
   c. if $f(x) > maxf$ then set $maxf = f(x)$
      else if $f(x) < minf$ then set $minf = f(x)$
   d. set K = K + 1
   e. set $y = K * EPS$
7. Print $maxf, minf$

Actually, a similar argument can be made with respect to the value of f to reduce the number of steps, but we will be satisfied with the above approach for the sake of simplicity.

The program follows, using the function

$$f(x) = 1/12 \cdot x^3 - 0.5 \cdot \cos 2x$$

To apply this program to a different function, several statements would have to be changed. Later we will discuss how this problem can be avoided.

EXAMPLE 3.1

```
      PROGRAM MINMAX
***************************************************************
* AUTHOR - J.A. HSU    6/2/87
* THIS PROGRAM COMPUTES APPROXIMATIONS TO THE MINIMUM AND
* MAXIMUM VALUES OF A REAL-VALUED FUNCTION OF A REAL VARIABLE IN
* AN INTERVAL [A,B] WHERE A AND B ARE READ FROM THE STANDARD
* INPUT UNIT.  TO APPLY THE PROGRAM TO A DIFFERENT FUNCTION,
* CHANGE THE TWO EXPRESSIONS BELOW THAT REPRESENT THE FUNCTION.
* THE PROGRAM SCALES THE INTERVAL TO THE RANGE [0,1] SO THAT ALL
* POSSIBLE MACHINE NUMBERS IN THE INTERVAL ARE TESTED.
*
* A, B--THE INTERVAL ENDPOINTS
* X--THE INDEPENDENT VARIABLE IN [A, B]
* Y--X SCALED TO THE INTERVAL [0, 1]
* FUN--THE FUNCTION VALUE AT X
* MAXF, MINF--THE MAXIMUM AND MINIMUM VALUES OF THE FUNCTION
* EPS--THE UNIT ROUNDOFF (COMPUTED)
* K--STEP MARKER IN INTERVAL [0, 1]
* N--USED FOR EPS DETERMINATION
* BMINA, D12--B - A, 1/12 TO AVOID RECOMPUTATIONS IN LOOP
***************************************************************
      REAL A, B, X, Y, MAXF, MINF, FUN, EPS, BMINA, D12
      INTEGER K, N
      READ *, A, B
      BMINA = B - A
      D12 = 1.0 / 12.0
*
* COMPUTE SMALLEST REPRESENTABLE NUMBER, EPS
*
      N = 1
*     WHILE UNIT ROUNDOFF NOT REACHED DO
10    CONTINUE
      IF (1.0 .NE. 1.0 + 2.0 ** (-N)) THEN
         N = N + 1
         GOTO 10
```

```
        ENDIF
*       ENDWHILE
        EPS = 2.0 ** (-N + 1)
*
* CHANGE THIS EXPRESSION TO MATCH THE FUNCTION AT X = A:
*
        FUN = D12 * A ** 3 - 0.5 * COS(2.0 * A)
        MAXF = FUN
        MINF = FUN
*
* SEARCH FOR EXTREMA
*
*       WHILE STILL IN THE Y INTERVAL (0,1) DO
        IF (Y .LE. 1.0) THEN
            X = BMINA * Y - A
*
* CHANGE THIS EXPRESSION TO MATCH THE FUNCTION AT X:
*
            FUN = D12 * X ** 3 - 0.5 * COS(2.0 * X)
            IF (FUN .GT. MAXF) THEN
                MAXF = FUN
            ELSE IF (FUN .LT. MINF) THEN
                MINF = FUN
            ENDIF
            K = K + 1
            Y = REAL(K) * EPS
        ENDIF
*       ENDWHILE
        PRINT *, 'THE MAX AND MIN VALUES OF THE FUNCTION ARE:'
        PRINT *, MAXF, MINF
        END
```

Exercises

Section 3.1

1. Let A = 1.0, B = 2.0, C = 3.0 (real), P = .TRUE., Q = .FALSE., and R = .TRUE. (logical). Which of the following are valid logical expressions or assignment statements? If one is invalid, rewrite it in a valid form (answers may vary).

   * **a.** A .AND. (B .OR. C)
   b. P = .NOT. R
   c. R = (A .LT. B) .OR. (B .GT. C) .AND. (C .GT. A)
   * **d.** B .GT. A .OR. Q
   e. A .LT. B .LT. C
   f. R = B .GT. A .OR. B .NE. C
   * **g.** R .AND. .TRUE.
   h. Q .NEQV. A .NE. B

    * **i.** P .NOT. Q
    j. .NOT. P .AND. R .EQV. A .EQ. B
    k. Q = (A .LT. B .OR. B .GT. C) .AND. (C .GT. A)
    * **l.** .NOT. .NOT. P .OR. .NOT. Q
    m. Q = Q .OR. .NOT. R
    n. P = A .LT. C .OR. .NOT. Q .EQV. B .GT. A .OR. Q

2. For those valid expressions and assignments in Exercise 1, what is the value?

3. Write FORTRAN logical expressions corresponding to the following:
     ***a.** $x < y < z$
     b. a is not greater than either b or c
     c. x is less than a and -100
     ***d.** neither x nor y is greater than $a + b$
     e. either $p = q = r$ or else p and q are both greater than or equal to N.

Section 3.2

4. Write an IF statement or block IF statement to do the following:
     ***a.** Add 1 to N if $|FX| \geq$ EPS and N < NMAX
     b. Print the smaller of X and Y
     ***c.** Assume an array GRADE exists with GRADE (1) = number of As on a test, GRADE(2) = number of Bs, and so forth. The IF block should add 1 to the appropriate grade count based on the value of MYGRAD. The ranges are: A (90–100), B (80–98), C (70–79), D (<70).
     d. If $r < 0$, print an error message; otherwise compute the volume of a sphere ($v = \frac{4}{3}\pi r^3$) and print r and v.

Section 3.4

5. Write a WHILE loop to do the following:
     ***a.** Compute the sum of all odd and even numbers in an integer array, NUM. Assume there are K values in the array.
     b. Print t and $f(t) = e^{-kt}$ for $t = 0, .5, 1.0, 1.5, \ldots$ until $f(t) <$ EPS. Assume k is given.
     c. Read a set of numbers and compute their standard deviation. Use the formula

$$S = \sqrt{\frac{1}{n-1}\left(\sum_{i=1}^{n} x_i^2 - \frac{\left(\sum_{i=1}^{n} x_i\right)^2}{n}\right)}$$

where n is the total number of values. Assume that n is not known in advance.

*d. Given a real array SAMPL of N values, print each value that is within EPS of CRIT, but exit from the loop if the difference between the largest and smallest values encountered in SAMPL is greater than MAXDIF.

e. Read a set of real numbers and compute their sum, but terminate the loop when you encounter a value of 0 or when the value just read is greater than twice the average of the three previous values; don't include this value in the sum. Read at least four numbers.

6. Write a REPEAT-UNTIL loop for each of the problems in Exercise 5 above. For each problem, which loop form do you prefer?

7. Write a program that reads a set of integers and prints the sums of the positive and negative values and the total number of positive and negative values.

* 8. Write a program to evaluate a polynomial, p, at a point $x = b$, where p is given by

$$p(x) = a_0 + a_1 \cdot x + a_2 \cdot x^2 + \ldots + a_n \cdot x^n$$

Read n, each of the coefficients a_i, and b. Evaluate p as shown and also by *Horner's method*, in which p is written in the form:

$$p(x) = a_0 + x \cdot (a_1 + x \cdot (a_2 + \ldots + x \cdot (a_{n-1} + x \cdot (a_n)) \ldots))$$

Count and print the number of multiplications and additions in both methods. Which one is more efficient?

9. A well-known formula relating the pressure, temperature, and volume of a confined gas is

$$\frac{P_1 V_1}{T_1} = \frac{P_2 V_2}{T_2}$$

Write a program that reads a list of measurements of a gas pressure P_1, volume V_1, and new volume V_2 and subsequently computes and prints the new pressure P_2 for each set. The temperature is to be held constant at 100°C. Use a negative pressure, P_1, to terminate the list. Also, first read in a value, MAXPR, which should be used to terminate the program if the pressure P_2 exceeds MAXPR.

10. Write a program to tabulate each of the following functions. Read the interval limits and the step size.
*a. $y = \frac{1}{3} \log [(1 + \cos x)/(1 - \cos x)]$ on (.5, 1.5) in steps of .1.
b. $y = \sin^2 x + \cos^2 x$ on $(0, \pi)$ in steps of $\pi/16$.

*Solution to this Exercise is given in Appendix D.

    c. $y = \sqrt{r^2 - (x^2/a^2)}$ on $[(r/a), (r/a)]$ in steps of $\frac{1}{8}$.
      Choose $a = 3$ and $r = 6$.
    d. $y = (\sin x/x)$ for x in $(-1, 1)$ in steps of $\frac{1}{16}$.

11. Write a program to read a list of Fahrenheit temperatures, convert them to Celsius ($C = \frac{5}{9} \cdot [F - 32]$), print both values, and then print an evaluation message according to the following list:

$C \le -20$	stay indoors
$-20 < C \le 0$	heavy coat
$0 < C \le 10$	lined jacket
$10 < C \le 20$	light jacket
$20 < C \le 30$	long sleeves
$30 < C \le 40$	short sleeves
$40 < C$	swim wear

12. Write a program to read a list of positive integers and determine whether each is a prime number.

13. A jet lands at v_0 miles per hour with a constant deceleration of 30 feet per second. Write a program to determine how far it will travel before it stops. Use the equation

$$d = \sum_{i=1}^{N} [v_0 + (v_0 - 30t)]^{1/2} \text{ for } t = 1, 2, 3, \ldots$$

seconds, where d is the distance in *feet*. Read various values of v_0 and print d in each case for each value of t.

4 Structured Programming and Modularity

This chapter introduces two important programming concepts that relate to the overall design of a program, rather than to the syntax or semantics of a specific programming language. As such, like loops and if-then-else structures, they may be discussed in the context of any language.

The first topic to be covered—*structured programming*—deals with methods for designing programs in an organized way so that they can be more easily understood by someone other than the original author. This methodology promotes program correctness and reliability. Since about 70 to 80 percent of all current programming efforts involve the maintenance of existing programs, structured programming has become a required practice for business, industrial, governmental, and military applications. It is likely that you have already had some exposure to structured programming methods, especially if you have learned Pascal or some other modern programming language.

The second topic—*modularity*—is related to structured programming in that it deals with the design of programs in order to promote correctness, understandability, and ease of modification. Specifically, modularity is about designing *modules*—which can be combined like a set of building blocks to form a complete program. By conceiving of the solution to a problem in terms of modules, one can reduce a complex, difficult problem into a set of smaller subproblems, each of which is relatively easy to understand and code. Procedures in Pascal or subroutines in BASIC (using GOSUB-RETURN statements) are implementations of modularity features in those languages.

To be sure, although structured programming and modularity are language-independent concepts, their implementations are language-specific, and languages vary greatly with regard to the support they provide. This chapter presents these topics in the context of FORTRAN. Thus, we recommend that you study this chapter even though you may already be familiar with its themes.

4.1 STRUCTURED PROGRAMMING IN FORTRAN

What is *structured programming*? It is difficult to give a formal definition. It is a methodology—a collection of rules and guidelines—which, if followed strictly, leads to programs that are easier to read and understand, easier to modify, and easier to debug than they might otherwise. Often the approach is a matter of degree, with some proponents more zealous than others regarding the use—and bending—of some of the rules. This text is perhaps less strict than some, in part because FORTRAN lacks some of the control structures that help to code programs in a structured manner.

However, no matter how rich the language is in control structures, structured programming still requires a great deal of self-discipline if the final result is to be satisfactory. For that reason a better name for this methodology might be *disciplined* programming, although we will continue to use the popular name.

Structured Programming Guidelines

Some guidelines of structured programming have already been recommended to you in earlier chapters, such as the WHILE loop simulation. In this section we describe the general characteristics of a well-structured program before presenting some guidelines on how to create one.

First, *a structured program should be conceived of in terms of blocks,* or control structures, rather than as sequences of individual statements. The entire program should consist only of simple sequences, selection structures, and loops. Blocks may be nested—an IF_THEN block may contain a loop and vice versa—but the nesting depth should be kept to a minimum where possible, as discussed in the section on IF statements. A depth of two or sometimes three is considered acceptable. If your procedure requires more than that, you might give some thought to designing another.

Figure 4.1 is characteristic of a program with a good structure, where each box represents a block, and boxes within boxes represent

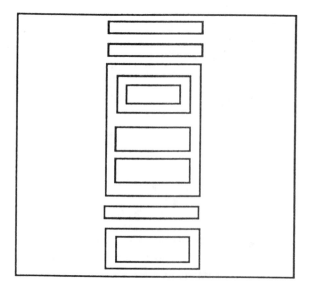

Figure 4.1
Example block structure of a well-structured program.

nested blocks. Control passes from top to bottom from one block to the next. Thus, *there is no jumping around a block and no jumping back*. Also, *each block should be entered only at its beginning and exited only at its end*. There should be no jumps out of or into the middle of loops. These are *critical* requirements of structured programming. They imply the avoidance of the GOTO except to implement loops, as described in the previous chapter.

Second, *the blocks used should be limited to those forms described in the previous chapter*. In particular, any loop can be constructed as one of the variations in the previous chapter or as a DO loop (Chapter 5). One important characteristic that is common to all of these variations is that *there is only one exit from the loop*. In other words there is only one statement in the loop that tests a logical expression for the continuation of the looping process.

On occasion, however, the single-exit limit may be awkward to enforce. Consider, for example, a loop in which data is read from a file, accumulated in a sum, and processed in other ways. Suppose also that it is necessary to exit from the loop and continue processing if the absolute value of the sum exceeds a certain value, MAXSUM. In this case there are two possible exit conditions: (1) the sum is too large or (2) the loop runs out of data.

One could still write this loop with a single exit by placing a sentinel at the end of the data stream and using a test for exit as in the following program segment.

```
          :
          :
       SUM = 0
       READ *, X
*      WHILE (DATA AVAILABLE AND SUM WITHIN LIMITS) DO
10     CONTINUE
       IF (X .NE. LAST .AND. ABS(SUM + X) .LT. MAXSUM) THEN
          SUM = SUM + X
          N = N + 1
          :
          :
          READ *, X
          GOTO 10
       ENDIF
*      ENDWHILE
          :
          :
```

Note that the READ is placed at the end of the loop and that an initial READ precedes the loop. This is a usual practice for loops involving I/O.

This approach is acceptable, but the use of a sentinel is often awkward. One can avoid it with the END = option if *multiple* exits are used, as in the following revision of the above sequence.

```
              ⋮
*        WHILE (DATA AVAILABLE) DO
10       CONTINUE
         READ (*, *, END = 20) X
            IF (ABS(SUM + X) .GE. MAXSUM) GOTO 20
            SUM = SUM + X
            N = N + 1
              ⋮
            GOTO 10
20       CONTINUE
*        ENDWHILE
              ⋮
```

In this example an IF statement in the loop body exits from the loop if the sum is too large. Consequently there are two exits from the loop. Some proponents of structured programming don't like this. Others—including the author—find it acceptable as long as the exits *jump to the statement immediately following the loop* (the line labeled 20). In this way the loop retains its block structure. An IF statement used this way is called a *break statement*. Some languages include explicit break statements for this purpose. They may appear anywhere in the loop body, but their use should be limited.

Observe that in both cases, a block IF may be required following the loop in order to handle the two exit conditions. That is, the program may proceed differently depending on the reason for the exit.

Third, *all of the style guidelines* mentioned in this and earlier chapters *should be used in constructing a program*. Descriptive prologues and comments, meaningful symbolic names, indenting of loop bodies and block IFs—all are necessary components of a well-structured program. Loops and block IFs should be easy to spot.

A fourth characteristic of a well-structured program is that *it can be read continuously from top to bottom*. There should be no jumping back to follow the code in order to understand what is going on. Review Example 1.1. Strict adherence to the guidelines described above should produce results of this kind.

A fifth and final characteristic of a well-structured program is that it is *modular*. Programs for complex problems are often broken down into smaller groups of blocks, each group—or *module*—representing the solution of a subproblem. One module might sort an array of numbers, another might process errors, and yet another might compute the boundary values for an object in a heat-transfer problem. Thus, just as statements are grouped into blocks to represent the logical completion of a task, so are blocks grouped into modules. Rather than being one long sequence of blocks, a program is subdivided into these logical units.

In FORTRAN, modules are represented by *subroutines* and *func-*

tions, which we introduce in the next section and cover in detail in Chapter 7. Pascal uses procedures and functions. Most versions of BASIC have only the GOSUB-RETURN combination, which is insufficient for true modularity.

In general the logic of the problem solution determines the module divisions. One guideline is that a module should solve only *one* problem. For example, sorting an array and printing a table of results is best done in two modules. A weaker guideline—more of a rule of thumb—is that an entire module should fit on a single page.

Consider the following example, which violates some of these rules. This program finds a *root* of a function, f (i.e., where the function value is zero), by means of the so-called *bisection method*. The process is illustrated in Figure 4.2.

Unstructured Example

We assume that values A and B are given, where $f(A) \times f(B) < 0$ (i.e., f has opposite signs at these points) and that the graph of f is a continuous unbroken line. This ensures that f crosses the x axis at least once. The bisection method proceeds by successively halving the interval containing the root until it is as small as desired. The midpoint of the final interval is taken to be the root. The interval containing the root is determined by comparing the signs of the function at the interval endpoints. In the figure the sequence of midpoints is $m_1, m_2, m_3, \ldots$.

An unstructured version of the bisection algorithm for the function $f(x) = x^3 - 2x - 1$ is given in Example 4.1. The prologue is omitted to save space.

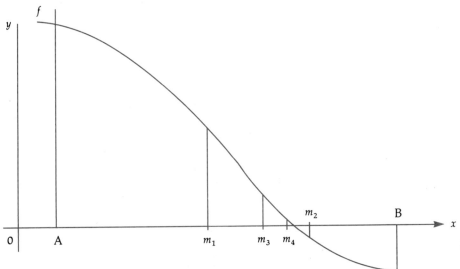

Figure 4.2
The bisection method.

EXAMPLE 4.1

```
        REAL A, B, TOL, ERROR, MIDPT, FA, FB, FM
        INTEGER N, MAXIT
        PARAMETER (MAXIT = 20)
        N = 0
        READ *, A, B, MIDPT, TOL
        FA = A ** 3 - 2. * A - 1.
        FB = B ** 3 - 2. * B - 1.
*   CHECK FOR OPPOSITE SIGNS
10      ERROR = ABS(B - A)
20      ERROR = ERROR / 2.
        MIDPT = (A + B) / 2.
        FM = MIDPT ** 3 - 2. * MIDPT - 1.
*   IS INTERVAL SUFFICIENTLY SMALL?
        IF (ERROR .LT. TOL) GOTO 40
        N = N + 1
*   IS ERROR REQUIREMENT TOO SMALL?
        IF (N .GE. MAXIT) GOTO 50
*   GET THE NEW INTERVAL ENDPOINTS
        IF (FA * FM .LE. 0.) GOTO 30
        A = MIDPT
        FA = FM
        GOTO 20
30      B = MIDPT
        FB = FM
        GOTO 20
40      PRINT *, 'THE SOLUTION, VALUE, ERROR:', MIDPT, FM, ERROR
        STOP
50      PRINT *, 'TOO MANY ITERATIONS - TOLERANCE TOO SMALL'
        PRINT *, 'OR FUNCTION NOT CONTINUOUS'
        STOP
        END
```

You will learn, in a later chapter, that there are better ways to evaluate a function in FORTRAN. The point of the example is that the unstructured code makes the program difficult to understand. To read it you are forced by the GOTOs to jump around statements or to jump back. We will design a much more readable structured version below.

This example leads us into the second question of this section: now that we know what a well-structured program should look like, how do we create one? This is by far the more difficult question to answer, since this is really what programming is all about. There are complete books on the subject, and to do it well requires a good deal of experience. It is possible only to give some general guidelines here and to demonstrate them by examples. If you learned programming with a language like Pascal or PL/I, you are probably accustomed to these ideas. If you learned with BASIC, you may have to forget some bad habits.

Structured Design

The first step in the writing of a program is the *design*. You design a program just as you would design an automobile engine. You think. You write down how you are going to solve the problem before you begin writing FORTRAN statements. This is the most important part of the programming process. A bad design will always result in a bad program.

To start, write down a detailed statement of the problem. You should put a reasonable amount of time into considering algorithms and heuristics for solving the problem. Be sure to consider alternative solutions and decide which one seems best, given how the program is to be used, the time constraints, and so forth.

Ask yourself questions about the problem and the proposed solution that will help you to write the program later. For example, consider the problem of finding the root of a function. Suppose you decide to use the bisection algorithm. How should the function be represented? What parameters should be provided on input, for example, interval endpoints where the function has opposite signs? Will   the input be interactive? What kinds of input errors are possible, and what should be done about them? What limits should be placed on the error tolerance? Should the program attempt to find all of the roots in the given interval or just one? Resist the temptation to begin writing code too early. Unless you first provide answers to questions like these, your program will most likely be a solution to the *wrong* problem.

Design your programs from the *top down*. Starting with the original statement of the problem, approach it as you would approach writing an essay. Write a rough outline of the program, specifying just the major steps. For example:

  I. Read the numbers into an array, A
 II. Sort the array A into ascending order
III. Locate and print the median value
      ⋮

The next step is to *refine* the outline. Take each step of the outline and expand it, specifying in greater detail the steps required to perform the task. For example, step III above could be expanded as follows:

III. Locate and print the median value in A
   A. If N (the size of A) is odd, then

$$median = A(N/2 + 1)$$

   else

$$median = (A(N/2) + A(N/2 + 1)) / 2$$

B. Print median

It is not necessary to write the outline and its refinements in FORTRAN. A popular approach is to use what is called *structured English*, or *pseudocode*, as in the above example. In that way you can concentrate on solving the problem without concerning yourself with distracting details of the language. An example of a pseudocode WHILE loop is

> while $|f(x_i)| >$ tolerance do:
> compute a new value for x_i
> increment the count
> print x_i, $f(x_i)$

An example of a counting loop (For, DO) is

> For $i = 1$ to n do
> add x_i to SUM
> compute the next term of the inner product
> compute the ith row of the difference table

Note that the pseudocode resulting from the refinement of a step in the previous stage may require further refinement. Each stage may suggest the inclusion of additional variable names or parameters. This process of repeatedly refining successive descriptions of the solution to the original problem is called *stepwise refinement*, a term suggested by Nicklaus Wirth, the designer of the Pascal language. As you proceed with the refinement, each stage will include more and more detail, until eventually the pseudocode will look more and more like statements in the *target* language—in our case FORTRAN.

The top-down design of a program is central to structured programming methodology. It has the advantage that a difficult problem may be logically subdivided into subproblems that are easier to handle. Also, once the lowest level of the design is finished, it is a simple matter to convert the pseudocode to FORTRAN. It does require practice and self-discipline, but the disciplined use of this technique has been shown to produce programs that have fewer bugs and are easier to understand and maintain.

A Structured Example

Let us now apply this methodology to finding the root of a function using the bisection method. To simplify the problem, we assume that the function is continuous and that we will find at most one root. We will represent the function as in the above example. Input values will be the endpoints of the interval supposedly containing the root, and the error tolerance, which we will use as an upper bound on the length of the subinterval containing the root. The program is assumed to be noninteractive. Finally, we will check for errors in which (1) the function value has the same sign at both end points, (2) the error tolerance requested is too small for our computer to handle, and (3) the function has no root in the interval or is not continuous.

We begin with a rough outline. We must read the data, check for opposite signs at the endpoints, and, if valid, keep reducing the size of the subinterval containing the root until we are satisfied. Thus we have:

  I. Read the endpoints A, B, and the error threshold TOL
 II. Evaluate F at A and B
III. If $F(A) * F(B) < 0$ then
      find the root
    else
      print error message: 'same sign at endpoints'

Step I requires no refinement; it is easily coded as a single FORTRAN statement.
Step II may be rewritten as

 II. Evaluate F at A and B
    A. $FA = A ** 3 - 2. * A - 1.$
    B. $FB = B ** 3 - 2. * B - 1.$

which needs no further refinement.

Now consider step III. We must decide what the phrase "find the root" means. We want to evaluate F at the midpoint of the current interval and then redefine the current interval to be the half-interval containing the root. We will do this repeatedly until we are "satisfied." This leads us to:

III. If $F(A) * F(B) \leq 0$ then
    find the root:
    A. while not satisfied do
        1. FM = value of F at midpoint of (A, B)
        2. reset (A, B) to be the half-interval
           containing the root
    B. root is the last midpoint
    C. print root, function value, and error
    else
      print error message: 'same sign at endpoints'

Let us concentrate on step III.A. We will be "satisfied" if the error—the absolute value of the difference between the exact root and the approximation—is less than the tolerance that was read in. Some thought will show that the error is bounded by $(B - A) / 2$, where (A, B) contains the root.

However, we must be concerned with possible errors of types (2) and (3) described above, which could cause our WHILE-structure to loop indefinitely. An easy way to prevent this from happening is to use a counter to limit the number of loop iterations.

Given these considerations we can now refine the WHILE loop in step III.A to obtain:

IIIA.
```
ERROR = ABS(B - A)
COUNT = 0
REPEAT
   MIDPT = (A + B) / 2.
   FM = MIDPT ** 3 - 2. * MIDPT - 1.
   ERROR = ERROR / 2.
   INCREMENT COUNT
   RESET (A, B) TO BE THE HALF-INTERVAL
                    CONTAINING THE ROOT
UNTIL COUNT > MAXIT OR ERROR < TOL
```

Note that we have replaced the WHILE loop with a REPEAT loop, which was observed to require fewer statements for this problem. Now, how can (A, B) be reset correctly? Suppose that the root is in the left half-interval. Then F(A) * F(MIDPT) will be negative, and we should reset B to be the midpoint, and similarly if the root is in the right half. With this in mind we will refine step III.A again. We will also replace the phrase "increment COUNT" with a more FORTRANlike statement.

IIIA.
```
ERROR = ABS(B - A)
COUNT = 0
REPEAT
   MIDPT = (A + B) / 2.
   FM = MIDPT ** 3 - 2. * MIDPT - 1.
   ERROR = ERROR / 2.
   COUNT = COUNT + 1
   IF FA * FM < 0 THEN
       B = MIDPT
       FB = B ** 3 - 2. * B - 1
   ELSE
       A = MIDPT
       FA = A ** 3 - 2. * A - 1
UNTIL COUNT > MAXIT OR ERROR < TOL
```

At this point step III.A is sufficiently detailed to be coded directly into FORTRAN. Upon exit from this loop, MIDPT can be taken as the approximation for the root, FM the function value, and ERROR the error of the approximation. The user should be informed if the maximum number of iterations was exceeded, thus implying an error of type (2) or (3). Therefore we refine step III.C as follows:

```
   IF COUNT > MAXIT THEN
      PRINT 'MAXIMUM ITERATIONS EXCEEDED--
          SELECTED TOLERANCE TOO SMALL OR DISCONTINUOUS
          FUNCTION'
      PRINT 'ROOT, VALUE, ERROR:', MIDPT, FM, ERROR
      PRINT 'NO. OF ITERATIONS:', COUNT
```

Note that we chose to print the values even if the count was too large.

We may now easily combine the refined sections of pseudocode to form the complete FORTRAN program shown below. All of the variables and parameters should be declared, and to be safe you should examine every statement in the pseudocode to be sure that each and every variable is declared properly.

EXAMPLE 4.2

```
      PROGRAM  BISECT
*********************************************************
* AUTHOR:  P. V. WOLF      5/86
*
* THIS PROGRAM COMPUTES A ROOT OF THE FUNCTION F(X) = X**3-2*X-1
* IN (A, B), WHERE F(A)*F(B) < 0 TO A GIVEN ERROR TOLERANCE USING
* THE BISECTION METHOD.  A MAXIMUM OF 20 ITERATIONS IS ALLOWED.
* TO APPLY THIS PROGRAM TO A DIFFERENT FUNCTION, CHANGE ALL
* REFERENCES TO FA, FB, AND FM ACCORDINGLY. F MUST BE CONTINUOUS
* IN (A,B).
* INPUT VALUES: A, B, TOL (ERROR TOLERANCE), ON STANDARD INPUT
* UNIT, ALL ON SAME LINE, SEPARATED BY AT LEAST ONE SPACE.
* PARAMETERS AND VARIABLES:
* MAXIT--MAXIMUM NUMBER OF ITERATIONS (20 HERE)
* A, B--LEFT AND RIGHT ENDPOINTS OF INTERVAL CONTAINING THE
*     ROOT (INPUT)
* TOL--ERROR TOLERANCE (INPUT)
* MIDPT--MIDPOINT OF CURRENT INTERVAL
* COUNT--CURRENT NUMBER OF TIMES THE INTERVAL HAS BEEN HALVED
* ERROR--CURRENT BOUND ON THE ERROR
* FA, FB, FM--VALUES OF F AT A, B, AND MIDPT, RESPECTIVELY
*********************************************************
      INTEGER COUNT, MAXIT
      REAL A, B, TOL, MIDPT, ERROR, FA, FB, FM
      PARAMETER (MAXIT = 20)
*
* DEFINE INITIAL VALUES
*
      READ *, A, B, TOL
      FA = A ** 3 - 2. * A - 1.
      FB = B ** 3 - 2. * B - 1.
```

```
            ERROR = ABS(B - A)
            COUNT = 0
            IF (FA * FB .LE. 0.) THEN
*
* FIND THE ROOT
*
*           REPEAT
10          CONTINUE
                MIDPT = (A +B) / 2.
                FM = MIDPT ** 3 - 2. * MIDPT - 1.
                ERROR = ERROR / 2.
                COUNT = COUNT + 1
                IF (FA * FM .LE. 0.) THEN
                    B = MIDPT
                    FB = B ** 3 - 2. * B - 1.
                ELSE
                    A = MIDPT
                    FA = A ** 3 - 2. * A - 1.
                ENDIF
            IF (.NOT. (COUNT .GT. MAXIT .OR. ERROR .LT. TOL)) GOTO 10
*           UNTIL (TOO MANY ITERATIONS OR ACCEPTABLE ERROR)
*
* CHECK REASON FOR LOOP EXIT
*
            IF (COUNT .GT. MAXIT) THEN
                PRINT *, 'MAXIMUM ITERATIONS EXCEEDED'
                PRINT *, 'TOLERANCE TOO SMALL OR DISCONTINUOUS FUNCTION'
            ENDIF
            PRINT *
            PRINT *, 'ROOT, VALUE, ERROR:', MIDPT, FM, ERROR
            PRINT *, 'NO. OF ITERATIONS IS', COUNT
        ELSE
            PRINT *, 'ERROR--F HAS SAME SIGN AT END POINTS'
        ENDIF
        END
```

Both examples have about the same length, but the second is much easier to follow. Note, however, that there is also room for improvement in Example 4.2. The evaluation of the function F is awkward and requires too many changes if the program is to be applied to a different function. The next section describes a better technique. Also, what would happen if the user of the program supplied a value of A greater than B? Would it still work? Finally, the program does not take into account the special cases where the root is found exactly (i.e., where F(MIDPT) = 0).

4.2 AN INTRODUCTION TO MODULARITY AND SUBPROGRAMS

As we indicated in the last section, modularity is really a design methodology that is part of structured programming. Subdividing a problem into subproblems, each essentially contained within its own module, eases the solution process, since we do not have to provide details of the solution to the complete problem all at once. Rather, we can concentrate on the subproblem at hand.

Once the detailed design is complete and we are ready to code the solution, it is desireable to have a programming language that supports the modular design in some way. If there is strong support, then we may store each module independently of the others. A carefully written, general-purpose module, such as a sort routine or a procedure to solve a system of linear equations, could then be used as a component in other programs. The user is relieved of the burden of rewriting what may be the same routine, or something nearly the same, again and again. This is another argument for writing procedures in as general a way as possible to make them applicable to a wide variety of problems.

Module support also allows for coding and testing various components of a program in parallel. Large programs require teams of programmers that can work independently to produce a program in a reasonable length of time. Of course, complete independence is not possible, since the team members must agree on what variables and data must be *passed*, or made available, from one module to another, and how they are to be passed. We will return to this concept in the next section.

FORTRAN provides strong support for modularity through *functions* and *subroutines*. In this section they are introduced in an informal way; Chapter 7 presents the full details. This approach gives you a more complete view of the structure of FORTRAN programs relatively early in the text.

Recall from the last section the initial design steps of a program to compute the median value in a list of numbers:

   I. Read the numbers into an array A.
  II. Sort A into ascending order.
 III. Compute and print the median value.

One could, of course, refine and code each of these steps into FORTRAN sequences and combine them into a single program. However, it would be just as easy, and in keeping with modularity guidelines, to define each of these steps as a separate (sub)program and to *call* (i.e., to execute) the subprograms in the proper sequence. Thus, the actual structure for such a program might look like the following:

Main Program:
  call the *Read* subprogram
  call the *Sort* subprogram
  call the *Median* subprogram
End Main Program
Read subprogram definition
Sort subprogram definition
Median subprogram definition

In the example, the main program—sometimes called the *driver program*— does nothing more than call the subprograms, although it would include some type statements and possibly some initializations of variables that are left out at this stage of the design.

Function Subprograms

Example 4.2 in the previous section computed an approximation to a root of a function using the method of bisection. Function evaluation was awkward; every reference required that the function be redefined; that is, that the expression be explicitly written at the point of reference. The program can be much improved by defining the function as a *function subprogram*.

Two components are involved in a function subprogram:

1. The function *definition*, which defines what the function computes.

2. One or more function *calls* (also termed *references*, or *invocations*), which use the code that represents the definition to compute values of the function.

The function call is exactly the same as that for an intrinsic function: use the function applied to a given argument or arguments in an expression. For example, in the statement

```
Y = 1.0 - SIN(X) ** K
```

there is a call to the function SIN. To understand how a function is defined, consider the following simple example.

For the function

$$g(x) = \begin{cases} \sin \pi x & \text{if } x < 0 \\ x \cos \pi x & \text{if } x \geq 0, \end{cases}$$

a corresponding function subprogram is defined as follows:

```
REAL FUNCTION G(X)
REAL PI, X
PARAMETER (PI = 3.1415926)
```

```
IF (X .LT. 0.0) THEN
   G = SIN(PI * X)
ELSE
   G = X * COS(PI * X)
ENDIF
END
```

It is only the first statement, called the *FUNCTION statement*, that distinguishes this sequence from an ordinary program. Note that there is a statement (two here) that defines the value of the function G corresponding to the argument X. G is the name of this function. Functions are named and typed according to the same rules used for variables.

Arguments—the variables in the list in parentheses following the function name—are called *dummy arguments* in FORTRAN and correspond to the *actual arguments*, which appear in the function call. Dummy arguments are akin to the formal parameters of a procedure definition in Pascal. They are the means by which data is passed to the function from the calling program. Note that the dummy arguments are assigned a type (REAL) along with the rest of the variables in the function definition. The function subprogram terminates with an END statement, after which control returns to the point where the function was called. Subprograms are usually placed following the main program definition.

An example of a call to this function is

```
Y = G(PVAL)
```

in which the value of PVAL would be used in place of X in the definition to compute the corresponding value of G.

Subroutines

Next, we briefly examine subroutine subprograms. A subroutine definition is a module that begins with a *SUBROUTINE statement*. Here is an example, with the name WELCOM, which prints a welcome message for the program user:

```
SUBROUTINE WELCOM
PRINT *, 'WELCOME TO THE OPIX DATA BASE SYSTEM'.
PRINT *, 'THIS PROGRAM CAN PROVIDE YOU WITH UP-TO-DATE'
PRINT *, 'DATA AND ANALYSES ON OCEAN CURRENTS.'
PRINT *, 'PLEASE SELECT AN OPTION FROM THE FOLLOWING MENU.'
END
```

A subroutine is called by means of a *call* statement as follows (for the above example):

```
CALL WELCOM
```

Subroutines, like functions, can have arguments too, although the above example has none. Here is a subroutine that computes the same value as the function G above:

```
SUBROUTINE GSUB(X, G)
REAL PI, X, G
PARAMETER (PI = 3.1415926)
IF (X .LT. 0.0) THEN
   G = SIN(PI * X)
ELSE
   G = X * COS(PI * X)
ENDIF
END
```

To assign the value G(PVAL) to Y, this subroutine could be called by the statement

```
CALL GSUB(PVAL, Y)
```

The arguments PVAL and Y are associated with the dummy arguments X and G, respectively. The arguments in the actual and dummy argument lists must match up in order and type.

Note that subroutines are named according to the rules for variables, except that no type is associated with the name. All values are passed back and forth between the calling program and the subroutine through the argument list.

Subroutines are considered more general-purpose than functions, which are generally restricted to returning a *single* value. Thus, although the function g above was represented both by the function G and the subroutine GSUB, the function form is more appropriate. A subroutine, on the other hand, would be used to sort an array.

The following is a simple example of how subroutines and functions can be used to support modularity. Imagine that you are to write an interactive program to be used by a high-school geometry class that will compute various parameters for geometry figures selected by the user. Assume that the program is to compute any of the following:

1. The volume and surface area of a sphere, given the radius
2. The volume and surface area of a right cylinder, given the radius and height.
3. The area of a triangle, given sides *a*, *b*, and *c*.

The main program will consist essentially of a menu to allow the user to choose an option. Three subprograms will be used.

For purposes of illustration, the PRINT statements for the triangle computation were included in the main program rather than in the calling program to allow arguments to be passed to the function. This approach is a more realistic use of subprograms. The main program loops in the menu until the user chooses to exit. Comments are deleted from the subprograms to save space here, but this should not be done in general.

EXAMPLE 4.3

```
      PROGRAM GEOM
***************************************************************
* AUTHOR: J.E. PERRY   6/14/87
*
* THIS PROGRAM COMPUTES VOLUMES, SURFACE AREAS, AND SO FORTH
* OF VARIOUS GEOMETRICAL OBJECTS, BASED ON INPUT FROM THE USER.
* THE PROGRAM DOES NO ERROR CHECKING.
*
* CHOICE--MENU ITEM NUMBER (INPUT)
* SPHERE--COMPUTE VOLUME AND SURFACE AREA OF SPHERE (SUB-
*        ROUTINE)
* CYLDER--COMPUTE VOLUME AND SURFACE AREA OF CYLINDER (SUB-
*        ROUTINE)
* TAREA--AREA OF A TRIANGLE (FUNCTION)
* A, B, C--SIDES OF TRIANGLE (INPUT)
***************************************************************

      INTEGER CHOICE
      REAL A, B, C, TAREA
*     REPEAT
10    CONTINUE
         PRINT *,'ENTER   1  TO COMPUTE VOLUME, AREA OF SPHERE'
         PRINT *,'        2  TO COMPUTE VOLUME, AREA OF CYLINDER'
         PRINT *,'        3  TO COMPUTE AREA OF TRIANGLE'
         PRINT *,'        4  TO EXIT'
         PRINT *
         READ *, CHOICE
         PRINT*
         IF (CHOICE .EQ. 1) THEN
            CALL SPHERE
         ELSE IF (CHOICE .EQ. 2) THEN
            CALL CYLDER
         ELSE IF (CHOICE .EQ. 3) THEN
            PRINT *, 'ENTER LENGTHS OF THREE SIDES OF TRIANGLE: '
            READ *, A, B, C
            PRINT *, 'THE AREA OF THE TRIANGLE IS:'
            PRINT *, TAREA(A, B, C)
         ENDIF
         PRINT *
         IF (CHOICE .NE. 4) GOTO 10
*     UNTIL (CHOOSE TO STOP)
      END

      SUBROUTINE SPHERE
      REAL PI, VOL, AREA, RADIUS
      PARAMETER (PI = 3.1415926)
```

```
PRINT *, 'ENTER RADIUS OF THE SPHERE: '
READ *, RADIUS
VOL = 4.0 / 3.0 * PI * RADIUS ** 3
AREA = 4.0 * PI * RADIUS * RADIUS
PRINT *, 'THE VOLUME AND SURFACE AREA ARE: ', VOL, AREA
END

SUBROUTINE CYLDER
REAL PI, VOL, AREA, HEIGHT, RADIUS
PARAMETER (PI = 3.1415926)
PRINT *, 'ENTER RADIUS OF THE BASE OF THE CYLINDER: '
READ *, RADIUS
PRINT *, 'ENTER THE HEIGHT OF THE CYLINDER: '
READ *, HEIGHT
AREA = PI * RADIUS * RADIUS
VOL = AREA * HEIGHT
AREA = 2.0 * (AREA + PI * RADIUS * HEIGHT)
PRINT *,'VOLUME AND SURFACE AREA (TOP AND BOTTOM) ARE: '
PRINT *, VOL, AREA
END

REAL FUNCTION TAREA (X, Y, Z)
REAL X, Y, Z, S
S = 0.5 * (X + Y + Z)
TAREA = SQRT (S * (S - X) * (S - Y) * (S - Z))
END
```

Sample output (user input is underlined):

```
ENTER    1    TO COMPUTE VOLUME, AREA OF SPHERE
         2    TO COMPUTE VOLUME, AREA OF CYLINDER
         3    TO COMPUTE AREA OF TRIANGLE
         4    TO EXIT
1
ENTER THE RADIUS OF THE SPHERE:
2.75

THE VOLUME AND SURFACE AREA ARE: 87.1137    95.0332

ENTER    1    TO COMPUTE VOLUME, AREA OF SPHERE
         2    TO COMPUTE VOLUME, AREA OF CYLINDER
         3    TO COMPUTE AREA OF TRIANGLE
         4    TO EXIT
4
```

Note that the type of the function TAREA is declared in the main program along with the variables and parameters. There are many other details to be covered in Chapter 7 regarding subprogram definitions, calls, argument lists, and so forth. The main purpose of this section is to get you thinking of problem solutions in terms of modules. In any case you should be able to use simple subprograms to solve various problems at this point. For example, the improvement of Example 4.2 to use function calls is left as an exercise.

4.3 TESTING MODULES

In general a modular design like that in Example 4.3 allows for more thorough testing of the logical components of a program. This is particularly important for large programs consisting of thousands or even tens of thousands of lines of code. More than one programmer can be assigned to the testing process, and the subprograms can be tested in *parallel*. Testing the lowest-level subprograms before the modules that call them is called *bottom-up testing*, which requires that higher-level programs, such as the main program, call the subprograms. Rather than writing a separate calling program for each subprogram, we can use the same one, after it has been tested.

Testing the program starting with the main program and then working down through the various sublevels is called *top-down testing*. Since it is likely that most of the subprograms will not have been completed in the early stages, we can accomplish this with the use of stubs. A *stub* is a skeleton of a subprogram that includes just enough structure for its call to be valid, and possibly a PRINT statement to show, in the testing stages, that the call was completed. For example, a stub for the subroutine CYLDER in Example 4.3 might be written as

```
SUBROUTINE CYLDER
REAL PI, VOL, AREA, HEIGHT, RADIUS
PARAMETER (PI = 3.1415926)
PRINT *, '******* CALL CYLDER'
END
```

The main program could then be run and tested using stubs like this one. After debugging, various programmers can replace the stubs with the complete subprograms and test them in parallel without changing any of the programs that call the stubs. Testing large programs usually involves a combination of the top-down and bottom-up approaches.

Real application programs are often large and complex, containing multiple *levels* of subprograms that call other subprograms, and so forth.

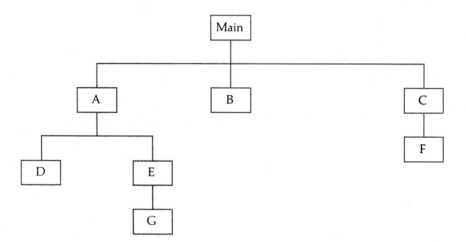

Figure 4.3
A structure chart.

To keep track of the overall organization, programmers may use *structure charts*. In a structure chart each module is represented by a rectangular box with lines joining the boxes below it to indicate the subprogram calls. Figure 4.3 is an example of a structure chart.

The chart shows that subprogram A calls subprograms D and E. Subprogram E in turn calls subprogram G. The chart displays no information on the logic, or even the type, of the subprograms, but it clearly shows their relationship to each other. This is very important for a large project.

Exercises

Section 4.1

1. Give specific reasons why Example 4.2 is a better program than Example 4.1.

*2. What does the following program do? Rewrite it in a well-structured form.

```
        REAL A, B, C
        READ *, A, B, C
        IF (A .GE. B) GOTO 20
        IF (B .GE. C) GOTO 60
        IF (B .GE. A) GOTO 70
10      PRINT *, A
        STOP
20      IF (A .GE. C) GOTO 30
        GOTO 10
```

*The solution to this exercise appears in Appendix D.

```
30      CONTINUE
40      IF (B .GE. C) GOTO 50
        PRINT *, C
        STOP
50      PRINT *, B
        STOP
60      CONTINUE
        IF (A .GE. C) GOTO 10
        GOTO 40
70      IF (B .GE. C) GOTO 80
        GOTO 50
80      CONTINUE
        IF (C .GE. A) GOTO 40
        GOTO 10
        END
```

3. Rewrite Example 3.2 using a WHILE loop instead of a REPEAT loop.

*4. How would you modify Example 4.2 to work correctly even if the user enters a value of A greater than B? What would happen if A = B?

5. As given, Example 4.2 is inefficient for cases where a midpoint turns out to be an exact root (which is unlikely). In fact, in that case the final result will not be as good. Modify the program to check for a root at the midpoint. It should also handle the case where the function has a root at points A or B.

6. The *binomial coefficient*, written as

$$C(n, k) = \binom{n}{k} = \frac{n!}{k!(n - k)!},$$

where $n!$ (called n *factorial*) $= 1 \times 2 \times \cdots \times n$, appears in many mathematical formulas and scientific applications. It represents the number of possible combinations of n items grouped k at a time. For example, $C(52, 5)$ could represent the number of possible five-card poker hands. Print $C(n, k)$ for $n = 2$ to 10 and $k = 1$ to n. Note that $C(n, k) = C(n - 1, k) + C(n - 1, k - 1)$ and that 0! is defined to be 1.

*7. Revise Example 2.1 to print the values of the Fibonacci sequence for $n = 0$ to 50, using both the direct formula from that example and the following recurrence formula:

$$f_{n+2} = f_{n+1} + f_n \qquad n = 0, 1 \ldots, f_n = 0, \text{ and } f_1 = 1$$

Try the recurrence formula using (1) reals and (2) integers. What happens to the integer sequence?

8. Write a program to read sets of coefficients a, b, and c, and compute

the roots of the corresponding quadratic $ax^2 + bx + c = 0$, using the quadratic formula. Be sure to print only one solution if there is only one root $(-b / 2a)$. For two complex roots, print them as

$$-\frac{b}{2a} \pm \left(\frac{\sqrt{b^2 - 4 \cdot a \cdot c}}{2a}\right)i$$

printing i as the character string 'I' following the imaginary part. Test the program on (a) $x^2 - 3x + 2 = 0$, (b) $x^2 - 6x + 9 = 0$, (c) $2x^2 + 4x + 9 = 0$.

Section 4.2

9. Revise Example 4.2 to employ a function definition and function calls in order to eliminate the awkwardness in the function evaluations.

*__10.__ Write a function subprogram to compute the following series approximation to the sine function:

$$\sin x = x - \frac{x^3}{3!} + \frac{x^5}{5!} - \frac{x^7}{7!} + \ldots \pm \frac{x^n}{n!}$$

Both x and n, the exponent of x in the last term of the approximation, should be arguments for the function.

11. Write a subroutine to compute the volume and surface area of a right circular cone. Add its call to the menu of Example 4.3. The formulas are:

$$v = \frac{\pi}{3}r^2h, \text{ and } a = \pi r \sqrt{r^2 + h^2} + \pi r^2.$$

*__12.__ Rewrite Example 4.3 to employ function calls for *each* quantity: the volume of the sphere, the surface area of the sphere, and so forth. All printing should be done in the main program.

13. Revise Example 4.3 to include some error checks. For example, negative values should not be accepted. Also, for the triangle, it must be possible to form the triangle with the given values a, b, and c. For example, it is necessary that $a + b \geq c$ and so forth.

14. Since most computers have only the arithmetic operations of addition, subtraction, multiplication, and division, how is a square root computed? One way is to approximate the square root of a number using *Newton's method*. Suppose we wish to find $\sqrt{a}$. We compute a sequence $x_1, x_2, x_3, \ldots, x_n$ of successive approximations to $\sqrt{a}$ via the formula

$$x_{i+1} = x_i - \frac{x_i^2 - a}{2x_i} = \frac{1}{2}\left(x_i + \frac{a}{x_i}\right),$$

where x_0 is a starting value provided on input. Write a program to compute $\sqrt{a}$ for various values of a. Stop the iteration when $|x_{i+1} - x_i| <$ eps, where eps is 10^{-6}. Let $x_0 = 1$. Count the number of iterations (i.e., the number of successive approximations), and compare your answers with those computed via the SQRT function. Use a subroutine to compute the root and the count. A and eps are input arguments.

*15. Compute an approximation to π using the formula given in Exercise 2.16 and the formula

$$\pi = \left\{8 + 16\left[\frac{1}{1^2 \cdot 3^2} + \frac{1}{3^2 \cdot 5^2} + \frac{1}{5^2 \cdot 7^2} + \cdots\right]\right\}^{1/2}$$

for n terms, where $n = 1, 2, \ldots , 10$. Compare to: 3.14159265. Which one is more accurate for each n? Which value of n yields the most accurate result?

16. In physics classes one may perform Young's double-slit experiment in which a laser beam shines on a screen that contains two parallel slits, usually on the order of a few wavelengths wide and separated by a few wavelengths. The light spreads onto the region behind the slits in a series of regularly spaced bright and dark areas. The intensity varies as a function of the observation angle in relation to the direction of the incident light as shown in the figure below.

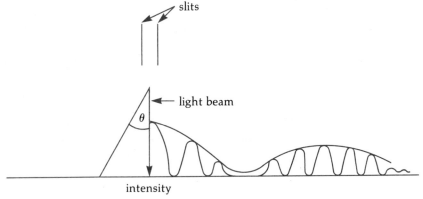

The formula for the ratio of the intensity I at the observed angle θ to the intensity I_0 of the initial beam is given by

$$I/I_0 = \left[\cos\left(\pi \cdot s \cdot \sin\theta\right) \cdot \frac{\sin\gamma}{\gamma}\right]^2,$$

where $\gamma = \pi \cdot w \cdot \sin \theta$, s is the ratio of slit separation to light wavelength, and w the ratio of slit width to light wavelength. Compute and print the value of I / I_0 for $\theta = 0$ to 5 degrees in steps of 0.1 and plot the result. Use $s = 9$ and $w = 2$. Employ a function to compute I/I_0. Note: $\sin \theta$ must be computed for θ in *radians* (i.e., compute $\sin [\theta \cdot \pi / 180]$).

17. Suppose a force of f pounds acting at an angle of θ degrees to the horizontal is sufficient to move a large box along the floor at a constant speed a distance of d feet. Write a program to read various combinations of f, θ, and d, and compute and print the *work* done, which is given by

$$w = f \cdot d \cdot \sin \theta,$$

where w is computed in foot-pounds. Use a function to compute w.

*18. A very important problem in computing is that of *sorting* an array of numbers, names, or other items. A relatively slow but easy-to-write sorting algorithm is the *bubble sort*, which works as follows. Suppose we intend to sort the array A of numbers into ascending order. First, compare A(1) with A(2), and exchange them if A(1) > A(2). Then compare A(2) with A(3) and exchange if necessary. Do the same for A(I) and A(I + 1) for I = 1, 2, . . . , N − 1. At the end of this pass A(N) will contain the largest value. Then repeat the process for I = 1, . . . N − 2, then for I = 1, . . . N − 3, until the last pass involves comparing only A(1) and A(2). To make the algorithms more efficient, you can stop if there were no exchanges throughout a complete pass. (Why?) Write a program to implement the bubble sort, and use a logical variable to exit from the loop if there were no exchanges in a given pass. First read the data into an array, and print the array before and after the sort.

19. You may remember from calculus that a definite integral may be crudely approximated by subdividing the interval of integration and adding the areas of the rectangles formed by using the subinterval length as the base and the function value at either end point of the subinterval as the height (area = base × height). Compute approximations to the following integrals for $n = 10$, 50, and 100 subdivisions of the corresponding interval and compare your results with the exact answers.

*a. $\displaystyle\int_0^{\pi} \sin x \, dx$ Answer: 2

b. $\displaystyle\int_0^1 e^x \, dx$ Answer: $e - 1$

c. $\int_{-2}^{0} x\sqrt{2x^2 + 1}\ dx$ Answer: $-13\ /\ 3$

d. $\int_{0}^{1} \dfrac{dx}{x^2 + 1}$ Answer: $\pi\ /\ 4$

20. We know that the equation for the temperature T at which a certain chemical has a given vapor pressure is:

$$5.08 \log_{10} T + \frac{3480.3}{T} - 21.13 = 0$$

Experimenting with a calculator will show that T is between 300 and 600 degrees on the Kelvin scale. Find T accurate to three decimal places using the bisection method.*

Section 4.3
21. Draw a structure chart for Example 4.3.

*From L.F. Shampine and R.C. Allen, *Numerical Computing: An Introduction*, W.B. Saunders Company, Philadephia, 1973. Reprinted by permission of Holt, Rinehart & Winston.

5 DO Loops and Arrays

A large part of the previous chapter was devoted to loops, but the discussion of a major loop type—the DO loop—was postponed until this chapter. The DO loop, which is a special case of the WHILE loop, is appropriate for processes that involve counting or for keeping track of the number of times the loop has been executed.

DO loops are especially convenient for processing arrays. The *DO variable*, which is automatically incremented or decremented after each loop iteration, can also be used as an index (or as part of an expression that is the index) of an array. In this chapter we will also complete our study of arrays, which we presented in an elementary form in Chapter 2. This material is presented in greater detail than that in the previous chapters to help readers who need a review of arrays.

5.1 THE DO LOOP

An example of a DO loop was given in lines 55 to 59 of Example 1.1. A DO Loop is similar to the FOR loop of BASIC or Pascal. Basically, a DO loop tests a variable, the *DO variable*, to determine if it satisfies a specified condition. If it does, the loop is executed. After each iteration the DO variable is incremented or decremented by a specified amount and tested again. When the condition is no longer true, execution proceeds with the statement immediately following the loop. Since the condition is tested at the beginning, the DO loop is really a special case of the WHILE loop.

Some simple examples of DO loops follow.

```
1.          :
            :
        SUM = 0.0
        DO 10   I = 1, N
            READ *, A, B
            SUM = SUM + (A - B)
    10      CONTINUE
            :
            :
```

This loop reads N pairs of numbers and accumulates the sums of their differences in SUM. The DO variable, I, is set to 1 initially and incremented by 1 after each loop iteration. The loop terminates when I > N. Note that the statement number 10 marks the last statement in the loop (10   CONTINUE). Note also the indentation of the READ and assignment statements for clarity, which is, again, the programmer's responsibility.

2.

```
        :
        :
        INTSUM = 0
        DO 100 K = -100, 2 * N, 2
            INTSUM = INTSUM + K
100     CONTINUE
        :
        :
```

In this example, which computes the sum of the even integers in the interval $(-100, 2 * N)$, the DO variable, K, takes on the values $-100, -98, -96, \ldots, 2 * N - 2, 2 * N$ (assuming $2 * N > -100$). Thus K is incremented by 2; the default increment is 1, as in the first example. Note that K is used in the arithmetic expression.

3.

```
        :
        :
        DO 30 N = 1, NMAX
            READ *, A(N)
30      CONTINUE
        :
        :
```

This loop reads NMAX numbers, one for each loop iteration, into the array elements A(1), A(2), . . . , A(NMAX). The DO variable does "double duty" here, acting as a counter for the loop and also as the index of the array element for the current READ operation.

4.

```
        :
        :
        DO 500  I = NMAX, 1, -1
            PRINT *, EEG(I)
500     CONTINUE
```

This loop prints the elements of the array EEG, 1 per line, in the order EEG(NMAX), EEG(NMAX − 1), . . . , EEG(1). The increment in this case is −1. The value −1 corresponds to the STEP value in a BASIC FOR-loop and to the *downto* version of a Pascal for-loop.

In general, a DO loop has the following structure:

```
        DO statement
        loop range:
        ⎡:            ⎤
        ⎢:            ⎥
        ⎣terminal statement⎦
```

consisting of a DO statement and a loop range that includes the loop's terminal statement. The *range*, or body, of a DO loop consists of all the executable statements up to, *and including*, the terminal statement. For example 1, the range is:

```
          READ *, A, B
          SUM = SUM + (A - B)
10        CONTINUE
```

The *terminal statement* must be an executable statement that does *not* involve transfer of control (e.g., a GOTO or another DO). Assignment, I/O, and restricted IF statements are allowed, but we strongly recommend that you strictly apply the convention of using only a CONTINUE statement as the terminal statement, just as in the above examples. Note that the terminal statement is always identified by the statement number that appears in the corresponding DO statement.

The *DO statement* controls the action of the loop. It is defined as follows:

DO Statement

Examples:

```
DO 50 PCON = 0, 10000
DO 10, IV = IN - 1, MAX
DO 90, J1 = LOW, HIGH, STEP
DO 5  X = X0, XN - 1., .1
```

DO statement

Remarks:

1. Executable.
2. The statement number must be the same as the one that labels the terminal statement.
3. Note that the comma following the statement number is optional.
4. The symbol v represents the DO variable, and e_1, e_2, and e_3 are arithmetic expressions, referred to respectively as the *initial parameter*, the *terminal parameter*, and the *incrementation parameter*. If e_3 is omitted, its value is assumed to be 1. Note that e_3 is not allowed to have a value of 0. Each of v, e_1, e_2, and e_3 may be of type INTEGER, REAL, or DOUBLE PRECISION, although it is common, and generally recommended, to use integer types for reasons of efficiency and other considerations (see Chapter 6).

Box 5.1 shows the steps that are carried out automatically when the DO statement is executed.

BOX 5.1   Execution of a DO Loop

1. Compute the values of the parameters e_1, e_2, and e_3.
2. Set $v = e_1$, applying any necessary type conversion.
3. Establish the *iteration count*; that is, an integer that is *the number of times the loop is to be executed* and is defined as:

$$ic = \text{MAX}(\text{INT}((e_2 - e_1 + e_3) / e_3), 0).$$

Therefore the iteration count can never be negative. Also, *ic* is 0 whenever:

$$e_1 > e_2 \text{ and } e_3 > 0 \qquad \text{or}$$
$$e_1 < e_2 \text{ and } e_3 < 0.$$

4. While *ic* > 0 do
   a.   execute the statements in the range of the DO loop, including the terminal statement.
   b.   set $v = v + e_3$, that is, increment the DO variable by the value of the incrementation parameter, applying any necessary type conversion.
   c.   set $ic = ic - 1$.

Step 4.c guarantees that the loop will terminate eventually. Some comments and examples will clarify the above process.

1. No statement in the range of the DO loop is allowed to modify the DO variable. If allowed, this practice could result in some very complex and error-prone code. Thus, the following loop is illegal.

```
            DO 100   L = 1, MAXIT
                SUM = SUM + L
                L = L - 1
   100      CONTINUE
```

2. Examples of *ic* evaluation:

For DO 10 K = 1, 50 $ic = \text{MAX}(\text{INT}((50 - 1 + 1) / 1), 0) = 50$

For DO 20 PIV = 2, 37, 3 $ic = 12$
For DO 30 X = .1, 7.5, .5 $ic = 15$
For DO 40 TAU = 100, 3, 2 $ic = 0$
For DO 50 GAM = 100, 3, -2 $ic = 49$

3. Clearly the loop will not be executed if the iteration count is 0 to begin with. However, the DO variable will have been assigned a value (step 2). After execution of the following sequence, K = 10 and I = 5.

```
            I = 5
            DO 50   K = 10, 1
                I = I + 1
     50     CONTINUE
```

4. Since *ic* is set at the beginning of the loop, changing the value of any of the initial, terminal, or incrementation parameters (e_1, e_2, or e_3) in the range of the DO will have no effect on the number of times the loop is executed. This is not recommended anyway; it is unnecessary and often confusing to a reader of the program. Consider the following example:

```
            LOW = 0
            HIGH = 10
            COUNT = 0
            DO 10 M = LOW, HIGH
                COUNT = COUNT + 1
                LOW = LOW + 1
                HIGH = HIGH - 1
     10     CONTINUE
```

At the completion of the loop, COUNT = 10, LOW = 10, and HIGH = 0.

5. The terminal statement *must* be executed at the end of each pass through the loop, or it will not decrement *ic* properly. For example,

```
           .
           .
           .
     10    DO 100 I = 1, N
               IF (X .GT. A(I)) THEN
                   X = X - 1.
                   GOTO 10
               ENDIF
               X = A(I)
     100   CONTINUE
           .
           .
           .
```

could result in an infinite loop since the loop variable I will be reset to 1 and the iteration count recomputed whenever the jump to the DO statement is taken via the GOTO.

6. A DO loop becomes *active* when its DO statement is executed. It becomes *inactive* when its iteration count becomes 0, or when control is transferred to a statement outside the range of the DO. However, execution of a function reference or CALL statement does not cause the DO loop to become inactive. Consider the following example:

```
          :
          :
          SUM = 0.0
          DO 10 I = 1, NMAX
              READ(*,*, END = 20) X
              SUM = SUM + X
10        CONTINUE
20        CONTINUE
          :
          :
```

This loop reads and adds a maximum of NMAX values; if it runs out of data, control is transferred to statement 20. It is important to remember that when a DO loop becomes inactive, *the DO variable retains its last defined value* (unlike the loop-control variable in Pascal). Thus, if NMAX = 50 and there are 50 or more records to be read then I will be equal to 51 when the statement labeled 20 is executed. However, if there are only 25 records, then I will be equal to 26.

7. Transfers into the range of a DO loop from outside, such as by means of a GOTO, are not allowed. The following example is illegal.

```
          DO 20 I = MIN, MAX, 2
10            PROD = A(I) * B(I + 1)
              SUMP = SUMP + PROD
              PRINT *, PROD, SUMP
20        CONTINUE
          IF (SUMP LT. MAXSUM) GOTO 10
```

8. A DO loop may be nested with the other DO loops and other control structures such as IF-THEN blocks or WHILE loops. Just be sure to follow the rule: If structure A begins within structure B then it should also end within structure B. The following overlapping DO loop and IF block combination is illegal.

```
          DO 20 I = 1, N
              READ *, RX
              IF (RX .GT. THRESH) THEN
                  SUM = SUM + RX
                  SUMSQ = SUMSQ + RX * RX
20        CONTINUE
              ELSE
                  PRINT *, RX, I
              ENDIF
```

The next example is proper, employing a pair of nested DO loops to evaluate and print the function $f(x, y)$ for x and y ranging from -1 to 1 in steps of 0.01, where

$$f(x, y) = \frac{x^2 - 0.0101y}{x^2 + y^2 + 1} \cdot \cos \pi x.$$

```
      PI = 3.1415926
      DO 10 X = -1.0, 1.0, 0.01
         DO 20 Y = -1.0, 1.0, 0.01
            FXY = (X * X - 0.0101 * Y)/(X * X + Y *
     $                        Y + 1.0) * COS(PI * X)
            PRINT*, X, Y, FXY
20       CONTINUE
10    CONTINUE
```

In this example X is set at −1.0 while Y varies from −1.0 to 1.0 in steps of 0.01. Thus X is increased by 0.01 to −.99 and Y varies from −1.0 to 1.0 again. This process continues until X is greater than 1.0. Actually a better version of this nested pair is given in Section 5.2.

Note that the loops have separate terminal statements. This is not required; the Standard allows nested loops to have the same terminal statement, as in:

```
      DO 100 I = 1, N
         DO 100 J = 1, M
            PRINT *, I, J, I * J
100   CONTINUE
```

If M = 3 and N = 2 this would print

1	1	1
1	2	2
1	3	3
2	1	2
2	2	4
2	3	6

However, we strongly recommend separate terminal statements as a matter of style and clarity.

Note also that nested loops may *not* have the same DO variable as the following example:

```
      DO 10 I = 1, M
         DO 20 I = 0, N + 1
            PRINT *, I
20       CONTINUE
10    CONTINUE
```

Clearly this pair would violate rule 1, since the DO variable of loop 10 is modified by the DO statement of loop 20.

5.2 DO LOOP STYLE

As a matter of style we recommend that you restrict the DO variable and the other loop parameters to integer values. At the expense of an occasional inconvenience you can avoid problems that might otherwise arise due to the accumulation of roundoff errors (see Chapter 6). The preceding example 8, which computes values of $f(x, y)$, might produce output such as

$$-1.00007E-2 \qquad -1.00007E-2 \qquad 2.00891E-4$$

and

$$-6.70552E-7 \qquad 9.99937E-3 \qquad -1.00973E-4$$

corresponding to the respective exact values

$$-1.00000E-2 \qquad -1.00000E-2 \qquad 2.00861E-4$$

and

$$0. \qquad 1.00000E-2 \qquad -1.00983E-4$$

Not only is the former output harder to read, but the accumulated errors can become relatively large for some problems. Rewriting the code for $f(x, y)$ to avoid the roundoff accumulation in x and y, we obtain:

```
      X0 = -1.0
      Y0 = -1.0
      DO 20 I = 0, 200
         X = X0 + REAL(I) / 100.0
         DO 10 J = 0, 200
            Y = Y0 + REAL(J) / 100.0
            FXY = (X * X - 0.0101 * Y) / (X * X + Y * Y
     $                            + 1.0) * COS(PI * X)
            PRINT *, X, Y, FXY
10       CONTINUE
20    CONTINUE
```

This approach computes the new values of X and Y directly from the integer steps I and J, and therefore errors induced in X and Y don't accumulate from step to step. We do pay a price: the code is more complex, and the execution time is greater. However, where there are such tradeoffs, it is generally better to aim for accuracy first.

It is possible to reduce the execution time of this latter pair of loops without sacrificing accuracy. A general principle you should use when you construct a loop (*any* loop, not just DO loops) is: within the range of a loop, *never compute a value that remains unchanged while the loop is active.* In the above example, X * X and COS(PI * X) are computed redundantly in the inner loop, which depends only on Y. The example, rewritten with the above principle in mind, becomes

```
      XO = -1.0
      YO = -1.0
      DO 10 I = 0, 200
         X = XO + REAL(I) / 100.0
         XSQ = X * X
         COSX = COS(PI * X)
         DO 20 J = 0, 200
            Y = YO + REAL(J) / 100.0
            FXY = (XSQ - 0.0101 * Y) / (XSQ + Y * Y + 1.0) * COSX
            PRINT *, X, Y, FXY
20       CONTINUE
10    CONTINUE
```

Again, there is a slight increase in complexity, which makes the code more difficult to follow. If the improvement in execution time is not critical, it may be advisable to leave the code in the previous "unoptimized" form. The optimization of source code is always a judgment call, based on the nature of the problem to be solved and the speed-complexity tradeoffs. Also, many compilers have an option to remove redundant operations from loops and to perform other steps to optimize the object code. In that case you should opt for clarity in the source program and let the compiler do the work.

Finally, this code could be improved further by defining the variables X0 and Y0 and the constants 100.0 and 200.0 as parameters, or as variables to be initialized by a READ statement. In this way different values could easily be defined for X and Y to allow for different spacing along the X and Y axes.

Style also dictates that you use the type of loop that is appropriate for the problem. READ-controlled loops, as illustrated in Figure 3.4, are best represented as WHILE loops, since the number of repetitions is indeterminate. However, for a loop whose termination condition includes—at least in part—a count reaching a limit, you should consider a DO loop. Ideally, you should know in advance, either from reading or computing the loop parameters, how many times the loop must be executed, but this is not necessary for a DO loop to be effective.

In general, guidelines for choosing the type of loop to use may be summarized as follows:

1. Use a *DO loop* if the exact number of iterations can be expressed as an arithmetic expression.

2. Use a *WHILE loop* if the number of iterations is indeterminate and the decision to repeat (or start) the loop body is appropriate at the *beginning* of the loop. A special case occurs when the WHILE loop is to be terminated on an end-of-data condition, in which case it is implemented with a READ (*, *, END = *n*) statement at the beginning of the loop.

3. Use a *REPEAT loop* if the number of iterations is indeterminate and the decision to repeat the loop body is appropriate at the *end* of the loop.

Unfortunately, the choice may not always be so straightforward, since there may be multiple conditions for terminating a loop.

Let us consider an example that could be written in either of two ways. In an exercise in Chapter 3 you were asked to write a program to compute the square root of a number with Newton's method, which generates a sequence $x_1, x_2, x_3 \ldots$ of successive approximations to $\sqrt{a}$ via the formula

$$x_{i+1} = \frac{1}{2}\left(x_i + \frac{a}{x_i}\right),$$

where x_0 ($\neq 0$) is a starting value provided by the user. Suppose we write such a program, which interactively asks the user to provide the value of *a* and a small positive number (e.g., 10^{-5}) that is used to terminate the process where the relative difference of two successive iterates is less than ε, that is, when $|x_{i+1} - x_i| / |x_i| < \varepsilon$. The number ε is a measure of the error in the approximation.

The problem is that a user may enter a value for ε that is unrealistically small, so that it is impossible for the halting condition to be satisfied. To prevent an infinite loop, then, we need to limit the number of iterations (to 20, say). Thus, there are two conditions that may terminate the looping process.

Suppose we write the loop as a DO loop:

```
       DO 100 I = 1, LIMIT
          XNEW = 0.5 * (XOLD + A / XOLD)
          IF (ABS((XNEW - XOLD) / XNEW) .LT. EPS) GOTO 200
          XOLD = XNEW
100    CONTINUE
200    CONTINUE
```

It is assumed that XOLD has been defined as x_0 earlier and that A and EPS have been read. We arrive at the statement labeled 200 either by reaching the limit or by satisfying the error condition. The IF statement acts as a break to exit from the loop.

This loop is compact and easy to understand. However, some programmers would prefer to use an equivalent WHILE loop to avoid the multiple exits:

```
       I = 1
       XNEW = 0.5 * (XOLD + A / XOLD)
*      WHILE (NO CONVERGENCE) DO
100    CONTINUE
       IF (I .LT. LIMIT .AND. ABS((XNEW - XOLD) / XNEW) .GE. EPS) THEN
          I = I + 1
          XOLD = XNEW
          XNEW = 0.5 * (XOLD + A / XOLD)
          GOTO 100
       ENDIF
*      ENDWHILE
```

Initialization of the loop required that XNEW be defined in some way, and so we might as well compute the first approximation. In this case there is only one exit from the loop, but the code is more complex. Which version do you prefer? A REPEAT loop could also do the job, but in the author's view the DO loop is best because it handles some of the messy details like the counting process automatically.

Pseudocode for the complete solution is given next, followed by the program. This example is intended only as a model for similar problems since one would ordinarily write X = SQRT(A) to complete the square root of A.

1. Repeat
    Get a and ε from the user input.
    Until a and ε are nonnegative
2. Set $x_{OLD} = x_0$ (parameter)
3. For $i = 1$ to limit (parameter)
    $x_{NEW} = 0.5 \ (x_{OLD} + a \ / \ x_{OLD})$
    if $(abs((x_{NEW} - x_{OLD}) / x_{NEW}) < \varepsilon)$ then break
    $x_{OLD} = x_{NEW}$
4. If error condition satisfied, then
    print x_{NEW} and i
  Else
    print error message − no convergence

EXAMPLE 5.1

```
       PROGRAM SQROOT
*******************************************************
* AUTHOR:  M. WRIGLEY       6/86
*
* THIS PROGRAM COMPUTES AN APPROXIMATION TO THE SQUARE ROOT OF
* A REAL NUMBER A USING NEWTON'S METHOD.
* HALT WHEN  ABS((X(I + 1) - X(I)) / X(I)) < EPS.
* INPUT VALUES:  A  AND  EPS.
```

```
*  PARAMETERS AND VARIABLES:
*  A - NUMBER WHOSE SQUARE ROOT IS DESIRED
*  EPS - REQUESTED APPROXIMATION TO RELATIVE ERROR.
*  X0 - INITIAL APPROXIMATION - DEFINED AS 1 HERE FOR LACK OF
*       MORE INFORMATION.
*  XOLD - THE CURRENT APPROXIMATION TO THE SQUARE ROOT OF A.
*       (CORRESPONDS TO X(I)).
*  XNEW - THE NEXT APPROXIMATION TO THE SQUARE ROOT OF A
*       (CORRESPONDS TO X(I + 1)).
*  LIMIT - BOUND ON THE NUMBER OF ITERATIONS (SET TO 20 HERE).
*  I - LOOP INDEX
*****************************************************************
       REAL A, EPS, XNEW, XOLD, X0
       INTEGER  I, LIMIT
       PARAMETER (X0 = 1.0, LIMIT = 20)
*      REPEAT
5      CONTINUE
       PRINT *,'ENTER A POSITIVE NO. WHOSE SQUARE ROOT YOU WANT'
       PRINT *,'AND A POSITIVE VALUE FOR THE DESIRED'
       PRINT *,'RELATIVE ERROR: '
       READ *, A, EPS
*
* ENSURE THAT  A  AND  EPS  ARE NONNEGATIVE
*
       IF (A .LE. 0.0 .OR. EPS .LE. 0.0) GOTO 5
*      UNTIL VALID PARAMETERS ENTERED
*
* NEWTON'S METHOD FOR SQUARE ROOT OF A
*
       XOLD = X0
       DO 10 I = 1, LIMIT
          XNEW = 0.5 * (XOLD + A / XOLD)
          IF (ABS((XNEW - XOLD) / XNEW) .LT. EPS) GOTO  20
          XOLD = XNEW
10     CONTINUE
20     CONTINUE
*
* CHECK REASON FOR LOOP EXIT AND PRINT APPROPRIATE MESSAGE
*
       IF (I .LT. LIMIT + 1) THEN
          PRINT *, 'NUMBER ENTERED: ', A
          PRINT *, 'REQUESTED ERROR: ', EPS
          PRINT *, 'APPROXIMATION TO SQUARE ROOT: ', XNEW
          PRINT *, 'NUMBER OF ITERATIONS: ', I
       ELSE
          PRINT *, 'THE PROCESS DID NOT CONVERGE IN ', LIMIT
          PRINT *, 'ITERATIONS FOR THE ERROR REQUEST ', EPS
       ENDIF
       END
```

Note that the check for convergence (I .LT. LIMIT + 1) after the loop depends on the fact that the DO variable I retains its last defined value when the loop becomes inactive.

Style Guide:
   1. Always use a CONTINUE statement as the terminal statement of a DO loop.
   2. Use separate terminal statements for each nested DO loop.
   3. Never alter the values of the parameters of a DO loop within the range of the loop itself.
   4. Always use integers for the DO variable and parameters.
   5. Remove unnecessary computations from the loop if the removal will not unduly complicate the code.
   6. Use the type of loop that is appropriate for the problem.

5.3 ARRAYS REVISITED

Arrays in computer languages are convenient structures for representing concepts in mathematics. As defined in Chapter 1, they correspond in a natural way to *vectors*. The array element X(I) corresponds to the element of x_i of a vector $x = (x_1, x_2, \ldots, x_n)$ of n elements. But arrays are also useful for other problems, such as sorting lists of names or printing a line of a digitized picture. They are useful for manipulating collections of data that are related in some way.

All of these arrays have a common characteristic: their *sizes* are specified in terms of *one dimension*—the *length*—which is the number of elements in the array. However, there are many problems that are not modeled conveniently as arrays of one dimension. For example, one may have to manipulate the pieces in a game of chess, or represent the coefficients of a linear system of equations, or describe the temperature distributions at discrete points in a solid object. Each of these problems is best described by an array of two or more dimensions. FORTRAN is well-equipped for dealing with such problems.

We now present a more general definition of arrays. Recall that an array declarator is used in a type statement to specify the name of an array and the range of its subscripts.

Array Declarator

Examples:

```
NAMES(500)     FREQ(0 : 100)     BASERD(-100 : 100)
A(20, 100)     TEMP(-50 : 75, 0 : 120)
CRDIST(10, -25 : 25)     MOT(20, 100, 50)
```

array declarator

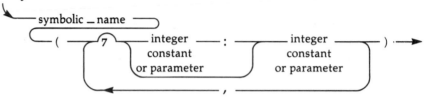

Remarks:

1. The numbers n_1 and n_2 in the pair $n_1 : n_2$ are called the *lower-dimension bound* and the *upper-dimension bound*, respectively. It is required that $n_1 \leq n_2$.
2. If n_1 is omitted, the value of the lower dimension bound is assumed to be 1.
3. The *size of a dimension* is: $n_2 - n_1 + 1$.
4. The maximum dimension (number of subscripts) of an array is seven.

Note that the size of an array—the number of elements in the array—is the product of its dimension sizes.

In the example BASERD, the range of the subscript values is -100 to 100, and in NAMES it is 1 to 500. The arrays A, TEMP, and CRDIST are two-dimensional arrays. MOT is a three-dimensional array.

Array Element   Array elements are defined in a manner similar to the restricted definition in Chapter 2.

Examples: `FREQ(37)     BASERD(-15)     A(I, J+1)     CRDIST(1, N)`

array element

Remark: The integer expressions representing the subscripts must evaluate to numbers that fall between their respective lower- and upper-dimension bounds.

Since any integer arithmetic expression is valid as a subscript, a subscript may also be a subscripted variable. For example, let PTR and VALUE be integer arrays. If N = 16, PTR(17) = 4, and VALUE(4) = -1, then VALUE(PTR(N + 1)) = VALUE(4) = −1. The array element PTR(17) acts like a pointer in Pascal, in a limited sense; it cannot be created during execution time like Pascal's pointer variables. Subscripted subscripts are useful for applications such as sorting (see Exercise 20).

Just as a one-dimensional array corresponds to a vector, a two-dimensional array corresponds to a *matrix*, which is a rectangular array of numbers, such as

$$
A = \begin{pmatrix} a_{11} & a_{12} & \cdots & a_{1n} \\ a_{21} & a_{22} & \cdots & a_{2n} \\ & & \cdots & \\ a_{m1} & a_{m2} & \cdots & a_{mn} \end{pmatrix}
$$

In a two-dimensional array you can think of the first subscript as representing a *row* number of the array and the second subscript as the *column*. Thus A(12, 30) is the element in row 12 and column 30 of array A. Adding a third dimension is analogous to adding pages, and so on. Most applications involve only one to three dimensions.

Next we present two examples that illustrate the kinds of problems that can be solved in an elegant way with arrays. Arrays are most useful when all, or a large part, of the data are required to be in the computer's memory during program execution. Both examples employ DO loops, which are convenient for working with arrays. For example, the full range of a subscript can be processed easily as a DO variable.

The first example finds the *median* of a set of real numbers, which could be measurements taken from an experiment, test scores, and so forth. The median is the middle value: half of the values are less than the median and half are greater. Like the mean, the median is a measure of the average value, but it is less affected by extreme values than is the mean. We first looked at this problem in Chapter 4.

Suppose there are N numbers in the set, sorted in increasing order as the array X: X(1), X(2), . . . , X(N). Then the median is defined as

$$
\text{MEDIAN} = \begin{cases} X(\text{INT}(N / 2) + 1) \text{ if N is odd;} \\ (X(\text{INT}(N/2)) + X(\text{INT}(N/2) + 1)) / 2.0 \text{ if N is even} \end{cases}
$$

In other words, the median is the average of the two middle values if N is even. For this problem we assume that the number of values is unknown and must therefore be counted.

This problem breaks up nicely into independent modules. As a design exercise you might try writing and refining a pseudocode solution to this problem before you read further (see Exercise 14).

Our pseudocode solution to this problem follows. Let NMAX be the maximum number of values the program will process (i.e., NMAX is the dimension of X):

1. Read the numbers into the array X.
2. Set N equal to the number of values in X (N ≤ NMAX).
3. Sort X into ascending order:

$$\text{For } I = 1 \text{ to } N - 1$$
$$K = I$$
$$\text{For } J = I + 1 \text{ to } N$$
$$\text{If } X(K) > X(J) \text{ then set } K = J$$
$$\text{Exchange } X(I) \text{ and } X(K)$$

4. Set N2 = INT (N / 2)
5. If N = 2 * N2 then (N is even)

$$\text{Set MEDIAN} = (X(N2) + X(N2 + 1)) / 2.0$$

Else (N is odd)

$$\text{Set MEDIAN} = X(N2 + 1)$$

6. Print MEDIAN

The sort procedure is a variant of the *exchange sort* algorithm, which is straightforward but inefficient. (Recall Exercise 1.22) Briefly, it makes N + 1 passes through the array, placing the smallest value among X(1), X(2), . . . , X(N) in X(1) on the first pass, placing the smallest value among X(2), X(3), . . . , X(N) in X(2) on the second pass, and so forth. This algorithm is roughly equivalent in speed to the bubble sort (Exercise 4.18). For efficiency the exchange takes place outside the inner loop.

Steps 4 and 5 define the median according to whether N is even or odd. Integer arithmetic is used to determine if N is divisible by 2.

The corresponding FORTRAN program is next. Note how a DO loop is used to implement steps 1 and 2.

EXAMPLE 5.2

```
      PROGRAM MEDIANR
*******************************************************************
* AUTHOR: H. BRUMLEY        6/86
*
* THE PROGRAM COMPUTES THE MEDIAN OF A SET OF REAL NUMBERS
* READ FROM THE STANDARD INPUT UNIT, FOUR NUMBERS PER LINE.
* AN EXCHANGE SORT ALGORITHM IS USED TO SORT THE NUMBERS.
* THE MAXIMUM NUMBER OF VALUES ALLOWED IS DETERMINED BY THE
```

```
* PARAMETER NMAX, WHICH CAN BE CHANGED TO ACCOMMODATE A LARGER
* SET. IF THERE ARE NMAX OR MORE VALUES, ONLY THE FIRST NMAX
* ARE USED.
* VARIABLES AND PARAMETERS:
* X - ARRAY TO HOLD THE INPUT VALUES
* NMAX - THE SIZE OF X
* N - THE NUMBER OF VALUES USED
* N2 - THE INTEGER QUOTIENT OF N/2.
* MEDIAN - THE MEDIAN
* K - PLACEHOLDER FOR CURRENT SMALLEST VALUE.
* TEMP - USED TO EXCHANGE INDEX VALUES
* I, J - LOOP INDICES
******************************************************************
      INTEGER NMAX, N, K, I, J, N2
      PARAMETER (NMAX = 500)
      REAL X(NMAX), MEDIAN, TEMP
*
* READ THE VALUES INTO X
*
      DO 10 I = 1, NMAX
         READ (*,*, END = 20)  X(I)
10    CONTINUE
20    CONTINUE
      N = I - 1

      IF (N .EQ. NMAX) THEN
         PRINT *, 'NOTE: THE PROGRAM HAS READ THE MAXIMUM'
         PRINT *, 'NUMBER OF VALUES THAT CAN BE PROCESSED BY'
         PRINT *, 'THE PROGRAM.  THIS SET OF VALUES WILL BE'
         PRINT *, 'PROCESSED.  TO ACCOMODATE A LARGER NUMBER,'
         PRINT *, 'CHANGE THE PARAMETER NMAX ACCORDINGLY.'
      ENDIF


*
* SORT THE NUMBERS INTO ASCENDING ORDER
*
      DO 40 I = 1, N - 1
         K = I
         DO 30 J = I + 1, N
            IF (X(K) .GT. X(J)) K = J
30       CONTINUE
*
* AT THIS POINT K POINTS TO CURRENT SMALLEST VALUE
*
         TEMP = X(K)
         X(K) = X(I)
         X(I) = TEMP
40    CONTINUE
*
```

```
* COMPUTE THE MEDIAN
*
      N2 = INT(N / 2)
      IF (N .EQ. 2 * N2)    THEN
         MEDIAN = (X(N2) + X(N2 + 1)) / 2.0
      ELSE
         MEDIAN = X(N2 + 1)
      ENDIF
      PRINT *, 'THE MEDIAN FOR THE ', N, ' VALUES IS: ', MEDIAN
      END
```

Some remarks are in order regarding the style of the program. First, choosing proper sizes for array dimensions always presents a problem, whether you are using FORTRAN, BASIC, or Pascal, since the dimensions must be known at compile time. If the values are too small, you will be forced to change them occasionally to fit the data. If they are too large, memory space is wasted, which can be costly if you are being charged for its use. The best you can do is to size the dimensions with values consistent with the class of problems you expect to handle.

Note that the variable I is used as an index for both DO loops 10 and 40. This is not a problem since the loops are not nested. However, some stylists recommend using a separate variable for each purpose and therefore different indices for each loop to avoid any possible unexpected interactions. In this book we take a middle position: with the exception of loop indices, don't reuse variables for different purposes in a single program unit (i.e., main program, subroutine, or function). A convention we do follow is to use variables I, J, K (and sometimes L, M, and N) strictly for loop indices.

A minor style point is to write statements and loops so that the statement numbers appear in increasing order. This can be helpful in debugging a long program.

Finally, it is awkward and inefficient to input the numbers one line at a time. Section 5.4 will introduce you to some additional I/O capabilities for arrays that will give you more flexibility.

Also, ordinarily one should echo-print the input data. This step was omitted to save space.

The next example employs an array to solve a *system of linear equations*. This problem arises in many areas of science, engineering and mathematics. An example of a system of linear equations is

$$
\begin{aligned}
15x_1 - 3x_2 + x_3 &= 13 \\
x_1 + 10x_2 - x_3 &= 10 \\
-2x_1 - 3x_2 + 12x_3 &= 7
\end{aligned}
$$

which is to be solved for the three unknowns x_1, x_2, and x_3. In this example $x_1 = x_2 = x_3 = 1$.

In general, for n equations in n unknowns $x_1, x_2, \ldots, x_n$ we have:

$$a_{11}x_1 + a_{12}x_2 + \ldots + a_{1n}x_n = a_{1,\,n+1}$$
$$a_{21}x_1 + a_{22}x_2 + \ldots + a_{2n}x_n = a_{2,\,n+1}$$
$$\cdots$$
$$a_{n1}x_1 + a_{n2}x_2 + \ldots + a_{nn}x_n = a_{n,\,n+1}$$

There are many computer algorithms for solving these systems. Since our intent is to illustrate the use of arrays, we will use the *Jacobi method*, which is easy to understand and program.

The Jacobi method is an iterative technique that produces a sequence of approximations $(x_1^{(j)}, x_2^{(j)}, \ldots, x_n^{(j)})$, $j = 1, 2, 3, \ldots$, which *converges*, under proper conditions, to the solution $(x_1, x_2, \ldots, x_n)$. Convergence means that, in the absence of roundoff error, the successive approximations will get as close as desired to the exact solution, after a sufficient number of iterations. It is convenient to store the values a_{ij} in a two-dimensional array, called the *coefficient matrix*. The procedure works as follows:

1. Provide an initial value—a guess if you will—for the x_i: $x_1^{(0)}$, $x_2^{(0)}, \ldots, x_n^{(0)}$

2. For $i = 1$ to n solve the ith equation for x_i in terms of the initial approximations to the other unknowns, to get the next set of approximations, $x_1^{(1)}, x_2^{(1)}, \ldots, x_n^{(1)}$:

$$x_1^{(1)} = [a_{1,\,n+1} - (a_{12}x_2^{(0)} + a_{13}x_3^{(0)} + \cdots + a_{1n}x_n^{(0)}] / a_{11};$$
$$x_2^{(1)} = [a_{2,\,n+1} - (a_{21}x_1^{(0)} + a_{23}x_3^{(0)} + \cdots + a_{2n}x_n^{(0)}] / a_{22};$$
$$\cdots$$
$$x_n^{(1)} = [a_{n,\,n+1} - (a_{n1}x_1^{(0)} + a_{n2}x_2^{(0)} + \cdots + a_{n,\,n-1}x_{n-1}^{(0)}] / a_{nn}.$$

3. Repeat step 2, computing the $j + 1$st approximation from the jth approximation, until satisfied or until the maximum number of iterations is reached.

Clearly, this procedure breaks down if any of the diagonal coefficients a_{ii} are 0. Therefore, we assume that this is not the case. Also, since a discussion of the criteria for convergence of this sequence is beyond the scope of this book, we will simply stop the process if the maximum number of iterations, MAXIT, is exceeded. Methods such as Jacobi's work best when the system is *sparse*; that is, when most of the coefficients a_{ij} are 0. Also, we know that the Jacobi scheme converges if the diagonal coefficients a_{ii} are greater in absolute value than the absolute value of the sum of the off-diagonal coefficients on the left-hand side.

In step 3, "until satisfied" means we are satisfied that convergence has occurred to within a certain accuracy, EPS. We will stop if

$$\max_{1 \le i \le n} |x_i^{(j+1)} + x_i^{(j)}| < \text{EPS};$$

that is, when the largest difference between the respective elements of two successive approximations is less than the value EPS. This difference is an approximation to the *absolute error* $|x_i - x_i^{(j)}|$, where x_i is the exact value. This approach contrasts with the use of the *relative error* approximation to terminate the iterative process in Newton's algorithm, in which the difference is divided by the most recent approximation. The choice of which test to use falls in the realm of numerical analysis and is outside the scope of this book. Often a relative error test is best, especially if x_i is very large or very small compared to 1. It can be tricky to define EPS and MAXIT properly—they actually should be input values. Here we will define them as parameters.

A pseudocode version of our Jacobi scheme is the following:

1. Read n, the number of equations.

2. Read the coefficients a_{ij} for $i = 1, \ldots, n$;
   $j = 1, \ldots, n + 1$

3. Echo-print the coefficients.

4. Redefine $a_{ij} = -a_{ij} / a_{ii}$ for $i, j = 1, \ldots, n, i \neq j$

5. Redefine $a_{i, n+1} = a_{i, n+1} / a_{ii}$ for $i = 1, \ldots, n$

6. Initialize $x_i^{(old)} = 0$ for $i = 1, \ldots, n$

7. For $k = 1$ to maxit
   set $x_i^{(new)} = a_{i, n+1} = (a_{i1}x_1^{(old)} + a_{i2}x_2^{(old)} + \cdots + a_{i, i-1}x_{i-1}^{(old)} + a_{i, i+1}x_{i+1}^{(old)} + \cdots + a_{in}x_n^{(old)})$
   compute maxdif $= \max_{1 \leq i \leq n} |x_i^{(new)} - x_i^{(old)}|$
   print $x_i^{(new)}$, maxdif for $i = 1, \ldots, n$
   if (maxdif < eps) then *break*
   set $x_i^{(old)} = x_i^{(new)}$ for $i = 1, \ldots, n$

8. If $k \leq$ maxit
   print 'convergence in', k, 'iterations'
   else
   print 'no convergence in', maxit, 'iterations'

To avoid excessive detail, we do not check for errors in the input data, which should be done in a production program. We carry out the divisions by the a_{ii} outside the loop for efficiency (steps 4 and 5). We use 0 for the initial approximation (step 6). Observe that two arrays, $x^{(old)}$ and $x^{(new)}$, are required for the previous and new approximations. The successive approximations are printed in the loop to show the details of convergence (or nonconvergence). Again, I/O is awkward, but additional capabilities will be covered in the next section. The program is next.

EXAMPLE 5.3

```
      PROGRAM JACOBI
*****************************************************************
* AUTHOR: R.M. HALLET           6/86
*
* THIS PROGRAM COMPUTES THE SOLUTION OF A SET OF N EQUATIONS IN
* N UNKNOWNS BY THE JACOBI METHOD.  THE PROGRAM ASSUMES THAT
* THE EQUATIONS ARE ARRANGED SO THAT THE COEFFICIENTS A(I,I)
* ARE NONZERO.  THE PROGRAM HALTS WHEN EITHER THE CONVERGENCE
* CRITERIA ARE SATISFIED OR WHEN THE MAXIMUM NUMBER OF
* ITERATIONS IS ATTAINED.  CONVERGENCE IS ASSUMED IF THE
* LARGEST DIFFERENCE BETWEEN THE CORRESPONDING ELEMENTS OF
* TWO SUCCESSIVE ITERATES IS LESS THAN EPS, A SUPPLIED
* PARAMETER.  THE COEFFICIENTS MUST BE PRESENTED ONE NUMBER
* PER LINE ON THE STANDARD INPUT UNIT IN ROW ORDER, FOLLOWED
* BY THE COEFFICIENTS ON THE RIGHT HAND SIDE.  THE VALUE N
* PRECEDES THE COEFFICIENTS.  THE ORIGINAL ARRAY A IS
* ALTERED.
* VARIABLES AND PARAMETERS:
* N - THE NUMBER OF EQUATIONS (INPUT)
* A - THE COEFFICIENT MATRIX (INPUT)
* XOLD - THE ARRAY OF PREVIOUS APPROXIMATIONS TO THE SOLUTION
* XNEW - THE ARRAY OF MOST RECENT APPROXIMATIONS TO THE
*        SOLUTION
* MAXDIF - THE CURRENT MAXIMUM DIFFERENCE BETWEEN ELEMENTS OF
*          XOLD AND XNEW
* MAXIT - THE MAXIMUM NUMBER OF ITERATIONS PERMITTED (PARA-
*         METER)
* EPS - THE ERROR BOUND (PARAMETER)
* TOOSML - A VALUE LESS THAN THIS IS ASSUMED TO BE ZERO
*          (PARAMETER)
* STARTV - VALUE ASSIGNED TO ELEMENTS OF INITIAL APPROXIMA-
*          TION (PARAMETER)
* DIM - THE MAXIMUM NUMBER OF EQUATIONS ALLOWED (PARAMETER)
* I, J, I1, J1, K - LOOP PARAMETERS
* SUM, TEMDIF - TEMPORARY VALUES
*****************************************************************
      INTEGER I, J, K, I1, J1, MAXIT, DIM, N
      REAL MAXDIF, EPS, TOOSML, STARTV, SUM, TEMDIF
      PARAMETER (DIM = 30, MAXIT = 25, EPS = 1.E-5, TOOSML
     $          = 1.E-20, DIMP1 = 31)
      PARAMETER (STARTV = 0.0)
      REAL A(DIM, DIMP1), XOLD(DIM), XNEW(DIM)
*
* READ THE COEFFICIENTS
```

```
*
      READ *, N
      IF (N .GT. DIM .OR. N .LE. 0)  THEN
         PRINT *, 'ERROR -- THE VALUE OF N IS OUT OF BOUNDS'
         STOP
      ENDIF
      DO 20 I = 1, N
         DO 10 J = 1, N + 1
            READ (*,*, END = 30) A(I,J)
10       CONTINUE
20    CONTINUE
30    CONTINUE
*
* ECHO-PRINT THE COEFFICIENTS
*
      PRINT *, 'THE COEFFICIENTS ARE: '
      DO 50 I1 = 1, I - 1
         DO 40 J1 = 1, J - 1
            PRINT *, A(I1, J1)
40       CONTINUE
50    CONTINUE
      IF (N .NE. I - 1 .OR. N .NE. J - 2)  THEN
         PRINT *, 'ERROR -- N DOES NOT MATCH NO. OF COEFFICIENTS'
         STOP
      ENDIF
*
* CHECK FOR ZERO DIAGONAL (DIVISOR)
*
      DO 60 I = 1, N
         IF (ABS(A(I,I)) .LT. TOOSML) THEN
            PRINT *, 'ERROR -- DIAGONAL ELEMENT TOO CLOSE TO ZERO'
            STOP
         ENDIF
60    CONTINUE
*
* PREDIVIDE THE COEFFICIENTS
*
      DO 80 I = 1, N
         DO 70 J = 1, I - 1
            A(I, J) = -A(I, J) / A(I, I)
70       CONTINUE
         DO 75 J = I + 1, N
            A(I, J) = -A(I, J) / A(I, I)
75       CONTINUE
         A(I, N + 1) = A(I, N + 1) / A(I, I)
80    CONTINUE
*
* DEFINE INITIAL APPROXIMATION
*
```

```
      DO 90 I = 1, N
         XOLD(I) = STARTV
90    CONTINUE
*
* COMPUTE NEXT APPROXIMATION (JACOBI) AND CHECK FOR CONVERGENCE
*
      DO 160 K = 1, MAXIT
         DO 120 I = 1, N
            SUM = 0.0
            DO 100 J = 1, I - 1
               SUM = SUM + A(I, J) * XOLD(J)
100         CONTINUE
            DO 110 J = I + 1, N
               SUM = SUM + A(I, J) * XOLD(J)
110         CONTINUE
            XNEW(I) = A(I, N + 1) + SUM
120      CONTINUE
         MAXDIF = ABS(XNEW(1) - XOLD(1))
         DO 130 I = 2, N
            TEMDIF = ABS(XNEW(I) - XOLD(I))
            IF (TEMDIF .GT. MAXDIF) MAXDIF = TEMDIF
130      CONTINUE
         PRINT *, 'THE NEXT APPROXIMATION IS: '
         DO 140 I = 1, N
            PRINT *, XNEW(I)
140      CONTINUE
         PRINT *, 'WITH A BOUND ON THE CHANGE IN: ', MAXDIF
*
* EXIT IF CONVERGED
*
         IF (MAXDIF .LT. EPS) GOTO 170
*
* NO CONVERGENCE YET -- SET UP FOR NEXT ITERATION
*
         DO 150 I = 1, N
            XOLD(I) = XNEW(I)
150      CONTINUE
160   CONTINUE
*
* PRINT CONCLUSIONS
*
170   CONTINUE
      PRINT *
      IF (K .LE. MAXIT) THEN
         PRINT *, 'CONVERGENCE IN ', K, ' ITERATIONS'
      ELSE
         PRINT *, 'NO CONVERGENCE IN ', MAXIT, ' ITERATIONS'
      ENDIF
      END
```

Some versions of FORTRAN, such as Ryan-McFarland's RMFORT compiler, do not accept parameters for subscript dimensions (except the first one) for arrays of dimension two or more. In this case you should replace A(DIM, DIMP1) by A(30, 31) in the REAL statement.

Note that the program checks that the number of coefficients matches the value of N. Echo-printing the coefficients allows the user to verify that the input data are correct. Also, the program works for a value of N less than or equal to the dimension of the arrays.

The program was tested on the example presented earlier. The results are shown in Table 5.1, but in a more compact form than the output from the above program. The sequence appears to converge nicely to the solution.

TABLE 5.1 Convergence of the Jacobi Method

x_1	x_2	x_3	j	MAXDIF
0	0	0	0	—
0.866667	1.00000	0.58333	1	1.00
1.02778	0.971667	0.977778	2	0.39
0.995815	0.995000	0.997546	3	3.20E-2
...	...	...	...	...
0.999984	0.999974	1.00000	6	1.80E-4
0.999975	1.00000	0.999991	7	2.76E-5
1.00000	1.00000	1.00000	8	8.64E-6

A final remark: subscript manipulation in FORTRAN and other languages can be computationally expensive. Therefore you should never use a two-dimensional array where a one-dimensional array will work just as well.

5.4 ARRAYS AND I/O

With your limited introduction to input and output functions in FORTRAN, the reading and printing of arrays has been very restricted, as illustrated by the two previous examples. In this section we will extend the READ and PRINT statements to enable you to deal with the input and output of arrays in a more flexible way.

Let us informally define *I/O list* as any list—items separated by commas—where the items may appear in a PRINT or READ statement. Thus, for example,

```
A, X, P(1), P(2), P(3)
```

is an I/O list. We have seen that for a PRINT statement the items in the

I/O list may be expressions, character strings, or array names. For READ statements, they may be variables, array elements, or array names.

We now add one more item to the I/O list, which is valid for both PRINT and READ statements. The *implied DO list* is used primarily for reading or printing a sequence of array elements. It is processed just like a DO statement. The effect is as if the list of items to be read or printed is expanded for each value assumed by the variable that corresponds to the DO variable.

Implied DO List

Examples:

1. `(A(I), I = 1, N)`
2. `(X(I), Y(I), I = LOW, HIGH)`
3. `(K, 'STEP IS:', VALUE(K), K = 1, MAX)`
4. `('-', I = 1, 30)`
5. `(ODD(N), N = 1, MAXODD, 2)`
6. `(N, N ** 3, N - K, N = -1, 50)`
7. `(VAR(I, J), J = 1, N + 1)`
8. `(MAT(I, J), J = 1, N), I = 1, M)`
9. `(A(I), (S(I, M), M = 1, L), I = 0, N)`

implied DO list

Remarks:

1. The variable v and the expressions e_1, e_2, and e_3 correspond to the DO variable and parameters of the DO statement. The iteration count and the values of v are established from e_1, e_2, and e_3 exactly as in a DO statement. The iteration count determines the number of items to be read or printed. The entire I/O list is repeated for each value taken on by the variable v.
2. None of v, e_1, e_2 or e_3 must appear in the associated I/O list of a READ statement.
3. Since an implied DO list is a valid item in an I/O list, an implied DO list may contain another implied DO list, as in the last two examples. The Standard does not specify a limit on the number of nested implied DOs, but each compiler will probably enforce some limit.
4. Take note of the comma preceding the variable v. Omitting it is a common error.

An implied DO list can be used to represent a list of array elements in a compact form. The example

```
PRINT *, X(1), X(2), X(3), X(4), X(5), X(6), X(7), X(8)
```

is equivalent to

```
PRINT *, (X(I), I = 1, 8)
```

which prints all eight values. The number of values per line depends on the compiler. The latter form is obviously preferred. It is shorter, and may be written in a more general form—the quantities 1 and 8 could be any valid expressions (e.g., those in the first and second examples in the definition).

Using a variable for the upper limit e_2 is especially important for READ statements since it enables the program to handle input data that is presented in various formats. For example, the statement

```
READ *, (A(I), I = 1, N)
```

will assign the first N values it finds to the array A. Thus the input values could be placed one per record, two per record, or even N per record, unlike the READ statements in Examples 5.2 and 5.3 which read only one value per record.

Let us use the rest of the examples in the definition as I/O lists for PRINT statements. For example 2 we would have

```
PRINT *, (X(I), Y(I), I = LOW, HIGH)
```

In this case the values would be printed in the order

```
X(LOW), Y(LOW), X(LOW + 1), Y(LOW + 1), . . . , X(HIGH),
Y(HIGH)
```

For

```
PRINT *, (K, 'STEP IS:', VALUE(K), K = 1, MAX)
```

suppose that MAX = 21 and VALUE(1) = 1.0, VALUE(2) = 2.0, and so forth. Its output would be similar to

```
1 STEP IS:  1.00000    2 STEP IS:  2.00000   ...
21 STEP IS:  21.0000
```

Example 4,

```
PRINT *, ('-', I = 1, 30)
```

illustrates that members of the I/O list need not be dependent on the value of v. This example prints a line of 30 consecutive dashes, useful, for example, as the axis of a graph.

In

```
PRINT *, (ODD(N), N = 1, MAXODD, 2)
```

the odd-numbered elements from ODD(1) to ODD(MAXODD) (or ODD(MAXODD − 1)) would be displayed.

If K = 2 in

```
PRINT *, (N, N ** 3, N - K, N = -1, 50)
```

the values will print as:

```
-1  -1  -3  0  0  -2  1  1  -1  2  8  0  3  27  1  . . .
```

illustrating that the variable v may be part of any expression in the I/O list (for printing).

The last three examples have two-dimensional arrays in their I/O lists. The statement

```
PRINT *, (VAR(I, J), J = 1, N + 1)
```

prints the first N + 1 elements in row I of array VAR, that is,

```
VAR(I, 1), VAR(I, 2), . . . , VAR(I, N + 1).
```

Assuming that the array MAT has M rows and N columns, the statement

```
PRINT *, ((MAT(I, J), J = 1, N), I = 1, M)
```

will print the elements in *row order*, that is, MAT(1, 1), MAT(1, 2), . . . , MAT(1, N), MAT(2, 1), MAT(2, 2), . . . , MAT(2, N), MAT(3, 1), . . . , MAT(M, N). First I is set to 1, then J runs through the values 1 to N. Then I is set to 2 and J runs from 1 through N again, and so forth. The function is exactly like that of a pair of nested DO loops. Note that the implied DO list (MAT (I, J), J = 1, N) is the I/O list for the outer implied DO list.

In the last example,

```
PRINT *, (A(I), (S(I, M), M = 1, L), I = 0, N)
```

the outer I/O list continues two items: A(I) and (S(I, M), M = 1, L).

The values will print in the order

```
A(0), S(0, 1), S(0, 2),..., S(0, L), A(1), S(1, 1),
S(1, 2),..., S(1, L),..., A(N), S(N, 1), S(N, 2),...,
S(N, L).
```

Thus, the nested DO loops 10 and 20 in Example 5.3 used to read the values of the coefficient matrix A could be replaced by the single statement

```
READ (*,*, END = 30) ((A(I, J), J = 1, N + 1), I = 1, N)
```

However, the Standard is ambiguous regarding the use of the END = clause in a READ statement with an implied DO list. For example, it would be convenient to replace the following loop that appears in Example 5.2

```
          DO 10 I = 1, NMAX
             READ (*,*, END = 20) X(I)
   10     CONTINUE
   20     CONTINUE
          N = I - 1
```

by the following sequence:

```
          READ (*,*, END = 20) (X(I), I = 1, NMAX)
   20     CONTINUE
          N = I - 1
```

The latter sequence is preferable in that it allows more than one input item to be placed on one line. Some compilers, however, do not allow this construction; they treat the loop variable I as undefined when the END = option takes effect. For example, this approach is allowed by DEC's FORTRAN compilers, but not by Ryan-McFarland's RM/ FORTRAN compiler. In this text we will use the latter version, but you may have to modify the code to make it work with your compiler.

In order to make a program as general as possible, it is a common practice to read the number of elements to be placed in an array or the number of rows and columns of a two-dimensional array before reading the data itself.

For example, the single statement

```
        READ *, N, (X(I), I = 1, N)
```

will read the first input value into N and the next N values into the array X.

The statement

```
        READ *, M, N, (A(I, J), J = 1, M), I = 1, N)
```

first defines the number of rows M and columns N of the array A and then reads the values, row by row, into A.

However, as a matter of style, if you are reading only *one* array with N elements it is better to use the END = option and let the program determine N rather than preceding the array values by the count. This approach avoids possible counting errors, especially for large arrays.

One may combine implied DO lists with DO loops to produce better-looking output. In Example 5.3 the coefficients of the matrix A were echo-printed one element per line, a wasteful practice for a large matrix. To echo-print the matrix one *row* per line, the DO loops 40 and 50 could be replaced by

```
      DO 40 I1 = 1, I - 1
         PRINT *, (A(I1, J1), J1 = 1, J - 1)
40    CONTINUE
```

Of course, each row of A could require more than one line of output.

Recall that using the array name alone in a READ (PRINT) list reads (prints) the entire array. For example,

```
.
.
.
REAL   A(LOW: HIGH)
.
.
READ *, A
.
.
.
```

is equivalent to

```
.
.
.
REAL   A(LOW: HIGH)
.
.
READ *, (A(I), I = LOW, HIGH)
.
.
.
```

Although it is convenient for testing and echo-printing purposes, the first approach has limited usefulness because it does not allow a programmer to refer to *part* of an array, which means that one would always have to modify the dimension specifications to match the data.

Style Guide:
1. Except for array indices, don't reuse variables for different purposes in the same program unit.
2. Write statements and loops so that the statement numbers appear in increasing order in the program.
3. Specify the dimensions of the arrays appropriately for the class of problems you expect the program to handle.
4. Use the fewest dimensions possible for an array, as long as clarity is not sacrificed.
5. Use array names for array I/O only where the generality of the program is not comprised. Ask: will a change in the data require that the program be recompiled?

5.5 ARRAY MEMORY ALLOCATION

To use implied DO lists properly for arrays of two or more dimensions, you should know how FORTRAN stores arrays in memory. Consider a two-dimensional array, A, defined by the statement

```
REAL A(2, 3)
```

Unlike most computer languages, FORTRAN will assign the elements of A to successive memory locations in *column* order rather than row order, as shown below.

location n: A(1, 1)
A(2, 1)
A(1, 2)
A(2, 2)
A(1, 3)
location $n + 5$: A(2, 3)

The first column of A begins at the first location, the second column at the third location, and so forth. The reason FORTRAN assigns locations this way is historical. It was more efficient for the particular computer model for which FORTRAN was originally developed, and it is now included in the Standard.

Therefore, if you read or print A using the array name alone, the data elements are assumed to be specified in column order. If you want to arrange your input data, say, in row order, you must specify the read order explicitly, as in

```
READ *, ((A(I, J), J = 1, 3), I = 1, 2)
```

In general, for arrays of two or more dimensions, you can think of arrays as being stored with *the subscripts varying most rapidly from left to right*. For example, if the array B is dimensioned as

```
REAL B(3, 4, 2)
```

the storage order will be B(1, 1, 1), B(2, 1, 1), B(3, 1, 1), B(1, 2, 1), B(2, 2, 1), B(3, 2, 1), . . . , B(3, 4, 1), B(1, 1, 2), B(2, 1, 2), B(3, 1, 2), . . . , B(3, 4, 2).

It often happens that not all of the memory locations reserved for an array by the compiler are used. Consider the array X dimensioned by

```
INTEGER X(4, 3)
```

and defined by

```
          READ *, M, N
          DO 20 I = 1, M
              DO 10 J = 1, N
                  X(I, J) = I + J
10            CONTINUE
20        CONTINUE
```

Suppose M = 2 and N = 3. Then X will be defined as shown in Table 5.2.

TABLE 5.2 Location of Assigned Array Elements

Relative location	Element	Value
1	X (1, 1)	2
2	X (2, 1)	3
3	X (3, 1)	
4	X (4, 1)	
5	X (1, 2)	3
6	X (2, 2)	4
7	X (3, 2)	
8	X (4, 2)	
9	X (1, 3)	4
10	X (2, 3)	5
11	X (3, 3)	
12	X (4, 3)	

Thus, there are *gaps* between the assigned array elements because of the way the array is mapped to memory. The other values are considered undefined, although many compilers will store 0s in all arrays and variables prior to execution. These gaps should be of no concern to you at this point, since you will explicitly reference the particular array elements. However, an awareness and understanding of this feature is critical for arrays used in subprograms, which are discussed in Chapter 7.

5.6 THE DATA STATEMENT

It often happens that we need to initialize a set of variables or an array just once when the program starts executing, such as the array XOLD in loop 90 of Example 5.3. Rather than using assignment statements and possibly a loop, we can use a *DATA statement* for this purpose.

   A DATA statement defines the values of the variables and arrays in its list when the program is compiled, not during execution. The formal definition allows for great variety in the specification, but basically the list consists of the variables to be defined followed by the respective values to be assigned, enclosed in slashes (/). For example, in

```
DATA N, B, C /1, -1.0, 0.27E3/
```

N is assigned the value 1, B the value −1.0, and C the value 0.27E3. The formal definition is next.

Examples:

```
DATA P(5), XOLD, YOLD /0.0, 1.0, 1.0/
```
     (P(5) = 0.0, XOLD = 1.0, and YOLD = 1.0)

```
DATA ANGLE, LEN /PI, 7.5/
```
     (PI is a parameter whose definition precedes the **DATA** statement.)

```
DATA X, Y, Z /3 * 0.0/
```
     (This is equivalent to `DATA X, Y, Z /0.0, 0.0, 0.0/`.)

```
DATA P /1, 2, 3/
```
     (P is an integer array of three elements: P(1) = 1, P(2) = 2, and P(3) = 3.)

```
DATA (X(I), I = 1, 100) /100 * 0.0/
```
     (This sets X(1), X(2), . . . , X(100) to zero.)

```
DATA L, C, D /.TRUE., (1.0, 3.0), 1.D - 5/
```
     (Variables of any type may be defined.)

```
DATA X1, X2 /0.0, 1.0 / N, M / 100, 500/
```
     (This defines two lists: X1 = 0.0, X2 = 1.0, and N = 100, M = 500.)

DATA statement

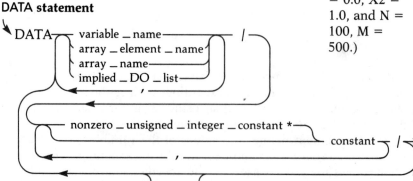

Remarks:

1. Nonexecutable.
2. DATA statements should be placed after the type statements but before any executable statement.
3. If an implied DO list is used, only constants can be used for the DO parameters.
4. The nonzero unsigned integer constant is called a *repeat factor*, which is used to specify a sequence of identical values, as in the third and fifth examples.
5. The number of items in the list of variables, arrays, and so forth must be equal to the number of constants assigned to them.
6. The types of the variables should match the types of the constants.
7. Parameters may be used in place of constants, as in the second example.

If an array name is used, as in the fourth example, the number of constants to be assigned must equal the size of the array.

The DATA statement is very convenient for initializing arrays. The following sequence initializes the array SOL to 1s:

```
REAL SOL(500)
DATA SOL /500 * 1.0/
```

So does the statement

```
DATA (SOL(I), I = 1, 500) /500 * 1.0/
```

The following sequence initializes the two-dimensional array A to 0:

```
REAL A(20, 50)
DATA ((A(I, J), J = 1, 50), I = 1, 20) /1000 * 0.0/
```

Exercises

Section 5.1

1. Write DO statements to perform loops for each of the following sequence of values:
   *a. P = 1, 4, 7, 10, . . . , 100
   b. IPCT = −25, −24, −23, . . . , 25
   *c. CNTDN = 10, 9, 8, . . . , 0
   d. BETA = −M, −M + 2, −M + 4, . . ., 2 * N − 1
   *e. INCR = 0.0, 0.01, 0.02, . . . , 5.0
   f. HAVS = 1.0, 1.5, 2.0, . . . , 10.0
   *g. MIL = all negative even numbers between −2 * N and 0.
   h. QNT = all integers from −100 to +100 in steps of N

2. Given the following DO statements, how many times will the loop be

executed, assuming there are no breaks from the loop? What is the value of the DO variable at the end of the loop?

*a. DO 10, I = 1, 20, 3
 b. DO 20 J = -12, 12
*c. DO 50, PH = 3.0, 9.5, 0.2
 d. DO 100, N = 10.0, -5.0, -0.5
*e. DO 40   MIN = 10, 80, -2
 f. DO 30 LV = 50, -50
*g. DO 10, K = M - 2, M + 2
 h. DO 20, X = -2 * Y, 4 * Y, Y

3. What is the value of N after the execution of the following loops?

*a.
```
        SUM = 0
        DO 10 N = 20, 1, -1
            SUM = SUM + N
10      CONTINUE
```

 b.
```
        SUM = 0
        DO 10 N = 20, 1, -2
            SUM = SUM + N
10      CONTINUE
```

4. When statement 30 is executed, what are the values of I, J, K, L, and N?

*a.
```
        N = 0
        DO 20 I = 1, 10
            J = I
            DO 10 K = 1, 5
                L = K
                N = N + 1
10          CONTINUE
20      CONTINUE
30      CONTINUE
```

 b.
```
        N = 0
        DO 20 I = 1, 10
            J = I
            DO 10 K = 5, 1
                L = K
                N = N + 1
10          CONTINUE
20      CONTINUE
30      CONTINUE
```

5. Write the equivalent to the following code without using a DO loop.

*a.
```
        SUM = 0.0
        DO 10, K = 0, N + 1, STEP
            IF (K .NE. L) THEN
                SUM = SUM + REAL(K ** 3) / REAL(K + 1)
            ENDIF
10      CONTINUE
```

b.
```
          SUM = 0
          DO 20 J = LOW, HIGH, 2
             PROD = 1
             SUM = SUM + (J - 1) ** 2
             DO 10 K = -N, N
                PROD = PROD * (SUM - K)
                PRINT *, J, K, PROD
10           CONTINUE
20        CONTINUE
```

6. Write the equivalent to the following code using a DO loop.

```
          SUM = 0.
          ICT = N
*         WHILE (COUNT INCOMPLETE) DO
10        CONTINUE
          IF (ICT .LE. NMAX) THEN
             SUM = SUM + REAL (ICT * ICT) - 1.0
             ICT = ICT + 2
             GOTO 10
          ENDIF
*         ENDWHILE
```

*7. Write a segment of FORTRAN code to compute

$$\sum_{\substack{i=1 \\ i \neq 10}}^{30} i^3 = 1 + 8 + 27 + \cdots + 9^3 + 11^3 + \cdots + 30^3$$

*8. Write a segment of FORTRAN code to find the least value of n such that

$$\sum_{i=1}^{n} i^5 < 5000$$

*9. Write a segment of FORTRAN code to compute

$$\sum_{i=0}^{n-1} \left(\sum_{j=0}^{n} (1 + ij) \right) \text{ for } n \geq 1$$

10. Write a program to read integers up to six digits long and compute the sum of the digits (e.g., for 71263 the sum is 19). Also compute the sum of all of the sums, and print the results.

11. A popular computer simulation problem is that of population growth and decline for predators and their prey, for example, foxes and rabbits. The fox population increases as it feeds on its food supply,

*The solution to this exercise appears in Appendix D.

rabbits, creating a corresponding decrease in their number. If there are too many foxes, there may not be enough rabbits to go around, and the fox population will begin to decline.

Write a program to simulate the daily population of foxes and rabbits. The daily changes in the fox-rabbit populations are given by the following equations:

$$f_{n+1} = (1 - d_f + p \cdot i_f \cdot r_n) \cdot f_n;$$
$$r_{n+1} = (1 + i_r - p \cdot f_n) \cdot r_n,$$

where f_n is the number of foxes that exist on day n, r_n the number of rabbits on day n, p is the probability that a fox will catch and eat a rabbit, d_f is the rate of decrease in foxes if there are no rabbits available, i_r is the rate of increase in rabbits if they are not eaten, and i_f is the rate of increase in the fox population corresponding to one rabbit being eaten.

Print the rabbit and fox population over a five-year period (1500 days). Print the values every 50 days, but be sure to update the population daily. Start with the following values:

$f_0 = 500$	$r_0 = 5000$	$d_f = .005$
$p = .0001$	$i_f = .01$	$i_r = .01$

Run the program several times, experimenting with different starting values.

12. Write a program to simulate the operation of a furnace in a home under control of a thermostat. When the inside temperature drops 4° below the current thermostat setting t, the furnace goes on. It shuts off when the temperature is 5° greater than t.

You may assume that the temperature in the house drops at a rate proportional to the difference between the inside temperature t_i and the outside temperature t_o, if the furnace is shut off. That is, let

$$t_d = k \, (t_i - t_o)$$

represent the temperature drop in degrees per hour. Let $k = .05$. If the furnace is on, the temperature increases at a rate given by

$$t_{inc} = \max(6 - t_d, 0)$$

Print out the temperature in the house over different 24-hour periods, and the total amount of time the furnace is running for the various values of t, t_o, and initial values of t_i. Draw graphs based on your output.

Section 5.2

***13.** Rewrite the following code so that it is more efficient and also uses integers for the loop parameters.

```
PI = 3.1415926
XSUM = 0.0
DO 200 T = 0.0, 10.0, 0.1
    KEL = -276.0
    YPROD = 1.0
    DO 100 VOL = VO, VN, 0.2
        SQ2 = SQRT(2.0)
        XSUM = XSUM+(T ** 3+KEL) * COS(VOL * PI/180.0)
        YPROD = YPROD * ABS(1.0 - T ** 3)
        FTV = XSUM - T * YPROD
        PRINT *, T, VOL, FTV
100     CONTINUE
        PRINT *, YPROD
200 CONTINUE
```

Section 5.3

14. Design a pseudocode solution to the median problem in Example 5.2. Consider the use of subprograms.

15. Try the Jacobi method (see Example 5.3) on the system

$$2x_1 + 5x_2 + 5x_3 = 12$$
$$5x_1 + 2x_2 + 5x_3 = 12$$
$$5x_1 + 5x_2 + 2x_3 = 12$$

What happens? Why?

16. Revise Example 5.3 to use the *Gauss-Seidel* method, instead of the Jacobi method, for solving systems of linear equations. The Gauss-Seidel method is similar to Jacobi's, except that each element of the new approximation to the solution vector is used immediately to compute the next element. That is,

$$x_1^{(j+1)} = [a_{1, n+1} - (a_{12}x_2^{(j)} + a_{13}x_3^{(j)} + \cdots + a_{1n}x_n^{(j)})] / a_{11};$$
$$x_2^{(j+1)} = [a_{2, n+1} - (a_{21}x_1^{(j+1)} + a_{23}x_3^{(j)} + \cdots + a_{2n}x_n^{(j)})] / a_{22};$$
$$\vdots$$
$$x_n^{(j+1)} = [a_{n, n+1} - (a_{n1}x_1^{(j+1)} + a_{n2}x_2^{(j+1)} + \cdots + a_{n, n-1}x_{n-1}^{(j+1)})] / a_{nn},$$

for $j = 1, 2, \ldots$. If both Gauss-Seidel and Jacobi converge for the same problem, Gauss-Seidel will converge almost twice as fast. Test your program on the problem used for Example 5.3.

17. Suppose that a biologist has collected several hundred grasshoppers that are classified into 15 different varieties. The biologist would like a table that lists the average length in centimeters for each variety.

Write a program to print the table. Assume that the data will be provided on the standard input unit as a list of pairs of numbers: the variety number (1 to 15) and the lengths in centimeters.

*18. Write a segment of FORTRAN code to compute the *inner product* of two vectors, x and y. If x and y have dimension n, then the inner product of x and y is defined by

$$x \cdot y = (x_1, x_2, \ldots, x_n) \cdot (y_1, y_2, \ldots, y_n)$$

$$= \sum_{i=1}^{n} x_i \cdot y_i = x_1 \cdot y_1 + x_2 \cdot y_2 + \cdots + x_n \cdot y_n.$$

19. A much more efficient sorting algorithm than the exchange sort used in Example 5.2 is the binary merge sort. For simplicity, assume that the array to be sorted contains 2^n elements. We will show how it works on a simple example. Suppose the array A, below, is to be sorted into ascending order. In the first pass A(1) is compared to A(2), and the smaller value (16) is copied first into the array B, followed by the larger element (35). Similarly for A(3) and A(4), A(5) and A(6), and so forth. The array B now contains four sublists of length 2, each in ascending order. In pass 2 the first sublist (B(1) and B(2)) is *merged* with the second sublist (B(3) and B(4)) into A to form a sorted sublist of 4 elements. The procedure is similar for the second half of B. The final step, pass 3, produces the sorted list in B.

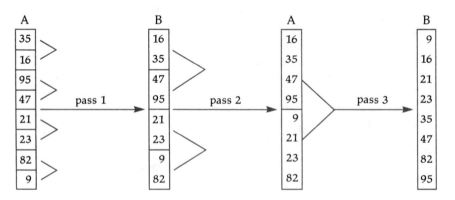

This process is easily extended to any list of length 2^n. Note that the number of merging steps is n (for example, $2^3 = 8$). The procedure can be made more efficient by using a two-dimensional array with 2 columns, each column replacing A and B, or by calling a subroutine to do the merging. Write a program to do the merge sort. [Extra credit: make it work for lists of arbitrary length, not just a power of 2.]

20. A college professor keeps a file of student ID numbers and test scores. Each record in the file looks like this:

ID	Test 1	Test 2	...	Test n	Average
781956	73	86		64	77.4

The ID is a five-digit integer. There may be from 1 to 10 tests. The test scores are all integers. The records are sorted on the ID, but the professor would like a printout ordered in descending order of the average score. Write a program to read the data and produce the desired printout.

Note however that when an interchange is called for in the exchange process (e.g., in the exchange sort), *all* of the fields corresponding to the average scores being compared must be interchanged. To make the sorting process more efficient, you should use an array of *pointers*. A pointer is a variable that points to, or marks the location of, another variable. You may be familiar with pointers if you have a Pascal background.

To sort the array of scores, then, all we do is sort the pointer array and then use the pointer array elements as subscripts for the ID and test arrays. A simple example should make this clear. Let AVG be an array of four values we wish to sort in ascending order, and let PTR be our pointer array.

	Before the sort		After the sort	
	PTR	AVG	PTR	AVG
1	1 ⟶ 78.1		1	2 ⟶ 78.1
2	2 ⟶ 47.3		2	4 ⟶ 47.3
3	3 ⟶ 92.5		3	1 ⟶ 92.5
4	4 ⟶ 69.5		4	3 ⟶ 69.5

After the sort, the elements of PTR point to the elements of AVG in ascending order, and none of the elements of AVG have been moved. Thus, PTR must be initialized according to

$$PTR(I) = I$$

and the Ith elements of AVG must be referred to as

$$AVG(PTR(I))$$

For example, note that after the sort AVG(PTR(1)) = AVG(2) = 47.3, AVG(PTR(2)) = AVG(4) = 69.5, and so forth. This technique is sometimes referred to as a *tag* sort.

21. Write a program to *normalize* a vector:
   a. Read n vector of n elements: $x = (x_1, x_2, \ldots, x_n)$.

b. Compute the *norm* of x:

$$|x| = \left(\sum_{i=1}^{n} x_i^2 \right)^{1/2}.$$

This number is called the *Euclidean norm* of the vector x, and is a measure of its length. If $n = 2$, $|x| = \sqrt{x_1^2 + x_2^2}$.

c. *Normalize* x: compute $x_i = x_i / |x|$ for $i = 1, 2, \ldots, n$. Be sure to check for a vector of all 0 elements.

d. Print the original and normalized vectors.

*22. Write a FORTRAN code segment to compute the product of two matrices. If A has *m* rows and *n* columns and B has *n* rows and *p* columns, the matrix product is a matrix $C = A \cdot B$ whose elements are defined by

$$c_{ij} = \sum_{k=1}^{n} a_{ik} \cdot b_{kj}$$

where a_{ik} and b_{kj} are elements of A and B respectively. Note that the number of columns of the left matrix, A, must equal the number of rows of B.

23. Write a program to solve a system of linear equations of the form

$$a_{11}x_1 + a_{12}x_2 = \cdots = a_{1n}x_n = a_{1,\,n+1};$$
$$a_{22}x_2 = \cdots = a_{2n}x_n = a_{2,\,n+1};$$
$$\vdots$$
$$a_{n-1,\,n-1}x_{n-1} + a_{n-1,\,n}x_n = a_{n-1,\,n+1};$$
$$a_{n,\,n}x_n = a_{n,\,n+1}.$$

That is, all of the elements below the diagonal on the left side are 0. This is called an *upper-triangular* system. To solve it, compute x_n from the last equation, and then use that value to compute x_{n-1} in the second-to-last equation, and so forth. This process is referred to as *back-substitution*.

*24. A forestry management team is studying the infestation of the Pine Bark beetle in the Rocky Mountains. They made a count of the number of infected trees found in a square unit of land at various altitudes and summarized their findings as shown below.

Altitude (ft.)	Number of infected trees
5000	310
5300	285
5700	202
6000	160
6500	110
7000	52
7500	8

They have theorized that the number of infected trees, t, is related to altitude, a, by the linear equation

$$t = b + m \cdot a$$

where b and m are constants. The team would like you to write a program that will compute b and m so that the above equation best fits the experimental data in a certain sense.

One way to do this is the *method of least squares*, which determines the values of b and m that minimize the sum of the squares of the deviations from the observed data. This can be done by solving the following system of linear equations for b and m:

$$\left(\sum_{i=1}^{n} a_i\right) \cdot b + \left(\sum_{i=1}^{n} a_i^2\right) \cdot m = \sum_{i=1}^{n} a_i t_i;$$

$$n \cdot b + \left(\sum_{i=1}^{n} a_i\right) \cdot m = \sum_{i=1}^{n} t_i,$$

where n is the number of observed pairs, a_i and t_i.

Section 5.4

25. Use implied DOs to construct PRINT statements equivalent to the following:
    *a. `PRINT*, X(0), Y(0), X(1), X(2), Y(2),..., X(M), Y(M)`
    b. `PRINT*, X(1), X(2), X(3), Y(1,1), Y(2, 1), Y(3, 1),`
       `Y(1, 2), Y(2, 2), Y(3, 2)`
    *c. `PRINT*, A(0) + 0, A(0) + 1, A(0) + 2, A(0) + 3, A(1)`
       `+ 0, A(1) + 1,..., A(3) + 3`
    d. `PRINT*, Z(1, 1, 0), Z(1, 1, 2), Z(1, 1, 4),...,`
       `Z(1, 1, 64), Z(1, 2, 0), Z(1, 2, 2),..., Z(2, 1,`
       `0), Z(2, 1, 2),..., Z(5, 10, 64)`

26. Write a single FORTRAN statement to print
    *a. The Ith row of a matrix, A, with M rows and N columns.
    b. the first L elements of the vector X followed by the first K elements in the Jth row of a matrix B.

27. Write a single FORTRAN statement to print the even-numbered columns of a matrix, H, with L rows and M columns.

28. Use a minimal number of FORTRAN statements to read elements into a checkerboard pattern of a matrix, A; for example:

$$a_{11}, a_{13}, a_{15}, \ldots, a_{1n}$$
$$a_{22}, a_{24}, a_{26}, \ldots, a_{2, n+1}$$
$$\vdots$$

Do it in

*a. row order

b. column order

*29. *A histogram* is a graph that displays the relative frequencies of a variable's distribution. The graph is usually displayed in terms of bars whose widths represent an interval of the variable, or a single value if the widths are all the same, and whose heights represent the frequencies.

Write a program to read integer data with values between 0 and 20, and print the corresponding histogram using "bars" that consist of a single line of asterisks to represent the 21 frequencies. Print the histogram horizontally, as shown in the example below. Also, print the actual value to the right of the bar, as shown.

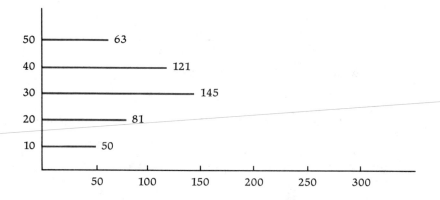

30. A meteorologist has tables of monthly rainfall totals in inches for various counties in the state. The entries look like this:

	J	F	M	A	M	J	J	A	S	O	N	D
County A	.3	.3	.5	1.2	1.8	.9	.8	.5	.2	.1	.2	0
County B	.2	.1	.6	1.0	1.5	1.0	.5	.2	0	.3	.1	.1

Write a program that will read and print such a table and print the average rainfall

a. by county for the year, and

b. by month for the whole state. What is the best way to read and print a table with this structure?

Section 5.5
31. Write DATA statements to do the following:
  *a. Initialize all 1000 elements of the integer array FREQ to 0.
  b. Set all 10 elements of the logical array FLG to .FALSE.
  c. Initialize X to 1.0, Y to −3.0, Z to 0.5, and N to 100.
  d. Initialize all elements P(−50), P(−49), . . . , P(20) to 0.5.

6

Errors: Avoidance, Detection, and Correction

This chapter deals with one of the most important aspects of program design and coding: How do you know, beyond a reasonable doubt, that your program is correct? Can you be sure that those numbers printed on the computer paper represent an accurate, or at least acceptable, solution to the problem you are trying to solve? Are there some input values for which it will not work?

For a program that prints a table of Fahrenheit and Celsius temperatures, written as a programming exercise, these questions may not be very important, and a brief examination of the output will tell you if the answers seem reasonable. If not, finding errors in programs with only 10 to 20 statements is usually straightforward. On the other hand, imagine being responsible for a program with 10,000 lines of FORTRAN that controls nuclear reactor processes. The questions become critically important in this context. Imagine the possible consequences of an undetected program error when control is turned over to the program.

Since a high percentage of programs in engineering, science, and mathematics applications involve numerical computations, we first examine how numbers are handled in FORTRAN. We will then study some specific examples of the kinds of serious errors that can arise because of the way numbers are represented in computers, and we will provide some guidelines on how to avoid them.

Next we will examine the problem of errors in a general sense. How can we detect and correct errors in a FORTRAN program? What trouble spots should we be wary of? What kinds of testing should we do in order to be confident that our program is error-free (or "bug" free)? In the current state of the art, we cannot guarantee that a program is bug-free, but only that the probability of error is very low. This chapter will give you guidelines for approaching that goal.

Finally, we will examine some issues of transportability and provide some guidelines to minimize the effect of machine dependencies.

6.1 INTEGER REPRESENTATION

The two principal number systems used in computers are *integer* systems and *real* (often called *floating-point*) systems. Each requires different concepts of computer arithmetic. Integers, as we have already seen, are useful for counting or indexing, for algorithms that employ integer arithmetic (such as a process that computes the greatest common divisor of two integers), and for much nonscientific computation. As long as the computed values do not exceed the range of integers that can be represented in the machine, integer computations are error-free.

First, consider how integer numbers are represented. Humans are accustomed to working with numbers in the decimal system, in which the digits represent coefficients of powers of 10. For example, the number 327 represents the expression

$$3 \times 10^2 + 2 \times 10^1 + 7 \times 10^0$$

The number 10 is the *base* of the system. Any decimal integer can be written in this way, with integral coefficients in the range 0 to 9. In general,

$$n = d_k d_{k-1} \ldots d_0 = d_k \times 10^k + d_{k-1} \times 10^{k-1} + \ldots + d_0 \times 10^0$$

where d_i is the ith digit in the k-digit integer n.

The decimal system is convenient for hand computation because we are used to it, but it is not the system used in most computers for scientific computing. Computers employ voltage levels that represent two basic states: *on* and *off, true* or *false, 0* or *1*. Therefore computer numbers (and other elements) are usually represented internally in the *binary* system, which has the base 2. Examples are

$$110 = 6 \text{ (decimal)}$$
$$110101 = 53 \text{ (decimal)}$$

The number 110101 represents the expression

$$1 \times 2^5 + 1 \times 2^4 + 0 \times 2^3 + 1 \times 2^2 + 0 \times 2^1 + 1 \times 2^0$$

In general,

$$n = d_m d_{m-1} \ldots d_0 = d_m \times 2^m + d_{m-1} \times 2^{m-1} + \ldots + d_0 \times 2^0$$

Where d_i is the ith digit in the m-digit binary integer n, and d_i is in (0, 1). Thus, in the binary system each nonzero digit represents the corresponding power of 2.

It is easy to convert a binary number to decimal form directly from the expansion. Thus,

$$110101 = 1 \times 2^5 + 1 \times 2^4 + 0 \times 2^3 + 1 \times 2^2 + 0 \times 2^1 + 1 \times 2^0$$
$$= 32 + 16 + 4 + 1 = 53.$$

There also exist algorithms to convert a decimal integer to binary form. We will not cover them here, but see Exercise 5.

We note briefly that two other systems are popular for dealing with computer representations. They are the *octal* (base 8) system and the *hexadecimal* (base 16) system. Binary representation uses lots of space. A 4-digit decimal number requires 10 or more binary digits. FORTRAN programmers usually work with decimal values, but they sometimes need to examine the binary representations generated by the computer. For convenience these values are often displayed in hexadecimal (*hex* for short) or octal, since it is very easy to covert from binary to octal or hex and back again. Table 6.1 shows the correspondence between the first 16 integers in the four bases.

TABLE 6.1   Numbers in Four Systems

Decimal	Binary	Octal	Hex
1	0001	1	1
2	0010	2	2
3	0011	3	3
4	0100	4	4
5	0101	5	5
6	0110	6	6
7	0111	7	7
8	1000	10	8
9	1001	11	9
10	1010	12	A
11	1011	13	B
12	1100	14	C
13	1101	15	D
14	1110	16	E
15	1111	17	F
16	10000	20	10

Observe that the letters A through F are used for the 6 hex digits beyond 9.

To convert a binary number to octal (hex), simply group the bits in groups of three (four) from right to left and use the table above to convert each group to a single digit. For example,

$$1101011110 = 001\ 101\ 011\ 110 = 1536\ (\text{octal})$$

and

$$1101011110 = 0011\ 0111\ 1110 = 27E\ (\text{hex})$$

Note the addition of the appropriate number of high-order 0s in each case.

To convert from octal (hex) to binary, simply expand each octal (hex) digit into 3 (4) bits according to the above table. For example,

$$375 \text{ (octal)} = 011\ 111\ 101 \text{ (binary)}$$

and

$$2C09 \text{ (hex)} = 0011\ 1100\ 0000\ 1001 \text{ (binary)}$$

Note the expansion of hex 0 to 0000 binary in the last example. The basis for these simple conversions is that $8 = 2^3$ and $16 = 2^4$; that is, the bases are all powers of 2.

As a FORTRAN programmer, you will usually work only with decimal numbers. The compiler provides the routines to do the conversion from the decimal data used in the program to their internal binary representation and back again to decimal for display purposes. It is important for you to be aware of this conversion—in the next section you will see that it is a source of certain errors.

Since integers are represented exactly, integer arithmetic does not usually produce any errors. However, in all computers the unit of memory used to store numbers is fixed in size; it is usually referred to as a *word.* Because of the fixed size, integers (and reals) have a finite range. Table 6.2 shows some common word sizes in bits, some computers that use them, and the maximum positive integer that can be stored in the word.

TABLE 6.2 Popular Word Sizes

Word size	Example computers	Maximum integer
16	DEC VAX series, IBM PC	$2^{15} - 1$
24	HARRIS H800	$2^{23} - 1$
32	IBM 4300 series	$2^{31} - 1$
60	CDC Cyber series	$2^{59} - 1$
64	Cray series	$2^{63} - 1$

The maximum positive integer for an n-bit word is $2^{n-1} - 1$ because the high-order (leftmost) bit is used to represent the sign (0 = positive, 1 = negative).

Some systems allow for *double integers,* which use two words to store the number. In either case there is a limit, and it is possible to generate an error, known as integer *overflow,* by computing an integer with a magnitude that is too large to represent in a word (or two words). The problem is that most versions of FORTRAN will not generate an error message on integer overflow. Therefore, you must take precautions, especially for computations involving large integers, such as printing your own warning message when values fall within a certain range of the limit. Some versions of FORTRAN allow you to specify an option that checks for integer overflow during execution.

If you check the FORTRAN standard, you will find that nothing is mentioned regarding ranges of integers or reals, since they are clearly machine-dependent. However, differences in word sizes can be one of the most serious impediments to the portability of programs.

6.2 REAL REPRESENTATION

Real arithmetic is used everywhere for scientific computation, from solving a system of linear equations to evaluating functions. Floating-point representation, which is akin to scientific notation, allows us to work with very large and very small numbers in a compact form. Although most computers perform the basic floating-point operations with high accuracy, the result of a computation involving several of these operations could be grossly in error (in contrast to integer computation).

We will use the terms *real* and *floating-point* interchangeably here, although floating-point is more generally used outside the context of a specific programming language.

Recall that real constants in FORTRAN can always be written in exponential form. For example,

$$273.5 = .2735E3$$

Real constants in FORTRAN are assumed to be in base 10.

In general, a floating-point number, x, in base β with k digits has the form

$$x = (.d_1 d_2 \ldots d_k) \beta^e$$

where the string of digits $d_1 d_2 \ldots d_k$ is called the *fraction*, or *mantissa*, and e is an integer called the *exponent*. The digits d_i and e are in base β. For calculators $\beta = 10$, but for computers $\beta = 2$, 8, or 16. Both the fraction and the exponent may have a sign as well.

Most computers operate on floating-point numbers in *normalized* form, in which $d_1 \neq 0$ (unless the number itself is 0). For example, $.35 \times 10^{-3}$ is normalized, but $.0035 \times 10^{-1}$ is not.

We can represent the fraction of a floating-point number, like an integer, as a sum of coefficients times powers of its base. For example,

$$.31416 = 3 \times 10^{-1} + 1 \times 10^{-2} + 4 \times 10^{-3} + 1 \times 10^{-4} + 6 \times 10^{-5}$$

and, in general, for $x = (.d_1 d_2 \ldots d_k) \beta^e$,

$$.d_1 d_2 \ldots d_k = d_1 \times \beta^{-1} + d_2 \times \beta^{-2} + d_3 \times \beta^{-3} + \ldots + d_k \times \beta^{-k}.$$

Floating-point numbers must also be converted to binary for computation, and FORTRAN provides routines to do this during compilation and execution. For example,

$.375 \times 10^0$ (normalized decimal)
$$= 3 \times 10^{-1} + 7 \times 10^{-2} + 5 \times 10^{-3}$$
$$= 0 \times 2^{-1} + 1 \times 2^{-2} + 1 \times 2^{-3} = .011 \text{ (binary)}$$
$$= .11 \times 2^{-1} \text{ (normalized binary)}$$

Such conversion takes place for every real decimal data number that is read during execution, and a similar conversion from binary to decimal takes place for printing results.

The digits in a binary fraction may also be grouped to form octal or hex fractions; for example:

$$.0110 \text{ (binary)} = .3 \text{ (octal)} = .6 \text{ (hex)}$$

We leave the details of these representations as exercises.

As for integers, the range of values for reals in FORTRAN varies according to the word size of the machine. The floating-point parameters for some specific computers are given in Table 6.3, in which m and M represent the bounds on the exponent: $m \leq e \leq M$. The value k is the number of digits in the fraction in the base β. Thus, on a Cray computer, a 48-bit fraction yields about 14 decimal digits of precision; this com-

TABLE 6.3 Floating-Point Parameters for Some Computers

Computer	β	k	M	m
IBM 4300 series	16	6	127	−127
DEC VAX series*	2	23	127	−127
CDC Cyber series	2	48	1071	−975
Cray series	2	48	8194	−8192

*The VAX actually uses two 16-bit words to store floating-point numbers.

pares to about 7 decimal digits on an IBM computer. One bit of the fraction is used for the sign of the number. The sign of the exponent is also included in its representation; on some machines the sign is explicit (a 1 bit for negative exponents, while on others the lower half of the range of possible numbers represents negative exponents.)

You should note that most computers have *double-precision* floating-point hardware, which uses two or more words to store a floating-point number and roughly doubles the precision of the fraction. In this context reals of one-word length—what FORTRAN refers to as REAL—are referred to as *single-precision* numbers.

A typical representation of reals is shown in Figure 6.1. Note that the decimal point is implied; it is not actually stored in the word. Both the fraction and exponent are represented in binary.

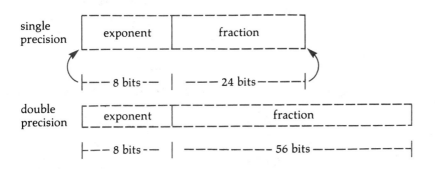

Figure 6.1
Floating-Point Formats

Some systems also increase the size of the exponent in the floating-point format with a corresponding reduction of the fraction.

Computing in double precision will usually greatly increase the accuracy of the result at the expense of doubling the storage space and usually increasing the execution time.

Double-Precision Constant

FORTRAN allows us to specify real variables and constants in double precision. The definition of double-precision constants is similar to that of real constants.

Examples: 3.5D2   −1.96D+4   93.D4   276D−5   .00375D10

double precision constant

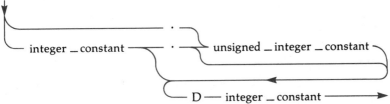

**DOUBLE
PRECISION
Statement**

Remark: In words, a double-precision constant looks like a real constant in exponential form with a D in place of the E.

Double-precision parameters, variables, and arrays must be explicitly declared (there is no default) using the *DOUBLE PRECISION* statement.*

Examples:

```
DOUBLE PRECISION X, Y
DOUBLE PRECISION ROOTS(1000), INITS(1000)
DOUBLE PRECISION LIMIT, CAPAC(350)
```

DOUBLE PRECISION statement

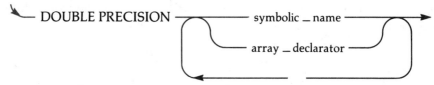

Remarks:

1. Nonexecutable
2. The Standard sets no limits on the number of elements in the list.
3. Double-precision complex values are not allowed. This limits the value of complex numbers in FORTRAN.

The following examples should clarify what happens in assignment statements with operands of different types. Let D1 and D2 be double precision variables, R1 a real, and I an integer.

Example 1: `R1 = D1 + D2`
The right-hand side is computed in double precision and is rounded, or truncated, to single precision before it is assigned to R1.

Example 2: `D2 = R1 + D1`
R1 is converted to double precision and added to D1, and the double-precision result is assigned to D2.

Example 3: `D1 = R1`
The value of R1 is converted to double precision before it is assigned to D1.

Example 4: `D2 = D1 + I`
I is converted to double precision and added to D1; the double-precision result is assigned to D2.

*More precise options will be available in the next FORTRAN standard, whose preliminary version is currently referred to as 8X.

Example 5: `I = D1`
D1 is truncated to the integer nearest to D1 that is between D1 and 0 before it is assigned to I. Thus, if D1 = 2.79D1, I will be 27; if D1 = −4.99D0, I will be −4.

Once again we emphasize that you should avoid mixed-mode right-hand sides where possible, and that type conversions should be explicit, not implicit as in the above examples. You can use the intrinsic functions DBLE, INT, and REAL for this purpose. The value of DBLE(X) is the double-precision value that corresponds to X. Thus, Example 2 above should be written as

$$D2 = DBLE(R1) + D1$$

and Example 5 should be

$$I = INT(D1)$$

Finally, you should note that all of the generic intrinsic functions defined in Table 2.3 may be applied to arguments of type DOUBLE PRECISION. See Appendix B for details.

As you gain experience with FORTRAN, you may encounter a statement such as

$$REAL*8 \ X, \ Y, \ P(100)$$

that defines the variables X and Y and the array P to be double precision. This variation became popular on IBM computers before the DOUBLE PRECISION statement was standardized. The statement indicates that X, Y, and P each require 8 bytes to represent their value(s); on a machine with 4 bytes per word, this representation was meaningful for double-precision variables. It is still used today in many versions of FORTRAN, but you should avoid its use in favor of the Standard. Note also, however, the potential changes in the forthcoming new standard, described in Chapter 11.

Remember that the use of double-precision arithmetic in an algorithm may give you the accuracy you want in the results, but at a cost of extra space and time. Not only is double precision slower than single precision—sometimes by a factor of 2 or more—but each conversion, such as those in the above examples, takes place at run time. If these conversions are embedded in a loop, their cost can also be significant.

What kinds of errors can occur in a floating-point system? First, regardless of whether one uses single- or double-precision arithmetic, floating-point numbers still have a finite range. For the following discussion, let us assume we are working on a machine with a five-decimal fraction.

Errors occur because a number must have a finite decimal expansion, within the number of digits available in the fraction, in order to be represented exactly. This is not possible in general. Consider

$$1/3 = .33333 \ldots$$

and
$$\pi = 3.141592 \ldots$$

In our five-digit decimal system, π would be represented in one of two ways:

$$\pi = \begin{cases} .31416 \times 10^1 & \text{if the number is } \textit{rounded}; \\ .31415 \times 10^1 & \text{if the number is } \textit{truncated (or chopped)}. \end{cases}$$

In a computer that rounds, the result chosen is the normalized floating-point number nearest the original value. With truncation, the result is the nearest normalized number between the original value and 0. In both cases the difference between the original value and the result of truncating or rounding is known as *roundoff error*. The roundoff error for π in the above example is:

$$r = \begin{cases} \pi - .31416 \times 10^1 = -.734 \ldots \times 10^{-5} & \text{(rounded)}; \\ \pi - .31415 \times 10^1 = .926 \ldots \times 10^{-4} & \text{(truncated)}. \end{cases}$$

Thus the roundoff error can be significantly larger in a truncated result compared to the corresponding rounded result.

In addition to numbers like π and $1/3$, a number with a finite expansion in one base may actually have an infinite expansion in another. For example,

$$1/10 = .1 \text{ (decimal)}$$
$$= .00011001100110011 \ldots \text{ (binary)}.$$

Thus roundoff error is often introduced in the conversion of a value to binary.

Roundoff errors also occur because of floating-point arithmetic operations. In most instances the result of each operation is normalized. Therefore, multiplying $x = .10101 \times 10^4$ times $y = .20081 \times 10^3$ yields

$$x \times y = .0202838181 \times 10^7 = .202838181 \times 10^6$$

$$= \begin{cases} .20284 \times 10^6 & \text{(rounded)} \\ .20283 \times 10^6 & \text{(truncated)} \end{cases}$$

in our five-digit system.

The extra digits (10 here) are usually retained until the operation is completed. This example illustrates another kind of error that occurs because of the finite length of the fraction. Roundoff errors due to arithmetic are much more serious than those due to conversion for input or output because the repetitive nature of the operations tends to compound the errors. We will examine some serious consequences of floating-point operations in the next section.

In floating-point addition (subtraction) the following steps take place:

1. Shift the fraction of the number with the smaller magnitude until the exponents of the two numbers are equal.
2. Add (subtract) the fractions.
3. Normalize the result.
4. Round or truncate the result.

Example:

$$(.27014 \times 10^5) + (.17381 \times 10^3) = \begin{array}{r} .2701400 \times 10^5 \\ .0017381 \times 10^5 \\ \hline .2718781 \times 10^5 \end{array}$$

normalize: $.2718781 \times 10^5$
round: $.27188 \times 10^5$

In floating-point multiplication (division) the steps are:

1. Multiply (divide) the fraction and add the exponents.
2. Normalize the result.
3. Round or truncate the result.

Example:

$(.27014 \times 10^5) \times (.17381 \times 10^5) = .0471094624 \times 10^{10}$
normalize: $.471094624 \times 10^9$
round: $.47109 \times 10^9$

In both examples all of the digits are retained throughout the intermediate stages. Most floating-point hardware uses *guard digits*, which are extra digits for storing the low-order bits of the intermediate result before normalization and rounding take place. Without guard digits, the errors due to rounding would be much worse.

Note that the exponent "takes up the slack" in the fraction, in a sense, when the number is normalized. However, if the exponent becomes too large ($e > M$), then an *exponential overflow* error occurs. If e is too small ($e < m$), which implies that the number is close to 0, the result is *exponential underflow*. Usually the system will terminate the program on exponential overflow. For underflow, which is generally not as serious, many systems simply replace the result by 0. The solution to the overflow problem depends on the conditions that caused it. Simply rerunning the process in double precision may solve the problem. Otherwise, you may have to scale the problem or use a different algorithm.

Because of the roundoff error usually present in a real number, comparing two reals for equality is a bad practice. For example, consider the following WHILE loop:

```
        ACLEV = 10.0
*       WHILE (SOLUTION NOT NEUTRALIZED) DO
10      CONTINUE
        IF (ACLEV .NE. 0.0) THEN
          .
          .
          ACLEV = ACLEV - 0.1
          GOTO 10
        ENDIF
*       ENDWHILE
```

This loop will most certainly never terminate: ALCLEV will never be exactly 0 because of accumulated roundoff error. A better way to write the test is:

```
        IF (ABS(ACLEV) .GT. EPS) THEN
```

where EPS is a previously defined parameter with a value much smaller than 0.1 but also much larger than the roundoff error threshold (i.e., the smallest number you can represent in your machine). In this case a value of 10^{-6} would do nicely.

To be safe you should also use a counter to limit the number of iterations in a loop such as the above example. That is, write the loop as

```
10      CONTINUE
        IF (ABS(ACLEV) .GT. EPS .AND. COUNT .LT. LIMIT) THEN
          .
          .
          ACLEV = ACLEV - 0.1
          COUNT = COUNT + 1
          GOTO 10
        ENDIF
```

where LIMIT is a suitable upper bound on the number of iterations.

Style Guide:
 1. Use double precision only where it is necessary to achieve the desired accuracy.
 2. Avoid mixed-mode arithmetic expressions. Where type conversion is involved, use explicit conversion functions INT, REAL, and DBLE.
 3. Never test for equality of real variables.

6.3 ERROR PROPAGATION

Roundoff error is an unavoidable consequence of the finite length of the floating-point fraction. Ongoing research will improve floating-point computation in the future, but we must still be wary of possible pitfalls to avoid disastrous consequences in certain instances. The intent here is not to turn you into a numerical analyst, but rather to encourage you to avoid blind acceptance of the results of numerical computation and to bring your questions to the experts when you are not sure.

Every floating-point operation may produce a roundoff error that may be amplified, or even reduced, in subsequent operations. One of the most common, and potentially serious, sources of these errors is the *loss of significant digits*, also called *cancellation*, which is due to subtraction, or to the addition of two numbers with different signs. The more nearly equal the two numbers, the more pronounced is the effect.

Consider the following example. We wish to compute $x - y$ on our five-digit machine, where $x = .763208372$ and $y = .7631501368$. The correct answer is $x - y = .0000547004$, while our rounded result is .00005, which is normalized to $.50000 \times 10^{-4}$, and which results from first rounding x and y to five digits and then subtracting. The error is .47 $\times 10^{-5}$, which may seem insignificant when compared to x or y. However, it is the *loss of digits* in the result that poses a problem. The computed difference, $.50000 \times 10^{-4}$, has only *one* significant figure of accuracy. That is, the four 0s following the digit 5 may be considered to be in error. They are not significant. They are provided as a result of rounding and normalizing the result, since no information about the true digits is available. Subsequent operations on these digits may severely amplify the error.

Suppose, for example,* that $x = .10005482410 \times 10^5$ and $y = .09997342213 \times 10^5$ represent the products of two five-digit floating-point numbers that have fractions of double length. The exact normalized value for $x - y$ is $.8140197 \times 10^1$. However, computing the difference on our five-digit system yields a very different result.

1. Round x and y to five digits: $x = .10005 \times 10^5$ and $y = .99973 \times 10^5$.
2. Compute $x - y$: $.10005 \times 10^5 - .99973 \times 10^5 =$

$$\begin{array}{r} .10005|00 \times 10^5 \\ -.09997|30 \times 10^5 \\ \hline .00007|70 \times 10^5. \end{array}$$

guard digits

---

*This example appeared in U. W. Kulisch and W. L. Miranker, "Arithmetic of the Digital Computer: A New Approach," *SIAM Review* (March 1986). Reprinted with the permission of the Society for Industrial and Applied Mathematics. All rights reserved. Copyright 1986 by the Society for Industrial and Applied Mathematics.

3. Normalize: $.7700000 \times 10^1$.
4. Round: $.77000 \times 10^1$.

Note that the subtraction step was *error-free* because of the guard digits. Even so, the final result, $.77000 \times 10^1$, is terrible; it agrees with the exact result only in magnitude. That is, rounded, they agree to the first decimal place. However, *none* of the digits of the two fractions agree. This example shows what can happen when cancellation takes place between two values that have already been rounded. Imagine the possibility for a calculation involving thousands, or even millions, of arithmetic operations.

How can one avoid cancellation? The remedy is to anticipate that this may occur and then revise the program. In many cases simply redoing the calculations in double precision will reduce the seriousness of the error. In the above example, if x, y, and $x - y$ are computed in double precision and the final result is rounded to single precision, we obtain a value of $.81402 \times 10^1$, which is as accurate as possible to five digits.

Even double precision may not help, however, if there is a serious cancellation of significant digits. In such cases we may be able to reformulate the solution to avoid the cancellation altogether, as in the following examples.

Recall that the formula

$$x = \frac{-b \pm \sqrt{b^2 - 4ac}}{2a}$$

is used to find the roots of the equation $ax^2 + bx + c = 0$. Suppose we use it to find the smaller root of

$$x^2 + .10101 \times 10^3 x + .12023 \times 10^1 = 0;$$

that is,

$$x = \frac{-b + \sqrt{b^2 - 4ac}}{2a}.$$

Using our five-digit system, we find that $x = -.10000 \times 10^{-1}$ whereas $-.1190418 \times 10^{-1}$ is the exact root to seven digits. The loss of accuracy is due primarily to cancellation, since $\sqrt{b^2 - 4ac}$ is very close to b. We can avoid the problem by rewriting the formula for the smaller root as follows:

$$x = \left(\frac{-b + \sqrt{b^2 - 4ac}}{2a}\right)\left(\frac{-b - \sqrt{b^2 - 4ac}}{-b - \sqrt{b^2 - 4ac}}\right) = \frac{-2c}{b^2 + \sqrt{b^2 - 4ac}}$$

In this case there is no subtraction between nearly equal values. Using our five-digit system again, we obtain $x = -.11904 \times 10^{-1}$, which is accurate to five digits.

For another example, suppose it is necessary to compute a value of the function $f(x) = 1 - \cos x$ for x near 0. Since $\cos x$ approaches 1 as x approaches 0, this function will be subject to severe cancellation there. Once again, we can rewrite the function:

$$f(x) = 1 - \cos x = \frac{1 - \cos^2 x}{1 + \cos x} = \frac{\sin x}{1 + \cos x},$$

which can be evaluated accurately for x close to 0.

The above examples illustrate computation involving only a few operations. When many operations are involved, errors will *propagate*, or multiply, with the number of operations, and cancellation can produce a result that is not even close in magnitude to the exact answer.

The function e^x is often approximated by the Taylor series:

$$e^x = 1 + x + \frac{x^2}{2!} + \frac{x^3}{3!} + \frac{x^4}{4!} + \cdots + \frac{x^n}{n!}$$

Generally, the more terms we use, the more accurate the approximation. However, this series was computed for $x = -20$ using 62 terms of the series on a floating-point system with six decimal digits in the fraction.* Note that the terms of the series alternate in sign (since x is negative) and that they first increase, then decrease, in magnitude. The correct answer is $.206115 \times 10^{-8}$, but the computed value is 181.496, a catastrophic error!

Errors can propagate in different ways. In iterative processes, some errors actually decrease in successive approximations and therefore have little effect on accuracy. Other errors grow, some to the point where the results of a computation will be completely invalid, as in the previous example.

Let $g(r)$ denote the rate of growth of an error, r. If $g(r)$ behaves as in

$$g(r) = c \times n \times r$$

where c is a constant and n is the number of arithmetic operations, the growth rate is said to be *linear*, since it depends linearly on n. If, however,

$$g(r) = c \times p^n \times r$$

*In Kulisch and Miranker, Ibid.

where p is a constant greater than 1, the growth rate is *exponential*. Linear growth is considered normal. It is usually not a problem, since r is generally very small relative to the numbers of interest in the process, having a relative magnitude on the order of the roundoff threshold of the machine (e.g., $2^{-24} \approx 10^{-7}$). Exponential growth, on the other hand, can be disastrous and should be avoided. If a process exhibits the exponential growth of error it is said to be *unstable*. The growth rate, g, depends on a number of factors, such as the physical system being modeled or the numerical algorithm being used.

The above computation of e^{-x} is an example of an unstable algorithm; therefore it should not be used for large values of x. How then could we compute e^{-20} in a stable manner?

We can avoid this particular problem by first using the series to compute e^{20} and then dividing the result into 1 (i.e., $e^{-20} = 1 / e^{20}$. However, in this case one would have to be very careful to avoid exponential overflow (see Exercise 26).

For example, if you evaluate the numerators and denominators separately, for example, $(20)^{60}$ and 60! for the 60th term, you will certainly generate an exponential overflow error. Instead, let a_n be the nth term of the series. Note that

$$a_{n+1} = \frac{x^{n+1}}{(n+1)!} = \frac{x}{(n+1)} \times \frac{x^n}{n!} = \frac{x}{(n+1)} \times a_n$$

In this way each term can be computed from the previous term without generating a numerator or denominator that is too large.

If you work in a field like astronomy, where all of the numbers related to the problem you want to solve are very large (or very small), you may be able to *scale* them—multiply them by 10^{-20}, for example, or use logarithms—so that the resulting values fall in the floating-point range of your computer.

Even where cancellation is not a factor, sums of a large number of terms can have large errors. Often the terms of a series decrease in magnitude, as in the series for π:

$$\pi^6 = 945 \times \left(1 + \frac{1}{2^6} + \frac{1}{3^6} + \cdots + \frac{1}{n^6}\right)$$

As one accumulates the sum, the difference between the sum and the subsequent terms increases markedly. Since floating-point addition requires shifting the fraction of the smaller number to the right, most of the digits in the later terms are lost. On the other hand, keeping the magnitudes of the two summands roughly the same keeps the shifting to a minimum. For that reason it is generally recommended that you accumulate the sum in order of increasing magnitude of the terms. Both the partial sums and the subsequent terms will increase.

Many numerical algorithms compute successive values at equidistant points in an interval, such as X in the loop

```
X = X0
DO 10 I = 1, 1000
    .
    .
    .
    X = X + H
    .
    .
    .
10   CONTINUE
```

Here H represents the *step size*, which is the distance between successive points. Because of roundoff error, the subsequent values of X can be increasingly in error as X increases. It is often (but not always) better to write the loop in the form

```
DO 10 I = 1, 1000
    .
    .
    .
    X = X0 + H * REAL(I)
    .
    .
    .
10   CONTINUE
```

The first loop is preferred if H is a power of 2, such as 1/64. (Why?) Recall that this technique was applied to an example in Chapter 4 to improve the accuracy and output of the evaluation of a function, $f(x, y)$.

In summary, then, you should now realize that floating-point computation can be a tricky business. You should always carefully examine the equations you are using to be sure that there is no danger of serious error due to the limitations of floating-point arithmetic. Remember the following guidelines:

1. Use double precision where it is appropriate. Remember that it can be expensive, and that it may not give you sufficient accuracy if cancellation is severe.
2. Reformulate the solution to avoid subtracting values of nearly equal magnitude. Avoid unstable algorithms. This may not always be as easy as in the above simple example.
3. Be wary of the possibility of exponential overflow. To avoid it you may have to compute terms of a series in a different way, break up the problem into different parts, or scale the numbers before using them in a program.
4. Accumulate sums starting with the smaller terms first.

The main point to remember is to be suspicious of your (or someone else's) results, and to ask for help from a qualified expert for important problems.

6.4 DESIGNING TO AVOID ERRORS

We have already considered structured programming as an effective design methodology. Writing programs in a style that promotes ease of understanding and readability goes a long way toward obtaining meaningful and accurate results. Building a large program by writing and testing it as a series of smaller components also helps to reduce errors, since each component will be less complex than the whole. Subprograms, which are required for this approach, are covered in Chapter 7. A third recommendation was to parameterize whenever possible. All limits —machine limits, parameters, and other constants (e.g., π)—should be defined as parameters for ease of reading and of possible alteration later.

Some other design suggestions from this section are summarized here:

1. Always use intrinsic functions or other FORTRAN library routines whenever possible, unless of course your purpose is to learn a programming language. Why should you expend effort on code that has already been written and debugged and runs efficiently?

2. If you can write a program to handle a more general problem than the one at hand, it may be worth the extra effort. Otherwise a program written to handle a particular set of numbers may have to be rewritten for a different set.

3. Be sure to check that the program will correctly handle the so-called *boundary cases* for the data. Verify that loops will operate correctly on data requiring only one or even no iterations. Will the program work on the largest or smallest acceptable values? What will it do if it reads a number that is outside the range of acceptable values? For example, suppose the program reads a negative integer that is to be used later as an array subscript for an array with positive subscript bounds. What will happen if all of the numbers in an array to be sorted are already in order, or in reverse order? In general, you should always write code with the thought: What will happen if the problem is bad or the method doesn't work as I expect it to?

How a program behaves as it is applied to problems outside the sphere of those for which it was intended is a measure of its *robustness*. A well-written, robust program should degrade gracefully when faced with bad data. Be sure to document your program with regard to its limitations and intended problem set. If input data or some computed value does not check as it should, print an appropriate diagnostic, set an error flag, or take some other action appropriate to the condition. Let the user know what is going on.

Examples of the kinds of conditions to check for are (1) that arguments for square roots are not negative, (2) that computed or inputted array subscripts are within bounds, (3) that a function to be integrated is continuous, (4) that the degree of a polynomial is positive, (5) that a function has opposite signs at the endpoints of an interval, (6) that the terms being accumulated in a series are getting small, or (7) that a request for accuracy is realistic (i.e., you should not allow a request for 10 digits of accuracy on a machine that provides only 7 digits.

You should provide other checks to reduce the chances that a program will produce invalid results. Limit all iterations to some maximum value. For arrays that should be ordered but are not, reorder them, or print a warning and stop, whichever is appropriate. Be sure that interval endpoints are in the right order. Make sure that arguments for intrinsic functions have logical values. Finally, you can force real variables that should have integer values to be integers by using the equivalent of the following statement (X is real):

```
X = INT(X + .5 * SIGN(X))
```

Please note that these suggestions are only guidelines that may not apply to all cases. The procedure used must have a realistic physical basis or theoretical foundation. For example, the terms in the *harmonic series*

$$\sum_{k=1}^{\infty} \frac{1}{k}$$

are strictly decreasing in magnitude, but as any student of calculus knows, this series does *not* converge to a finite value.

Once you have written a FORTRAN program, there remain some steps you can take to help ensure its correctness:

1. Be sure to trace through the program statements by hand, using a typical but simple example. This process, called *desk-checking*, is often forgotten, given the present day availability and convenience of terminals and interactive programming, but it is generally considered to be well worth the effort.
2. As part of the desk-checking process, examine carefully all the variables and parameters in the program. Be sure that each appears in the intended type statement and that each instance of the variable or parameter is spelled correctly. Be sure you have not used I where 1 was intended and vice versa. Similarly for O and 0. Unlike Pascal and other strongly-typed languages, FORTRAN will not check these for you.
3. You should also scan the entire program to make sure that every variable has been initialized before it is used. If a variable

appears in an IF condition, the right-hand side of an assignment statement, or in a PRINT statement, it should previously have been assigned a value. An easy way to do this, as you scan the program listing, is to place a check mark over the variable after its initialization has been verified or to make a list of the initialized variables to compare against the code. Better yet, many FORTRAN compilers have an option to automatically check for uninitialized variables for you. This process will also help you to find any misspellings.

4. Where possible, avoid *side effects* associated with subprogram use (see Chapter 7). If portability is an issue, document the problem code well with appropriate comments.

6.5 TESTING AND VERIFICATION

Once the design is complete and the code written, we must verify that the program is correct. A great deal of effort has been put into finding methods for *proving* programs correct. While this research has generated a number of useful ideas, no method yet exists that can be applied in general. We may attempt to prove partial correctness, for example, that all array subscripts are within their declared ranges, but the techniques for doing so are beyond the scope of this book.

Therefore we are left with the prospect of *testing* a program in order to verify that it is correct. Ideally, we test a program using "live" data, in the environment in which it is to be used. A program might control the precisely timed addition of a catalyst into a chemical process. Another might perform the real-time correction of the flight path of an unmanned satellite. Clearly it is too expensive or too dangerous to test programs in these and other environments, especially in the early stages. (Imagine trying to test a nuclear missile warning system this way.) In cases like these, the environment is *simulated*: input data is generated that supposedly reflects all possible real-life conditions that the program would be subjected to. Eventually a person or group approves the program for use in the real environment, but in critical cases the program is likely to undergo prolonged testing. Experienced computer users can describe errors they have discovered in complex programs such as operating systems and compilers, even after they were released for general use. It is generally agreed that such programs will always contain some bugs. We always hope that, for critical programs, the very unusual conditions necessary to create an unanticipated error will never take place.

Testing Suggestions

In any case, testing is the only practical means we now have for verifying that a program is correct. Following the design suggestions in the previous section will help to reduce the number of bugs in your program and will correspondingly ease the burden of the testing process. Testing may reveal so many bugs in a poorly designed program that it may have to be thrown out and completely redesigned. In this section we present a number of suggestions for testing your programs.

1. Before you begin work on a serious program, familiarize yourself with the various error messages produced by the FORTRAN compiler, the loader, and other system programs you will use. Make intentional errors on a relatively simple program (let an array exceed its declared dimension) and observe what happens. Often the messages can be cryptic, misleading, and even incorrect. Most messages must be taken seriously, but some can be ignored. Some compilers provide numeric classifications of errors according to their seriousness; classes 0 and 1 may be warnings, while 7 to 9 may be very serious errors. Errors that cause the computer system to terminate the compilation or execution of your program are called *fatal* errors. With experience you will be more likely to understand quickly what the messages really mean; as a beginnner, the effort needed to decipher them may seriously impede your progress on a difficult program.

2. Use all the compiler options available to help you find errors. Every compiler will identify all syntax errors, but some compilers can also provide code that will (1) check for array subscripts that are out of bounds (which can otherwise be *very* difficult to diagnose and locate), (2) provide a traceback that indicates the FORTRAN source statement that failed as a result of an error like exponential overflow, (3) mark statements that cannot be reached during execution (e.g., an unlabeled statement immediately following a GOTO), and (4) mark statement numbers that are not referenced anywhere. Once initial testing is complete, some or all of these options can be omitted for the sake of efficiency. Sometimes other programs, called *software tools*, are available for in-depth analyses of programs.

3. Always *echo-print* the input data. That is, print out the data immediately after reading it. This is the only way to be sure that the program is reading the data correctly. If the data items are voluminous, print out every *n*th value, for some reasonable *n*.

4. Insert PRINT statements at judicious points throughout the program to verify that it has reached a certain point, or to print key variables when they change values. PRINT statements are helpful in verifying that the program is (or is not) performing as expected at various stages in its execution. The absence of a printed line can indicate that a section of code was never

executed. Such PRINT statements, and those used for echo-printing of input data, can be easily changed to comments by inserting asterisks in columns 1 through 5 when initial testing is complete, so that someone reading the listing can tell easily that these statements are "commented out" and are there for debugging purposes.

5. If execution time is a problem, be aware that most compilers include options that produce *optimized* object code. The compilation step is slower, but the program will execute much faster. Additionally, there are software tools that analyze the execution performance of a program and indicate the percentages of time used by each section of code. If one small loop used 50% to 75% of the execution time, it might be worthwhile to rewrite the loop and make it more efficient. Your local computer center should have information about software tools for this purpose.

6. If your program fails or gives incorrect results for unknown reasons, you may be able to take advantage of other compiler options to help you analyze the process. The following tools may be available:

   a. A *trace*, which serves essentially the same purpose as the PRINT statements described in suggestion 3. With a trace option you may specify the variables you wish printed whenever they change value or the statement numbers that are reached during execution. Because such output can be voluminous, you can usually limit the trace to a specific section of code, and you can also limit the number of lines of output.

   b. *Breakpoints*, which are used in an interactive environment. You specify points in the program where it is to halt and display values of selected variables. You often have the option of changing one or more of the variables before proceeding with the execution. In this way you could step through the program one statement at a time, emulating the desk-checking process.

   c. *Dumps*, which display the state of the program at the time it was terminated. All of the relevant machine registers are displayed, along with the object code and memory areas for arrays and variables. Usually dumps are of little value to a FORTRAN programmer, especially if some of the other tools are available.

7. The test data provided as input to the program is very important to the testing process. Ideally, the data should exercise the program so that it executes every statement, takes every branch, and follows every path. This is unrealistic in practice; the best we can do is to provide representative sets of data (probably more

than one) to reflect what will happen when the program is used in production. Try to test the boundary conditions, as we recommended earlier.

8. Suppose you write a program to solve a particular problem or class of problems. Before you apply it to the problem, test it first on a related problem whose solution is known. For example, if you are writing a program to solve a system of linear equations, apply it to a system whose solution is given in a textbook. (But be careful here; many textbook solutions are incorrect.) For most classes of problems, published test problems exist in the relevant literature. Ask an expert in the area for help in finding such sources.

Classes and Sources of Errors

Suppose your program produces correct results for one or more test problems, and you apply it to the problem you wanted to solve in the first place. How confident should you be that the answer is accurate? How accurate is it? Since there is no exact answer available (otherwise you wouldn't need the program), this can be a difficult question to answer.

Let x represent the exact solution to a problem and x_n our computed approximation. Sometimes we are interested in the value

$$x - x_n$$

which is called the *absolute error* in x_n. More frequently, however, we are interested in the quantity

$$\frac{x - x_n}{x}$$

which is called the *relative error* in x_n. It usually gives us a better sense of how serious the error is, as long as x is not zero. For example, if $x = .1 \times 10^9$ and $x_n = .10001 \times 10^9$, the absolute error is

$$x - x_n = -.1 \times 10^5 = -10,000$$

which may seem very large in magnitude, but it is very small compared to the value of x. The relative error is

$$\frac{x - x_n}{x} = -\frac{.1 \times 10^5}{.1 \times 10^9} = -10^{-4}$$

which is comparatively small. A similar conclusion can be made for x

very small. Naturally both types of errors must be approximated since the exact value of x would not generally be known.

There exist three sources of possible errors in your results. First, the *model* may contain errors. A program represents a model of physical reality. Equations used in the program might represent the motion of a particle in a magnetic field or the growth of trees in a forest. However, the physical theory could be incorrect, and the model may not reflect reality.

Second, there may be errors in the *software*. Your program may still contain undetected bugs, and, although it is rare, even the compiler may produce incorrect object code in certain cases. You should be particularly wary when a new version of a compiler has just been released. Compare results on a known problem using the previous version and the new version of the compiler. They should be the same.

Third, there may be significant *numerical* errors. Roundoff may have contaminated the solution; worse, the algorithm may be unstable, and the result may not even be close to the true result. This is another reason for using prewritten software routines wherever possible: they are usually based on well-established, stable algorithms.

It should be clear that a good understanding of the physical system is a prerequisite for producing a reasonable computer model. Furthermore, a model is often refined over time as developers and researchers study its behavior. For example, models of global weather patterns have undergone extensive study and refinement for years. To validate a model, most experts first test it on cases for which the results are known and then refine it until it compares favorably with reality. For critical problems, such as a nuclear reactor control system, often two or more groups will work independently and compare their results.

We have already given a number of guidelines for detecting and correcting software errors. It should be noted that most numerical computations involve *heuristics*, (i.e., rules of thumb, or procedures that are expected to work most of the time but are not guaranteed), even though the algorithm that is the core of the process may be based on sound mathematical principles. Choices of how frequently a given function is evaluated, criteria for accepting a result as accurate to so many digits, decisions on whether a function is continuous in a certain interval, are all based on heuristics. Errors in a program may just be the result of a poor choice for a heuristic.

Measuring Accuracy

Heuristics are part of the suggestions given in Section 6.3 for avoiding cancellation errors. Of course, the construction of stable algorithms for numerical computation falls in the realm of numerical analysis and is beyond the scope of this book. However, we will describe some general methods that are used to measure the accuracy of a result. For specific algorithms, there may also be specific, more effective, methods.

1. A relatively easy way to estimate the accuracy of a numerical result is to do the computation twice: once in single precision and once in double precision. If the results agree to n digits, we often accept those digits as accurate. The difference between the two values is a measure of the error due to roundoff. For example, if the computed solution to a problem is given by

$$y = \begin{cases} .7319526 \times 10^2 \text{ in single precision} \\ .7314838 \times 10^2 \text{ in double precision} \end{cases}$$

then we might accept $.731 \times 10^2$ as the value of y, and the magnitude of the roundoff error in the single-precision result could be estimated to be 1×10^{-1}. Alternatively, we could accept more digits of the double-precision result as correct, but we would not have an estimate of the error.

2. Numerical algorithms commonly subdivide an interval and compute values at the *nodes*, or points of the subdivision. This approach is used in numerical integration schemes, for example. Computing the values at common nodes for two or more subdivision sizes and comparing them as done in method 1 above is another way to estimate the error in a result and verify its correctness. Usually, increasing the number of nodes in a given method improves the accuracy. However, Figure 6.2 shows what happens to the error in general, as the *stepsize, h*—the distance between successive nodes—changes. As h decreases, the error decreases until the magnitudes of the values used approach that

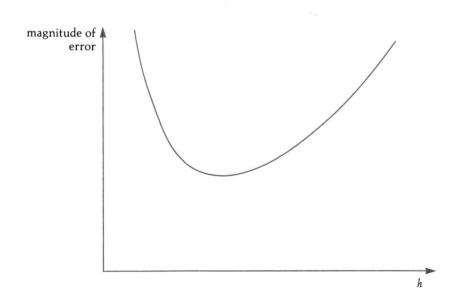

magnitude of
error

h

of the roundoff threshold of the computer; then the error begins to increase again as the roundoff error grows. Sophisticated software routines can warn you when roundoff error begins to contaminate the results.

For example, the following program was written to experiment with the accuracy of a numerical computation as a function of h. From calculus, the *slope* of a function, f, at the point x is given by the *derivative* of f, which is defined by the formula

$$f'(x) = \lim_{h \to 0} \frac{f(x + h) - f(x)}{h}$$

We can simulate this limit process by computing the value

$$\frac{f(x + h) - f(x)}{h}$$

using the following sequence of values for h:

$$h = \frac{1}{2}, \frac{1}{4}, \frac{1}{8}, \cdots \frac{1}{2^n}$$

This value is called a *divided difference* approximation to $f'(x)$. Using powers of 2 means that no roundoff error will be generated as a result of the division.

A program to do this for $f(x) = e^x$ (answer: $f'(x) = e^x$) at $x = 1$ follows.

EXAMPLE 6.1

```
INTEGER N, I
REAL X, H, FX, FXH, DERIV, ERR
PARAMETER (N = 30)
X = 1.0
FX = EXP(X)
H = 1.0
DO 10 I = 1, N
    H = H / 2.0
    FXH = EXP(X + H)
    DERIV = (FXH - FX) / H
    ERR = ABS(DERIV - FX)
    PRINT *, I, H, DERIV, ERR
10      CONTINUE
END
```

Output (excerpts):

1	0.500000	3.52681	0.808533
2	0.250000	3.08824	0.369963
3	0.125000	2.89548	0.177197
4	6.25000E-02	2.80503	8.67453E-02
⋮	⋮	⋮	⋮
10	9.76563E-04	2.71948	1.20068E-03
11	4.88281E-04	2.71875	4.68254E-04
⋮	⋮	⋮	⋮
17	7.62939E-06	2.71875	4.68254E-04
18	3.18470E-06	2.68750	3.07817E-02
19	1.90735E-07	2.75000	3.17183E-02
⋮	⋮	⋮	⋮
24	5.96046E-08	4.00000	1.28172
25	2.98023E-07	0.	2.71828

Observe that the absolute error in DERIV (the last column), the approximation to the derivative, decreases uniformly as H decreases until $H = 2^{-11}$, after which the error flattens out and then increases again. In fact, when $H = 2^{-25}$, DERIV becomes identically 0. The increase results from the contamination due to roundoff error. As the value of H approaches the roundoff error threshold for the machine, $2^{-24} \approx 10^{-7}$ here, the difference in the function values EXP(X + H) and EXP(X) becomes correspondingly small. Divided difference approximations to the derivative are therefore regarded as unstable for small values of H.

3. Many numerical processes are *iterative* in nature, generating successive values (e.g., $x_1, x_2, x_3, \ldots, x_n$) which are (we hope) increasingly better approximations to the unknown exact solution. For these methods one usually compares two or more successive approximations, as above, assuming that if they agree to n digits, then the exact solution must agree with those values to n digits too. Sometimes this is an incorrect assumption. This approach is also used as a criterion for stopping the iteration: iterate until $|x_i - x_{i+1}|$, or $|x_i - x_{i+1}| / |x_{i+1}|$, is less then some small, predetermined constant.

4. A more expensive way to verify the correctness of a result is to use two or more different algorithms. This may not be too difficult if the program is modular. Also, if all of the methods yield essentially the same result, your level of confidence in the result should be correspondingly high.

5. A method is considered stable if "small" changes in the data (e.g., .01 percent) produce correspondingly small changes in the

results. Therefore one way to validate your program is to perturb the data at random, up to a small percentage, and study the changes in the outcome. There are published programs that test other programs in this way for instability.

We have presented a number of general suggestions for checking the validity of your results. Their use presumes varying degrees of expertise with the given techniques, knowledge about the problem you are trying to solve, and understanding of the algorithm. The intent was to make you aware of the various heuristics available to avoid, detect, and measure errors, and encourage you not to accept numerical results as correct without question. The fact that a number was generated by a computer doesn't make it correct.

6.6 TRANSPORTABILITY ISSUES

We have promoted strict adherence to the FORTRAN 77 standard in order to achieve transportability, or machine-independence. Unfortunately the Standard alone is not sufficient to guarantee this. There are hundreds of FORTRAN dialects, and many of the differences are actually restrictions on the way the language may be used. Does manufacturer ABC's FORTRAN compiler, version 4.3 for computer model XYZ/100, really adhere to the Standard? Part of the problem is that the Standard is ambiguous in places and therefore gives the compiler-writer some leeway. Unfortunately this means that you cannot always rely on "standard FORTRAN" working the same way on all systems.

An example of how standard FORTRAN compilers may differ is in the way they treat constants that are specified with more digits of accuracy than the machine can handle. If you specify the value of π to 12 digits, the compiler may generate a fatal error on some systems. Another example involves a compiler's explicit dependence on the word size of the machine, which affects the specific number of characters that can be packed into a "word." Other "danger" areas will be described as we present the relevant material.

These and other features are often called *hardware dependencies*. Some programs, such as one whose algorithm depends heavily on the word size of the machine, may be easier to rewrite than move to a different computer. It can be extremely difficult, time-consuming, and expensive to scan through a program, try to understand its logic, identify *all* of the dependencies, and make the appropriate modifications. Some such programs have no comments or documentation to help the person assigned to make the changes.

Many hardware dependencies are unavoidable. What can you do to minimize their effects and improve the transportability of your programs? We list seven measures:

1. Try to write your program to avoid hardware dependencies in the first place. For example, you may pack more than one number into a word in order to save memory space, but you should avoid this approach if possible. Perhaps memory space is not that critical, or perhaps the data should be subdivided and manipulated in chunks.

2. Include comments in the prologue describing all of the hardware dependencies.

3. Insert comments in the body of the program that explain a particular dependency.

4. Define the variables that determine the dependencies (e.g., the roundoff thresholds of the computer), and assign their values once, early in the program. Usually a parameter will do nicely for this purpose.

5. Use a FORTRAN compiler that checks for standard FORTRAN. There are other tools, such as PFORT, a program written at Bell Telephone Laboratories, that check FORTRAN source code and identify any statements that may cause transportability problems. PFORT is available in many computer centers.

6. If possible, test the program on two or more different systems.

7. Some computer systems include special functions in their FORTRAN libraries (see Chapter 7) that provide information about the hardware. If the program that uses these functions is moved to a new computer, you must be sure that the new system also includes these functions. If not, it is a relatively simple matter to write your own functions to provide these services (see Chapter 7). Among the functions which are proposed for inclusion in the set of intrinsic functions in the forthcoming new standard are the following:

`DIGITS(X)` = number of significant digits (in the base of the model)

`RADIX(X)` = base of the number system in the computer model

`TINY(X)` = smallest number that can be represented

`HUGE(X)` = largest number that can be represented

`EPSILON(X)` = number that is "almost negligible" compared to 1

`EFFECTIVE_PRECISION(X)` = effective decimal precision

`MAXEXPONENT(X)` = maximum exponent

The argument X for each function is only used to determine the *type* of the associated number. For example, HUGE(1) determines the largest integer in the system, HUGE(1.0) the largest real, and HUGE(1.DO) the largest double-precision value.

It should be clear that the using these and similar functions will help to improve the transportability of FORTRAN programs. For example, convergence in Example 4.3 (Jacobi's method for solving linear systems of equations) might be assumed if MAXDIF is less than 50 times the roundoff threshold, EPSILON. That is, replace the line

```
IF (MAXDIF .LT. EPS)  GOTO 170
```

by the code

```
CONV = 50. * EPSILON(1.0)
  :
  :
IF (MAXDIF .LT. CONV)  GOTO 170
```

Exercises

Section 6.1

1. What are the values of the following binary integers in decimal?
   *a. 1100111   *c. 111111   e. 10111010011
   b. 101010   d. 100000001

2. What are the values of the binary integers in Exercise 1 in octal? In hexadecimal?

3. What are the values of the following octal integers in binary? In decimal? In hexadecimal?
   *a. 707   b. 1234   *c. 6000   .d. 31242   e. 10000

4. What are the values of the following hexadecimal integers in binary? In decimal? In octal?
   *a. A05   b. F9   *c. 2090   d. CDE   e. 100

5. One way to convert a decimal integer to binary is to divide the number and successive quotients by 2, saving all the remainders. The remainders, written down in the order opposite to that in which they were obtained, are the digits of the binary number. For example,

Quotients	Remainders
2 ⌐ 87	1
2 ⌐ 43	1
2 ⌐ 21	1
2 ⌐ 10	0
2 ⌐ 5	1
2 ⌐ 2	0
2 ⌐ 1	1
0	

Therefore, 87 (decimal) = 1010111 (binary). A similar scheme can be used to convert a decimal integer to octal or hexadecimal. Convert the following decimal integer to binary, to octal, and to hex.

*a. 99   b. 204   *c. 64   d. 63   e. 123

6. Negative binary numbers are often stored in *twos complement* form in computers. The twos complement is obtained by reversing each bit (0 to 1 and 1 to 0) and adding 1. Thus, the twos complement of the 8-bit binary number 00010011 (decimal 19)—assuming an 8-bit word with the sign bit in the high-order position—is determined by:

$$\frac{\begin{array}{r} 11101100 \\ 1 \end{array}}{11101101} \quad (-19 \text{ decimal})$$

Subtraction is thus accomplished by complementing the subtrahend and adding. For example,

$$\begin{array}{ll} 00010011 & (19 \text{ decimal}) \\ -00000101 & (-5 \text{ decimal}) \end{array} \qquad \frac{\begin{array}{l} 00010011 \\ 11111011 \end{array}}{00001110} \quad (14 \text{ decimal})$$

Write the twos complement of the following binary numbers. Check your answers by taking their twos complement, which should be the same as the original number.

*a. 00111010   *c. 01111110
b. 00000001   d. 11110110 (negative)

Section 6.2

7. What are the values of the following binary numbers in decimal?
   *a. .111   *c. .0001   e. 11.011
   b. .10101   d. .110110

8. What are the values of the binary numbers in Exercise 6 in octal? In hex?

9. What are the values of the following octal numbers in binary? In decimal?
   *a. .702   b. .011   *c. .612   d. 7.31   e. .777

10. What are the values of the following hex numbers in binary? In decimal?
    *a. .AE   b. .011   *c. .FOB   d. A.B   e. .99

11. One way to convert a decimal fraction to binary is to multiply the number and fraction parts of successive products by 2, saving all of the integer parts. The integer parts, written down in the order obtained from the decimal point represent the binary digits. Since the expansion may not terminate, you should stop the expansion when you achieve the desired accuracy. For example,

Products	Integer part
$2 \times .17 = .34$	0
$2 \times .34 = .68$	0
$2 \times .68 = 1.36$	1
$2 \times .36 = .72$	0
$2 \times .72 = 1.44$	1
$2 \times .44 = .88$	0
$2 \times .88 = 1.76$	1
. . .	

Therefore .17 (decimal) = .0010101 (binary). A similar scheme can be used to convert decimal fractions to octal or hex. Convert the following decimal fractions to binary, to octal, and to hex.

*a. .99   *c. .111   e. .555
b. .07   d. .875

12. Perform the following additions using five-digit, normalized, rounded, decimal arithmetic.

*a. $.90512 \times 10^3$ *c. $.58269 \times 10^{-3}$
   $.81723 \times 10^3$ $.24787 \times 10^{-6}$

b. $.72368 \times 10^4$ d. $.17935 \times 10^2$
   $.40654 \times 10^6$ $.92483 \times 10^{-4}$

13. Perform the following multiplications using three-digit, normalized, rounded decimal arithmetic.

*a. $.214 \times 10^2$ *c. $.817 \times 10^0$
   $.081 \times 10^3$ $.795 \times 10^{-4}$

b. $.100 \times 10^{-3}$ d. $.111 \times 10^7$
   $.102 \times 10^2$ $.555 \times 10^6$

14. In the floating-point number system of your computer, there are numbers x such that $y + x = y$ for a fixed value y and $x \neq 0$. Why? What is the set of integers, N, such that $1.0 + 2.0 ** (-N) = 1.0$? Write a FORTRAN program to find the smallest value of N—call it

N_0—for which this is true in both single and double precision. The value 2^{-N_0+1} is the roundoff error threshold of your computer, called *unit-roundoff*.

15. A *stochastic matrix* has all nonnegative elements, and the sum of all the elements in each row equals 1. Write a program to read coefficients for five-by-five matrices and test them to verify whether they are stochastic. Try your program on at least three cases: two that are stochastic and one that is not.

Section 6.3

16. Given the following expressions, for which values of x and/or y would you expect to encounter difficulties in computing accurately? Rewrite the expressions to eliminate the problem.
   *a. $4 - (4 + x^2)$ *c. $\sin x - \sin y$ e. $\log x - \log y$
   b. $\dfrac{x - \sin x}{\tan x}$ d. $x - \sqrt{x^2 - a}$

17. How would you evaluate $e - e^x$ for x close to 1 if full precision were needed?

18. Test the accuracy of the single- and double-precision version of the FORTRAN function COS in your computer. Use the routines to evaluate $\cos x$ for x near $\pi/2$. Compute x as accurately as possible. Since $\cos x \approx \pi/2 - x$ for x near $\pi/2$, you can hand-compute $\pi/2 - x$ and use it as a check. Note that

$$\pi/2 = 1.5707963267948966192313 2169 \ldots$$

*19. Evaluate the hyperbolic cosine function $\cosh x$, using

$$\cosh x = (e^x + e^{-x}) / 2$$

with the standard single-precision routine for EXP(X). Compare to the intrinsic function value COSH(X) for various values of x.

20. The Taylor series for the sine function is given by

$$\sin x = x - \frac{x^3}{3!} + \frac{x^5}{5!} - \frac{x^7}{7!} + \cdots + (-1)^{n+1} \frac{x^{2n-1}}{(2n - 1)!}$$

It can be shown that the error due to dropping the trailing terms

*The solution to this exercise appears in Appendix D.

from the series is less, in absolute value, than the absolute value of the first neglected term. For example,

$$\left| \sin 1 - \left(1 - \frac{1}{6} \right) \right| < \frac{1}{120}$$

Try to use the series to compute sin 100 correct to 10 digits. Why does it fail?

21. The rational function

$$\frac{120 + 60x + 12x^2 + x^3}{120 - 60x + 12x^2 - x^3}$$

can be used to approximate e^x for x positive and near 0. Compare this value to **EXP (X)** in single and double precision for various values of x.

*22. How would you evaluate sinh $x = (e^x - e^{-x}) / 2$ at $x = .001$, assuming that the intrinsic functions **SINH** and **EXP** are not available?

$$\left[Hint\text{: the Taylor series for } e^x = 1 + x + \frac{x^2}{2!} + \frac{x^3}{3!} + \cdots + \frac{x^n}{n!} \right]$$

23. The following *continued fraction* can be used to approximate e^{-x} for x near 0.

$$1 + \cfrac{1}{1 - \cfrac{x}{2 + \cfrac{x}{3 - \cfrac{x}{2 + \cfrac{x}{5 - \cfrac{x}{2 + \cfrac{x}{7 - \frac{x}{2}}}}}}}}$$

Compare this value to EXP(−X) for various values of X in single and double precision.

24. What difficulties might you encounter when trying to translate the code for a square root routine from one computer to another?

*25. What advantage is there to computing the next step in a numerical algorithm using X = X + H, where H is a power of 2?

26. Try computing e^{-x} for large x without the EXP function to get as much accuracy as possible using single-precision arithmetic. Use some of the suggestions following the example of e^{-20} in the text: compute the $(n + 1)$st term from the nth term; add the positive and negative terms separately; add the terms in order of smallest to largest (for this you will first need to determine the number of terms required of a given accuracy); note that $e^{-x} = 1 / e^x$. Compare your answers to the double-precision result from the EXP function.

27. Write a program to compute $\sqrt[3]{x}$ for some $x > 0$, using the following three versions of Newton's method:

a. $x_{k+1} = x_k - \dfrac{x_k^3 - x}{3x_k}, \ k = 0, 1, 2, \ldots, n$

b. $x_{k+1} = x_k - \dfrac{x_k^2 - x/x_k}{2x_k + x \cdot x_k^2}, \ k = 0, 1, 2, \ldots, n$

c. $x_{k+1} = \dfrac{1}{2} \cdot x_k + \dfrac{\frac{3}{2}x}{2x_k^2 + x/x_k}, \ k = 0, 1, 2, \ldots, n$

Start each sequence with $x_0 = 1$. Iterate until

$$\frac{|x_{k+1} - x_k|}{|x_{k+1}|} < \frac{1}{2}\varepsilon,$$

where $\varepsilon = 10^{-6}$, say. Count the number of iterations in each case, and compare the results to X ** (1./ 3.). Which method requires the fewest iterations?

28. Compute the value of

$$83521y^8 + 578x^2y^4 - 2x^4 + 2x^6 - x^8$$

for $x = 9478657$ and $y = 2298912$. Use single and double precision. The correct answer is -179689877047297.0. This is another example of a catastrophic error due to the limitations of floating-point arithmetic.

*29. Compute the sum:

$$10^{50} + 812 - 10^{50} + 10^{35} + 511 - 10^{35} = 1323.$$

Explain your result.*

*30. Define $r_n(x) = n!\left[e^x - \left(1 + x + \frac{x^2}{2!} + \cdots + \frac{x^n}{n!} \right) \right]$, $n = 0, 1, 2, \ldots$.

Then $r_n(x)/n!$ represents the error in the n-term Taylor series approximation to e^x. It is known that

$$r_{n+1}(x) = (n + 1) \cdot r_n(x) - x^{n+1}, n = 0, 1, 2, \ldots.$$

Compute the latter sequence for $x = 1$ and $r_0(1) = e - 1 = 1.71828183 \ldots$, for n ranging from 0 to 10 and 0 to 20. Compare the values of $r_n(1) / n!$, using both formulas, and note how different they are. The latter formula is another example of an unstable algorithm.

31. Revise Example 5.1 to change EPS if the input value of EPS is too small. Set EPS = MAX (EPS, 2 × U) where U is the unit roundoff of your computer. Print a message to the user if you change EPS.

Section 6.5

32. Study the error messages that your FORTRAN compiler and other system programs generate under controlled circumstances. Compute A(I) for I = 1 to 50 where A is dimensioned at size 10. Compute 10 ** N for N = 1 TO 100. Divide by 0 using both integers and reals. Devise other intentional errors. Could you tell where the execution error took place?

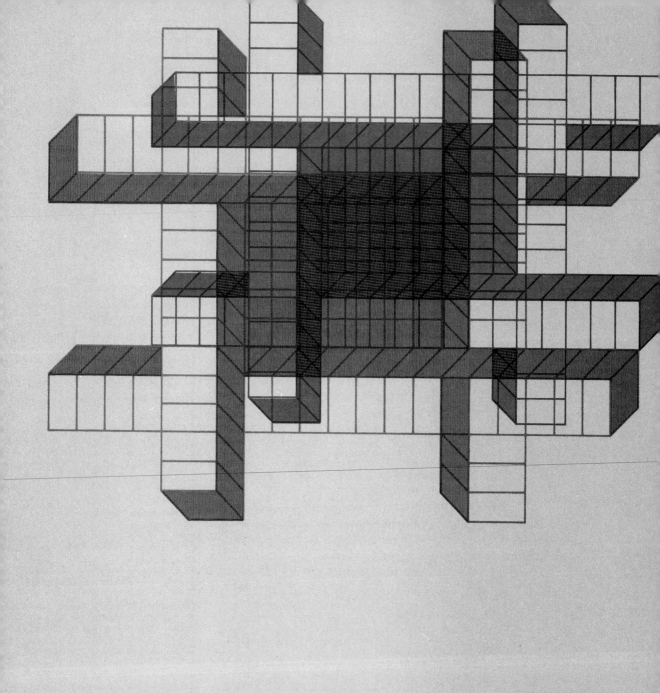

7 *Subprograms*

We introduced subprograms in Chapter 4 as constructs for supporting structured programming and modularity. In this chapter we review the concepts and continue the study of FORTRAN subprograms in detail.

A subprogram, as the name implies, is a unit, or module, that forms part of a program. It is defined independently of the rest of the program, although it cannot function outside the context of the program as a whole. It is employed by the program and possibly other subprograms to carry out specific tasks.

You were introduced to one form of subprogram, the intrinsic function (e.g., SQRT and SIN), in Chapter 2. A whole library of these functions is available to your FORTRAN program.

Intrinsic functions are so convenient that you may wish there were more of them. Actually, most computer installations do include one or more additional libraries of subprograms to perform common computational tasks. Examples include functions for generating pseudorandom numbers and routines for solving systems of linear equations. However, if the one you need is not available, FORTRAN provides powerful facilities that will allow you to write your own subprogram to accomplish the task.

The subprograms of FORTRAN are sometimes classified as *external* subprograms because, unlike the procedures of Pascal or the GOSUB-RETURN sequences in BASIC, they may be written and compiled independently of the rest of the program, and if desired, they may be saved in a library and used just as if they were intrinsic functions. Some versions of BASIC and Pascal do have provisions for user-written external subprograms.

There are a number of advantages to using subprograms.

1. As we pointed out in regard to intrinsic functions, using a subprogram from a program library saves you time and effort; it relieves you of the task of selecting a stable and efficient algorithm, designing and coding the routine, and testing it for correctness.

2. You may be able to modify an existing subprogram to solve your problem much more efficiently than trying to write the whole routine from scratch.

3. Often a program will require the same or very similar code at several points. Providing references to a single subprogram at these points will save you the time of entering and debugging all

of the extra copies of the code; it will also save the memory space required for the object code.

4. Sometimes procedures should be designed with the idea that they might have to be changed in the future. For example, you might want to replace an algorithm for solving systems of equations with a better, recently published algorithm. The details of the algorithm can be hidden in a subprogram; a program that uses it need not know *how* a subprogram solves a problem, but only *what* it does. This approach to programming is part of what is called *information hiding* and *data abstraction*.

5. Most importantly, the use of subprograms promotes modularity.

You can usually design a program as a collection of independent logical units that can be represented as subprograms. These smaller units are easier to comprehend and test for correctness. A subprogram can first be debugged independently and then combined to form the complete program, which will also require a thorough test to make sure that the pieces fit together properly. This approach is desirable for programs of any size and is mandatory for large ones. The subprograms, or modules, are often referred to as *program units* in FORTRAN, and we will use this convention from now on.

In this chapter we will examine the FUNCTION and the SUBROU-TINE in detail. Then we will discuss some examples of subprograms provided by some popular FORTRAN libraries, such as IMSL and LINPACK. Finally, we will point out some possible pitfalls to avoid when writing and using your own subprograms.

7.1 FUNCTION SUBPROGRAMS

Some examples of user-defined functions were presented in Section 4.2. Before we give a formal definition, let us consider some additional examples.

Our first example is the frequently used *factorial function*:

$$f(n) = n! = \begin{cases} 1 \cdot 2 \cdot 3 \cdots \cdots n & \text{for } n \geq 1 \\ 1 & \text{for } n = 0 \\ \text{undefined} & \text{for } n < 0 \end{cases}$$

for which the following function subprogram is defined:

```
INTEGER FUNCTION FAC(N)
INTEGER N, MAXN, I
PARAMETER (MAXN = 13)
```

```
*
*      MAXN IS THE LARGEST VALUE OF N SUCH THAT N! DOES NOT
*      CAUSE INTEGER OVERFLOW ON A 32 BIT MACHINE
*
       IF (N .GT. MAXN .OR. N .LT. 0) THEN
          FAC = -1
          RETURN
       ENDIF
       FAC = 1
       DO 10 I = 1, N
          FAC = FAC * I
10     CONTINUE
       END
```

This function returns a value of −1 for **FAC** if N is too large or negative. Note that the function name *alone*—FAC, not FAC (N)—is used just like an ordinary variable in the body of the function definition. The *RETURN* statement returns control to the calling program at the point immediately following the function call. The action of a RETURN is the same as END in a subprogram. Observe that this function also employs a *local variable* I, which is not one of the dummy arguments. The *value* of FAC is the *last* value assigned to it before control returns to the calling program via a RETURN or END.

The following function returns the sum of the first N elements of an array.

```
       REAL FUNCTION SUM(SAMPLE, N)
       INTEGER N, I
       REAL SAMPLE(N)
       SUM = 0
       DO 100, I = 1,N
          SUM = SUM + SAMPLE(I)
100    CONTINUE
       END
```

This function has two dummy arguments: the array SAMPLE and the dimension variable N. Note that N defines the dimension of the array, which is legal and proper in a function (or subprogram) definition. The statement

```
       GSUM = SUM(GRADES, 50)
```

would place the sum of the 50 values in the array GRADES into GSUM.

One feature that all of these examples have in common is that they all compute a *single value*, which is represented by the function name. A second feature is that *all of the actual arguments are defined* when the function is called.

In general, a function subprogram definition has the following structure:

```
FUNCTION statement
⎡function body --
⎢contains at least one statement
⎣that assigns a value to the function name⎦
END
```

The END statement is required as the last statement in the function definition.

FUNCTION Statement

The *FUNCTION statement*, which must be the first statement in a function definition, is defined as follows:

Examples:

```
REAL FUNCTION RAD(ALPH, THETA, RHO)
INTEGER FUNCTION COUNT(INC, FLG)
DOUBLE PRECISION FUNCTION FORM(XNEW, XOLD, EPS)
LOGICAL FUNCTION ACCPT(P, Q)
REAL FUNCTION TIME( )
FUNCTION MAXOUT(A, N)
```

FUNCTION statement

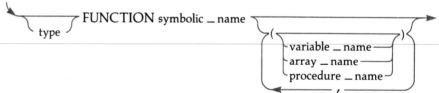

Remarks:

1. Nonexecutable.
2. The type is any one of the legal type specifications, such as REAL or LOGICAL. Although it is optional, as in the last example, we strongly recommend that you specify the type of every function. If no type is specified, it is determined by the I through N rule for variables. That is, implicit typing occurs on the basis of the first letter of the function name.
3. The function name has the same form as an ordinary variable and is used just that way in the function definition.
4. The variables, array names, and procedure names enclosed in parentheses are called *dummy arguments* (which correspond to formal parameters for procedures in Pascal). A *procedure* name is the name of a function subroutine, intrinsic function, or *statement function* (see Chapter 11).
5. The dummy arguments should be assigned a type in the function body.

6. A dummy argument may not be defined as a PARAMETER in the function definition.
7. It is legal for a function to have *no* arguments, as in Example 5, which might, for example, return the time of day.
8. A dummy argument may not be initialized by a DATA statement.

The *RETURN statement* has the simple form

RETURN
Statement

```
RETURN
```

It functions like an END statement in a subprogram, returning control to the point immediately following the most recent call to the sub-program. Multiple RETURNs are allowed in a subprogram.

A complete FORTRAN program generally consists of a sequence of program units, which is a sequence of statements terminated by an END statement. The first program unit is almost always the *main program*, which is given initial control when the program is executed and calls the various subprograms it needs. The rest of the program units are function subprograms (and subroutines) that are not part of the FORTRAN libraries; they are placed following the main program, as shown below:

Program Units

```
PROGRAM ABC
    :
    :
END
INTEGER FUNCTION X(N)
    :
    :
END
REAL FUNCTION Y(T, V)
    :
    :
END
SUBROUTINE PL(A, B)
    :
    :
END
```

References to intrinsic functions are handled automatically by the compiler. Note that since a main program is not called, it may not contain a RETURN statement. Likewise, a PROGRAM statement may not appear in a subprogram.

Each program unit is compiled independently of the others. The compiler needs no information about other units in order to compile a given program unit. The program units may be grouped together as previously shown in a single file and then compiled with a single compiler command. Alternatively, each unit may be placed in a separate file for maximum flexibility and compiled with a separate command. Calls to other subprograms—those that follow the main program, and nonintrinsic library subprograms—that require jumps to the code of the subprogram definition and other information are filled in later during the linking and loading steps. Because the program units are treated independently, *variables, parameters, and statement numbers in different program units are not related.* Thus, in the following example the variable X in the definition of function F is not the same as X in the main program. They represent different memory locations altogether. Both variables are said to be *local* to their program unit. Similarly, the duplicate statement numbers (100) are allowed because they are in different program units. At the same time, the function name is a *global* value, and therefore should not be used to identify any other entity in the program.

```
          PROGRAM MAIN
          .
          .
          X = 1.0
100       CONTINUE
          .
          .
          END
          REAL FUNCTION F(A, B)
          .
          .
100       CONTINUE
          .
          .
          X = 2.0
          .
          .
          END
```

What process actually takes place when a function is called? Generally you can think of the value of each actual argument in the call replacing the value of the corresponding dummy argument in the definition. The call generates a jump to the function, which is executed given the above replacement. When a RETURN or END is encountered, control returns to the point immediately following the call. The value of the function is the value most recently assigned to the function name in the definition. This process is illustrated in Figure 7.1.

Just as for intrinsic functions, the actual arguments may be any valid expressions. They may also be procedure names (see below). Figure 7.2 shows the relationship between the actual and the dummy arguments.

In this call A assumes the value of X, B assumes the value of A + 3.0 * ABS(T) (again, A in this expression is not the same as the first dummy argument, A), N is set to 21, and L is assigned the value of .TRUE.. In general the values of the actual arguments are assigned in the same order as the dummy arguments.

How do the dummy arguments actually assume the values represented by the actual arguments? In general, there are two ways. In the

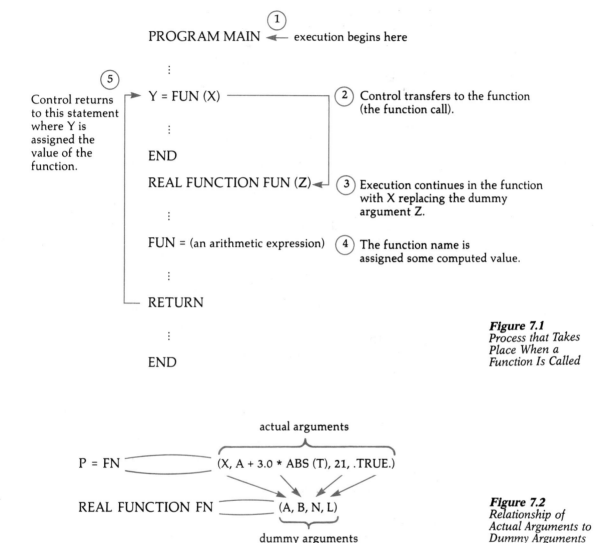

Figure 7.1
*Process that Takes
Place When a
Function Is Called*

Figure 7.2
*Relationship of
Actual Arguments to
Dummy Arguments*

scheme referred to as *call by reference*, the *address* of the actual argument is provided to the subprogram. Any subsequent reference to the corresponding dummy argument in the subprogram is to the location of the actual argument. In the method of *call by value*, the *value* of the actual argument, not its address, is provided to the subprogram.

Standard FORTRAN uses call by reference exclusively for functions and subroutines, although some versions of FORTRAN include options for call by value as well. Call by reference can be more efficient, but it is also prone to side effects (see Section 7.7).

1. When the corresponding arguments are scalar variables, the call-by-reference method is straightforward. The address of the actual argument is referenced directly in the subprogram. Thus, any change to the dummy variable results in a direct change in the corresponding actual argument.

2. When the arguments are arrays, the address of the *first* element in the actual array is passed to the subprogram, and references to the other array elements are *relative* to the first one (see Section 7.6).

3. When the actual argument is an expression, there is no address to pass. In this case the expression is evaluated and stored in a temporary location whose address is then passed to the subprogram. (Some would argue that this is an instance of call by value, but in the author's view it is still a call by reference, since an address is transferred.)

4. Finally, if the actual argument is a constant, some FORTRAN compilers will pass its address to the subprogram; others will make a temporary copy of the constant and pass the address of the copy to the subprogram. Arguments that are expressions or constants should obviously be used as *input* to the subroutine only. That is, the dummy argument should not be altered during execution of the subprogram (see Section 7.7). The five rules regarding the call are given in Box 7.1.

You must verify that the rules for function calls (Box 7.1) are satisfied since most computer systems will not provide checks for their violations, especially for the first two. The results are often unpredictable, and the error may be hard to spot. For example, if you provide a real actual argument to an integer dummy argument, it is likely that the program will accept the bit pattern that represents the real number as an integer, resulting in a very large number. The program may halt unexpectedly, during the computation of the function value, with an unrelated error message.

The fifth rule is not required by the Standard, but you should treat it as a rule; the inconsistant typing of program elements is an easy error to make and can be difficult to detect.

You should also understand that any change in the value of a dummy argument will result in the same change in the corresponding actual argument upon return from the subprogram. For you Pascal programmers, this means that all dummy arguments in a function subprogram are like *variable* parameters. For example, the program

BOX 7.1 Rules for Function Calls

1. The number of actual arguments in the function call must equal the number of dummy arguments in the FUNCTION statement.
2. Each actual argument in the function call must be of the same type as the corresponding dummy argument in the FUNCTION statement.
3. A function may call another subprogram, but it may not call *itself*. That is, a statement such as

$$Q = FN(A, B, K, L)$$

is not allowed in the function definition of FN. A function that calls itself is a *recursive* function. They are allowed in Pascal and in some versions of **BASIC**, but not in FORTRAN.
4. If a subprogram reference causes a dummy argument to become associated with another dummy argument in the same subprogram, neither dummy argument may become defined during execution of the subprogram. Otherwise, redefining one argument would mean an implicit change to the other, and then also to its corresponding actual argument. For example, if the function headed by

$$REAL \ FUNCTION \ ALPHA(A, B)$$

is called by

$$Y = ALPHA(X, X)$$

then the dummy arguments A and B become associated with the same actual argument X and therefore with each other. Neither A nor B may be defined during the execution of this function. That is, they could represent input values for the function, but they could not be assigned value in the function body by an assignment statement, for example.
5. You should always specify the type of the function in the program unit where the call is made to match the type in the function definition. For example, the following specification is appropriate:

```
REAL INCAMT
.
.
Y = INCAMT(P, R-1.0)
.
.
END
REAL FUNCTION INCAMT(X, Y)
.
.
END
```

```
INTEGER N, P, F
N = 1
P = F(N)
PRINT *, P, N
END
INTEGER FUNCTION F(M)
INTEGER M
F = M
M = M + 1
END
```

will print

1   2

that is, P = 1 and N = 2. One should avoid changing the values of the
dummy arguments in a function definition. We will discuss this characteristic in more detail later.

The following example illustrates the interaction between the function and the calling program. Suppose we need a program to compute
and print the value of a polynomial at various points in an interval. We
would like to allow the user to specify the polynomial and the spacing
between the points. We will evaluate the polynomial in a function
subprogram using *Horner's method* (recall Exercise 3.8). Horner's method evaluates the polynomial

$$p(x) = a_0 + a_1 \cdot x + a_2 \cdot x^2 + \cdots + a_n \cdot x^n$$

as

$$p(x) = a_0 + x\{a_1 + x \times [a_2 + \cdots + x \times [a_{n-1} + x \times (a_n)] \cdots]\},$$

which requires half as many multiplications as the former equation.

EXAMPLE 7.1

```
PROGRAM POLYN
****************************************************************
* THIS PROGRAM PRINTS THE VALUE OF A POLYNOMIAL AT EQUALLY-SPACED
* POINTS IN AN INTERVAL (L, R). THE VALUES OF L AND R, THE
* NUMBER OF POINTS IN (L, R) (INCLUDING L AND R), THE DEGREE OF
* THE POLYNOMIAL, AND THE COEFFICIENTS OF THE POLYNOMIAL A(0),
* A(1), ..., A(N) MUST BE PROVIDED IN THAT ORDER AS DATA ON THE
* STANDARD INPUT UNIT.
* PARAMETERS, AND VARIABLES:
* L, R -- THE LEFT AND RIGHT INTERVAL BOUNDARIES (INPUT)
* NP -- THE NUMBER OF POINTS WHERE THE POLYNOMIAL IS TO BE
```

```
*         EVALUATED (NP >= 2) (INPUT)
* N -- THE DEGREE OF THE POLYNOMIAL (INPUT)
* MAXDEG -- THE MAXIMUM VALUE OF N ALLOWED.
* A -- THE ARRAY CONTAINING THE COEFFICIENTS OF THE POLYNOMIAL
*      (INPUT)
* H -- THE SPACING BETWEEN SUCCESSIVE POINTS
* X -- THE CURRENT ABSCISSCA VALUE
* HMIN -- MINIMUM VALUE OF H ALLOWED
* POLY -- THE VALUE OF THE POLYNOMIAL AT THE MOST RECENT VALUE
*         OF X
* I -- LOOP INDEX
* TEMP -- TEMPORARY VARIABLE FOR EXCHANGE OF ENDPOINTS IF OUT OF
*         ORDER
* FUNCTIONS AND SUBROUTINES:
* HORNER -- FUNCTION THAT RETURNS THE VALUE OF THE POLYNOMIAL AT
* X.
*********************************************************************
      INTEGER NP, N, I, MAXDEG
      REAL L, R, X, H, POLY, HMIN, TEMP, HORNER
      PARAMETER (MAXDEG = 20, HMIN = 1.E-5)
      REAL A(0: MAXDEG)
*
* READ AND CHECK THE INPUT PARAMETERS
*
      READ *, L, R, NP, N
      IF (R .LT. L) THEN
         TEMP = L
         L = R
         R = TEMP
         PRINT *, 'ERROR -- RT. ENDPT. < LEFT ENDPT.; EXCHANGED'
         PRINT *, 'AND CONTINUING'
      ENDIF
      IF (NP .LT. 2) THEN
         NP = 2
         PRINT *, 'ERROR -- REQUESTED NO. OF PTS. TOO SMALL;'
         PRINT *, 'SET TO 2 AND CONTINUING'
      ENDIF
      IF (N .GT. MAXDEG) THEN
         PRINT *, 'FATAL ERROR -- REQUESTED DEGREE EXCEEDS MAX:'
         PRINT *, MAXDEG
         STOP
      ENDIF
*
*   COMPUTE SPACING AND CHECK SIZE
*
      H = (R - L) / REAL(NP - 1)
      IF (H .LT. HMIN) THEN
         PRINT *, 'FATAL ERROR -- NO. OF PTS. TOO LARGE'
         STOP
      ENDIF
      PRINT *
```

```
*
* READ THE COEFFICIENTS
*
      DO 10 I = 0, N
          READ (*, *, END = 15) A(I)
10    CONTINUE
*
* REDEFINE N IN CASE OF INSUFFICIENT NO. OF COEFFICIENTS
*
15    N = I - 1
*
* ECHO PRINT THE DATA
*
      PRINT *, 'L = ', L, ' R = ', R, ' NO. PTS. = ', NP
      PRINT *, 'DEGREE = ', N
      PRINT *
      PRINT *, 'COEFFICIENTS:'
      PRINT *, (A(I), I = 0, N)
*
* COMPUTE AND PRINT THE POLYNOMIAL VALUES
*
      PRINT *
      PRINT *, '     ABSCISSA', '      POLYNOMIAL VALUE'
      DO 20 I = 0, NP - 1
         X = L + H * REAL(I)
         POLY = HORNER(A, N, X)
         PRINT *, X, POLY
20    CONTINUE
      END

      REAL FUNCTION HORNER(COEF, N, Z)
******************************************************************
* HORNER COMPUTES THE VALUE OF THE POLYNOMIAL OF DEGREE N WITH
* COEFFICIENTS IN THE ARRAY COEF AT THE POINT Z.
* VARIABLES:
* COEF -- THE ARRAY OF COEFFICIENTS (DUMMY ARG.)
* N -- THE DEGREE OF THE POLYNOMIAL (DUMMY ARG.)
* Z -- THE VALUE WHERE THE POLYNOMIAL IS EVALUATED
* K -- LOOP INDEX
******************************************************************
      INTEGER K, N
      REAL COEF(N), Z
      HORNER = COEF(N)
      DO 10 K = N - 1, 0, - 1
         HORNER = COEF(K) + Z * HORNER
10    CONTINUE
      END
```

The actual arguments A, N, and X are passed to the dummy arguments COEF, N, and Z, respectively. The arguments agree in number, order, and type.

Note that a prologue is provided for both the subprogram and the main program. The function HORNER could easily be compiled separately and stored in a FORTRAN library for use by POLYN or any other FORTRAN program unit, including other subprograms.

Finally, you should recall that the END = option may not work with an implied DO loop, as it is used above, on some compilers; I may be undefined. In this case the READ statement must be imbedded in a DO loop.

7.2 SUBROUTINES

To review, a subroutine is a program unit that begins with a SUBROUTINE statement. Here is an example, which initializes each of the elements of the array PTR to its index.

```
      SUBROUTINE PTINIT(PTR, LOW, HI)
      INTEGER I, LOW, HI, PTR(LOW : HI)
      DO 10 I = LOW, HI
         PTR(I) = I
10    CONTINUE
      END
```

Subroutines are called by means of a CALL statement, e.g.,

```
      CALL PTINIT(INDX, 0, NMAX)
```

Subroutine names are governed by the same rules as variables (e.g., maximum of 6 characters) except that *no value or type is associated with the name*; the name is used for reference only. Therefore it is meaningless, and illegal, to assign a value to the name in a subroutine definition. All values are passed back to the calling program through the argument list (or through COMMON—see Section 7.4). In the example call above, the elements of the array INDX are initialized by the call to the subroutine PTINIT through its association with the dummy array argument PTR. Like functions, subroutine definitions may contain one or more RETURN statements.

SUBROUTINE Statement

The *SUBROUTINE statement* has the following formal definition.

Examples:
```
SUBROUTINE MIX(K, N, PNG)
SUBROUTINE INTEGR(A, N, EPS, FLG)
```

```
SUBROUTINE EIGEN5(MAT, MAXROW, MAXCOL, M, N, X, B)
SUBROUTINE RAND( )
```

SUBROUTINE statement

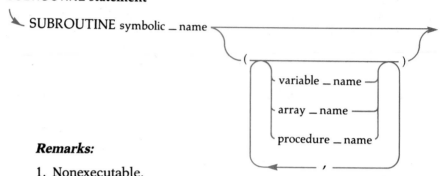

Remarks:

1. Nonexecutable.
2. No type is associated with the subroutine since it is not a variable.
3. The arguments in the list are called *dummy arguments* and are processed the same as dummy arguments in function subprograms. They should be assigned a type in the subroutine definition.
4. A dummy argument may not be defined as a PARAMETER in the subroutine definition.
5. There is a fourth argument type, the *asterisk* (*), which allows for a return to a statement other than the one immediately following the CALL (called an *alternate return*). Since this is a violation of structured programming methodology we do not describe it here.

CALL Statement

The *CALL statement* is defined as follows:

Examples:
```
CALL CVX (N, LIMIT, 1.E-5)
CALL TRACE ((X + Y) / 2.0, 50, N - 1)
CALL AREA (BND, M, X(N), .FALSE.)
CALL TIME
```

CALL statement

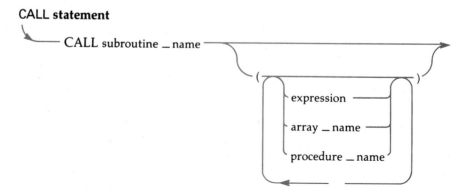

Remarks:

1. Executable.
2. The arguments in the CALL statement are referred to as *actual arguments*. Just as in function calls, they may be any valid expressions.
3. The rules regarding a call to a subroutine and passing values of actual arguments (or, equivalently, their addresses) to the corresponding dummy arguments and back are precisely the same as for functions (Figure 7.1).

The call to a subroutine is similar to that for a function call. The values of the actual arguments are passed to their corresponding dummy arguments. When a RETURN or END is encountered, control returns to the statement immediately following the CALL. The main difference is that no value is assigned to the subroutine name. Therefore the usual result of a subroutine call is that one or more of the actual arguments is defined, or redefined.

Figure 7.3 illustrates the relationship between the actual arguments in the subroutine call and the dummy arguments in the subroutine definition.

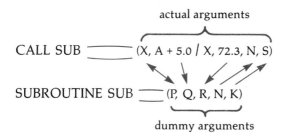

Figure 7.3
Subroutine argument relationships.

Data passes to and from the subroutine through the argument list. Therefore, as the arrows indicate, some arguments, like A + 5.0 / X and 72.3, are strictly input values to the subroutine; others, like N and S, are output values (i.e., are defined) from the subroutine; and others, such as X, serve both roles, since their values may be changed in the subroutine.

FORTRAN novices are often confused about when to use a function and when to use a subroutine, since one could easily be written to replace the other. A FORTRAN function may only compute a *scalar* quantity: a real number, an integer, a logical value, and so forth. It cannot return an array of values. Therefore, a general rule of thumb is the following: *When a subprogram is written to compute a single value, such as a sum or a function value, use a function subprogram with the function name assigned to the value; otherwise use a subroutine.*

To illustrate the use of functions and subroutines as tools for modular design, let us rewrite Example 5.2, which computes the median of an array of numbers, and compute the mean as well this time. An initial pseudocode solution, for which the pseudocode preceding Example 5.2 could be a refinement, is the following:

1. Read the numbers into the array X.
2. Sort X into ascending order.
3. Compute the median.
4. Compute the mean.
5. Print the results.

You could design and write each of these steps as a subprogram. Since this would allow you to focus your attention on each module as a smaller, independent problem, it is likely that the resulting program would have fewer errors. The program is next. Prologues have been omitted to save space. Note that the number of values, N, is assigned in READX.

EXAMPLE 7.2

```
        PROGRAM MSTATS
        INTEGER NMAX, N
        PARAMETER (NMAX = 500)
        REAL X(NMAX), MEDIAN, MEAN, MEDF, MEANF
        CALL READX (X, N, NMAX)
        CALL SORT (X, N)
        MEDIAN = MEDF(X, N)
        MEAN = MEANF(X, N)
        PRINT *, 'FOR TOTAL NO. OF VALUES: ', N
        PRINT *, 'THE MEDIAN = ', MEDIAN
        PRINT *, 'THE MEAN = ', MEAN
        END


        SUBROUTINE READX (LIST, N, MAX)
        INTEGER N, MAX, I
        REAL LIST(MAX)
        DO 10 I = 1, MAX
           READ (*,*, END = 20) LIST(I)
10      CONTINUE
20      N = I - 1
        END


        SUBROUTINE SORT (NUMBRS, N)
        INTEGER N, I, J, K
```

```
        REAL NUMBRS(N), TEMP
        DO 20, I = 1, N - 1
           K = I
           DO 10 J = I + 1, N
              IF (NUMBRS(K) .GT. NUMBRS(J)) K = J
10         CONTINUE
           TEMP = NUMBRS(K)
           NUMBRS(K) = NUMBRS(I)
           NUMBRS(I) = TEMP
20      CONTINUE
        END

        REAL FUNCTION MEDF (NUMBRS, N)
        INTEGER N, N2
        REAL NUMBRS(N)
        N2 = INT(N / 2)
        IF (MOD(N, 2) .EQ. 0) THEN
           MEDF = (NUMBRS(N2) + NUMBRS(N2 + 1)) / 2.0
        ELSE
           MEDF = NUMBRS(N2 + 1)
        ENDIF
        END

        REAL FUNCTION MEANF (X, N)
        INTEGER N, I
        REAL X(N), SUM
        SUM = 0.0
        DO 10 I = 1, N
           SUM = SUM + X(I)
10      CONTINUE
        IF (N .GT. 0) THEN
           MEANF = SUM / N
        ELSE
           MEANF = 0.0
        ENDIF
        END
```

Observe that dummy arguments with the same name, such as N and NUMBRS, have been used in several subprograms. They are completely independent of each other except for the values passed to them by the main program. Likewise, the actual argument X in the main program is related to the dummy argument X in MEANF only through the function call. SUM, I, J, and K are all local variables. Note that the function MEANF calls two other functions, INT and MOD.

The main program is nothing more than a series of calls followed by the printing of the answers. If the printing process were complicated, it too might be written as a subprogram. Another task commonly relegated to a subprogram is the extensive checking of input data.

What is the proper size of a subprogram or main program? Since each subprogram in turn could be further subdivided into smaller and smaller modules, where does one stop this process? At the extreme, each subprogram would consist of a single statement.

In general, the logic of the problem to be solved suggests proper subdivisions. A common rule of thumb is that a half-page to a page of code is probably a reasonable upper limit for a subprogram or program without subprograms.

7.3 THE EXTERNAL AND INTRINSIC STATEMENTS

FORTRAN allows an actual argument in a subprogram call to be a procedure name. This feature is particularly useful for subprograms that reference other subprograms. Consider the following example.

```
REAL FUNCTION WAC (FUN, X)
REAL FUN, X
WAC = FUN(X) + 1.
END
```

The argument FUN is the dummy name of another subprogram. A call to WAC might look like

```
Y = WAC(MYFUNC, T)
```

where MYFUNC is the name of another actual subprogram. This feature enhances the generality of a program by allowing WAC and similar subprograms to use any function passed to them by the calling unit. They do not have to be rewritten to use a different function.

EXTERNAL
Statement

However, the FORTRAN compiler needs a way to tell that MYFUNC is a subprogram name rather than a variable; otherwise MYFUNC, which is external to the calling program, would not be passed to WAC correctly. This information is supplied by an *EXTERNAL statement in the calling program*:

```
EXTERNAL MYFUNC
```

The *EXTERNAL statement* is defined as follows:

Examples:
```
EXTERNAL DSTATS
EXTERNAL VMC, DIFFEQ, ERRMES
```

EXTERNAL statement

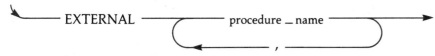

Remarks:

1. Nonexecutable.
2. The EXTERNAL statement must be placed with the other descriptive statements (e.g., after the type statements but before any executable statement) in the program unit that contains the subprogram name as an actual argument.
3. The corresponding actual and dummy procedure names should agree as to form (i.e., either both represent functions or both represent subroutines). If both are functions, they should also agree as to type.
4. If the actual argument is to be an intrinsic function such as SIN, the name should appear in an INTRINSIC statement rather than in an EXTERNAL statement.

INTRINSIC Statement

Intrinsic functions are handled differently by the compiler than user-written or external library subprograms. Therefore, an intrinsic function that is to be passed as an argument to subprograms must be listed in an *INTRINSIC statement*.

Examples:

```
INTRINSIC SQR
INTRINSIC SIN, COS, TAN
```

INTRINSIC statement

Remarks:

1. Nonexecutable.
2. Placement is the same as the EXTERNAL statement.
3. The names of intrinsic functions for type conversion (e.g., INT or REAL), for choosing the largest or smallest value (e.g., MIN or MAX), and for lexical relationship (e.g., LGE or LLE—see Chapter 8) must not be used as actual arguments.

To illustrate the utility of the EXTERNAL statement, let us rewrite Example 3.2 to make use of an external function definition. This example computes an approximation to a root of a function by the method of bisection. Our improved version allows the function to be replaced by another with minimal changes to the program. Read it carefully.

EXAMPLE 7.3

```
        PROGRAM ROOTF
****************************************************************
* AUTHOR:  A.B.ARTHUR  7/86
* THIS PROGRAM COMPUTES A ROOT OF A FUNCTION IN AN INTERVAL.
* INPUT DATA ARE THE LEFT AND RIGHT INTERVAL ENDPOINTS AND AN
* UPPER BOUND ON THE ACCEPTED TOLERANCE. THE EXTERNAL AND TYPE
* STATEMENTS AND SUBROUTINE CALL MUST BE CHANGED TO INCLUDE THE
* NAME OF THE USER-SUPPLIED FUNCTION, OR THE USER-SUPPLIED
* FUNCTION MUST BE GIVEN THE NAME FUN.
* VARIABLES AND PARAMETERS:
* A, B -- LEFT AND RIGHT INTERVAL ENDPOINTS, RESPECTIVELY (INPUT)
* TOL -- ERROR TOLERANCE (INPUT)
*
* FUNCTIONS AND SUBROUTINES:
* FUN -- FUNCTION WHOSE ROOT IS DESIRED
*     CALL: Y = FUN(X)
*     ARGUMENT:  X - THE INDEPENDENT VARIABLE
* BISECT -- SUBROUTINE THAT COMPUTES A ROOT OF FUN IN (A, B) WITH
*           THE BISECTION METHOD.
*     CALL: CALL BISECT (FUN, A, B, TOL, ROOT, FROOT, ERRBND, FLG)
*     ARGUMENTS: (RETURNED) ROOT -- APPROXIMATE ROOT OF FUN
*                 FROOT -- FUNCTION VALUE AT ROOT: FUN (ROOT)
*                 ERRBND -- COMPUTED ERROR BOUND ( <= TOL )
*                 FLG -- STATUS FLAG
*                         = 0 -- ROOT IS VALID; NORMAL COMPLETION
*                                OF BISECTION SCHEME.
*                         = 1 -- FUN (ROOT) IS CLOSE ENOUGH TO
*                                ZERO FOR ROOT TO BE CONSIDERED
*                                EXACT.
*                         = 2 -- FUN IS OF SAME SIGN AT INTERVAL
*                                ENDPOINTS
*                         = 3 -- MAXIMUM NUMBER OF ITERATIONS
*                                EXCEEDED.
****************************************************************
        INTEGER FLG
        REAL A, B, TOL, ROOT, FROOT, ERRBND
*
* CHANGE THE NEXT TWO STATEMENTS, IF NECESSARY, TO MATCH THE NAME
* OF THE FUNCTION.
*
        REAL FUN
        EXTERNAL FUN
        READ *, A, B, TOL
```

```
*
* CHANGE THE NAME FUN, IF NECESSARY, TO MATCH THE NAME OF THE
* FUNCTION.
*
      CALL BISECT (FUN, A, B, TOL, ROOT, FROOT, ERRBND, FLG)
      IF (FLG .EQ. 2) THEN
         PRINT *,'ERROR -- FUNCTION IS OF SAME SIGN AT ENDPOINTS'
         STOP
      ENDIF
      IF (FLG .EQ. 0) THEN
         PRINT *, 'NORMAL COMPLETION OF BISECTION SCHEME'
      ELSE IF (FLG .EQ. 1) THEN
         PRINT *, 'BISECTION TERMINATED -- ROOT ASSUMED EXACT'
      ELSE
         PRINT *, 'ERROR -- MAXIMUM ITERATIONS EXCEEDED'
      ENDIF
      PRINT *, 'ROOT IS: ', ROOT, ' FUNC. VALUE IS: ', FROOT
      PRINT *, 'ERROR BOUND IS: ', ERRBND
      END

      SUBROUTINE BISECT (F, A, B, EPS, ROOT, FROOT, ERRBND, STAT)
***************************************************************
* AUTHOR:  J.A.L. LEWIS  6/85
* APPROXIMATES A ROOT OF A FUNCTION VIA THE BISECTION METHOD.
* LOCAL VARIABLES AND PARAMETERS:
* I -- LOOP INDEX.
* A1, B1 -- LOCAL VARIABLES CORRESPONDING TO A AND B, RESPECT-
*           IVELY,
* MAXIT -- MAXIMUM NUMBER OF ITERATIONS ALLOWED
* FTOL -- IF ABS (F(ROOT)) IS LESS THAN THIS VALUE, ROOT IS
*         ACCEPTED AS A ROOT.
*
* ARGUMENTS:
* F -- FUNCTION NAME (INPUT)
* A, B -- LEFT AND RIGHT ENDPOINTS (INPUT)
* EPS -- ERROR TOLERANCE (INPUT)
* ROOT -- APPROXIMATION TO THE ROOT (OUTPUT)
* FROOT -- F(ROOT)
* ERRBND -- COMPUTED ERROR BOUND
* STAT -- STATUS OF COMPUTATION
*         0 = VALID ROOT; NORMAL CONVERGENCE OF BISECTION
*         1 = F(ROOT) CONSIDERED TO BE EXACTLY ZERO; BISECTION
*             TERMINATED
*         2 = ERROR -- F OF SAME SIGN AT ENDPOINTS
*         3 = ERROR -- MAXIMUM NUMBER OF ITERATIONS EXCEEDED
***************************************************************
      INTEGER I, STAT, MAXIT
      REAL FTOL, F, A, B, EPS, ROOT, FROOT, ERRBND
      PARAMETER (MAXIT = 20, FTOL = 1.E-6)
*
```

```
*       PRESERVE INTERVAL ENDPOINTS
*
        A1 = A
        B1 = B
        STAT = 0
        ERRBND = ABS(B1 - A1)
*
* CHECK FOR OPPOSITE SIGNS
*
        IF (F(A1) * F(B1) .GT. 0.0) THEN
           STAT = 2
           RETURN
        ENDIF
*
* THE BISECTION ALGORITHM
*
        DO 10 I = 1, MAXIT
           ROOT = .5 * (A1 + B1)
           ERRBND = .5 * ERRBND
           FROOT = F(ROOT)
*
* ROOT CONSIDERED EXACT
*
           IF (ABS(FROOT) .LT. FTOL) THEN
              STAT = 1
              RETURN
*
* NOT EXACT -- SUBDIVIDE THE INTERVAL
*
           ELSE IF (F(A1) * FROOT .LT. 0.0) THEN
              B1 = ROOT
           ELSE
              A1 = ROOT
           ENDIF
           IF (ERRBND .LE. EPS) GOTO 20
10      CONTINUE
20      CONTINUE
*
* WAS MAXIT EXCEEDED?
*
        IF (ERRBND .GT. EPS) STAT = 3
        END

        REAL FUNCTION FUN (X)
        REAL X
        FUN = EXP(-2.0 * X) - SIN(X)
        END
```

Note that the subroutine BISECT preserves the interval endpoints by assigning their values to the local variables A1 and B1 and using them instead. The use of a status code is typical of general subroutines like BISECT. The code allows for some flexibility, in that users of the routine are able to deal with the various conditions in whatever way they choose. One important characteristic of a routine like BISECT is that it can be applied to *any* function (FUN here) with *no* change to the subroutine itself.

7.4 THE COMMON STATEMENT

Functions and subroutines have been characterized as independent program units that are compiled separately. Communication between various program units has been through the argument lists. The values of actual arguments are used by the subprograms; values computed by the subprograms are passed back to the calling program through the function name in the case of functions and as other arguments in the case of subroutines.

Actually, program units may also pass data to each other by means of the *COMMON statement*. The COMMON statement is used by the FORTRAN compiler to reserve a block of storage—called a *COMMON block*—for use by the variables and arrays that appear in the COMMON statement list. Each program unit with a matching COMMON statement has access to the data in the COMMON block.

COMMON Statement

The author prefers the use of argument lists over COMMON for reasons to be clarified later. We present it here in some detail since its frequent use in existing programs dictates that you understand its function well.

The *COMMON statement* is defined as follows:

COMMON statement

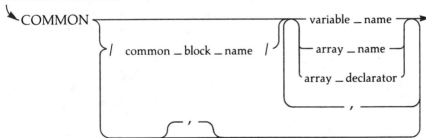

Examples:

```
COMMON A, B, N
COMMON T(100), C(50)
COMMON /COEFF/ A(50, 50), B(50)
COMMON /BASE/ PIC, VEC, NAME(500)
COMMON /BLK1/ N(100), M(100) /BLK2/ R, I, V, POT
COMMON // X(1000)
```

Remarks:

1. Nonexecutable.
2. The *common block name*, if used, can be any valid symbolic name (as in the third, fourth, and fifth examples).
3. If there is an array name in the COMMON list, the array must be dimensioned in a statement that (usually) precedes the COMMON statement, for example:

   ```
   REAL Y(100)
   COMMON Y
   ```

   which is equivalent to

   ```
   COMMON Y(100)
   ```

   However, the first combination is best because it explicitly types Y as a real array.
4. The same name cannot appear more than once in the same COMMON list, or in different COMMON lists in the same program unit. For example, both

   ```
   COMMON A, B, C, A
   ```

   and

   ```
   COMMON X, Y
   COMMON /AREA2/ A(100), X
   ```

   are illegal.
5. COMMON statements should be placed toward the beginning of the program unit before any executable statement and usually just after the type statements.
6. An element in a COMMON list may not appear as a *dummy* argument in the subprogram containing the COMMON statement.

You can see that there are two types of COMMON blocks: (1) *blank COMMON*, as specified by the first, second, and last examples (a null COMMON block name indicates a blank COMMON block), and (2) *named COMMON*, as specified by the third through the fifth examples. In the fifth example, arrays N and M are in COMMON block BLK1 and R, I, V, and POT are in block BLK2. The principal difference between the two is in the options available for initializing the COMMON variables: variables in named COMMON can be initialized by a DATA statement that appears in a BLOCK DATA subprogram (see below); variables in blank COMMON cannot be initialized by a DATA statement.

Blank COMMON and different named COMMON lists represent different areas in storage. Program units share access to the same COMMON blocks that are specified in them. Therefore if

```
COMMON /ALPHA/ X(3), M, N
```

appears in one program unit, and

```
COMMON /ALPHA/ A, B, C, P, Q
```

appears in another, then A = X(1), B = X(2), C = X(3), P = M, and Q = N, that is, since A and X(1) represent the *same place*, they are really different names for the *same* variable. Suppose in the first program unit we set

$$X(1) = 1.0$$
$$X(2) = 2.0$$
$$X(3) = 3.0$$
$$M = 5$$
$$N = -1$$

Box 7.2 illustrates the layout of storage for the COMMON block ALPHA.

BOX 7.2 The Layout of a COMMON Block

X(1) =	1.0	= A
X(2) =	2.0	= B
X(3) =	3.0	= C
M =	5	= P
N =	−1	= Q

Therefore, unlike the list in a type statement, the order in which the elements appear in the COMMON list is very important because the elements are actually stored in that order. If we want the variable A to correspond to the array element X(1) in another program unit, then we must know which common block X is in *and* where it appears in the list. Variables in COMMON are said to be *global* because, unlike local variables, they are accessible to more than one program unit.

A variable in COMMON may also appear as an actual argument in a subprogram call. However, if a call associates a dummy argument with an item in COMMON in the subprogram, or in a subprogram *called by* the subprogram, then neither the dummy argument nor the item in COMMON may be defined in the subprogram. For example, given

```
SUBROUTINE BETA(A)
COMMON X
```

that head a subroutine called by a program containing the statements

```
COMMON B
CALL BETA(B)
```

then A becomes associated with B, which is associated with X, which is in COMMON. Thus neither A nor X may be defined in BETA. Clearly this is not something you would normally do. Why pass the value as an argument if it is available in the COMMON block?

It is important that the types of corresponding variable names in a COMMON list be the *same* (e.g., that both M and P above are of type INTEGER). This is not required by the Standard, but we strongly recommend it, since violating it can produce unexpected results. In the past, this recommendation was sometimes violated for the sake of "tricky" programming, resulting in code that was hard to understand and maintain.

We also recommend that you keep the corresponding COMMON lists the *same length*, (i.e., the same number of words of memory). This is required of named COMMON but optional for blank COMMON.

One advantage of named COMMON is that you can specify a particular COMMON block in only those program units that you want to share the listed variables.

**BLOCK DATA
Statement**

Another advantage of named COMMON is that its variables can be initialized by a DATA statement. However, the DATA statement must appear in a *BLOCK DATA subprogram*.

A BLOCK DATA subprogram contains no executable statements; only declaration statements, such as REAL and COMMON, may be used. It has the form

```
BLOCK DATA NAME
[declaration statements]
END
```

It should be placed with the other subprograms when compiling your program. The *BLOCK DATA statement* is defined as follows:

Examples: BLOCK DATA BEGIN
BLOCK DATA

BLOCK DATA statement

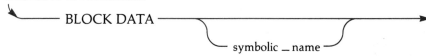

Remarks:

1. Nonexecutable.
2. The name, if used, is global, just like any other subroutine name.
3. The BLOCK DATA subprogram may define items in more than one named COMMON block.
4. The same named COMMON block may not be specified in more than one BLOCK DATA subprogram.

The following example initializes the array X and the variables P and Q. Note that we do not need to initialize all of the variables in the common lists.

```
BLOCK DATA INIT
REAL X(50)
INTEGER P, Q, R, N(100)
COMMON /ARRAYS/ X, N
COMMON /VARS/ P, Q, R
DATA X, P, Q /50 * 1.0, 20, 100/
END
```

The main advantage of COMMON is *efficiency*. When variables are passed as arguments to a subprogram, the linkage from the actual arguments to the dummy arguments via the variable addresses must be redefined repeatedly. This can involve a significant percentage of the execution time, especially if the argument list is long and there are many calls. On the other hand, with COMMON no such linking process is required because the corresponding common variables represent the same locations.

However, recall that we recommend avoiding COMMON in general, in favor of argument lists. The current trend in programming is certainly in that direction; in fact there are programming languages that allow communication between program units only through the equivalent of argument lists. One reason for this is that the use of COMMON and global variables can obscure what is going on. For example, in the sequence

```
COMMON A
  .
  .
CALL SUB(X, N)
  .
  .
END
SUBROUTINE SUB (P, M)
```

```
          .
          .
          .
COMMON B
          .
          .
          .
B = B + 1
          .
          .
          .
END
```

it is not at all apparent that the value of A will change in the calling program as a result of the call to SUB. Also, the use of global variables can sometimes result in undesirable *side effects* (see below). The required replication of the COMMON statements in each program unit that uses them is also a source of errors. Finally, if you insist on using global variables, you should know that the next version of FORTRAN will have a better way to treat them.

7.5 THE SAVE STATEMENT

Subprograms are usually called many times during the execution of a program, and it is occasionally useful for local variables to retain their values from one call to the next. Such a feature helps to encapsulate the implementation details of an algorithm within a program module to prevent unanticipated, and possibly invalid, uses of a data structure. An example of this usage is given below.

Unfortunately, various compilers handle local variables differently. Some retain the values while others treat them as undefined upon return from the subprogram. Variables in named COMMON blocks may also be treated as undefined.

SAVE
Statement

However, you can guarantee that the value of local variables will be retained by means of the SAVE statement, in which you list all of the local variables you want to save. The SAVE statement is defined as follows:

> ***Examples:*** `SAVE X, Y, Z`
> `SAVE`
> `SAVE /BBLK/, /CBLK/`

SAVE statement

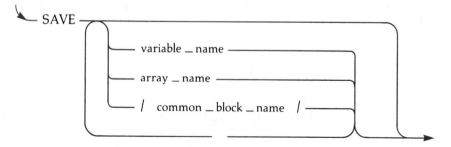

Remarks:

1. Nonexecutable.
2. A statement with an empty list (the second example) retains *all* of the local variables and named COMMON blocks in the subprogram.
3. Dummy arguments, procedure names, and names of items in a COMMON block may not appear in a SAVE statement.
4. The saved item (i.e., in a named COMMON block) may be redefined in another program unit.

The SAVE statement is useful for applications that need to hide the implementation details of a data structure within a subprogram. The following example illustrates the utility of the SAVE statement. A *stack* (sometimes called *pushdown stack*) is a data structure that is used frequently in computer operating systems and in numerous algorithms in computer science. It allows for the convenient storage of items and for their removal in reverse order; that is, the last item stored is the first one removed (as with a stack of plates in a cafeteria).

There are two operations that can be applied to a stack: (1) to *push* (or *push down*), a value onto the stack means to add a value to the top of the stack; (2) to *pop* (or *pop up*) a value from the stack means to remove the top value from the stack.

Let us implement a stack for integer numbers in FORTRAN. To do so we will use an array in a named COMMON block inside a pair of subroutines. Using a local array will ensure that we *hide* the implementation from the user of the routine. Also, the user can get to the stack only through the subroutines, thereby ensuring correct use of the stack.

The following subroutine defines the push operation for the stack. Study it carefully.

```
      SUBROUTINE PUSH (ITEM, FLG)
      INTEGER STACK(500)
      INTEGER MAX, PTR, ITEM
      LOGICAL FLG
      PARAMETER (MAX = 500)
      COMMON /STKBLK/ STACK, PTR
      SAVE
*
* PTR POINTS TO THE CURRENT TOP OF STACK
*
* CHECK FOR STACK OVERFLOW (STACK FULL)
*
      IF (PTR .EQ. MAX) THEN
         FLG = .FALSE.
      ELSE
*
* PUSH ITEM ONTO THE STACK
*
```

```
            PTR = PTR + 1
            STACK(PTR) = ITEM
            FLG = .TRUE.
        ENDIF
        END
```

Note that the SAVE statement will retain the values of STACK and PTR for subsequent calls to PUSH (and for calls to a routine to pop values from the stack). The statement

```
        CALL PUSH (ADDR, VALID)
```

will push the value of ADDR onto the stack, as long as the stack is not full to begin with. You can check the status of the logical variable VALID to determine if the push operation was successful.

For this routine to work properly, the variable PTR should be initialized to 0. Since it is in a named COMMON list, you could use the following BLOCK DATA subprogram:

```
        BLOCK DATA INPTR
        INTEGER STACK(500), PTR
        COMMON /STKBLK/ STACK, PTR
        DATA PTR / 0 /
        END
```

A routine similar to PUSH could be written to pop items from the stack (see Exercise 7.27).

7.6 ARRAYS IN SUBPROGRAMS

Arrays must be dealt with carefully as arguments for subprograms. A dummy array argument must be dimensioned in the subprogram definition. You may dimension such an array using bounds that are constants or parameters, but the usual practice is to use dummy arguments instead, as in the third example of function definitions above (SAMPLE) and in the following example that computes the largest value in the array NUM.

```
        INTEGER FUNCTION MAX (NUM, LOW, HI)
        INTEGER LOW, HI, NUM(LOW:HI)
        MAX = NUM(LOW)
        DO 10 I = LOW + 1, HI
            IF (MAX .LT. NUM (I)) MAX = NUM(I)
   10   CONTINUE
        END
```

The array dimension bounds are the variables LOW and HI (called *adjustable dimensions*), which are passed as arguments to the function.

This approach allows greater flexibility since the function need not provide fixed, specific limitations on the size of an array. Instead, the limits are determined by the program unit that calls the function, where the array is *not* a dummy argument for that program unit. Whether the array dimensions of a dummy array are specified by constant or by dummy arguments, they may not exceed the corresponding dimensions of the actual array. Note that adjustable dimensions may not be used for arrays in COMMON.

Although it is not a requirement, we recommend that dummy arrays have the same *shape* as the corresponding actual arrays. Since arrays are simply contiguous blocks of memory, it is possible to have, for example, a two-dimensional actual array corresponding to a one-dimensional dummy array, and vice versa. This approach is generally regarded as a programming trick and should be avoided, because it is very easy to reference the wrong array element.

Arrays of two or more dimensions must be treated with care. Recall from Chapter 5 that two-dimensional arrays are stored in column order, and that there may be gaps between defined values if the full dimensions are not used. Consider the following example that computes the sum of all of the elements in the M-by-N array X.

```
      REAL FUNCTION ASUM (X, M, N)
      INTEGER M, N, I, J
      REAL X(M, N)
      ASUM = 0.0
      DO 20 I = 1, M
         DO 10 J = 1, N
            ASUM = ASUM + X(I, J)
10       CONTINUE
20    CONTINUE
      END
```

This function definition may appear straightforward and proper, but it is actually quite limited; it will compute the correct answer only if M and N are equal to the dimensions of the actual array in the calling program.

Suppose, for example, that the following code appears in the calling program:

```
      INTEGER P, Q, I, J
      REAL T(4, 2)
      REAL ASUM, SUM
      P = 4
      Q = 2
      READ *, ((T (I, J), J = 1, P), I = 1, Q)
      :
      :
      SUM = ASUM(T, P, Q)
      :
      :
```

Then M and N will take on the values 4 and 2, respectively, and each of the elements T(I, J) will map correctly to the dummy reference X(I, J). However, if the values assigned to P and Q are changed to

$$P = 2$$
$$Q = 2$$

the result will be incorrect! In fact, the program may even halt due to your referencing unassigned values.

The reason for this is the way the array elements are stored in memory. Figure 7.4 shows how the elements of T are ordered and how they are mapped to the elements of X.

Thus X(1, 2) and X(2, 2) correspond to T(3, 1) and T(4, 1), respectively, which are undefined. We would obviously prefer that X(1, 2) = T(1, 2) and X(2, 2) = T(2, 2).

The relative location of an array element T(I, J) from the first element in the array is determined from the *storage-mapping function*. For the two-dimensional array T, dimensioned as T(P, Q), the function is:

```
LOC(T(I, J)) = (location of T(1, 1)) + P * (J - 1) + (I - 1)
```

because T is stored in column order. The function would be slightly different if lower bounds other than 1 were used (see Exercise 7.28).

When an array is an argument for a function (or subroutine), the array elements are not actually copied to the elements of the corresponding dummy array. That would be too inefficient. Instead the address of the starting location of the actual array is used as the starting location for the dummy array. Dummy array elements are then retrieved and stored via its storage-mapping function.

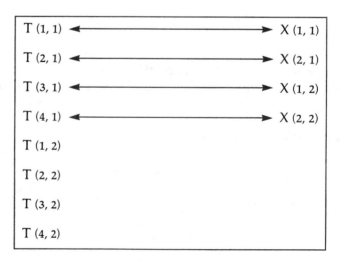

Figure 7.4
Correspondence between Actual and Dummy Array Elements

The storage-mapping function for the array X is:

```
LOC(X(I, J)) = (location of x(1, 1)) + M * (J - 1) + (I - 1)
```

Therefore

```
        LOC(T(1, 2)) = (location of T(1, 1)) + 4
```

but

```
        LOC(X(1, 2)) = (location of T(1, 1)) + 2
```

Because of the need to process arrays that may be smaller than their dimension sizes, *two* sets of dimensions should be passed as arguments: (1) the dimensions of the actual array and (2) the dimensions that represent the portion of the array being used. (However, it should be clear that this is not necessary for arrays of one dimension.) Therefore the function ASUM should be rewritten as follows:

```
            REAL FUNCTION ASUM (X, P, Q, M, N)
            INTEGER P, Q, M, N, I, J
            REAL X(P, Q)
            ASUM = 0.0
            DO 20 I = 1, M
                DO 10 J = 1, N
                    ASUM = ASUM + X(I, J)
    10          CONTINUE
    20      CONTINUE
            END
```

The corresponding function call is:

```
            SUM = ASUM(T, 4, 2, 2, 2)
```

or its equivalent. Now the dimension sizes of the actual and dummy arrays will always agree, and the corresponding storage-mapping functions will be the same.

Actually there is no need to pass Q as an argument in this example since it is not used by the storage-mapping function. Therefore, you will often see dummy array declaratives written as in these examples:

```
            REAL A(M, 1)
            INTEGER X(LOW:HIGH, *)
            DOUBLE PRECISION Y(M, N, *)
            REAL MNT(*)
```

The '*' is allowed as a dimension specifier in the *last* (rightmost) dimension. These arrays are called *assumed-size* dummy arrays. The author's preference is to use a dummy argument in the case of one-dimensional arrays, as in

```
            REAL MNT(N)
```

7.7 SIDE EFFECTS AND SUBPROGRAM STYLE

Using FORTRAN subprograms raises the possibility of *side effects*. Briefly, a side effect is a change made by a function or subroutine in addition to those it was designed to compute. They result from the fact that changes to dummy arguments within the subprogram definition are assigned to the corresponding actual arguments in the calling program unit. For example, a change to the value of the argument N in

```
REAL FUNCTION F(X, N)
```

would be a side effect. Similarly, a change to the value of MAX in the following subroutine to sort the array A would be a side effect:

```
SUBROUTINE SORT(A, MAX)
```

You can use side effects to your advantage, but they often produce undesirable results. Some of the most difficult errors to detect result from side effects. Therefore you should procede with extreme caution whenever side effects are possible.

Consider the following example:

```
INTEGER FUNCTION DBLE(N)
INTEGER N
N = N * 2
DBLE = N
END
```

The third statement, which redefines the value of N, produces a side effect. After the sequence

```
M = 8
M2 = DBLE(M)
```

M will have the value 16. This is perfectly legal in FORTRAN, but it is also obscure since you could not tell from this sequence, without knowing how the function DBLE was written, what M would be equal to afterward, or even that it would be changed at all.

This example may not seem very serious, but note that the following sequence

```
K = 8
K2 = DBLE(8)
L = 8
PRINT *, K, K2, L
```

would print the line

```
              8    16    16
```

in most versions of FORTRAN. That is, the value of L is 16, not 8! Thus even the value of a *constant* can be changed, because the subprogram uses the location of the actual argument in its reference to the dummy argument. Any later references to 8 will also produce a value of 16. This kind of bug can be very hard to find.

This kind of side effect can be avoided by rigid adherence to the following principles:

1. As a safety measure, avoid the use of constants and parameters for actual arguments in the call to a subprogram. For example, replace

```
Y = F(X, 50, 0.0)
```

by

```
F50 = 50
FZERO = 0.0
Y = F(X, F50, FZERO)
```

where F50 and FZERO are not used for any other purpose. Never change the values of any of the dummy arguments in a function definition.

2. Don't assign values to the dummy arguments in a subroutine except those for which the subroutine was written to define. For example, if arrays A and B are to be merged into array C, and A, B, and C have lengths L, M, and N, respectively, then in

```
SUBROUTINE MERGE(A, B, C, L, M, N)
```

only C and possibly N, should be assigned values.

3. Assign local variables to the dummy arguments that would otherwise be changed in a subprogram definition. For example, replace

```
REAL FUNCTION P(X, Y, N)
INTEGER N, I
REAL X, Y
DO 10 I = 1, N
    X = X + REAL(I)
    ⋮
P = X + Y
    ⋮
```

by

```
REAL FUNCTION P(X, Y, N)
INTEGER N, I
REAL X, Y, XLOC
XLOC = X
```

```
      DO 10 I = 1, N
         XLOC = XLOC + REAL(I)
         .
         .
   P = XLOC + Y
         .
         .
         .
```

In the latter case the variable X is not altered by the function definition, but the value of P is the same.

Unfortunately, functions can give rise to side effects that are even more subtle than those described above that are related to the way various FORTRAN compilers evaluate expressions. The following program,

```
      PROGRAM SIDEF
      INTEGER M, MSUM, ADD
      COMMON M
      M = 1
      MSUM = M + ADD(5)
      PRINT *, MSUM
      END
      INTEGER FUNCTION ADD(X)
      INTEGER X, N
      COMMON N
      N = N + X
      ADD = N
      END
```

will display a value of either 7 or 12 depending on the code produced by the compiler to evaluate the expression for MSUM. The Standard offers no guidance for the order of evaluation of such an expression. This example is another argument for avoiding the use of COMMON. To ensure that the expression will yield the expected result 7, you might replace the statement

```
      MSUM = M + ADD(5)
```

by

```
      MSUM = M
      MSUM = MSUM + ADD(5)
```

although you must be careful that an optimizing compiler will not produce the equivalent of the first statement again! Testing and clear documentation of this potential portability problem are mandatory here.

As far as style is concerned, a subprogram should usually be responsible for a *single* logical function (e.g., sort an array, perform *one* Jacobi iteration, perform the input operations, and so forth). Don't try to pack too much into a subprogram. One common rule of thumb is that the FORTRAN source code for a subprogram should not be more than one page long, excluding comments. The longer a routine, the harder it is to write correctly, to understand, and to modify. If it is longer, break it up into a series of calls to other more specific subprograms. Realize that this is just a guideline and that exceptions will often be required. This suggestion and others mentioned previously are summarized in the Style Guide below.

Finally, there are two features of subprograms that we do not recommend. We have already mentioned briefly the *alternate return* mechanism. The second is the *ENTRY statement*, which allows a subprogram call to begin execution of the subprogram at a statement other than the first one. These features are discussed briefly in Chapter 11.

Style Guide:
1. Use a function for a subprogram that is to define a single scalar value; otherwise use a subroutine.
2. Don't assign values to the dummy arguments in a function definition. In a subroutine, assign values only to the dummy arguments that represent output values.
3. Be careful to avoid side effects whenever possible.
4. Keep dummy array bounds dimensioned at the same size as the corresponding actual array in all but the last (rightmost) dimension.
5. Set a status flag for errors encountered in a subroutine; let the calling program decide what to do with the errors.
6. Use prewritten subprograms wherever possible; avoid writing programs that don't need to be written. (See the next section).
7. Restrict each subprogram to performance of a single logical function.

7.8 FORTRAN LIBRARIES

Writing software for various general domains of computational problems is a challenging and difficult task. You must have a thorough understanding of the problem and of the pitfalls you may encounter in the solution process. Given that, try to select the best algorithm available that is appropriate for the problem domain. Considerations of execution time, storage requirements, and stability (Chapter 6) become important. You must account for boundary conditions; for example, you must decide what the root-finding program should do if the function is discontinuous. How can the program determine that there is a discontinuity in the first place?

Attempting to make the routines transportable compounds the difficulties. Some existing, well-designed commercial computational software has required the equivalent of more than a year of developmental effort.

This is a strong argument against writing your own procedures. Unless you have a very specialized problem for which existing software packages are not adequate, or if the appropriate package is not available to you at your site, you should seriously consider using a prewritten FORTRAN library subprogram, or even a package of routines that doesn't require programming at all!

There are many FORTRAN libraries of subprograms. If the computer system you are using is anything other than a personal computer it is quite likely that it includes a FORTRAN library that was provided by the computer's manufacturer. For example, the CDC Cyber series has FTLIB, and Cray systems include SCILIB. Unfortunately many of these procedures may take advantage of the architecture of the machine, thereby rendering the procedures nontransportable.

However, there are a large number of FORTRAN libraries and packages that are more or less independent of the manufacturer and computer model. That is, they are either highly transportable or they include different versions for the various machines.

The following list is only a small sample of the hundreds of available software packages:

IMSL a library of numerical algorithms written in FORTRAN.

LINPACK a collection of FORTRAN subprograms for solving problems in linear algebra.

NAG a library of numerical algorithms written in FORTRAN.

Protran a preprocessor that translates mathematical statements into FORTRAN programs.

SAP a structured analysis program; allows analysis of structure for stress and load.

DISSPLA a library of FORTRAN subroutines for graphics

SPSS a large package of statistical procedures. It has its own language, which bears some similarity to FORTRAN. There is also a version which contains subprograms that can be called from FORTRAN programs.

MINITAB a statistical package designed primarily for relatively small samples of data (compared to SPSS).

ISPICE a package for solving circuit analysis problems.

A large computer center is likely to have copies of many of these packages. Deciding which package is best to use may be a real problem. Even when you choose one that appears to meet your needs, you may find many options available within the package itself. IMSL, for example, has over 500 subprograms described in four large volumes of documentation. Whatever you do, don't simply apply the first routine you find that "looks good." Follow these guidelines:

1. Be sure you have a thorough understanding of the problem you want to solve.
2. Read the documentation carefully for the procedure you think you will use. It may have some limitations that render it useless for your problem. Also, some packages have online, interactive documentation that will help you to decide if a given routine is right for you, and, if so, how it should be used.
3. Many computer centers offer periodic seminars and workshops on the various packages. If so, sign up for those of interest to you.
4. Discuss your problem with a knowledgeable consultant.

The packages vary greatly with regard to their ease of use. Some require that you learn a special language; some require essentially no programming. When using a library of FORTRAN subprograms, you will probably have to inform the loader, through JCL, that you are calling one or more of its routines, for example:

```
LIB = FTLIB, IMSL
```

This may not be necessary if you are using only the default library supplied by the manufacturer.

To give you a sense of how such packages might be used, consider a couple of examples from the IMSL library* (IMSL is a product of IMSL, Inc. of Houston, Texas). The package is available for a wide variety of machines, from personal computers to supercomputers. Some of the routines perform relatively simple tasks, such as exchanging the elements in two vectors; others are very complex. It includes routines for (1) the solution of linear equations, integrals and differential equations; (2) linear programming; (3) interpolation and smoothing; (4) root finding; (5) evaluating the special functions of mathematical physics, such as the various Bessel, Gamma, and Kelvin functions; (6) factor analysis; (7)

---

*For the purpose of this book only, IMSL has authorized the reprint of selected routines/subroutines taken from The IMSL Libraries. The subroutines and other material are subject to copyright protection and are considered to be proprietary information of IMSL. Use, duplication, or distribution of the IMSL subroutines without authorization is strictly prohibited.

regression analysis; (8) cluster analysis; and (9) analysis of variance.

Extensive documentation is included with each IMSL subprogram. For example, the documentation for the routine RNUNF begins as follows:

IMSL ROUTINE NAME:	RNUNF
PURPOSE:	Generate a pseudorandom number from a uniform (0, 1) distribution
USAGE:	RNUNF( ) (function)
ARGUMENT:	RNUNF—function value, a random uniform (0, 1) deviate (output)

Remarks:

1. The IMSL routine RNSET can be used to initialize the seed of the random number generator.
2. This function has a side effect: it changes the value of the seed, which is passed through a common block.

Algorithm:

Let S_0 = ISEED. Then deviate R is generated by
S_o = ISEED
$S = 7^5 S_0 \pmod{2^{31} - 1}$
$R = 2^{-31} S$

The documentation also includes a set of references that describe the algorithm, including the theory behind it, in more detail, and an example of its use, including a sample call and the resulting output.

Let us use the routine RNUNF to generate a sequence of *random numbers* in the interval (0, 1). (Actually they are *pseudorandom* numbers; computer-generated "random" numbers are not truly random because the sequence can be reproduced.) Random numbers are used extensively in such areas as computer games and simulation. They could be used to represent trees growing in a forest or the growth of bacteria subject to random variations in radiation levels. The distribution pattern can be selected to fit the application. In RNUNF, the distribution is *uniform*; that is, if you were to plot them, they would fall approximately on a straight, horizontal line. RNUNF, like all random number generators, requires a *seed* (ISEED), which is a starting value used to generate the sequence. If you call the function again with the same seed, the same sequence will be generated. Some random number generators use the computer's clock to produce the time of day as a seed.

The following program prints a table of 100 random numbers uniformly distributed over the interval (0, 1). The numbers are in single precision.

EXAMPLE 7.4

```
        PROGRAM RANTAB
        INTEGER N, I, ISEED
        REAL RAN, RNUNF
        ISEED = 123457
        CALL RNSET(ISEED)
        N = 100
        DO 10 I = 1, N
            RAN = RNUNF()
            PRINT *, RAN
   10   CONTINUE
        PRINT *, 'ISEED = ', ISEED
        END
```

Output: .96622
.51385
.
.
.
.37306
ISEED = 801129

The preceding problem is relatively simple. Consider again the problem of solving a system of N linear equations in N unknowns (recall Example 5.3). The IMSL library includes a variety of routines for this problem; which one is appropriate depends on the size of N, the special structure of the coefficient matrix, and so forth. The routine LSARG in the following example is a general one that you can use to solve systems of the form

$$A \ X = B$$

where A is a matrix and X and B are vectors. This matrix equation represents a set of linear equations with the coefficients in matrix A and right-hand sides in B.

Error checking and echo-printing have been omitted to save space. The comments in the prologue regarding the call to LSARG are the same as the IMSL documentation. Note that if the matrix A is "algorithmically singular," then the system has no solution. If A is "ill conditioned," then the matrix is too poorly structured for the procedure to compute an accurate solution.

EXAMPLE 7.5

```
      PROGRAM LINEQ
*******************************************************************
* SOLVES A SYSTEM OF LINEAR EQUATIONS A X = B. THE COEFFICIENTS
* OF A MUST BE READ IN ROW ORDER FOLLOWED BY THE COEFFICIENTS OF
* B. THE NUMBER OF ROWS OF A AND B MUST BE READ FIRST. CALLS
* IMSL ROUTINE LSARG.  THE SOLUTION IS STORED IN X.
*
* SUBROUTINE -- LSARG
*
* PURPOSE           -- SOLVE A GENERAL SYSTEM  OF LINEAR EQUATIONS
*                      WITH REAL COEFFICIENTS
* USAGE             -- CALL LSARG (N, A, LDA, B, IPATH, X)
*
* ARGUMENTS     N       -- NUMBER OF EQUATIONS (INPUT)
*               A       -- N BY N MATRIX CONTAINING THE COEF-
*                          FICIENTS OF THE LINEAR SYSTEM (INPUT)
*               LDA     -- ROW DIMENSION OF A EXACTLY AS
*                          SPECIFIED IN THE DIMENSION STATEMENT
*                          IN THE CALLING PROGRAM.  (INPUT)
*               B       -- VECTOR OF LENGTH N CONTAINING THE
*                          RIGHT-HAND SIDE OF THE SYSTEM (INPUT)
*               IPATH   -- IPATH = 1 MEANS THE SYSTEM A X = B IS
*                          SOLVED. IPATH = 2 MEANS THE SYSTEM
*                          TRANS(A) X = B IS SOLVED, WHERE
*                          TRANS(A) IS THE TRANSPOSE OF A (INPUT)
*               X       -- VECTOR OF LENGTH N CONTAINING THE
*                          SOLUTION TO THE LINEAR SYSTEM (OUTPUT)
* NOTE: A CODE 1 ERROR MESSAGE IS PRINTED IF THE MATRIX A IS
*       TOO ILL-CONDITIONED.  A CODE 2 ERROR MESSAGE INDICATES
*       THAT THE MATRIX IS SINGULAR.
*******************************************************************
      INTEGER N, LDA, IPATH, I, J, DIM
      PARAMETER (DIM = 25)
      REAL A(DIM, DIM), B(DIM), X(DIM)
      READ *, N
      READ *, ((A(I, J), J = 1, N), I = 1, N)
      READ *, (B(I), I = 1, N)
      LDA = DIM
      IPATH = 1
      CALL LSARG (N, A, LDA, B, IPATH, X)
      PRINT *, 'THE SOLUTION MATRIX IS:'
      PRINT *, (X(I), I = 1, N)
      END
```

Note again that DIM may have to be replaced by a constant for some FORTRAN compilers.

Clearly, the above approach is superior to that used for Example 5.3. It uses a rigorous, well-tested procedure and requires no effort on your part to code and debug it. Only the *driver* program—the main program—must be provided, which is a relatively simple task. A program that might otherwise require months of work can be written in minutes.

Exercises

Section 7.1

1. Write function subprograms to evaluate each of the functions in Exercise 3.10.

*2. Write a function subprogram to compute the inner product of two vectors (see Exericse 5.18.)

*3. Example 7.3 uses a heuristic to determine when the computed approximation represents an exact root of a function. Can you think of an example in which this heuristic will yield an incorrect result?

4. Write function subprograms to determine the values of
   *a. TINY
   b. EPSILON
   that were described in Section 6 of Chapter 6.

5. Write a function subprogram called SUMS to compute the sum of the following, depending on the value of a variable, CHOICE:
   a. All the elements
   b. The odd-numbered elements
   c. The even-numbered elements of an array

*6. Write a function subprogram that computes the *trace* of a double-precision square (N-by-N) matrix in double-precision. The trace of a square matrix is the sum of its diagonal elements.

7. A *permutation* of n objects is an arrangement of the objects in a row. A problem common to many applications is to determine the number of *distinct* permutations of the objects a, b, and c:

$$a\,b\,c \qquad b\,a\,c \qquad a\,c\,b \qquad b\,c\,a \qquad c\,a\,b \qquad c\,b\,a$$

The formula for the number of permutations of k objects taken from a collection of n objects is given by the formula

$$p(n, k) = n! \,/\, (n - k)!$$

---

*The solution to this exercise appears in Appendix D.

Write a function subprogram to compute p.

8. Write a program to tabulate the function

$$f(c, u, t) = c\left[\log\left(\frac{1 + u}{1 - u}\right)\right]^{t-1}$$

using the function subprogram with input parameters c, u, the step h, and the interval endpoints, for t varying over the interval.

9. Example 7.1 reads the coefficients of a polynomial into the array A, and jumps to the statement labeled 15 immediately following the loop if the number of coefficients does not agree with N. Make a case here for jumping to a location other than the one immediately following the input loop on an input data error.

10. **a.** Write a function to compute the mean of an array of test scores.
   b. Write a function to compute the median of an array of test scores, assuming that the scores are already sorted into ascending order.
   c. Write a function to compute the *mode* of the array of test scores, assuming that they are sorted into ascending order. The mode is the most frequently occurring score.
   d. Write a function to return the highest score in the sorted array of scores.
   e. Same problem as (d) for the lowest score.
   f. Write a function that will check the array of scores and return .TRUE. if the scores are sorted into ascending order and .FALSE. otherwise.
   g. Write a function to compute the standard deviation of the test scores (see Exercise 3.5 c).
   h. Write a main program to read a set of test scores and print an error message if they are not in ascending order; otherwise compute and print each of the descriptive statistics listed in parts a through g of this exercise.

Section 7.2

11. Write a subroutine that will compute and return the roots of a quadratic $ax^2 + bx + c = 0$, given a, b, and c as input parameters. It should also return a flag, RTTYP, to indicate if there were two real roots, one real root, and so forth. Return the roots as complex numbers. Test the program on the examples given in Exercise 3.16.

*12. Write a subroutine to exchange two vectors of the same length.

13. Write a subroutine to compute the product of two matrices. Be sure to check for valid dimensions. See Exercise 5.22.

14. Write a subroutine to compute *one* iteration of the Jacobi method for solving a system of linear equations (Example 5.3).

15. Redo Example 7.1 using a subroutine to produce the error messages.

16. Redo Example 3.2 using functions and subroutines, where appropriate.

17. In your calculus classes, all of the integrals you were exposed to could be solved exactly by hand, using techniques like a change of variable or integration by parts. However, many integrals that arise in real applications can only be approximated by numerical methods such as the *trapezoidal rule*:

$$\int_a^b f(x)dx \approx h\left[\frac{1}{2}(f(a) + f(b)) + \sum_{i=1}^{n-1} f(a + ih)\right]$$

where $h = (b - a) / n$ and n is a positive integer equal to the number of subintervals used. In general, the accuracy improves as n increases, until the accumulated roundoff error becomes too large (recall Chapter 6.) Write a program that uses a subprogram to compute the value of the integral to compute the integral of a function. Try it on

*a. $\int_0^2 e^x \, dx$ (exact answer: $e^2 - 1$)

b. $\int_1^{10} \frac{1}{x} \, dx$ (exact answer: $\ln 10$)

for various values of n. Try to find the value of n that yields the best accuracy. Note: roundoff error is minimized when h is a power of 2.

18. Use the subprogram you wrote for Exercise 17 to evaluate the integrals

a. $\int_0^\pi e^x \cos nx \, dx$ **b.** $\int_0^\pi x \sin nx \, dx$ **c.** $\int_0^\pi x^2 \cos nx \, dx$

for $n = 0, 1, 2, \ldots, 10$. These integrals are used in the evaluation of Fourier series.

19. Another method for numerical integration, which is usually more accurate than the trapezoidal rule, is *Simpson's rule*:

$$\int_a^b f(x)dx \approx \frac{h}{6}\left\{f(a) + f(b) + 2\sum_{i=1}^{n-1} f(a + ih) + 4\sum_{i=1}^{n-1} f\left[a + \left(i - \frac{1}{2}\right)h\right]\right\}$$

Do Exercise 17 using Simpson's rule in place of the trapezoidal rule. Compare your results for the *same number of function evaluations*; that is, N (Simpson) = 2N (trapezoidal).

20. The function

$$E(t) = -\gamma - \ln t + \int_0^t (1 - e^{-x}) \frac{dx}{x}$$

arises in applications in radiative transfer and transport theory, where $\gamma = 0.5772157\ldots$, which is Euler's constant. Use Simpson's rule (Exercise 19) to evaluate $E(t)$ for $t = 1, 2, 3$. Note: There is an apparent problem at $x = 0$ because $(1 - e^{-x})/x$ must be evaluated there. However, since

$$\lim_{x \to 0} \frac{1 - e^{-x}}{x} = 1,$$

just evaluate the function as

$$f(x) = \begin{cases} 1 & \text{for } x = 0 \\ \dfrac{1 - e^{-x}}{x} & \text{for } x > 0 \end{cases}$$

The solutions for $t = 1, 2, 3$ are 0.2193839, 0.0489005, and 0.0130484, respectively.†

*21. Often a function cannot be written as a formula but is represented instead by a set of tabular values. In such cases the function can easily be approximated at points other than the tabulated values by *linear interpolation*. If the function $f(x)$ is known at the points $x_1, x_2, \ldots, x_n$ and if $x_k < x < x_{k+1}$, then $f(x)$ can be approximated by

$$f(x) = \frac{1}{x_{k+1} - x_k} [f(x_{k+1}) \cdot (x - x_k) - f(x_k) \cdot (x - x_{k+1})]$$

Write a program to read N pairs of numbers $x_1, f(x_1), x_2, f(x_2), \ldots, x_N, f(x_N)$, where $x_i < x_{i+1}$. Then read a set of numbers x, where $x_1 < x < x_N$, and compute and print the value of $f(x)$ using the above formula. Use functions and/or subroutines where appropriate.

22. Given the equation $Ax = \lambda x$, where A is an n-by-n matrix, x is a vector of length n, and λ is a scalar, x is called an *eigenvector*, and λ is called an *eigenvalue* of A. The problem of finding the eigenvalues and eigenvectors of a matrix A is important in scientific and engineering applications. Write a program to compute the dominant (largest in magnitude) eigenvalue of an N-by-N matrix and its corresponding eigenvector using the *power method*, which is described by the following pseudocode:

1. Let $u^{(0)}$ = vector of all 1s
2. Compute $v^{(k)} = Au^{(k-1)}$ for $k = 1, 2, \ldots$
   $u^{(k)} = v^{(k)} / v_{max}^{(k)}$

†From L. F. Shampine and R. C. Allen, *Numerical Computing: An Introduction*, (Philadelphia: W. B. Saunders, 1973). Reprinted by permission of Holt, Rinehart & Winston.

where $u^{(k)}$ and $v^{(k)}$ are vectors of length n and $v^{(k)}_{max}$ = maximum element of vector $v^{(k)}$. With this method $v^{(k)}_{max}$ converges to the dominant eigenvalue of A, and $u^{(k)}$ converges to the eigenvector corresponding to $v^{(k)}_{max}$. Stop the iteration when

$$\max_{1 \leq i \leq N} \left| \frac{u_i^{(k)} - u_i^{(k-1)}}{u_i^{(k)}} \right| < 10^{-5}$$

where $u_i^{(k)}$ is the ith element of $u^{(k)}$. Try your program on

$$A = \begin{bmatrix} 1 & 2 & 0 \\ 2 & 1 & 0 \\ 0 & 0 & -1 \end{bmatrix}$$

The exact answer is $\lambda = 3$ with $x = (1, 1, 0)^T$.

Section 7.4

*23. Example 7.3 doesn't validate that A and B are the left and right endpoints of the interval, respectively. Why not?

24. Modify either your version of the trapezoidal rule (Exercise 17) or Simpson's rule (Exercise 19) so that the function name is an argument to the subprogram call.

25. Write a program to tabulate a trigonometric function of the user's choice (e.g., sine, cosine, tangent, and so forth). Input to the subprogram should be the interval limits, the stepsize, and the function name.

Section 7.5

26. Using *no arguments* (*Note*: This is generally not recommended.) write the subprogram and corresponding call for
   *a. Exercise 2
   b. Exercise 12
   c. Exercise 13

Section 7.6

27. You were introduced to the concept of a stack in Section 7.5. Write a routine similar to that in the text to *pop* a value from the stack (i.e., to remove the top value from the stack). Set an error status flag appropriately if you try to pop a value from an empty stack.

Section 7.7

28. Write down the storage-mapping function for
   a. a two-dimensional array, assuming the array is stored in *row* order.

*b. a two-dimensional FORTRAN array with lower bound that may have a value other than one.

c. A three-dimensional FORTRAN array.

Section 7.8

29. How do you think the FORTRAN compiler can tell that the statement

$$P = F(I)$$

is an array reference rather than a function call? Also, what will the following program print? Try it.

```
INTEGER P, L(10)
L(5) = -1
P = L(5)
PRINT *, P
END
INTEGER FUNCTION L(X)
INTEGER X
L = X
END
```

*30. What will the following program print?

```
INTEGER A(2), N, Y, F
A(1) = 1
A(2) = 2
N = 2
Y = F(A(N), N)
PRINT *, N, Y, A(1), A(2)
END
INTEGER FUNCTION F(X, K)
INTEGER X, K
K = K - 1
F = X + 5
END
```

Section 7.9

31. If you have IMSL or another mathematical computation package available, find and use a routine to compute *all* of the roots of a polynomial. How would you proceed to do this with a method like bisection?

32. Use an IMSL or other library routine to compute the integral of a function. Compare the result with that of your trapezoidal or Simpson method (Exercises 17 and 19).

33. Use Example 7.4 to generate a sequence of random *integers* between 1 and N.

34. Use the algorithm for Example 7.4 to write your *own* random number generator function. Compare your results with those obtained from RNUNF or an equivalent library function.

8 *Character Data*

FORTRAN 77 provides one data type that we haven't discussed yet: the *character data type*. It is akin to a string type in BASIC and the packed array of character type in Pascal. Character variables are used for nonnumeric problems, such as sorting lists of names, manipulating text in a word-processor, implementing queries in expert systems, or printing reports that consist in part of character strings. Character-string manipulation, including string I/O, concatenation (combining strings), extracting substrings, and comparing strings, will be covered in detail in this chapter.

Character variables were added to FORTRAN as part of the 77 standard. Since FORTRAN was, and still is, intended primarily for computation, the character features are weak relative to those available in many versions of BASIC and are comparable to those in Pascal. However, as you will see, it is relatively easy to build additional functions and subroutines to accomodate your needs.

8.1 CHARACTER CONSTANTS, VARIABLES, AND ASSIGNMENTS

A *character* is a single letter, digit, or symbol, such as * . Some systems restrict characters to the FORTRAN character set; others allow additional characters, such as lowercase letters. A *character string* is a sequence of one or more characters, and a *character constant* is a character string enclosed in single quotes (i.e., apostrophes), just as in Pascal and in some versions of BASIC. For example,

```
'VELOCITY'
```

is a character constant with a length of 8 characters.

Blanks are significant in a character constant, as in

```
'ESCAPE VELOCITY'
```

Also, single quotes may be represented in a character constant by two consecutive quotes (e.g., 'IT''S' represents the constant IT'S).

Character variables, which are used to store and manipulate character strings, are defined by the *CHARACTER type statement*. It specifies the names and lengths of the character variables.

CHARACTER Statement

Examples:

```
1. CHARACTER * 20, PLANET, STAR, CONSTL
2. CHARACTER NAME * 20, ADDRES * 18, CITY * 8, STATE * 2
3. CHARACTER * 12, INSTR, CRSE * 4, DESCR, LOC
4. CHARACTER LET1, LET2, LET3
5. CHARACTER PSTAT * (2 * 72 - 7)
6. CHARACTER RESIST(50) * 10
7. CHARACTER *(*), ERMES1

   PARAMETER (ERMES1 = 'NEGATIVE VALUES ARE ILLEGAL')
```

where *length-specification* is defined by:

CHARACTER statement

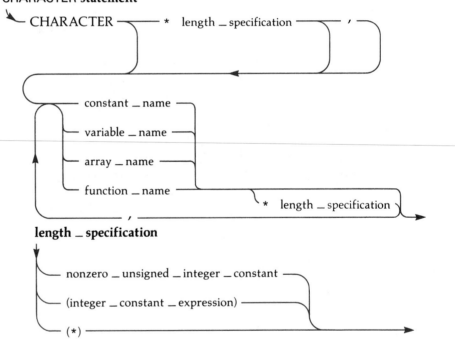

length _ specification

Remarks:

1. Nonexecutable.

2. The *default length specification*—the asterisk and integer after the word CHARACTER—applies to all variables in the list. Thus, PLANET, STAR, and CONSTL all have length 20 in the first example.

3. Each variable can be given a length explicitly; the length specifi-

cation follows the variable name. In the second example the variables NAME, ADDRES, CITY, and STATE have lengths 20, 18, 8, and 2, respectively. An explicit length specification overrides the default, as in Example 3. CRSE has length 4; the rest of the variables in the list have length 12.

4. If there is no length specification, the length is equal to 1. In Example 4, each of LET1, LET2, and LET3 has length 1.

5. A constant integer expression may be used to represent the length, as in Example 5. This feature has limited usefulness. It would allow a programmer to express the length of a character variable as the sum of its component parts, for example.

6. An array of character strings may be defined as in Example 6 where each element of the array RESIST is a character string of length 10.

7. The last example illustrates the use of the CHARACTER statement to define a *symbolic character constant*, ERMES1. The asterisk used for the length specification means that FORTRAN will use the actual length of the string as defined in the companion PARAMETER statement (27 here). This saves you the trouble of counting the characters in the string. You may also use this form for dummy character variables in a subprogram.

CHARACTER Assignment Statement

Just as there are arithmetic operators and operations for manipulating numeric operands, there are operations designed to manipulate strings. Let us consider the *CHARACTER assignment statement* first.

A CHARACTER assignment statement has the same form as other assignment statements we have considered. Its form is

```
cname = cexpression
```

where *cname* is a character variable or *substring name*, and *cexpression* is a valid character expression. Both sides *must* be of type CHARACTER. For now, assume that a character expression may be a character constant or a character variable and that *cname* is a character variable. We will explore other possibilities and present the formal definition in Section 8.3. For example,

```
CHARACTER * 10 PREXY
PREXY = 'WASHINGTON'
```

stores the name WASHINGTON in the character variable PREXY.

A character variable is represented internally as a sequence of bytes together with an integer that specifies its length, or the number of bytes it can store.

Therefore one must be careful to consider the defined length of the character variable when making an assignment. The following rules apply:

1. If the length of *cexpression* is *less than* the length of the variable *cname*, then the value of the expression is stored *left-justified* in the space represented by the variable, and the remaining space is *padded* (filled) with blanks.
2. If the length of the variable is less than the length of the expression, then the value of the expression is *truncated* on the right; only the leftmost characters are stored in the variable.

Consider the following program fragment.

```
CHARACTER LOCATN(3) * 9, SHLOC * 3
:
:
LOCATN(1) = 'POMONA'
LOCATN(2) = 'LOS ANGELES'
LOCATN(3) = 'SAN DIEGO'
SHLOC = LOCATN(3)
:
:
```

After these assignments, the values of the variables are as follows:

```
LOCATN(1):   POMONA
LOCATN(2):   LOS ANGEL
LOCATN(3):   SAN DIEGO
SHLOC:       SAN
```

8.2 INPUT AND OUTPUT OF CHARACTER STRINGS

One way to assign a character string to a character variable is to read it using a list-directed READ statement. For example, if the sequence

```
CHARACTER FORML * 5, CNAME * 15
READ *, FORML, CNAME
```

is applied to the input record

```
'HNO3' , 'NITRIC ACID'
```

then FORML will have the value 'HNO3_' and CNAME the value 'NITRIC ACID____', where _ represents a *blank* space. Note that input string data *must* be enclosed in quotes for a list-directed READ. As with assignment statements, short strings are left-justified in the space represented by the variable, and the remaining space is padded with blanks.

If the input string is *longer* than the variable's declared length, it is *truncated* on the right. Thus, if the input record for the above sequence is

'HCL' , 'HYDROCHLORIC ACID'

then FORML will have the value 'HCL__' and CNAME will be equal to 'HYDROCHLORIC AC'.

Character variables may be printed using list-directed PRINT statements. For example, given the preceding assignment, the statement

PRINT *, FORML, CNAME, 'IN STOCK'

would print

HCL___HYDROCHLORIC_AC_IN_STOCK

although the items may be separated by more blanks, or commas plus blanks, depending on the implementation of FORTRAN 77.

It would be nice from the standpoint of a FORTRAN programmer to be able to ignore the internal character code, but sometimes this is not possible. Consider first the problem of comparing single characters. In FORTRAN they can be compared using the relational operators .GT., .EQ., and so forth.

For example,

'X' .LT. 'Y'

is true since 'X' precedes 'Y' in alphabetical order. Likewise it is true that

'N' .GT. 'B'

However, what about

'9' .GT. 'B'

or

'*' .LE. '+' ?

The answer lies in the *collating sequence* of the particular computer being used—the order in which the characters appear in its coding scheme. This order, sometimes called the *lexical* order, is determined by the internal binary representation of the characters. Thus in the ASCII coding scheme, the character 'A' is represented by the binary number

01000001

while '9' is given by

00111001

Thus, if ASCII is used, then it is true that

'9' .LT. 'A'

in the sense that the binary number 00111001 is less than 0100001. The ASCII, EBCDIC, and CDC Scientific coding schemes are given in Appendix A.

The Standard is not much help in all this. It requires only that the following orderings be observed:

1. 'A' < 'B' < ... < 'Z'
2. '0' < '1' < ... < '9'
3. (space) ' ' < 'A' and ' ' < '0'
4. All of the digits must precede 'A' or follow 'Z'; the letters and digits must not be intermixed, nor must the special characters be intermixed between the letters or the digits.

Nothing is specified regarding the order of the special characters. Therefore, in ASCII, the following is true:

'*' .LT. '+'

but

'*' .GT. '+'

is true in EBCDIC.

Similarly, there is no uniformity regarding relationships between uppercase and lowercase letters. For example,

'A' .LT. 'b'

is true in ASCII and false in EBCDIC.

All of this variability in the collating sequences causes potential transportability problems. Many machines allow a choice of collating sequence through options provided by the operating system. We will examine another solution below, after we illustrate how character strings are compared.

We compare character strings just as we examine words for their alphabetical order: character by character, left to right. Their order is the same as that of the *first* two corresponding characters that are different. Thus, the following are all true:

```
'ABERCROMBE' .LT. 'FITCH'
'SMITH' .LT. 'WESSON'
'PETERSEN' .LT. 'PETERSON'
'917-32-0717' .LT. '917-32-0719'
'JOHN E. SMYTH' .LT. 'JOHN E SMYTHE'
```

Note that the lengths of the strings do not influence the relations in these examples. The length is important, however, if one string is exactly the same as the leftmost part of a longer string. In this case the effect of the comparison is as if the shorter string were padded on the right with blanks to make it as long as the other string. Thus, for example, it is true that

'ATOMIC' .LT. 'ATOMICITY'

and

'AB9*/' .LT. 'AB9' (in CDC Scientific since '*/' < '__')

Consider now the problem of reading a list of chemical formulas into an array, sorting the array, and printing it out. You may already be familiar with some simple sorting algorithms, such as the bubble sort or exchange sort. Here we will employ a much more efficient algorithm, the *Shell sort*, named after its discoverer, D. L. Shell. Where the bubble sort requires on the order of one-half million comparisons to sort an array of 1000 elements, the Shell sort requires only about 30,000. To be sure, there are more efficient sorting procedures, but the Shell sort, which is a generalization of the bubble sort, is relatively easy to implement and serves as an appropriate illustration. A proof that the procedure works can be found in textbooks on algorithm design.

The algorithm sorts an array, CFORM, of N strings by sorting N/2 pairs (CFORM(I), CFORM(N/2 + I)) for $1 \le I \le N/2$ on the first pass, N/4 four-tuples (CFORM(I), CFORM(N/4 + I), CFORM(N/2 + I), CFORM(3N/4 + I)) for $1 \le I \le N/4$ on the second pass, N/8 eight-tuples in the third pass, and so forth. In each pass sorting is done using an exchange sort in which corresponding elements that are out of order between the various tuples are interchanged. We exit from the innermost loop as soon as 2 elements are found that are already in order. You may wish to work through the algorithm by hand with a list of 10 numbers, say, to attain a better understanding.

A pseudocode version of the Shell sort algorithm is as follows:

```
Let NTPL be the number of tuples on each pass.
Set NTPL = N
While NTPL > 1 do
    Set NTPL = NTPL/2  (integer)
    For I = NTPL + 1 to N
        Set J = I - NTPL
        While J > 0  do
            If CFORM(J) > CFORM(J + NTPL) then
                Switch (CFORM(J), CFORM(J + NTPL))
                Set J = J - NTPL
            Else
                Set J = 0  (exit from inner loop)
```

The entire solution can be written nicely as a set of independent modules. A structure chart for the solution appears in Figure 8.1.

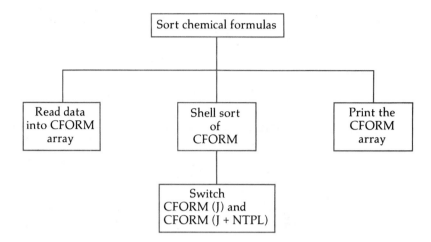

Figure 8.1
Structure chart for sorting program.

The problem of interest here, however, is to ensure that the compounds will be sorted in the same way, *regardless of the collating sequence of the character set*. Note that

$$\text{'HCL' .GT. 'H2O'}$$

is true in the ASCII collating sequence but false in EBCDIC and CDC Scientific.

This problem could require a complicated solution, but fortunately FORTRAN 77 provides four intrinsic functions to facilitate the comparison of strings in a standard way. These functions always compare strings *according to the ASCII sequence*, no matter which coding scheme is used. The functions are defined in Table 8.1, in which the arguments a_1 and a_2 are character-string expressions. LGE, for example, stands for *lexically greater than or equal to*.

TABLE 8.1   Intrinsic String-Comparison Functions

Function	Definition	Example	Value
LGE(a_1, a_2)	true if $a_1 \geq a_2$	LGE('HYDROCHLORIC', 'HYDROCARBON')	true since 'H' > 'A'
LGT(a_1, a_2)	true if $a_1 > a_2$	LGT('H2S04', 'HN03')	true since '2' > 'N'
LLE(a_1, a_2)	true if $a_1 \leq a_2$	LLE('CO2', 'CO2_')	true since they are equal; the first argument is extended with a blank
LLT(a_1, a_2)	true if $a_1 < a_2$	LLT('H20' 'H20+')	true since ' ' < '+'

These functions should be used for comparing strings in a FOR-TRAN program if there is any possibility that it might be used on another system, unless the strings are limited to a subset of the collating sequence for which any collating sequence will yield the same result (e.g., all uppercase letters).

If the ASCII sequence is inappropriate for some reason, you may define you own sequence (see Section 8.3).

Using the functions from Table 8.1 for the comparison in the pseudocode version of the Shell sort enables us to produce the following transportable program to sort our lists.

EXAMPLE 8.1

```
      PROGRAM CFSORT
*****************************************************************
* AUTHOR:  DON VERDE  3/87
*
* THIS PROGRAM SORTS A LIST OF UP TO NMAX CHEMICAL NAMES PROVIDED
* AS DATA ON THE STANDARD INPUT UNIT.  (ACTUALLY, IT WILL SORT
* ANY CHARACTER STRINGS OF LENGTH 12 OR LESS.)  INPUT DATA MUST
* BE ONE NAME PER RECORD.  THE SORTED LIST IS PRINTED ON THE
* STANDARD OUTPUT UNIT.
*
*                 VARIABLES, PARAMETERS, SUBPROGRAMS
* NMAX --   MAXIMUM NUMBER OF STRINGS -- THE ARRAY DIMENSION
*           (PARAMETER)
* N -- ACTUAL NUMBER OF STRINGS TO SORT (N <= NMAX)
* CFORM -- ARRAY OF CHEMICAL FORMULAS (STRINGS)
* TEMPST -- A TEMPORARY VARIABLE USED IN THE SWITCH ROUTINE
* READIN -- READS CHARACTER STRINGS INTO THE ARRAY CFORM
*           (SUBROUTINE)
* PRTOUT -- PRINTS ARRAY ELEMENTS (SUBROUTINE)
* SHELL -- SHELL SORT PROCEDURE (SUBROUTINE)
*****************************************************************
      INTEGER N, NMAX
      PARAMETER (NMAX = 1000)
      CHARACTER * 12, CFORM(NMAX), TEMPST
      CALL READIN (CFORM, NMAX, N)
      CALL SHELL (CFORM, N, TEMPST)
      PRINT *, 'CHEMICAL FORMULAS'
      PRINT *, '-----------------'
      CALL PRTOUT (CFORM, N)
      END

      SUBROUTINE READIN (CSTRNG, NMAX, N)
*****************************************************************
```

```
      * THIS ROUTINE READS CHARACTER STRINGS INTO THE ARRAY
      * CSTRNG.
      *
      * CSTRNG -- THE ARRAY OF CHARACTER STRINGS (OUTPUT)
      * NMAX -- THE DIMENSION OF CSTRNG (INPUT)
      * N -- THE ACTUAL NUMBER OF STRINGS IN THE INPUT LIST (OUTPUT)
      *****************************************************************
            INTEGER NMAX, N
            CHARACTER *(*), CSTRNG(NMAX)
            N = 1
      *     WHILE (NOT END OF DATA)  DO
      10    CONTINUE
                READ (*,*, END = 20) CSTRNG(N)
                N = N + 1
                GOTO 10
      20    CONTINUE
      *     ENDWHILE
            N = N - 1
            END

            SUBROUTINE PRTOUT (CSTRNG, N)
      *****************************************************************
      * THIS ROUTINE PRINTS THE N CHARACTER STRINGS IN THE ARRAY
      * CSTRING ON THE STANDARD OUTPUT UNIT.
      *
      * CSTRNG -- THE ARRAY OF CHARACTER STRINGS (INPUT)
      * N -- THE ACTUAL NUMBER OR STRINGS IN THE ARRAY (INPUT)
      * I -- LOOP INDEX
      *****************************************************************
            INTEGER N, I
            CHARACTER *(*), CSTRNG(N)
            DO 10, I = 1, N
                PRINT *, CSTRNG(I)
      10    CONTINUE
            END

            SUBROUTINE SHELL (CSTRNG, N, TEMPST)
      *****************************************************************
      * THIS ROUTINE SORTS THE CHARACTER STRING ARRAY CSTRNG INTO ASCII
      * LEXICAL ORDER USING A VARIANT OF THE SHELL SORT ALGORITHM.
      *
      * CSTRNG -- THE ARRAY OF CHARACTER STRINGS (INPUT/OUTPUT)
      * N -- THE ACTUAL NUMBER OF STRINGS IN THE ARRAY (INPUT)
      * TEMPST -- A TEMPORARY CHARACTER VARIABLE USED IN THE SWITCH
      *           ROUTINE
      * NTPL -- THE NUMBER OF TUPLES ON EACH PASS
      * I, J -- LOOP INDICES
      *****************************************************************
```

```
      INTEGER N, I, J, NTPL
      CHARACTER *(*), CSTRNG(N), TEMPST
      NTPL = N
*     WHILE NO. OF TUPLES > 1 DO
10    CONTINUE
      IF (NTPL .GT. 1) THEN
          NTPL = INT(NTPL / 2)
          DO 30, I = NTPL + 1, N
             J = I - NTPL
*            WHILE NO. OF UNSORTED TUPLES > 0 DO
20           CONTINUE
             IF (J .GT. 0) THEN
                 IF (LGT(CSTRNG(J), CSTRNG(J + NTPL))) THEN
                     CALL SWITCH (CSTRNG(J), CSTRNG(J+NTPL), TEMPST)
                     J = J - NTPL
                 ELSE
*                    EXIT FROM INNER LOOP
                     J = 0
                 ENDIF
                 GOTO 20
             ENDIF
30        CONTINUE
          GOTO 10
      ENDIF
*     ENDWHILE
      END

      SUBROUTINE SWITCH(STR1, STR2, TEMPST)
******************************************************************
* THIS ROUTINE EXCHANGES THE FIRST TWO ARGUMENT STRINGS.
* TEMPST IS PASSED AS AN ARGUMENT TO ALLOW ITS LENGTH TO VARY
* WITH THAT OF THE OTHER STRINGS.
*
* STR1, STR2 -- THE STRINGS TO BE SWITCHED (INPUT/OUTPUT)
* TEMPST -- TEMPORARY PLACEHOLDER IN THE SWITCH PROCESS
******************************************************************
      CHARACTER *(*), STR1, STR2, TEMPST
      TEMPST = STR1
      STR1 = STR2
      STR2 = TEMPST
      END
```

Note that the lexical function LGE is required only once in the SHELL subroutine, but its use is critical for transportability. It should be noted that LGE and the related functions are very efficient. In a test of 10,000 comparisons on a minicomputer, LLE required 76 seconds, and .LE. required 75 seconds.

TEMPST could be defined as a local variable in the SWITCH subroutine, but then its length would be fixed, which would result in the truncation of longer strings. As an argument, however, its length is tied to that of the input strings.

From a logical standpoint, the above example was conveniently subdivided into a set of subroutines. However, it is unlikely that a production program would be subdivided to this extent because of the time overload of calling subroutines. Also, the READIN routine should be modified to prevent reading a number of strings in excess of the size of the array. This modification is left as an exercise.

Style Guide:
1. Always use the string comparison functions, LLE, LGT, etc., to compare strings if transportability is an issue.
2. Use the *(*) expression to declare the lengths of string arguments in subprograms in order to maximize flexibility.

8.3 CHARACTER-STRING EXPRESSIONS AND FUNCTIONS

In this section we examine additional types of character expressions. Besides input/output and lexical comparisons, two other operations that may be performed on strings are *concatenation* and *substring extraction*. These operations would be required in a word-processing program, for example, or in a natural-language interpreter in an artificial intelligence application.

String Concatenation

To *concatenate* two strings means to put them together into a single string. The FORTRAN concatenation operator is the double slash (//), which works like the plus sign (+) in most versions of BASIC and in some versions of Pascal that have the string type. For example,

```
CHARACTER  TYPE1 * 7, TYPE2 * 9
TYPE1 = 'ELASTIC'
TYPE2 = 'IN' // TYPE1
```

would result in TYPE2 being assigned the value 'INELASTIC'.

Likewise, the sequence

```
CHARACTER TYPE * 7, SCHOOL * 11, MAJOR * 22
SCHOOL = 'ENGINEERING'
TYPE = 'NUCLEAR'
```

```
MAJOR = TYPE // ' ' // SCHOOL
PRINT *, MAJOR
TYPE = 'MECHANICAL'
MAJOR = TYPE // ' ' // SCHOOL
PRINT *, MAJOR
TYPE = 'CIVIL'
MAJOR = TYPE // ' ' // SCHOOL
PRINT *, MAJOR
```

would result in an output of

```
NUCLEAR ENGINEERING
MECHANI ENGINEERING
CIVIL   ENGINEERING
```

The truncated word in the second line and the extra blank spaces in the third line occur because TYPE has a length of 7. We will solve this problem after we examine some additional language features for manipulating character strings.

We can now give the formal definition of a character expression:

character expression

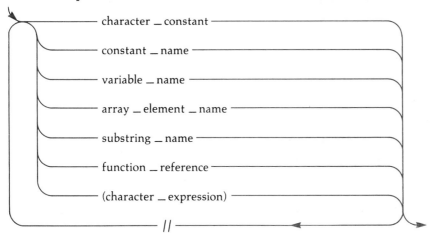

Remarks:

1. Each of the items in the diagram must be of type CHARACTER.
2. A constant_name as used above is a symbolic character constant defined by a PARAMETER statement.
3. Substring names and specific character functions will be defined shortly.
4. Note that the concatenation operator (//) can be applied repeatedly in an expression, as demonstrated in the above example.

Remember, just as the *value* of a number expression is a number, so the *value* of a character expression is a character string.

Substrings

Let us now consider how *substring names* are represented and manipulated. As the term implies, a *substring* of a character string, C, is a string of 0 (the *null string*) or more contiguous characters from C.

Examples: Given the sequence

```
CHARACTER * 16 STRING, SLIST(3)
STRING = 'ABCDEFGHIJKLMNOP'
SLIST(3) = '0123456789*/+-'
N = 8
```

the following are some possible substrings:

Substring name	Value
STRING(3:9)	'CDEFGHI'
STRING(N – 2:N + 2)	'FGHIJ'
STRING(:6)	'ABCDEF'
STRING(N:)	'HIJKLMNOP'
SLIST(3)(4:8)	'34567'
SLIST(3)(11:)	'*/+-'
STRING(N:3)	Error
STRING(10:20)	Error

substring name

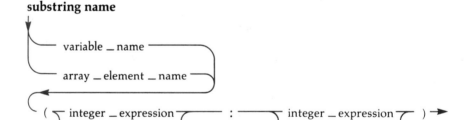

Remarks:

1. The two integers separated by the colon represent the first and last positions of the substring in the original string.
2. For a substring name to be valid, the corresponding character variable must be defined in a CHARACTER statement.
3. For a substring name of the form S(F:L), the following relationship must hold:

$$1 \leq F \leq L \leq \text{the length of S}$$

Consequently the last two examples are in error.

4. A substring name of the form S(:N), such as the third example, includes all of the characters up to and including character N. Likewise S(N:) consists of all characters from position N through the end of S.

5. Note that in an array substring name, the substring limits are specified *after* the subscript(s).

6. The concatenation operator is restricted to *assignment statements* only in subprograms if an assumed length declaration is used. Thus, in

```
SUBROUTINE(C1, C2, COUNT)
INTEGER COUNT
CHARACTER *(*) C1, C2
   :
   :
C1 = C2 // 'ACID'
```

is valid, but

```
IF (C1 // C2 .EQ. 'WEAK ACID') COUNT = COUNT + 1
```

is invalid.

7. An important limitation of character expressions is that none of the character positions on the left side of an assignment statement can be referenced on the right side. For example, the following assignments are invalid:

```
CNAME = CNAME(N:M)
SENTC = SENTC // WORD
NEWFRM = NEWFRM(1:5) // NEWFRM(6:N)
```

A substring name may be used wherever a character variable is used, subject to the above rules.

You may assign values to substring names and concatenate them, as in

```
CHARACTER PHRASE * 14, ALTPHR * 16
PHRASE (:7) = 'KINETIC'
PHRASE (8:8) = ' '
PHRASE (9:11) = 'ENE'
PHRASE (12:) = 'RGY'
ALTPHR = 'POTENTIAL' // PHRASE (8:)
PRINT *, PHRASE, ALTPHR
END
```

which prints the string

```
KINETIC ENERGY   POTENTIAL ENERGY
```

As is the case with character variables, strings assigned to substring names may be truncated or padded with blanks on the right to fit the substring.

Likewise you may read and print substring names:

```
CHARACTER SCIENT * 15
READ *, SCIENT(1:7), SCIENT(8:10), SCIENT(11:)
PRINT *, SCIENT, SCIENT(11:)
END
```

Given an input record of

'ALBERT', 'EIN', 'STEIN'

the above code would print

ALBERT EINSTEIN STEIN

The intrinsic functions like LLE (see Table 8.1) are useful for manipulating CHARACTER data types. FORTRAN provides four additional functions defined in Table 8.2.

TABLE 8.2   More Intrinsic Character Functions

Function	Argument type	Function type	Definition	Example
LEN (c)	Character	Integer	Length of c	LEN('STAR') is 4
ICHAR(c)	Character*1	Integer	Relative position of c in collating sequence	ICHAR('A') is 65(ASCII)
CHAR(i)	Integer	Character*1	ith character in the collating sequence	CHAR(57) is '9' (ASCII)
INDEX(c_1,c_2)	Character	Integer	Staring location of substring c_1 in string c_2	INDEX('DEF', 'ABCDEFG') is 4

Most versions of BASIC provide similar functions. ICHAR and CHAR are the analogues of the *ord* and *chr* functions, respectively, of Pascal.

Note that the arguments for the LEN and INDEX functions may be any valid character expressions, but the length of the argument for ICHAR must be 1. Note also that INDEX computes the starting location of *the first occurrence* of substring c_1, in c_2. The value is 0 if c_1 is not in c_2.

The LEN function allows us to avoid using the declared length of a string throughout a program. We can use this function with a substring name to eliminate the awkward spacing exhibited in the second example for the // operator.

The following function, TRUNC, finds the location of the rightmost nonblank character in its string argument by scanning the string character-by-character from the right.

```
              INTEGER FUNCTION TRUNC(CSTR)
              CHARACTER *(*) CSTR, BLANK
              PARAMETER (BLANK = ' '),
              DO 10, TRUNC = LEN(CSTR), 1, -1
                  IF (CSTR(TRUNC:TRUNC) .NE. BLANK) RETURN
    10        CONTINUE
    *         TRUNC IS ZERO IF THE ENTIRE STRING IS BLANK
              END
```

Let us now rewrite the concatenation example using this function.

```
          INTEGER I
          CHARACTER TYPE(3) * 10, SCHOOL * 11, MAJOR * 22
          DATA TYPE /'NUCLEAR', 'MECHANICAL', 'CIVIL'/
          DATA SCHOOL /'ENGINEERING'/
          DO 10, I = 1, 3
              MAJOR = TYPE(I) (:TRUNC(TYPE(I))) // ' ' // SCHOOL
              PRINT *, MAJOR
    10    CONTINUE
          END
```

This example will print the following strings:

```
              NUCLEAR ENGINEERING
              MECHANICAL ENGINEERING
              CIVIL ENGINEERING
```

which is a distinct improvement over the earlier example.

Note that ICHAR and CHAR are the inverse of each other. Therefore,

```
        CHAR(ICHAR('P')) = 'P'
```

and

```
        ICHAR(CHAR(32)) = 32
```

for example.

One application for the CHAR function is to send *control characters* to output devices such as printers to control spacing, subscript printing, and so forth. Control characters have an ICHAR value less than 32 in the ASCII collating sequence. Since control characters are not generally printable, one should use the corresponding CHAR values to control devices. For example,

```
        PRINT *, CHAR(13) // CHAR(10)
```

will send a carriage return/line feed sequence to an ASCII device. We will study another example of these functions shortly.

A common operation in word-processing programs is replacing one string of characters with another. The INDEX function is useful for this purpose. The following sequence will replace *all* occurrences of the word RECTANGLE by the word SQUARE in the character-string variable PARAGR. It repeatedly concatenates the substring preceding the target word, the replacement word, and the substring following the target word. For this approach to work, PARAGR generally must be defined as large enough to hold the revised string.

```
        INTEGER L
        CHARACTER TARGET*9, REPL*6, PARAGR*1000, TEMPAR*1000
        TARGET = 'RECTANGLE'
        REPL = 'SQUARE'
        TLEN = LEN(TARGET)
        L = INDEX(TARGET, PARAGR)
*       WHILE TARGET STILL PRESENT IN PARAGRAPH DO
10      CONTINUE
        IF (L .NE. 0) THEN
            TEMPAR = PARAGR(1:L - 1) // REPL // PARAGR(L +
     $              TLEN - 1:)
            PARAGR = TEMPAR
*       RESTART SEARCH AFTER INSERTED WORD
            L = INDEX(TARGET, PARAGR(L + TLEN - 1:))
            GOTO 10
        ENDIF
*       ENDWHILE
        :
        :
```

We must use TEMPAR because PARAGR cannot be referenced on both sides of an assignment statement.

These are the only intrinsic character functions available in the current Standard. It is a small set, but you can easily augment it with your own character functions. Earlier examples illustrated the use of CHARACTER type arguments, but the function values themselves may also be of type CHARACTER. The following examples illustrate character-valued FUNCTION statements:

```
        CHARACTER * 12, FUNCTION PTYP(LIST, N)
        CHARACTER * 1, FUNCTION LET(APLHA)
        CHARACTER FUNCTION SML(X,Y) * 3, LRGE(Z) * 100
        CHARACTER *(*), FUNCTION ELEMNT(CLIST)
```

In the last example the length of ELEMNT is determined by the corresponding declaration in the program or subprogram that references ELEMNT, as in the sequence

```
CHARACTER * 12, ELEMNT
    .
    .
    .
PRINT *, ELEMNT(CFORMS)
    .
    .
    .
```

Consider the following problem. Several versions of FORTRAN compilers accept programs written in both uppercase and lowercase letters. Suppose you have written a large collection of such programs, but now you have changed jobs and must run them on a system that accepts uppercase only. You could use the following program to read your source programs as data and produce an output source program that uses only uppercase.

EXAMPLE 8.2

```
      PROGRAM LCTOUC
*************************************************************
* AUTHOR: A. WANG 5/87
*
* THIS PROGRAM READS A FILE OF TEXT ON THE STANDARD INPUT UNIT
* AND CONVERTS ALL LOWERCASE LETTERS TO UPPERCASE.  ALL OTHER
* CHARACTERS ARE UNCHANGED.  THE INPUT TEXT IS ASSUMED TO BE
* PROVIDED ON 80-CHARACTER RECORDS.
*
* INLINE -- CURRENT RECORD FROM INPUT TEXT
* OUTLIN -- FUNCTION VALUE CORRESPONDING TO INPUT RECORD
*************************************************************
      CHARACTER * 80, INLINE, OUTLIN
*     WHILE SOURCE DATA REMAINS DO
10    CONTINUE
      READ (*,*, END = 20) INLINE
         PRINT *, OUTLIN(INLINE)
         GOTO 10
20    CONTINUE
*     ENDWHILE
      END

      CHARACTER *(*) FUNCTION OUTLIN(TEXT)
*************************************************************
* THIS FUNCTION REPLACES EACH LOWERCASE LETTER IN THE ARGUMENT
* WITH THE CORRESPONDING UPPERCASE LETTER.  THE OUTPUT STRING
* MUST BE THE SAME LENGTH AS THE INPUT STRING.  THE INPUT STRING
* IS UNCHANGED
*
* TEXT -- INPUT CHARACTER STRING
* ALPHUC - ALPHABET OF UPPERCASE LETTERS
```

```
* ALPHLC -- ALPHABET OF LOWERCASE LETTERS
* L -- INDEX OF LOWERCASE LETTER IN INPUT STRING
* I -- LOOP INDEX
*******************************************************************
      INTEGER L, I
      CHARACTER *(*), TEXT
      CHARACTER * 26, ALPHUC, ALPHLC
      ALPHUC = 'ABCDEFGHIJKLMNOPQRSTUVWXYZ'
      ALPHLC = 'abcdefghijklmnopqrstuvwxyz'
      DO 10, I = 1, LEN(TEXT)
         L = INDEX(ALPHLC, TEXT(I:I))
         IF (L .GT. 0) THEN
            OUTLIN(I:I) = ALPHUC(L:L)
         ELSE
            OUTLIN(I:I) = TEXT(I:I)
         ENDIF
10    CONTINUE
      END
```

Sample input and output:

Input:
```
      program letest
**********************************************************
* This is a test program
**********************************************************
      integer UC, lc, var, i
      Character * 10 cRazY, XxX
      read *, var
      Do 10, i = 1, var
       . . .
```

Output:
```
      PROGRAM LETEST
**********************************************************
* THIS IS A TEST PROGRAM
**********************************************************
      INTEGER UC, LC, VAR, I
      CHARACTER * 10 CRAZY, XXX
      READ *, VAR
      DO 10, I = 1, VAR
       . . .
```

Exercises

Section 8.1

1. Write CHARACTER statements to define character items as follows:
   *a. INVTYP, INVPRT, and CORPL, each to have length 20.
   b. SENT, WRD, CHR to have lengths 80, 10, and 1, respectively.
   *c. PTITL = 'HYDROSTATIC PRESSURE' is a parameter. Include the PARAMETER statement for this one.
   d. TEMPMH is to be an array of 100 character elements of length 10 each.

2. What is the value of the character variable CPART in each of the following:
   *a. `CHARACTER * 5 CPART`
      ```
          :
          :
      CPART = 'SULPHURIC ACID'
      ```
   b. `CHARACTER CPART * 10`
      ```
          :
          :
          :
      CPART = 'CARBON'
      ```
   c. `CHARACTER CPART * 12, APART * 6`
      ```
      APART = 'NITRIC OXIDE'
      CPART = APART
      ```

Section 8.2

3. What values are assigned to the character variables in the following sequence, given the data that follows?
   ```
   CHARACTER * 7 ST(5)
   READ * ST(1), ST(2)
   READ *, ST(3)
   READ *, ST(4), ST(5)
       :
       :
   'MICHIGAN', 'IOWA', 'ILLINOIS'
   'CALIFORNIA', 'WASHINGTON'
   'MINNESOTA'
   'TEXAS', 'FLORIDA'
   ```

Section 8.3

4. Write the value of each of the following expressions for machines with the ASCII, EBCDIC, and CDC Scientific collating sequences (see Appendix A). If an expression is invalid, explain why.

   *a. `'X' .EQ. '2'`
   b. `'X' .EQ. 'X_'`
   c. `'_X' .LT. 'X_'`
   *d. `'PI' .LT. 'PIE'`
   e. `'H2O' .GT. 'HYDROGEN'`
   *f. `'9' .LT. 'A'`
   g. `LGT('9', 'A')`
   h. `'OXYGEN' .LT. 'OXYGEN%'`
   *i. `'OXYGEN' .LT. '%OXYGEN'`
   j. `'#PRES1' .GE. '#PRESS'`

5. The *selection sort* procedure sorts an array, A, in the following way: it searches A for the minimal element and exchanges it with A(1). The next pass finds the minimal element among the entries A(2) . . . A(n) and exchanges it with A(2). This process continues until A(n − 1) and A(n) are compared and exchanged, if necessary. Write a FORTRAN subroutine that uses the selection sort algorithm to sort an array of character strings.

6. The *binary merge sort* is an efficient sorting procedure that uses a second array as a work space. See Exercise 4.19, and revise it to work for an array of character strings.

7. Modify the subroutine PRTOUT in Example 8.1 so that it prints five compounds per line, rather than one. Be sure to account for the last few elements of the array where the total number of elements, N, is not a multiple of 5.

8. Modify the sort routines in Example 8.1 to sort a *pair* of arrays. The first is the list of chemical formulas and the second is the list of names for the corresponding chemicals. For example, perhaps CFORM(I) = 'HCL' and CNAME(I) = 'HYDROCHLORIC ACID' for some value of I. Sort the arrays in lexical order according to the formula.

Section 8.4

9. What is the value of CSTR in each of the following sequences?

```
*a. CHARACTER * 7 CSTR
    CSTR = 'ST' // 'AT' // 'IC'
 b. CHARACTER C1, C2, CSTR * 6
    C1 = 'H2S'
    C2 = 'CO4'
    CSTR = C1 // '-' // C2
*c. CHARACTER * 4 CSTR, CSTR2
    CSTR2 = 'POL'
    CSTR = CSTR2
    CSTR = CSTR // CSTR
 d. CHARACTER*3 CSTR2, CSTR*5
    CSTR2 = 'MICIN'
    CSTR = CSTR2
```

10. What is the value of the character variable B in each of the following, where B and C have a length of 8 and C has an initial value of 'ENGINEER'?

```
*a. B = C(8:8) // C(7:7) // C
 b. B = C(5:) // C(:5)
```

```
*c. B = C(8:8) // C(1:1) // C(1:2) // C(4:4) // C(3:3) // C(5:6)
 d. B(5:) = C
    B(:5) = C(3:)
*e. B(:5) = C(5:)
```

11. What is printed by each of the following segments? Assume that the ASCII character set is used. Answer the same question for EBCDIC.

    *a.
    ```
            DO 10, I = 65, 90
                PRINT *, CHAR(I), CHAR(I + 32)
       10   CONTINUE
    ```

    b.
    ```
            DO 20, I = 1, 26
                PRINT*, CHAR(ICHAR('A') + I - 1),
          $                         CHAR(ICHAR('A') + I - 31)
       20   CONTINUE
    ```

    *c.
    ```
            CHARACTER CSTR * 30
            CSTR = 'CHEMISTRY IS A REAL GAS'
            PRINT *, LEN(CSTR), INDEX('GAS', CSTR), CSTR(11:19)
    ```

    d.
    ```
            CHARACTER CNAME *18, CPRFX * 6
            CNAME = 'CHLOROFLUOROCARBON'
            CPRFX = 'FLUORO'
            PRINT *, INDEX(CNAME, CPRFX), INDEX(CPRFX, CNAME)
    ```

12. Write a FORTRAN character function whose value is the reverse of the value of the input character argument. For example, if the input string is

    'PHYSICS IS FUN!'

    then the function value should be

    !NUF SI SCISYHP

    Discard trailing blanks in the input string.

*13. Revise the program in Example 8.2 to convert only noncomments to uppercase.

14. Write a logical-valued function that performs like the LGE function for the EBCDIC collating sequence. Use the INDEX function and a string of characters in EBCDIC order.

15. Write a program that reads a FORTRAN program as character strings and count the number of occurrences of the following statement types: DO, IF, READ, PRINT, GOTO, assignment, CONTINUE, and comments. Print the original program and a table of the frequencies of occurrence.

*The solution to this exercise appears in Appendix D.

16. Write a program that reads names entered in the form

> last, first middle

and prints out the name in the form

> first middle_initial last

For example the name read as

> EHRLICH, PAUL RALPH

should be printed as

> PAUL R. EHRLICH

17. Write a program to translate Morse code strings into English and vice versa. Assume that the "characters" are separated by a single space. The Morse code alphabet is as follows:

A	·-	H	····	O	---	V	···-
B	-···	I	··	P	·--·	W	·--
C	-·-·	J	·---	Q	--·-	X	-··-
D	-··	K	-·-	R	·-·	Y	-·--
E	·	L	·-··	S	···	Z	--··
F	··-·	M	--	T	-		
G	--·	N	-·	U	··-		

18. Write a program to encipher lines of uppercase text. Using **DATA** statements, define two character strings:

a. 'ABCDEFGHIJKLMNOPQRSTUVWXYZ' (called a *plain* sequence)
b. 'NDXTYPQARTSMOW IUKZEJAVCDFG' (called a *cipher* sequence)

Use any permutation of the letters in string that you like.

    The program should read in a line of text, replace each letter in the text by the corresponding letter in the cipher sequence (e.g., replace a blank space by N, A by D, B by X, and so forth), and then print out the resulting cipher string along with the original string. To verify that the program works correctly, it should also *decipher* the cipher string by applying the above two character strings in reverse (i.e., replace N by a blank space, D by A, and so forth). This kind of enciphering algorithm is called a *substitution cipher*.

*19. Do Exercise 18, but simply use the normal alphabetic sequence shifted left or right *n* places for the cipher sequence. For example, for *n* = 3, the cipher sequence is 'DEFGHIJKLMNOPQRSTUVWXYZ ABC'

20. Write a program that reads lines of text and computes the frequencies of various word lengths. Store the frequency counts in an array, WORD. WORD(1) contains the count of words of length 1, WORD(2) is the count for words of length 2, and so forth. Assume no words are longer than 25 characters.

21. Modify the Shell sort routines in Example 8.1 so that TEMPST is a local variable in SWITCH. SWITCH should then return an error flag if the input strings are longer than TEMPST, which has a length of 15, say. The sort should be terminated with an error message.

9 Input and Output Control

Up to now we have used list-directed READ and PRINT statements to make data available to a program and to display the results. These statements are easy to use and have been sufficient for the problems we have met so far. However, their usage is limited for some applications because they offer *little control* over the source and organization of the input data and the destination and appearance of the output. You might, for example, want to specify the number of decimal places in a real number displayed on the output line, the placement of a column of numbers, or the reading of data from a source other than the standard input unit.

The full Standard input/output capabilities of FORTRAN will enable you to solve these problems and to deal with other input and output issues in a sophisticated way. Although output formatting capabilities are available in BASIC through the PRINT USING statement and in Pascal through *format* specifiers, FORTRAN's input and output formatting capabilities are much more powerful.

This chapter is loaded with necessary but—frankly—uninteresting details. A suggestion for a first reading is to study Sections 9.1, 9.2, and 9.6 carefully and skim the others. This study should give you a sufficient understanding of the basics of formatting. You can then look up the necessary details later to handle a specific problem.

9.1 INPUT/OUTPUT STATEMENTS AND THE CONTROL INFORMATION LIST

In this section we will describe another form of output statement, the *WRITE statement*, and the complete *control information list* that is part of all input/output statements in FORTRAN. This list specifies information such as the unit from which input data is to be read, the statement that describes the appearance of an output record, or the place to begin execution when the end of the input data stream has been detected.

Actually, you have already seen limited forms of the control information list. The asterisk for list-directed I/O is a special case; the specification (*,*, END = 100) is another.

There are many options, and rather than providing an exhaustive set of examples to go with the formal syntax diagrams, we will show only a few cases at this point to give you a sense of what can be specified. We will present examples of the rest of the options later.

I/O Statements   We can now give a complete definition of each of the *FORTRAN I/O statements*. Like the PRINT statement, the WRITE statement prints data, but it also has more capabilities. Earlier versions of FORTRAN used *only* the WRITE statement; the PRINT statement was introduced as part of the FORTRAN 77 standard.

> ***Examples:***
>
> ```
> READ (*,*, END = 100) (X(T), Y(T), Z(T), T = 1, N)
> WRITE (6, 500, ERR = 999) NAME, SSN, ADDR
> PRINT 50, NITER, ERRCDE, EPS, ROOT
> READ (UNIT = 5, FMT = 200, END = 500, ERR = 100)
> $                        (SDAT(I), I = 1, NPTS)
> ```

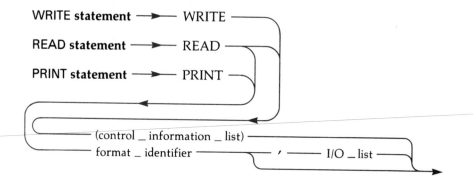

> ***Remarks:***
>
> 1. The I/O_list is the list of items to be read or printed and is the same as the I/O_list for list-directed output.
> 2. The format identifier, which is underlined for emphasis in the above examples, is usually either an asterisk, which means that the I/O is list-directed, or a statement number that labels a *FORMAT statement*. The FORMAT statement, discussed in the next section, specifies the layout of the input or output data. Other options for the format identifier are also covered in the next section. If the optional phrase FMT = is omitted, then the format specifier *must* be the *second* item in the control information list, and the first item *must* be the *unit specifier* (defined below), *without* the optional phrase UNIT =, as shown in the first two examples.
> 3. Note that the READ and PRINT statements may optionally specify only the format identifier, as illustrated by the third example. In this case the standard input/output units are used.

In addition to allowing I/O statements to specify the format of the data, the control information list also provides for handling end-of-data and error conditions, and alternates to the standard units for data input and output. Examples are given above as part of the I/O statements. The list is defined formally by the following syntax diagram.

Control Information List

control information list

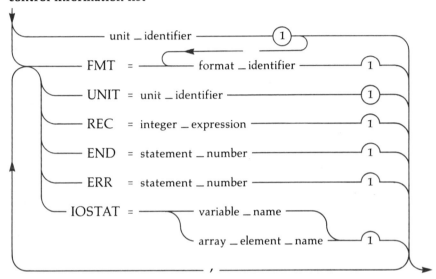

Remarks:

1. The list must contain *exactly one unit identifier*. The unit identifier specifies the unit (e.g., a specific terminal or a tape drive) from which data will be read or to which it will be written. It must be of type INTEGER or CHARACTER, or it must be an asterisk, which implies the standard input/output unit. Observe that the PRINT statement can write data only to the standard output unit. This item is related to file I/O and will be explained further in the next chapter.

2. The REC specifier is used for *direct-access file* input and will also be covered in the next chapter.

3. The END specifier must not appear in a WRITE statement.

4. The ERR specifier works as follows: If an I/O statement causes an error (e.g., when a READ statement attempts to read a character string into an integer variable) the I/O statement is terminated, and execution continues with the statement labeled by the statement number in the ERR clause.

5. The IOSTAT specifier allows the operating system to provide status information regarding the I/O operation. The variable in the IOSTAT clause is set to 0 if there is neither an error nor an end-of-data condition. The Standard does not specify values for the IOSTAT variable for other conditions. They are dependent on the particular processor being used. One FORTRAN implementation sets the variable to the system error number corresponding to the type of error, for example:

4543	Illegal character encountered on input
4545	Exponential overflow during input
4558	Subscript out of range

One could use such values to write a detailed and exhaustive error-handling routine, although it would have limited transportability.

We have already used the END specifier, and we are postponing discussions of the REC specifier and formats until later.

Regarding control over error- and status-checking, the combination of the ERR and IOSTAT specifiers gives you some flexibility. For most cases it is sufficient to detect an error and then either terminate the program in a controlled way, or, if the I/O is done in a subprogram, pass the status code as an argument back to the calling program. A relatively simple technique is to have the ERR code print out the value of the IOSTAT variable, allowing the user to look up the error in a manual or on a terminal with a help facility. The following skeleton is an illustration of this approach.

```
      INTEGER STATUS, N, I
         .
         .
      READ(*,*, END = 200, ERR = 900, IOSTAT = STATUS)N,
     $         (X(I), I = 1, N)
         .
         .
900   PRINT *, '*** ERROR 900 *** STATUS CODE:', STATUS
         .
         .
```

Using this scheme to the limit, each I/O statement with a potential error would require its own error message that would uniquely identify it. The preceding example uses the statement number as the identifier.

9.2 AN INTRODUCTION TO FORMATTED OUTPUT

Formatting, or controlling the layout of the input and output data, is an absolute necessity in data processing applications that print large volumes of reports and special forms, such as paychecks. On the other hand, it is usually not required for scientific or engineering applications, although many such applications benefit by improved readability of the output data or by efficient, compact representation of the input data. In other languages, formatting is sometimes described as *editing*.

FORMAT Statement

The format is usually specified in the *FORMAT statement* referenced by the corresponding I/O statement. The FORMAT statement is essentially a list of format codes, called *edit descriptors*, each usually corresponding to a value to be read or printed. There is a rich variety of edit descriptors, but the structure of the FORMAT statement itself is simple. The following examples illustrate some typical cases for output; other variations will be described later. Formatted output is generally of more interest than formatted input and is therefore presented first. We will cover the formatting of input data in another section. Bear in mind that the formatting of output values does not change the corresponding variables in memory; it only affects the way their values are displayed.

Examples: Let N = −157 (integer), R = 10.6666 (real) and C = 'ABCDEFGH' (character with a declared length of 8); A(1) = 1, A(2) = 2, A(3) = 3 (integer array). The output is shown following each PRINT/WRITE-FORMAT pair. An underscore (_) indicates a blank space.

```
          PRINT 100, N, R
100       FORMAT (' ', I5, 3X, F6.2 )

          _-157____10.67

          PRINT '(1X, I2, 4X, E12.5)', N, R
          **_____0.10667E+02

          WRITE (*, 150) (A(I), I = 1, 3)
150       FORMAT (' ', I2)

          _1
          _2
          _3

          WRITE (*, 200) C, N
200       FORMAT (' ', A, 2X, 'N IS', I5)

          ABCDEFGH__N_IS__-157

          PRINT 250
250       FORMAT ('1', 'TEMPERATURE', 5X, 'VELOCITY')

          TEMPERATURE_____VELOCITY
```

FORMAT statement

→— FORMAT (format _ specification _ list) ————————————→

Remarks:

1. Nonexecutable—therefore FORMAT statements may be placed anywhere in the body of a program unit (i.e., main program or subprogram). The usual conventions are to place them all at the end of the program, the beginning of the program, or immediately following their associated I/O statements. We will use the latter convention.

2. The format specification list is the list of edit descriptors. The structure of this list will be illustrated throughout the rest of this chapter and is described by the remaining remarks. Note that an empty list implies that a blank output line will be written or that an input record will be skipped.

3. Each variable in the I/O list must be associated with an edit descriptor of the proper type. Thus the order of these descriptors in the list must match their order in the variable list. These descriptors are called *repeatable*, for reasons to be made clear later. However, some of the descriptors, such as those that control spacing, are not associated with any variables; they are referred to as *nonrepeatable*.

4. The input/output line can be thought of as a sequence of *fields*, which are consecutive sequences of columns. Most of the edit descriptors specify, among other things, the size of the field. Thus the I5 descriptor in the first example specifies an integer field of 5 characters.

5. Realize that the edit descriptors—not the FORMAT statement itself—are required for data layout specifications. In the second example, the format identifier is a character string in the first position in the PRINT list and therefore functions as the format specification.

6. Generally the first descriptor in the FORMAT statement may be used to control vertical spacing, especially if output is to a printer. For example, a descriptor ' ' will result in single-spaced output, whereas '1' may force the data to be printed at the top of the next page.

In the first example, the descriptor I5 corresponds to the variable N. Since the value of N happens to require only four spaces, it is *right-justified* in the field. The descriptor 3X inserts a field of three blank spaces after the I5 field. The floating-point descriptor F6.2 displays the value of R in a field of six spaces, including the decimal point, and *rounded* to two digits to the right of the decimal point.

In the second example, the format specification is contained in the PRINT statement, which is explained further in a later section. Asterisks are displayed in the output field because the specified field size (2) is too small to hold the current value of N. The displayed character is system-dependent. This time the value of R is displayed in exponential form, using the descriptor E12.5. The value 12 is the field width, and the value 5 specifies the number of digits. The mantissa is normalized to between 0.1 and 1.0.

In the third example there are three variables in the I/O list but only one repeatable descriptor (I2). In this case the list is reused, resulting in one number per line.

In the fourth example, the character variable C is handled by the edit descriptor A. Since no size is specified, the size of the field is determined by the length of the character string being written (8 here). Note that any character string in the list (except for vertical spacing control) is printed as is.

The last example illustrates how column headers, page titles, and other character constants can be displayed. The character strings to be printed are enclosed in single quotes. They are printed in the output record according to their placement in the format specification list. Note that the I/O list is empty in this example.

You have seen enough formatting at this point so that a complete but simple example should be meaningful. The following program computes and prints a table of sines and cosines for an angle between 0 and $\pi/2$ radians (0° to 90°). The values are displayed to three decimal places.

EXAMPLE 9.1

```
      PROGRAM SICOTB
****************************************************************
* THIS PROGRAM PRINTS A TABLE OF SINES AND COSINES FOR AN ANGLE
* BETWEEN 0 AND PI/2 RADIANS.
*
* INCR -- THE INCREMENT BETWEEN SUCCESSIVE ANGLES (PARAMETER)
* PI -- 3.14159 ... (PARAMETER)
* THETA -- THE ANGLE IN RADIANS
* DEGR -- THE ANGLE IN DEGREES
* DCONV -- 180 / PI (PARAMETER)
* NTABE -- THE NUMBER OF TABLE ENTRIES -1
* I -- LOOP INDEX
****************************************************************
      INTEGER NTABE, I
      REAL THETA, DEGR, PI, INCR
      PARAMETER(PI = 3.1415926, INCR = 0.01, DCONV = 180.0 / PI)
      NTABE = INT((PI / 2) / INCR)
      WRITE (8,100)
100   FORMAT ('1', 25X, 'TABLE OF SINES AND COSINES')
      WRITE (*, 200)
```

```
200     FORMAT('0', 15X, 'RADIANS', 6X, 'DEGREES', 9X, 'SINE', 10X,
        $    'COSINE')
        DO 10, I = 0, NTABE
            THETA = INCR * REAL(I)
            DEGR = THETA * DCONV
            WRITE (*, 300) THETA, DEGR, SIN(THETA), COS(THETA)
300         FORMAT (' ', 12X, E10.3, 3X, E10.3, 5X, E10.3, 5X, E10.3)
10      CONTINUE
*
*       PRINT LAST LINE OF TABLE
*
        WRITE (*, 300) PI / 2, 90.0, 1.0, 0.0
        END
```

Sample output:

```
            TABLE OF SINES AND COSINES

        RADIANS        DEGREES          SINE          COSINE
        0.000E+01      0.000E+01      0.000E+01      0.100E+01
        0.100E-01      0.573E+00      0.100E-01      0.100E+01
        0.200E-01      0.115E+01      0.200E-01      0.100E+01
          . . .          . . .          . . .          . . .
        0.156E+01      0.894E+02      0.100E+01      0.108E-01
        0.157E+01      0.900E+02      0.100E+01      0.796E-03
        0.157E+01      0.900E+02      0.100E+01      0.000E+01
```

The format of the four columns of data is due to the FORMAT statement labeled 300. It would be easy to alter the program to include more, or fewer, digits of accuracy. Note that this FORMAT statement is referenced by *two different* WRITE statements. It used to be a common practice to have I/O statements share FORMAT statements, but this is not generally recommended unless the sharing I/O statements are closely related, as in this example. Otherwise errors may be introduced if one of the I/O statements must be modified at a later time.

9.3 REPEATABLE EDIT DESCRIPTORS (OUTPUT)

The next task is to describe the repeatable edit descriptors in detail. In this and the next section we continue to describe the effects of these descriptors in the context of output, because you are more likely to require formatting for output than for input.

There are two forms of the integer edit descriptor: Iw and Iw.m where w is the field width and m is the minimum number of digits that will be displayed on output. Obviously it is required that $m \leq w$. For example, Table 9.1 shows the output, given the value of the integer variable N in

```
        WRITE (*, 100) N
100 FORMAT (' ', I6)
```

and in

```
        WRITE (*, 200) N
200 FORMAT (' ', I6.4)
```

An underscore (_) indicates a blank space.

TABLE 9.1   Integer Edit Descriptors

Value of N	Output using I6	Output using I6.4
164	___164	__0164
-57	____-57	__0057
27123	_27123	_27123
-91286	-91268	-91286
0	_____0	__0000
-123456	******	******

Note that leading 0s are added, if necessary, in the case of I6.4 to make the result four digits long. Also, the special case where the value of the variable is 0 and $m = 0$ (e.g., as in I6.0) will yield an output field consisting of only blanks.

Regarding errors, if the value of the variable is too large to fit in the specified field, asterisks are displayed in the field. If an I edit descriptor is applied to noninteger data, a run-time error will result, but it can be trapped using the ERR specifier.

There are essentially two ways to edit real or double-precision numbers, corresponding to whether or not exponential representation is preferred. The F edit descriptor, of the form Fw.d, indicates that the field width is w and that the fractional part of the number consists of d digits; no exponent is displayed. Note that the width should include one space for the decimal point and another for the sign.

Table 9.2 illustrates the output resulting from the execution of the following PRINT statements, where X is real or double-precision:

```
        PRINT 150, X
150     FORMAT (' ', F7.2)

        PRINT 160, X
160     FORMAT (' ', F7.0)
```

TABLE 9.2   The F Edit Descriptor

Value of X	Output using F7.2	Output using F7.0
127.6	_127.60	____128.
1972.5283	1972.53	__1973.
-905.0	-905.00	__-905.
0.005	____0.0	_____0.
0.06823	____0.07	_____0.
0.175E+2	__17.50	_____18.
0.175D+2	__17.50	_____18.
123456.1	*******	123456.
-123456.78	*******	*******
5.0E+5	*******	500000.

From these examples it is evident that the result is rounded to the number of specified digits on output. Also, real and double-precision numbers are displayed in the same way.

Again, a field of asterisks results if the number, including its sign, decimal point, and d digits of the fraction, is too large to fit in the field. In general, then, if k is the number of digits in the integral portion of the number, you should be sure that

$$w \geq k + d + 2$$

The number 2 is for the sign and decimal point. Clearly, you should therefore be sure that w is large enough to handle *all* values of the corresponding variable that are generated for output during the execution of the program.

If exponential notation is desired, then the E or D edit descriptor should be used. This form is appropriate when the values to be displayed vary greatly in magnitude. Both E and D may be used interchangeably for editing either real or double-precision numbers, but generally you should use E for real numbers and D for double-precision to make your output consistent and clear. These descriptors have the forms Ew.d, Dw.d, and Ew.dEe where w is the field width and d is the number of digits in the fraction. The third form allows for a display of the exponent in e digits rather than the default two; there is no such form for the D descriptor.

Table 9.3 illustrates the use of the E descriptor, given the following output statements:

```
         PRINT 300, X
    300  FORMAT (' ', E10.3)
```

and

```
            PRINT 350, X
     350    FORMAT (' ', E10.3E3)
```

TABLE 9.3   The E Edit Descriptors

Value of X	Output using E10.3	Output using E10.3E3
7537.0	_0.754E+04	0.754E+004
0.0004193	_0.419E-03	0.419E-003
349.6E17	_0.350E+20	0.350E+020
349.6D17	_0.350E+20	0.350E+020
-5.0	-0.500E+01	**********
-2500000.0	-0.250E+07	**********

In general the digits are normalized to a value between 1.0 and 0.1 on most systems, and a leading digit is always displayed. The last two examples show that the value of w is too small to account for negative numbers. For the Ew.d or Dw.d descriptor, you should choose w so that

$$w \geq d + 7$$

and for the Ew.dEe descriptor you should have

$$w \geq d + 5 + e$$

to account for the sign, leading 0, decimal point, and so forth.

A third edit descriptor is available to edit reals and the like: the G descriptor, like the E descriptor, has the forms Gw.d and Gw.dEe. The form of the corresponding output value will vary according to its magnitude. For example, if its magnitude is less than 0.1 or greater than or equal to 10^d, it will be displayed in E format. The position of the decimal point also varies with the magnitude, and blank spaces are added at the right end of the field. Basically, it prints in F format if the number will fit in the field; otherwise it will print in E format. Because it is rarely used, we do not present any detail here.

Finally, we should note that complex numbers, which consist of pairs of separate real numbers, are edited by two successively interpreted F, E, D, or G edit descriptors. The two descriptors may be different, and nonrepeatable edit descriptors may appear between them, as in the following example. Let X be complex and equal to (127.6, −34125.0E4). Then

```
            PRINT 100, X
     100    FORMAT (' ', '(', F7.2, ',', E11.3, ')')
```

would produce the following output (_ indicates a blank space):

$$(\_127.60,\_-0.341E+09)$$

Note that the printing of the enclosing parentheses and separating comma is the user's responsibility.

Character-String Editing

Two forms of a descriptor are available for editing output: A and Aw, where w is the field width. For the first form the number of characters in the field is the length of the corresponding data item.

Table 9.4 illustrates the use of the A descriptor for the following cases:

```
          PRINT 100, ALPHA
100       FORMAT (' ', A5)
```

and

```
          PRINT 200, ALPHA
200       FORMAT (' ', A)
```

where it is assumed that the defined length of ALPHA is the same as the length of the character string shown in each case. The underscore character indicates a blank space in the field.

TABLE 9.4 The A Edit Descriptor

Value of ALPHA	Length of ALPHA	Output (A5)	Output (A)
'ABCDE'	5	ABCDE	ABCDE
'ABC'	3	ABC__	ABC
'ABCDEFG'	7	ABCDE	ABCDEFG

Just as in other character-string operations, if the specified field width is too small, the output string is truncated on the right. If it is larger than the length of the string, the field is padded with blanks. Clearly, the A version is generally more convenient.

Editing Logical Values

Logical values may be written using the L edit descriptor, of the form Lw, where w is the field width. The output value is represented by a letter T or F, right-justified in the field. Thus, the sequence

```
          LOGICAL ALPHA, OMEGA
          ALPHA = .FALSE.
          OMEGA = .TRUE.
          WRITE (*, 300) ALPHA, OMEGA
300       FORMAT (' ', L3, 2X, L5)
          END
```

would produce

$$\text{\_\_F_____T}$$

(␣ marks a blank space).

The edit descriptors in this section are called *repeatable* because you may precede any of them with an optional, nonzero, unsigned, integer constant called a *repeat specification* (or *repeat factor*) that represents the number of repetitions. The general form is then *r f*, where *f* is a format specification, and *r* is the repeat factor, as in 2I3. For example, the FORMAT statement

```
150      FORMAT (' ', I6, I6, I6, I6)
```

is equivalent to

```
150      FORMAT (' ', 4I6)
                        ↑
                        └── repeat factor
```

Note that a whole group of edit descriptors may be repeated by enclosing it in parentheses and preceding it with a repeat specification. The group may include nonrepeatable edit descriptors, such as 2X, as in the following example. The FORMAT statement

```
50   FORMAT(' ',F6.1, 2X, I2, F6.1, 2X, I2, F6.1, 2X, I2, E10.1)
```

can be written more economically in the form

```
50       FORMAT (' ', 3(F6.1, 2X, I2), E10.1)
```

The following example would print a line of 30 question marks:

```
         PRINT 400
400      FORMAT (' ', 30('?'))
```

The parentheses around the '?' are necessary because character strings in quotes are classified as nonrepeatable.

9.4 NONREPEATABLE EDIT DESCRIPTORS (OUTPUT)

The nonrepeatable edit descriptors do not correspond to data to be read or displayed. Instead they control such factors as vertical spacing on output or the spacing and placement of the fields in the input or output record.

Character Constants

To review, any character string appearing in the FORMAT statement (except for the descriptor used for vertical spacing, to be described next) is printed as is. Thus, if N = 27, then

```
          PRINT 200, N
   200    FORMAT (' ', 'THE CLASS SIZE IS: ', I2)
```

would print

```
          THE CLASS SIZE IS: 27
```

Earlier versions of FORTRAN used the H (Hollerith)* edit descriptor to display character strings.

The general form of the Hollerith specification is

$$wHxxxx \ldots x$$

$$\underbrace{\qquad\qquad}_{w \text{ characters}}$$

where w is an integer specifying the length of the character string following the H. For example,

```
          10HFREQUENCY=
          1H0
          14HTABLE OF SINES
```

are all Hollerith fields. They are equivalent to

```
          'FREQUENCY='
          '0'
          'TABLE OF SINES'
```

respectively. The Hollerith form is available in FORTRAN 77, but it is awkward to use because the length w must be precisely specified. Always use the quoted form instead.

Vertical Spacing

The *carriage control character* is the first edit descriptor in the list and controls the vertical spacing of the output record. Although it is not part of the formal standard, carriage control is available on most systems, and because of its usefulness, it is covered here. On most systems it is required for output and is not used for input. Table 9.5 defines the actions of the various control characters.

The plus ('+') character is used for complex overprinting applications such as computer-generated maps or pictures that are displayed on a character-oriented printer. The idea is to provide graphics capability on a nongraphic device.

It is important that you include a carriage control specification in

*Named for Herman Hollerith, the inventor of the punched card.

TABLE 9.5 Carriage Control

Carriage Control Character	Action
' '	Single space *before* printing the line
'0'	Double space *before* printing the line
'1'	Skip to the top of the next page *before* printing the line
'+'	Do not space before printing (overprint)
other	System-dependent action (not standard)

your format—otherwise *the first character* in your output line will be used for this purpose. For example, if N = 12345, the sequence

```
            PRINT 200, N
     200    FORMAT (I5)
```

would display 2345 at the top of the page. The first digit, 1, was used to control spacing and does not print. Likewise if S = 'TNT', the effect of

```
            PRINT 500, S
     500    FORMAT (A)
```

is unpredictable. The letter *T* would be used for carriage control, and only the substring 'NT' would be printed.

You should also realize that the effect of the carriage control character on the particular output device is system-dependent. A carriage control character of '1' may clear the screen on one terminal; on another it may be ignored. Some printers will also ignore the character.

You can also force the output unit to skip to a new line with the *slash (/) edit descriptor*. Each slash encountered in the format causes a skip to the beginning of the next line. This is one way that a single PRINT or WRITE statement can produce more than one line of output. The use of the slash is illustrated by the following examples.

Let X = 538.2 and Y = 79.5

```
            PRINT 300, X,Y
     300    FORMAT (1X, F5.1 / 1X, F5.1)
```

output:
```
                538.2
                 79.5
```

```
            PRINT 400, X, Y
     400    FORMAT (1X, F5.1 //// 1X, F5.1)
```

output: 538.2

                                                                      ⎫
                                                                      ⎬ Three blank lines
                                                                      ⎭

                                                  79.5

```
     WRITE (*, 500) X
500  FORMAT(1X,'THE INDEPENDENT VARIABLE IS:' / '0', F5.1)
```

output: THE INDEPENDENT VARIABLE IS:

                   538.2

Horizontal Spacing

As you have seen in earlier examples, the *X edit descriptor* is used to move the next field to the right the specified number of spaces. Its form is nX, where n is the number of spaces to skip. Therefore, if N = 123,

```
          WRITE (*, 120) N
120       FORMAT (' ', 20X, I3)
```

would print a field of 20 blank spaces, followed by the value of N starting in column 21. Note that the X descriptor field is sometimes used for carriage control. Thus the FORMAT statement

```
120     FORMAT (1X, 20X, I3)
```

would produce the same result. So would the FORMAT statement

```
120     FORMAT (21X, I3)
```

The author prefers the former version because it explicitly exhibits the carriage control character.

The *T edit descriptor* is also used for horizontal spacing, but it *tabs* to a given column, rather than skipping spaces like the X descriptor. There are three versions:

1. Tc means to tab *to* column c (c is an integer constant) on the output unit. Thus the next field will start *in* column c (not to the right of column c).
2. TRc means to tab *to the right of the current position c columns.*
3. TLc means to tab *to the left of the current position c columns.*

In no case may the value of c define the next column position to be beyond the range of the record. Note that column 1 of a page is actually located at position T2 because of the carriage control character.

For example, then, if N = 925, and R = 34.62,

```
          PRINT 150, N, R
150       FORMAT (' ', T6, I3, T11, F5.2)
```

would print (‿ means a blank space)

```
‿‿‿‿925‿‿34.62
```

and

```
            PRINT 250, N, R
   250      FORMAT (' ', T6, I3, TR10, F5.2)
```

would print

```
‿‿‿‿925‿‿‿‿‿‿‿‿‿34.62
```

and

```
            PRINT 350, N, R
   350      FORMAT (1X, T11, I3, TL10, F5.2)
```

would print

```
   ‿‿34.62‿‿925
```

Note in the first example that the value of N starts *in* column 5 (tab position 6), not after column 5. Also, as the third example shows, it is possible to display the data in an order different from that of the output list, but this is not recommended.

The T descriptor is most useful for printing column and page headings since you don't need to count spaces between them. For example,

```
      PRINT 500
 500  FORMAT ('1', T11, 'FAHRENHEIT', T31, 'CELSIUS')
```

would print the headings FAHRENHEIT and CELSIUS starting in columns 10 and 30, respectively.

Sign Control

Sometimes users prefer to have plus signs explicitly displayed on output. The S, SS, and SP descriptors control the display of the plus sign and apply to the I, F, E, D, and G descriptors. Note that once an S, SS, or SP descriptor is specified, it applies to all of the numeric descriptors that follow, unless another sign control descriptor is encountered.

S and SS are identical; they indicate that leading plus signs are to print as blanks. SP causes leading plus signs to print. Be sure to make the field width large enough to include the sign.

If N = 346 and R = 74.35E2, then

```
            PRINT 200, N, R
   200      FORMAT (1X, SP, I4, 2X, E11.4)
```

would print

```
   +346‿‿+0.7435E+04
```

Scale Factors

Similar to the S descriptor, the *scale factor edit descriptor*, P, applies to all subsequent E, D, and G descriptors in the FORMAT until another is encountered. In some systems it also applies to F, but this is not part of the Standard. Its form is kP, where k is a *signed* integer constant. With kP in effect, each output fraction is multiplied by 10^k, and the exponent is reduced by k. Thus, for example, if X = 0.98765E5, then

```
         PRINT 100, X
100      FORMAT (' ', 2P, E12.5)
```

{alternatively written (' ', 2PE12.5)}

would print

```
98.76500E+03
```

The effect, then, is to change the normalization.

9.5 FORMATTED INPUT

In this section we describe briefly how the various edit descriptors apply to input records. Formatting is applied to input records primarily to save space. Numbers and other data can be packed into adjacent fields without intervening spaces. Decimal points can be omitted from real data. The disadvantage is that you must be very careful to place the data elements correctly in their fields, which occupy fixed columns in the input record, since the FORMAT sequence is really a description of the placement and type of data in the record.

For example, given the statements

```
         READ (*, 200) COUNT, FORM, DENS
200      FORMAT (I4, 2X, A3, F5.1)
```

and the input record (_ means a blank)

```
            _ _ 7 9 _ _ H C L 4 9 1 . 4
column   1 2 3 4 5 6 7 8 9 1 1 1 1 1
                           0 1 2 3 4
```

the following assignments would be made: COUNT = 79, FORM = 'HCL' and DENS = 491.4. Changing the locations of the data elements in the record would most likely result in different values. If the input record were instead

```
            _ _ _ 7 9 _ H C L _ _ 4 9 1 . 4
column   1 2 3 4 5 6 7 8 9 1 1 1 1 1 1 1
                           0 1 2 3 4 5 6
```

then the result would be COUNT = 7, FORM = 'HCL', and DENS = 49.1.

On input, blanks in a numeric field are normally treated as 0s. **Numeric Input**
Therefore integers *must* be right-justified in the field—otherwise the
trailing blanks would be evaluated as 0s and the number would, in
effect, be multiplied by the corresponding power of 10. The integer 45
left-justified in an I4 input field would yield a value of 4500. Also, on
input the descriptors Iw and Iw.d are equivalent.

Note, however, that some compilers normally *ignore* blanks in
numeric input fields, which is in disagreement with standard FORTRAN.
In any case, you may change the default by using the BN or BZ format
specifiers (see below) or the BLANK specifier in the OPEN statement
(Chapter 10).

You will have more flexibility with F, E, D, and G editing. A decimal
point in the input field overrides the edit descriptor specification. For an
Fw.d descriptor, if the decimal point is absent from the number, the
rightmost *d* digits are interpreted as the fraction. The value may have an
optional exponent of the form S*i*, E*i*, or D*i*, where S*i* is a signed integer
and *i* is an integer with or without a sign.

Table 9.6 contains illustrations of edited numeric input, assuming a
READ statement of the form:

```
         READ 550, X
550      FORMAT (f)
```

where X is either an integer or real variable corresponding to the given
edit descriptor *f*.

TABLE 9.6 Editing Numeric Input

Input field	Edit descriptor	Result
columns 1234567890		
127	I10	127
42___	I10	42000
-51	I10	-51
523.0__	F10.2	523.0
- 1493	F10.2	-14.93
5___	F10.2	50.00
357	F10.5	0.00357
-1.9E02	F10.3	-1.9E+02
24364	E10.3	24.364
276E-01	F10.3	.0276
625.0+3	E10.3	625000.0
625+2_	F10.3	625E+20

It should be clear from Table 9.6 that there are many ways to
represent a number in an input field, and that the result actually read

can vary accordingly. To avoid potential input errors, be sure to adhere to these guidelines:

1. Be sure you know where the boundaries of the input fields are.
2. If space is not severely constrained, use a decimal point in the real number input data.
3. Always right-justify integers and real numbers without decimal points. Note that any exponent must be right-justified since it is an integer.

Character-String Input

Both the A and Aw forms may be used to edit input character strings. Let l be the length of the corresponding character variable. If A is used, the length assumed for the input field is equal to l.

Note that the effect of the Aw form is different for input than for output: if the specified field width w is greater than l, only the *rightmost l* characters will be assigned. If $w < l$ then the value is padded on the right with $l - w$ blanks, just as on output. Table 9.7 shows a few examples, given the input statement

```
        READ 250, BETA
250     FORMAT (f)
```

where f is the edit descriptor, and BETA has a length of 5.

TABLE 9.7 Editing Character Input

Input field	Edit descriptor	Result stored in BETA
columns 1 2 3 4 5 6 7		
ABCDEFG	A	ABCDE
ABCDEFG	A5	ABCDE
ABCDEFG	A3	ABC__
ABCDEFG	A7	CDEFG

Logical Data Input

The stored result will be .TRUE. if the first nonblank character string encountered in the field starts with a T or .T (therefore .TRUE. is a valid logical input value). Likewise, the result is .FALSE. if F or .F is encountered.

Nonrepeatable Input Edit Descriptors

The slash (/) descriptor causes the remaining portion of the current record to be skipped, and the next data element, if any, is read starting at the beginning of the next record. For example, the sequence

```
        READ 300, I, J, K
300     FORMAT (I2 / I2 / I2)
```

would read 3 records, assigning the numbers in the first 2 columns of each one to I, J, and K respectively.

Horizontal spacing using the X, T, TL, and TR descriptors works essentially the same way for output and input. However, on input the T descriptor allows parts of the record to be processed more than once, possibly with different editing. If the following example

```
        READ (*, 500) A, B, C
   500  FORMAT (F5.2, T1, F6.1, T1, F6.4)
```

is applied to the input data

```
              col. 1
              ↓
              123456
```

the result will be that A = 123.45, B = 12345.6, and C = 12.3456.

For scaling of the form kP applied to F, E, D, or G descriptors, the variable will be equal to 10^{-k} times the input value if it has no exponent. There is no effect if the input item includes an exponent. Thus, if

```
        READ 200, A, B
   200  FORMAT (2PE6.2, F4.1)
```

reads the input data

```
        2.51E273.6
```

then A = 2.51E+02, and B = 0.736.

The S descriptors are ignored for input. However, the BN and BZ descriptors apply *only* to input. Normally, blanks in a numeric input field are interpreted as 0s, but if BN is encountered in an input format sequence, then in all succeeding numeric fields blanks will *not* be interpreted as 0s. BZ, in a like manner, causes blanks to be 0s. Therefore, if the digit 5 is in column 1 of an input record, then

```
        READ 100, L
   100  FORMAT (I3)
```

would assign 500 to L, but

```
        READ 200, M
   200  FORMAT (BN, I3)
```

would assign 5 to M.
Like the S and P descriptors, BN and BZ apply to all subsequent relevant descriptors until another BN or BZ is encountered. Thus, you can temporarily turn on an option, as in the following example. Apply the sequence

```
        READ 700, N1, N2, N3
   700  FORMAT (BN, I3, BZ, 2I3)
```

to the record

```
        _1_2___3_
```

Then N1 = 1, N2 = 200, and N3 = 30.

9.6 INTERACTION BETWEEN THE FORMAT AND THE INPUT/OUTPUT LIST

So far we have assumed that the number of repeatable edit descriptors (counting those implied by the repeat factors) is equal to the number of items in the input/output list. This need not be the case.

If there are *fewer* items in the I/O list than there are repeatable edit descriptors, then the extra repeatable descriptors are ignored. However, any nonrepeatable descriptors that are placed in the format list between the last-used repeatable descriptor and the first unused repeatable descriptor are processed as usual.

Let N = 502, R = 312.57, and SUM = 1295.5 in the following examples.

```
          PRINT 150, R
    150   FORMAT (' ', F7.2, 5X, I5)
```

will display 312.57. The I5 descriptor is ignored.

```
          PRINT 300, SUM
    300   FORMAT (1X, 'THE SUM IS', F7.1 / 1X, 'THE AVERAGE IS ',
      $              F6.1 / 1X, 'END OF REPORT')
```

will print

```
          THE SUM IS 1295.5
          THE AVERAGE IS
```

To prevent unwanted trailing character strings such as "THE AVERAGE IS" from printing after the last item in the output list, place a *colon* (:), which is the only nonrepeatable edit descriptor we haven't yet mentioned, immediately preceding the unwanted strings in the format sequence. The colon terminates all further format control if there are no more items in the output list. Thus the revised example

```
          PRINT 300, SUM
    300   FORMAT (1X, 'THE SUM IS ', F7.1 ,: / 1X,
      $'THE AVERAGE IS ', F6.1 / 1X, 'END OF REPORT')
```

will print

```
          THE SUM IS 1295.5
```

Now if there are *more* items in the I/O list than there are repeatable edit descriptors, then the sequence of format specifications, or a subsequence of them, will be reused according to the following rules:

1. A new record is read or printed.

2. If there are no parenthesized groups of edit descriptors, the format specifications are reused from the beginning.

3. If there are one or more parenthesized groups of edit descriptors, the format specifications are reused from the *rightmost* group, including the repeat factor, if any, to the right end of the specification sequence.

4. Repetition of the sequence continues according to rules 1 to 3 until the I/O list is exhausted.

The following examples illustrate these rules. Assume that the variables in the output lists have already been assigned the displayed values and that they are of the proper types. The underscore (_) marks a blank space.

1.
```
          PRINT 100, (I, TEMP(I), I = 1, 100)
     100  FORMAT (1X, 'TEMP(', I3, ')= ', F5.1)
```
would print
```
          TEMP(__1)=__72.3
          TEMP(__2)=__69.1
          TEMP(__3)=__67.5
                 .
                 .
                 .
          TEMP(100)=__43.8
```

In this case the entire format specification is reused for each pair I and TEMP(I), resulting in 100 lines of output.

2.
```
          WRITE (*, 150) ((A(I, J), J = 1, 4), I = 1, 3)
     150  FORMAT ('1', 'THE COEFFICIENT MATRIX :' //
        $      4(1X, E11.3))
```
would produce the following output:
```
THE COEFFICIENT MATRIX:

__0.537E+02___0.175E+03___0.902E+01___0.772E+01
__0.695E+01__-0.935E+01___0.557E+02__-0.173E+03
__0.410E+02__-0.851E+02___0.375E+02___0.207E+03
```

The repeat group of specifications on the second line of the FORMAT statement is reused for each output line after the first, according to rule 3. This is a common approach to making a single I/O statement do the work of several.

3.
```
          READ 300, (X(I), I = 1,50)
     300  FORMAT (2F10.2)
```
In this case 25 records will be read, two real numbers per record, in columns 1 to 10 and 11 to 20 respectively.

4.
```
          PRINT 500, N, M, (SINTAB(I), I = 1, N)
     500  FORMAT (1X, 2(3X, I4) / 3(2X, F5.2))
```

The output from this example would be similar to the following:

```
----293---2557
--76.53--27.41--61.10
--14.87--88.44--30.43
    ⋮
    ⋮
```

Note that only the rightmost parenthesized group is reused and that the first space in the group is used for carriage control.

9.7 ALTERNATE FORMAT SPECIFICATIONS

An alternative to the FORMAT statement for specifying the layout of data in an I/O operation was illustrated in Section 9.2. The format identifier can actually be any of the following types:

1. Statement number—identifying the corresponding FORMAT statement
2. Asterisk (*)—for list-directed I/O
3. Character expression—containing the parenthesized list of edit descriptors that would otherwise represent the FORMAT statement
4. Variable or array name—having a value that is a character expression of the type described in (3).

Nearly all of the examples you have seen so far are of types (1) or (2). The third variation eliminates the FORMAT statement, as in the following examples:

```
PRINT '(1X, 2I4, 3X, E12.4)', ROW, COL, X(ROW, COL)
PRINT '(''0'', ''GRAND TOTAL ='', F8.2)', SUM
WRITE (*, '(1X, 3(I3, 2X))') A, B, C
READ '(I2 / 10(I5, 2X))', N, (MCNT(I), I = 1, N)
```

Note that parentheses are required to begin and end the string. If a character string is part of the format, then its quotes must each be represented by a pair of apostrophes, as in the second example.

Run-Time Formats

For most applications a constant format identifier is sufficient, but FORTRAN also allows for generating or modifying a format specification during execution. The identifier may be a variable or array name whose value is the character string representing the format specification.* An array format specification is considered to be a concatenation of all of

---

*The variable or array name may also be of type INTEGER and contain Hollerith characters, but we assume here that they are of type CHARACTER.

the array elements of the array in the order given by the array element ordering.

Suppose, for example, we specify

```
CHARACTER * 20, F
    :
READ *, F
    :
WRITE (*, F) ROW, COL, X(ROW, COL)
    :
```

where '(1X, 2I4, 3X, E12.4)' is the input character string that is read. Then this sequence will produce the same result as the first example above.

We conclude this chapter with an example that uses dynamic formats to its advantage. Imagine a program that reads data into a matrix, applies some transformations to it, and prints it out.

Suppose we want to print the matrix *centered* horizontally on the page, *regardless of the size of the matrix*. Assume that the numbers are in double precision with up to 14 significant digits. We require at least two spaces on both sides of each number. If the entire row can fit on one line, all digits will be displayed; otherwise the field width in the edit descriptor will be reduced by 1 from D21.14 until the row fits or until the minimum D10.3 is reached. If the row is still too long to fit on one line, it is carried over to successive lines. We will double-space between rows of the matrix.

We must compute the values to be used in the format specification during execution. The basic format has the form

$$(\underline{5}(\underline{5}X,D\underline{21}.\underline{14}))$$

but each of the underlined values must be allowed to vary according to the row-size of the matrix. The following pseudocode sequence describes a solution, which centers the matrix as best it can, given equal gaps to the left of each number.

Let LLEN = the length of the line (typically 132 characters)
   GAPS = the gap size between the numbers
   NUMS = the total field width of a number
   DIGS = the number of digits to be displayed for each number
   NVAL = the number of values per line
   NCOL = the number of columns of the matrix A
    LEN = the space required to print a row of A
  NSTAB = array of character string equivalents to its index (e.g., NSTAB(15) = '15')

1. Initialize GAPS to 2 (minimum)
2. Compute NVAL = MIN(NCOL, 11) (Fit the entire row or a maximum of 11 per line.)
3. Compute the largest acceptable number size:
   a. Set NUMS = 22
   b. Set LEN = LLEN + 1
   c. While NUMS > 10 and LEN > LLEN do
      Set NUMS = NUMS − 1
      Compute LEN = NVAL * NUMS + (NVAL + 1) * GAPS
   d. Set DIGS = NUMS − 7
4. Compute the largest possible gap size:
   a. While LEN < LLEN do
      Set GAPS = GAPS + 1
      Compute LEN = NCOL * NUMS + (NCOL + 1) * GAPS
   b. Set GAPS = GAPS − 1
5. Look up the character-string equivalents to these specifications in NSTAB: NSTAB(NUMS), NSTAB(DIGS), NSTAB(GAPS), NSTAB(NVAL)
6. Concatenate the pieces to form the format specification string FMAT:
   FMAT = '(' // NSTAB(NVAL) // '(' // NSTAB(GAPS) //' X, D'
            // NSTAB(NUMS) // '.' // NSTAB(DIGS) // ') /)'
7. Print the matrix.

Steps 3 and 4 are implemented as another subroutine and a function, respectively. The code is given next as a subroutine followed by some sample output. The calling program is not shown.

EXAMPLE 9.2

```
       SUBROUTINE MPRINT (A, M, N, NROW, NCOL)
**********************************************************************
* THIS ROUTINE PRINTS THE NROW BY NCOL MATRIX A IN D-FORMAT
* CENTERED HORIZONTALLY ON THE PAGE WITH EQUALLY-SPACED GAPS TO
* THE LEFT OF EACH NUMBER
*
* A -- THE MATRIX (ARGUMENT)
* M, N -- ROW AND COLUMN DIMENSIONS OF A (ARGUMENTS)
* NROW, NCOL -- THE NUMBER OF ROWS AND COLUMNS USED IN A (ARGU-
*               MENTS)
* MINGAP -- MINIMUM GAP SIZE (PARAMETER)
* MAXW, MINW -- MAXIMUM AND MINIMUM FIELD WIDTHS (PARAMETERS)
* LLEN -- THE OUTPUT LINE LENGTH (PARAMETER)
* GAPS -- THE GAP SIZE     NVAL -- THE NUMBER OF VALUES PER LINE
* NUMS -- FIELD WIDTH OF A NUMBER   DIGS -- THE NUMBER OF DIGITS
*                                         DISPLAYED
```

```
*  NSTAB -- ARRAY OF CHARACTER STRING EQUIVALENTS TO ITS INDEX
*            (DATA)
*  FMAT -- CHARACTER VARIABLE CONTAINING THE FORMAT SPECIFICA-
*            TIONS
*  FIELDW -- SUBROUTINE THAT COMPUTES NUMS AND DIGS
*  GAPSIZ -- FUNCTION THAT RETURNS THE GAP SIZE

*******************************************************************
      INTEGER M, N, NROW, NCOL
      DOUBLE PRECISION  A(M, N)
      INTEGER MINGAP, MAXVAL, MAXW, MINW, LLEN
      INTEGER GAPS, NVAL, NUMS, DIGS
      INTEGER GAPSIZ
      CHARACTER FMAT * 16, NSTAB(65) * 2
      PARAMETER (LLEN = 132, MINGAP = 2, MAXVAL = 11, MAXW =
     $         21,MINW = 10)
      DATA NSTAB / '1','2','3','4','5','6','7','8','9','10','11',
     $'12','13','14','15','16','17','18','19','20','21','22',
     $'23','24','25','26','27','28','29','30','31','32','33',
     $'34','35','36','37','38','39','40','41','42','43','44',
     $'45','46','47','48','49','50','51','52','53','54','55',
     $'56','57','58','59','60','61','62','63','64','65'/
*
* COMPUTE THE NUMBER OF VALUES PER LINE
*
      NVAL = MIN(NCOL, MAXVAL)
*
* COMPUTE THE LARGEST ACCEPTABLE NUMBER SIZE AND DIGITS
*
      CALL FIELDW(MAXW, MINW, LLEN, NVAL, MINGAP, NUMS, DIGS)
*
* COMPUTE THE LARGEST POSSIBLE GAP SIZE
*
      GAPS = GAPSIZ(LLEN, NCOL, MINGAP, NUMS)
*
* BUILD THE FORMAT SPECIFICATION
*
      FMAT = '('// NSTAB(NVAL) // '('// NSTAB(GAPS) // 'X,D'
     $         // NSTAB(NUMS) // '.' // NSTAB(DIGS) // ')/)'
*
* PRINT THE MATRIX
*
      DO 30, I = 1, NROW
         WRITE (*, FMAT) (A(I, J), J = 1, NCOL)
30    CONTINUE
      END

      SUBROUTINE FIELDW(MAXW, MINW, LLEN, NVAL, MINGAP, NUMS,
     $                    DIGS)
```

```
**************************************************************
* COMPUTE THE FIELD WIDTH SPECIFICATIONS NUMS AND DIGS
*
* ARGUMENTS -- SEE MAIN PROGRAM PROLOGUE
*       MAXW, LLEN, NVAL, MINGAP -- INPUT
*       NUMS, DIGS -- OUTPUT
* LEN -- SPACE REQUIRED TO PRINT A ROW
**************************************************************
      INTEGER MAXW, MINW, LLEN, NVAL, MINGAP, NUMS, DIGS, LEN
      NUMS = MAXW + 1
      LEN = LLEN + 1
*     WHILE ROW DOESN'T FIT OR MIN SIZE NOT REACHED, DO
10    CONTINUE
      IF (NUMS .GT. MINW .AND. LEN .GT. LLEN) THEN
          NUMS = NUMS - 1
          LEN = NVAL * NUMS + (NVAL + 1) * MINGAP
          GOTO 10
      ENDIF
*     ENDWHILE
      DIGS = NUMS - 7
      END

      INTEGER FUNCTION GAPSIZ(LLEN, NCOL, NUMS, MINGAP)
**************************************************************
* COMPUTES AND RETURNS THE MAXIMUM ALLOWABLE GAP SIZE
*
* ARGUMENTS -- SEE MAIN PROGRAM PROLOGUE
* GAPS -- GAPSIZE CURRENTLY TESTED FOR FIT
* LEN -- SPACE REQUIRED TO PRINT A ROW
**************************************************************
      INTEGER LLEN, NCOL, NUMS, MINGAP, GAPS, LEN
      GAPS - MINGAP
      LEN = LLEN - 1
*     WHILE THE ROW STILL FITS DO
20    CONTINUE
      IF (LEN .LT. LLEN) THEN
          GAPS = GAPS + 1
          LEN = NCOL * NUMS + (NCOL + 1) * GAPS
          GOTO 20
      ENDIF
*     ENDWHILE
      GAPSIZ = GAPS - 1
      END
```

Output: (for 80 columns)

```
0.10000000000000E+01      0.40000000000000E+01      0.70000000000000E+01
0.20000000000000E+01      0.50000000000000E+01      0.80000000000000E+01
0.30000000000000E+01      0.60000000000000E+01      0.90000000000000E+01
```

For this three-by-three matrix the following format specification was generated:

$$(3\_(4\_X,D21.14)/)$$

Note that the first space in the nX field is used for carriage control. Also, any remainder blank spaces appear at the end of the line. It would be easy to modify the program to include half of these spaces at the beginning. The program could also be somewhat more efficient: the number of choices is small enough so that all of the required values could be looked up in a table (see Exercise 9.25).

In conclusion, FORTRAN provides a great deal of power and flexibility for describing the layout of the input/output data. For most scientific or engineering applications, however, formatting should be simple and straightforward.

Style Guide: In general, keep it simple.
1. Use list-directed I/O whenever possible.
2. Don't try to cram everything into one format. Unless execution time is at a real premium, use multiple READ/WRITE statements with simpler formats.
3. Use formatted input when it is necessary to save space on input. Use decimal points in real number data if not inconvenient; right-justify numbers without decimal points in the field.

Exercises

Section 9.1

1.*a. Write a READ statement to read the variables A, B, and C from unit number 6, with a FORMAT statement labeled 400, that will jump to statement number 900 if an end-of-file record is encountered or to 1000 if there is an error.
   b. Write a WRITE statement that prints the array elements X(I), for I = 1 to N on unit number 12, using FORMAT statement number

*The solution to this exercise appears in Appendix D.

100, and sets the variable WSTAT equal to the status of the operation.

Section 9.2

2. Suppose that I = 12345, J = −28, K = 3, X = 9.24, Y = 0.72, and C = 'FORTRAN' (where C has a length of 7). What is printed by the following statements?

*a.
```
          WRITE (*, 100) I, J, X
100       FORMAT (1X, I7, 3X, I3, 3X, F6.2)
```

b.
```
          WRITE (*, 200) I, J, K
200       FORMAT (' ', I5)
```

c.
```
          PRINT 300, X, C, Y
300       FORMAT (1X, E10.3, 2X, A, F7.1)
```

d.
```
          PRINT 400, X, X
400       FORMAT (' ', 'X IS ', F7.2, ' ANOTHER X IS ',
     $          F5.0)
```

3. Write a program to print a table of tangent values for angles between 0 and π radians where the stepsize between successive angles is read as an input item. Print the angle x, tan x, and the ratio sin x/cos x to seven decimal places and look for differences in the two function values for each x. Be careful around $x = \pi/2$.

Section 9.3

4. For each FORMAT statement, indicate what would be printed by the statement

```
                    WRITE (*,100) -973.8257
```

*a. 100	FORMAT (1X, F10.4)		d. 100	FORMAT (' ', F8.4)
b. 100	FORMAT (' ', F9.3)		*e. 100	FORMAT (1X, F11.6)
*c. 100	FORMAT (1X, F5.0)		f. 100	FORMAT (' ', F7.2)

5. For each PRINT statement, indicate what would be printed if the following FORMAT statement is used:

```
             200 FORMAT (1X, E10.4)
```

*a. PRINT 200, -5.0		d. PRINT 200, -293.58E-5
b. PRINT 200, 3573.92		*e. PRINT 200, 79.0D+5
*c. PRINT 200, 0.0000527		f. PRINT 200, 1.004

6. Write WRITE and FORMAT statements to print SUM and COUNT on a single-spaced line in the form

```
     __SUM_IS_XXXXXXXXXXXX__AND_COUNT_IS_XXXX
```

where SUM is printed in E-format and COUNT in I-format. The Xs represent the positions in the numeric fields.

*7. Write a PRINT and FORMAT statement pair that will print the single-spaced line described as follows:

Item	Columns	Type
Part no.	5–9	INTEGER
Description	12–33	CHARACTER
Unit price	35–40	REAL (2 dec. places)
Unit wt. (kg)	43–48	REAL (3 dec. places)
Quantity ordered	50–52	INTEGER
Total price	55–63	REAL (2 dec. places)
Total wt. (kg)	65–73	REAL (3 dec. places)

8. Suppose N elements of the arrays ALEV and PCB have been computed. Write the necessary WRITE and FORMAT statements to print the following table:

a. The title

```
        ACID AND PCB LEVEL
         MEASUREMENTS IN
          SONOMA COUNTY
            MAY, 1987
```

should be centered on an 80-column page at the top.

b. The column headers should be printed as:

```
   COUNT        ACID LEVEL     PCB LEVEL

   -----        ---- -----     --- -----
```
   In col. 15–19   In col. 35–44   In col. 55–63

c. The values I, ALEV(I), and PCB(I), for I = 1 to N, should be centered under their respective columns. N is less than 1000; typical values for ALEV(I) and PCV(I) are, respectively, −3.1746 and 0.5492E−3.

9. Write a program that will read two character strings of digits, each up to 50 digits in length, convert the digits to integers, and compute the sum of the two numbers. Store the sum as a sequence of digits in an array, one digit per array element. Print the sum without intervening spaces between the digits.

Section 9.4

10. Given the following declarations, show what will be printed in each of the cases:

```
CHARACTER LET * 26
DATA LET /'ABCDEFGHIJKLMNOPQRSTUVWXYZ'/
```

*a.
```
      WRITE (*, 100) (LET(I:I), I = 1, 26)
100   FORMAT ('+', A)
```

b.
```
            WRITE (*, 200) LET
200         FORMAT ('+', A)
```

c.
```
            DO 10 I = 1, 26
              WRITE (*, 300) LET(I:I)
300             FORMAT ('+', A)
10          CONTINUE
```

11. Show what will be printed by each of the following sequences:

*a.
```
            N = 9237
            WRITE (*, 100) N, N, N
100         FORMAT ('1', T5, I4, 2X, I6, T20, I4)
```

b.
```
            PRES = 437.52
            WRITE (*, 200) PRES, PRES, PRES
200         FORMAT (' ', F6.2 / '0', F7.3 / ' ', F8.4)
```

*c.
```
            CHARACTER M * 3, W * 5
            M = 'MAN'
            W = 'WOMAN'
            PRINT 300, M, W, M
300         FORMAT (' ', 'SUPER', T7, A / '+', T11, A /
     $                                   '+', T17, A)
```

d.
```
            CHARACTER * 6   C(4)
            C(1) = 'FIRST'
            C(2) = 'SECOND'
            C(3) = 'THIRD'
            C(4) = 'LAST'
            PRINT 400, (C(I), I = 1, 4)
400         FORMAT ('0', T24, A, T10, A, T17, A, T2, A)
```

e.
```
            X = 1923.75
            WRITE 500, X, X, X
500         FORMAT (' ', E12.5, 2X, 3PE13.5, 2X, -2PE12.5)
```

Section 9.5

12. Write READ and FORMAT statements that will read the five values shown and assign them to the integer variables I and J, the real variables X and Y, and the logical variable L, in that order.

```
--5--   ---7---   ----10----   -----12-----   -------15------   -3-
   3      -5959                    37.5E01         .0058E-04    T
```

13. An input record contains this data, starting in column 1:

79356-2053+812879394

If this data is read by

READ (*, 100) A, B, C

for each of the following FORMAT statements, what values are assigned to A, B, and C?

```
 *a. 100    FORMAT (F5.0, F5.0, F8.4)
  b. 100    FORMAT (F5.2, F4.0, 3X, F6.2)
 *c. 100    FORMAT (F4.3, 1X, F5.2, F10.4)
  d. 100    FORMAT (F2.0, F3.0, 1X, F3.0)
  e. 100    FORMAT (F3.2, 8X, F4.1, F5.2)
```

14. Two input records contain the following data, starting in column 1:

$$3026150284$$
$$2883005241$$

What values are assigned to the variables in each of the following?

```
 *a.         READ (*, 100) A, B
     100     FORMAT (F6.2 / F4.1)

  b.         READ (*, 200) I, J, X
     200     FORMAT (2X, I5 / 4X, I2, F4.1)

 *c.         READ (*, 300) X, P, I, J
     300     FORMAT (F5.0 / F4.0, T1, I4, T2, I4)

  d.         READ (*, 400) M, N, X, Y
     400     FORMAT (T3, I2, T1, I6 / T4, F6.1, T1, F6.1)
```

15. An input record contains this data, starting in column 1:

$$781\_\_\_\_\_\text{-}294\_\_\_503\_\_\_TIP\_\_$$

What values are assigned to the variables in each of the following? Assume that I, K, N are integers, X and Y are real, L is logical, and C is a character variable of length 3.

```
 *a.         READ (*, 100) I, N, K
     100     FORMAT (I3, I8, I6)

  b.         READ (*, 200) I, X, K
     200     FORMAT (I5, F7.2, 3X, I3)

 *c.         READ (*, 300) X, N, L
     300     FORMAT (F5.1, BN, 5X, I5, 4X, L3)

  d.         READ (*, 400) I, K, N
     400     FORMAT (BN, I5, 5X, I2, BZ, 2X, I5)

  e.         READ (*, 500) X, I, Y, C
     500     FORMAT (F3.1, 5X, I2, F5.0, A)
```

*__16.__ Write a READ and FORMAT statement to read the following input record for a mailing list:

Input Record	Column
a) name of member	1–20(character)
b) street address	21–45(character)
c) city	46–58(character)

(Continued)

d) state   60–61(character)
e) zip code   62–66(character)
f) telephone #   70–79(character)
g) number of years in organization   80–81(integer)
h) principal area of interest code   83–85(character)
i) member of SIAM (true or false)   86   (logical)
j) member of IEEE (true or false)   87   (logical)

17. Revise Exercise 9.9 to read two strings up to 25 digits in length into two integer arrays, each array element to contain one digit. Compute the *product* of these two numbers and display it without intervening spaces between the digits.

Section 9.6

18. Simplify each of the following FORMAT statements where possible by using repetition and/or grouping:
*a. FORMAT (I3, I3, I3)
 b. FORMAT (F8.2, A5, A5, 2X, I3, F6.1, F6.1)
*c. FORMAT (I3, F7.1, I3, F7.1, E12.2, 2X, E12.2)
 d. FORMAT ('0', I5, 2X, I5, 2X, F7.0 / '0', I1, A, I1)
 e. FORMAT (' ', F5.1, 2X, F5.1, 2X, F5.1)

19. Write a single PRINT and FORMAT statement pair to print out *all* 25 rows of the array A, 5 elements per row, using E10.3 format for each element, separated by 3 spaces, and with the rows double-spaced.

20. Write a single WRITE and FORMAT statement pair to print the table described in Exercise 9.8.

21. Two input records contain the following data, starting in column 1:

```
1073528264
8824169026
```

What values are assigned to the variables in each of the following?
*a.   READ 100, I, J, M, N
   100   FORMAT (2(I3, I2 /))

 b.   READ 200, X, Y
   200   FORMAT (/ 2(2X, F3.0))

*c.   READ 300, I, J, X, K, L, M, N
   300   FORMAT (2I2, F3.1 / 4(I2, 1X))

 d.   CHARACTER * 2, C1, C2
           READ 400, I, C1, C2, K
   400   FORMAT (3X, I4 / 2(A, 2X), I2)

22. An independent automobile testing company has been contracted by a popular automobile magazine to do a comparison of the gas mileage obtained for a group of compact cars. The data has been collected and is to be entered on records in the following format:

Column	Data item
1–10	car make
12–20	car model
22–25	engine size (cubic inches)
27–31	starting odometer reading
33–37	ending odometer reading
40–42	gallons of gas used

Write a program that will read the data and calculate the miles per gallon for each car. Then print a report that has the following structure:

```
               INDEPENDENT AUTO MPG TEST


CAR MAKE    MODEL     ENGINE    GALLONS USED    MILES    MPG
  FORD      TAURUS     250         32.85        1200    36.53
    .          .         .           .            .        .
    .          .         .           .            .        .
    .          .         .           .            .        .
```

The report should be sorted in descending order by miles per gallon.

Section 9.7
23. Convert the following pairs into a single READ or WRITE statement. Also, use repeat factors and parenthesized grouping where possible.

    *a.
    ```
           READ 90, P, Q, T
           READ 100, A, B, V, I, J, CH
      100  FORMAT ( F3.0, 2X, F6.1, 3X, I2, I2, A4)
       90  FORMAT (F5.0, 2X, F5.0, 2X, I4)
    ```

    b.
    ```
           WRITE (*, 100)
      100  FORMAT ('1', 'ATMOSPHERIC DATA:')
           WRITE (*, 200) YR, MO, DAY, LOC, ELEV, TEMP
      200  FORMAT ('0', 'GRID: ', I1, '/' , I2 '/' I2,
        $           T20, A10, T33, I5, T40, F6.2)
    ```

24. Read a character string that represents a report title and then print it, centered at the top of the page
    *a. without the use of execution-time formats (*hint*: append blanks to the left end of the string).
    b. using an execution-time format.

25. Improve Example 9.2 so that the columns are centered more precisely on the page. Allow the number of columns per page to be an input parameter. Also, based on the value of NVAL, the number of values per line, look up the values of GAPS, NUMS, and DIGS in a table, rather than computing them.

26. Revise Exercise 8.7 so that it will print N compounds per line, where N is an input parameter.

27. Write a program to produce and print snowflake patterns. Use a random number function, such as RNUNF (Chapter 7), to produce random integers x and y in the range 0 to 30. The pairs (x, y) can be

thought of as points in a grid. Initialize the character array SNOW(−30:30, −30:30) to blanks. For each generated pair (x, y) set each of the following array locations to an asterisk: (x, y), $(x, -y)$, $(-x, y)$, $(-x, -y)$, (y, x), $(y, -x)$, $(-y, x)$, and $(-y, -x)$. Generate N pairs (x, y), where N is an input value, and print the array SNOW centered on the page. Experiment with different values of N.

28. Redo Exercise 5.29 to print a histogram, but use what you have learned regarding character strings and formatting to produce a better display than the one in Exercise 5.29. Use the line length of the output media as an input variable to expand the histogram to better fit the page. Allow the range of data values to be variable as well, and *scale* the histogram to fit the data as well as the page. For example, one asterisk might represent 55 kilometers.

29. Write a program to simulate the game "Life" (the one invented by John Conway: *Scientific American*, October 1970, p. 120). The game generates interesting patterns that are produced by a colony of "living organisms."

    Use a 30-by-30 character array that is initialized to blanks; organisms are placed on the array in the form of asterisks, or some other character. The organisms give birth to others, survive to the next generation, or die according to the following rules. Note that a *neighbor* is an organism on an adjacent—including the diagonal—element (each organism has at most eight neighbors).

    a. *Birth*: each empty position with exactly three organisms as neighbors gives rise to a birth in the next generation.
    b. *Death*: organisms with fewer than two neighbors die from isolation; those with four or more die from overcrowding. They are replaced by a blank space in the next generation.
    c. *Survival*: organisms with exactly two or three neighbors survive to the next generation.

    For example:

1st generation	2nd generation	3rd generation
*	* * *	*
* * *	* *	* *
*	* * *	* *
		* *
		*

    Read in the row and column positions of a set of organisms. Print out 10 successive generations of the array to the screen but stop sooner if the array is empty (the population has died out). Use two arrays, each the next generation of the other. In order to handle the borders in an elegant way, include a border of array elements around the array that is initialized to blanks and treated as an infertile region in which no organisms can grow.

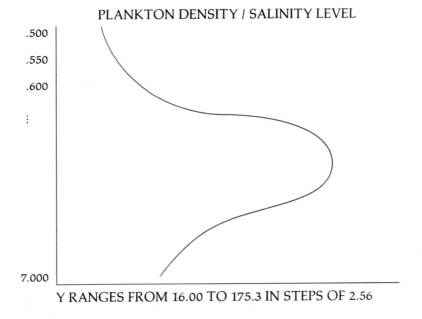

PLANKTON DENSITY / SALINITY LEVEL

.500

.550

.600

⋮

7.000

Y RANGES FROM 16.00 TO 175.3 IN STEPS OF 2.56

Figure 9.1
*Sample function
plot.*

This program can produce interesting sequences of patterns. Some have been designed that seem to "move" off the page! Others die out, oscillate, or grow without bounds.

30. Write a program to plot the graph of a function, $y = f(x)$. The function values should be computed by a FUNCTION subprogram. Input to the program should be the minimum and maximum values of x, a title for the graph, and labels for the x and y axes. Print the graph with the abscissa (x) running vertically. Scale the graph by computing approximate minimum and maximum values for y. Print a border to the left and below the graph. Vary the scaling according to the page size, an input value. The x values should be printed to the left of the area and the range of y values should be printed below the graph, as illustrated in Figure 9.1.

10 *Data Files*

All of the input and output operations we have considered in the previous chapters have involved the standard input/output unit. For interactive FORTRAN programs, this unit was probably a video device for input and either the same video device or a printer for output. For batch programs the input data was most likely included in the job stream, and output went directly to a printer. Record sizes have generally been fixed at 80 or 132 characters to match the input/output units.

In this chapter we will consider alternatives for the provision of data. Data will be stored in a *file*, which in this context can be defined as a named collection of records. You may have some prior experience with files in BASIC or Pascal, which have relatively limited file-handling capability. Just as you can store your FORTRAN program in a file, so you can enter and save data in a separate file, by means of either the same text editor used to edit programs, or another program.

Files that can be manipulated by the text editor are, by necessity, stored on the same media as the programs, most likely a disk, floppy disk, or other so-called *direct-access device*, although it is common to store *sequential files* on these devices too. In a sequential file records are written one after another, in sequence, and are read in the same order. All of the applications we have considered so far have read and written data sequentially. *Direct-access files*, on the other hand, allow records to be read or written in any order. The application will dictate which file type is best.

Another common storage medium, especially for large files, or infrequently used files, is *magnetic tape*, on which data is recorded in a sequential manner by a *tape drive*. This medium is appropriate for sequential files only; to read the 1000th record on a tape file you will normally read the 999 records that precede it in the file.

Additionally, record sizes can vary greatly from file to file, depending on the application. It is not unusual for a file to hold records thousands of characters in length.

Generally, data are stored in files for the following reasons:

1. The volume of data is very large, so that it would be impractical to enter it via a keyboard, store it in the computer's memory, or even print it on paper. An example is the set of billions of data bits collected from satellite transmissions over a given time period.
2. The collection of data will be used only occasionally, as is the case for a course master file in a university's registration system.

There is no need to keep it immediately accessible in the computer's memory.

3. The data will be accessed frequently by a number of programs. Placing the data in a separate file avoids duplication. It is necessary to store only one copy of the data rather than storing a copy with every program that uses it. Files in on-line data bases fall into this category.

4. Only a small percentage of the data records will be accessed at any time. An example is a large collection of dragonfly data from which random samples are read for various statistical analyses.

5. A large set of data must be read and processed at high speed. An example might be data in pure binary form that has been collected by laboratory instruments interfaced to a computer. Such data could be read without the overhead of converting it from ASCII to binary for internal use. For efficiency reasons, records may be very long as well.

6. It may be convenient to reformat the data at times from one form to another (e.g., from INTEGER to CHARACTER type).

In addition to reading and writing, additional operations are necessary for data stored in a file. Reading and writing operations in FORTRAN are designed to be *independent* of any unit or device to provide as much flexibility as possible. Before these operations commence, however, they must be *connected*, or linked, to the given file. Also, it may be necessary to manipulate the device in some way, such as rewinding a tape so that a file may be written on it from the beginning. We will consider all of these operations in this chapter.

The first five sections deal with files, such as tape or disk files, that are external to the main memory of the computer. For this reason they are often referred to as *external files. Internal files*, which are entirely memory-resident, are covered in Section 10.6. Unless we specify otherwise, the term *file* will mean external file in this book.

10.1 INPUT/OUTPUT AND THE UNIT SPECIFIER

All of the I/O operations we have employed so far have been sequential, as when we read data entered at a terminal keyboard or display results on a printer. Input data are accessed by the program in the order in which they were written. Extending this approach to files is straightforward. One does not need to know anything about the physical representation of the data. In fact, very little additional information is required in the READ or WRITE statements to apply them to data files, although there are a few restrictions that we will cover in this chapter.

In Chapter 9 we introduced the *unit specifier*, which was part of the control information list. Most often the unit is specified by an asterisk, for the standard unit, or by an integer that is used to designate a specific file or device. For example, a unit number 6 might be used for printer output, number 5 for terminal input, and 20 for a particular data file on disk. Other forms of the unit specifier will be discussed later.

The following examples should clarify its usage.

1. `READ (10, 500, END = 999) CLASS, LENGTH, WT`

   will read the data from unit number 10, using a FORMAT statement labeled 500. Unit 10 could refer to a file on disk, for example. The particular input file that is used is the one that is associated with the unit number 10 by means of the connection operation, which we will cover in the next section.

2. `WRITE (6, 150) (A(I), I = 1, N)`

   will write the data on unit number 6 using the FORMAT statement labelled 150. Note again that the PRINT statement can be used for output to the standard unit only.

3. `WRITE (FMT = 1000, UNIT = 20, END = 5000, ERR = 500) X, SIN(X)`

   will write the data on unit 20 using FORMAT 1000. This example illustrates the explicit declaration of the unit and format specifiers, sometimes called *keyword* specifiers. If the UNIT clause is omitted, the unit specifier *must* be the first specifier in the control information list.

4. `READ (5, *) CNAM1, CNAM2, DIV`

   is a list-directed version of the READ statement that accesses the data on unit 5.

We should note that some systems limit the range of possible unit numbers (e.g., between 1 and 250).

It is not uncommon for an application program to read data from more than one file (as in merging two or more alphabetical lists) or to write to more than one file. Consequently there may be numerous I/O statements scattered throughout the program that employ several different unit numbers.

To keep them straight and to provide clear documentation, we recommend that you parameterize the unit numbers. For example, if a

WRITE statement is to print lab equipment inventory data to a file, it might best be written as follows:

```
INTEGER LABEQP
PARAMETER (LABEQP = 12)
    .
    .
    .
WRITE (LABEQP, 200) PNO, SERNO, DESCR, LABNO, SIZE, WT
    .
    .
    .
```

The WRITE statement writes to unit 12.

10.2 THE OPEN AND CLOSE STATEMENTS

The unit number is the means by which FORTRAN programs maintain independence from particular data files. Without them each I/O statement would have to name the file it is to access. Changing the data file would require changing all of the corresponding I/O statements.

However, the unit numbers must become associated with their corresponding files or devices at some point. We say that the unit is then *connected* to the file. Before any read or write operations take place on a file, it must be connected. The connection process takes place in any of three ways.

1. Some of the unit numbers are reserved for use by the compiler and are said to be *preconnected* to a device or file. The unit numbers in this category are system-dependent. For example, it is common for FORTRAN compilers running on large IBM series computers to have units 5 and 6 associated with the standard input and output units, respectively, by default. Thus, for example,

```
WRITE (6, 300) A, B, C
```

would send output to the system printer. Although these defaults can often be changed, it is best to use different numbers for files and devices other than the standard ones.

2. JCL (Job Control) statements are most likely available that enable you to connect units to files or devices *outside* of your FORTRAN program. This approach promotes the greatest independence of the program from its data files, but the statements are obviously system-dependent.

3. The OPEN statement, to be covered next, performs a number of functions, including establishing the file connection. The file names themselves are system-dependent. On many systems they

must begin with a letter and are limited in length to 6 or 8 characters.

To *open* a file means to prepare it for processing. In general, an *OPEN statement* specifies a unit number and file name, thereby establishing the connection; it also describes various attributes of the file, such as the length of the records it holds or will hold. Its form is similar to the control information list of an I/O statement. It performs the functions of the reset and rewrite operations in Pascal. We now present a formal definition of the OPEN statement.

OPEN Statement

OPEN statement

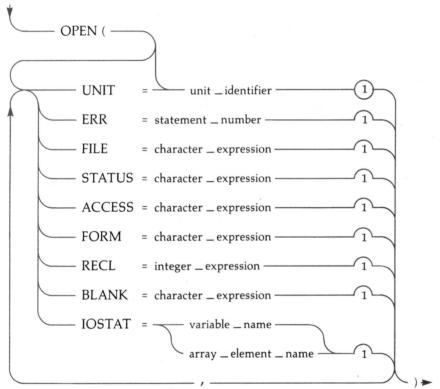

Examples:

1. OPEN (UNIT = 25, FILE = 'SATFIL')

   This statement connects a file named SATFIL to unit number 25.

2. OPEN (10, FILE = 'AIRQAL', STATUS = 'NEW',
   $ ACCESS = 'DIRECT', RECL = 120)

   This statement connects a file named AIRQAL to unit number 10.

The fact that STATUS = 'NEW' means that the file does not exist and is to be created as part of the OPEN process. The file is to be of type DIRECT and will contain records of length 120. When a file is created this way, or externally by means of JCL statements, the file name and its attributes are saved as an entry in the computer system's file directory.

3.
```
CHARACTER * 6 FNAME
PRINT *, 'ENTER FILE NAME:'
READ *, FNAME
OPEN (UNIT = 7, FILE = FNAME, FORM = 'FORMATTED',
$      BLANK = 'ZERO')
```

In this sequence the user interactively enters the name of the file, which is then connected to unit number 7. The file is assumed to be formatted (to be discussed below), and blanks in numeric fields are treated as 0s.

4. OPEN (UNIT = 12)

In this example the file name is not specified, and unit 12 is therefore connected to a processor-determined file (i.e., the standard input or output unit, whichever is appropriate).

Remarks:

1. Executable. The list of specifiers must contain exactly one unit specifier and at most one of each of the other specifiers. An OPEN statement can be applied to a file that had been previously OPENed but not *closed* (see below), but then only the BLANK specifier can be different from the one currently in effect. Note that some FORTRAN implementations will *rewind* a sequential file (i.e., position it at the beginning) as part of the OPEN operation, but the Standard has nothing to say about this.

2. We have already discussed the unit specifier. The ERR specifier works the same as that for a READ or WRITE statement. An example of a situation that would activate this error trap is the specification of a file name that already exists but whose STATUS is given as 'NEW'. The file specifier must evaluate to the file name that is to be connected to the given unit.

3. The STATUS specifier must evaluate to one of the following: 'OLD', 'NEW', 'SCRATCH', or 'UNKNOWN'. 'OLD' means that the file already exists. It could have been created by another program or by the text editor. If 'NEW' is specified, the file must not exist. The OPEN statement changes the status of the newly created file to 'OLD'. A *scratch file* is a temporary file that is available for storage during execution and is usually deleted upon termination of the program. If 'SCRATCH' is specified, the

file name must be omitted. A scratch file is then created and connected to the given unit. 'UNKNOWN' is the default if this clause is omitted, and it is useful if the user doesn't care about the file status. The danger is that it could allow an unintentional rewriting of an existing file. Its use is system-dependent.

4. The ACCESS specifier must evaluate to either 'SEQUENTIAL' or 'DIRECT' to specify the file type. The default value is 'SEQUEN-TIAL'. A corresponding 'OLD' file must have the same attributes as this specifier.

5. The FORM specifier must evaluate to either 'FORMATTED' or 'UNFORMATTED'. If it is omitted, 'UNFORMATTED' is assumed for direct files, and 'FORMATTED' is assumed for sequential files. Note, however, that formatted direct files and unformatted sequential files are also valid.

   A formatted file is similar to a text file in Pascal. The data are stored in records in character form and can therefore be read directly (by a word processor, for example) or printed on a printer. An unformatted file is one in which the data are stored in pure binary form, like the data in a Pascal binary file. Unformatted I/O and its advantages will be covered in Section 10.5.

6. The RECL specification gives the length of the records in a direct-access file. It is required for direct-access files and must be omitted for sequential files. All records must be of the same length for direct-access files.

7. The BLANK specifier must evaluate to 'NULL' if blank characters in numeric fields are to be ignored, and to 'ZERO' if blanks are to be treated as 0s, according to the Standard. Contrary to popular opinion, the default setting is 'NULL', *not* 'ZERO', according to the Standard. This specifier can only be used for formatted files.

   For example, given the input record and corresponding READ statement

   ```
        _53__7___672E+2__
   ```

   ```
             READ (20, 100) M, N, P
   100       FORMAT (2I5, E7.0)
   ```

   with BLANK = 'NULL' specified in the OPEN statement, the result will be that M = 53, N = 76, and P = 72.0E+2.

8. The IOSTAT specifier works exactly the same way as it does as part of the control information list in a READ or WRITE statement. It enables the program to recover from errors or at least to print diagnostic messages rather than allowing the operating

system to abort the program. The values assumed by the IOSTAT variable are system-dependent.

The following subroutine illustrates the use of the STATUS and IOSTAT specifiers. The program loops until the user enters the name of a file with the proper attributes. This example presumes that list-directed output and input are directed to and from the user's interactive terminal.

EXAMPLE 10.1

```
      SUBROUTINE GETFIL (INFIL, FNAME, FSTAT)
*************************************************************
* THIS ROUTINE OPENS A SEQUENTIAL FILE BASED ON USER INPUT.
* LIST-DIRECTED I/O IS FROM/TO THE USER'S TERMINAL.
*
* INFIL -- UNIT IDENTIFIER (INPUT)
* FNAME -- FILE NAME (OR STOP TO TERMINATE) (OUTPUT)
* FSTAT -- FILE STATUS (OLD OR NEW)
* STAT -- IOSTAT FLAG
*************************************************************
      INTEGER INFIL, STAT
      CHARACTER FNAME * 8, FSTAT * 3
      FNAME = 'GO'
      STAT = 1
*     WHILE (STATUS SHOWS ERROR AND WANT TO RETRY OPEN) DO
10    CONTINUE
      IF (STAT .NE. 0 .AND. FNAME .NE. 'STOP') THEN
         PRINT *, 'ENTER NAME OF INPUT FILE OR STOP TO HALT '
         READ *, FNAME
         IF (FNAME .NE. 'STOP') THEN
            PRINT *, 'ENTER FILE STATUS (OLD OR NEW) '
            READ *, FSTAT
            OPEN (UNIT = INFIL, FILE = FNAME, STATUS = FSTAT,
     $            ACCESS = 'SEQUENTIAL', IOSTAT = STAT)
            IF (STAT .NE. 0) PRINT *, 'STATUS ERROR NO. ',
     $            STAT, ' ON FILE ', FNAME
         ENDIF
         GOTO 10
      ENDIF
*     ENDWHILE
      END
```

An OPEN statement must be executed once for each unit prior to that unit's reference by an I/O statement. Once the program has finished accessing a file (for example, after it has read the file's contents into an array), it is customary to *close* the file. Closing a file *disconnects* it from the associated unit number. Information stored in the file's directory entry, such as the time and date of last access, is updated at this time.

The FORTRAN statement that closes a file is the *CLOSE statement*, which is defined next. It is not necessary to close a file explicitly since FORTRAN will close it for you when the program terminates. Therefore the use of CLOSE is optional, although from the standpoint of good style, we recommend that all files be explicitly closed. Also, files should be closed as soon as they are no longer needed by the program to reduce the possibility of complications due to system crashes and related problems. In some instances this practice may also accelerate the completion of the program by freeing up additional memory space.

CLOSE Statement

Examples:
```
CLOSE (UNIT = 10, ERR = 900)
CLOSE (5)
CLOSE (UNIT = 25,IOSTAT = TVAR,ERR = 5000,STATUS = 'KEEP')
```

CLOSE statement

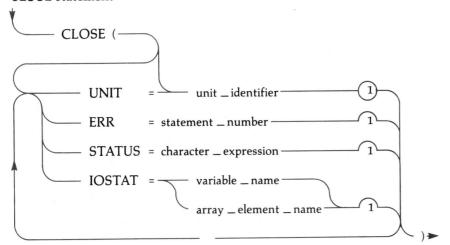

Remarks:

1. Executable. The list of specifiers must contain exactly one unit specifier and may contain at most one of each of the others. If there is no file connected to the specified unit, no action takes place. Both the unit and the file, if it exists, may be connected to each other again or to a different file and unit, respectively, by another OPEN statement.

2. The UNIT, IOSTAT, and ERR specifiers are the same as those for the OPEN statement. The STATUS specifier must evaluate to either 'KEEP' or 'DELETE' and tells FORTRAN to save or delete the file accordingly, after it has been closed. 'KEEP' must not be specified for a file whose OPEN status is 'SCRATCH'.

The following example illustrates a case in which the STATUS specifier would be useful. Imagine an experimenter who is running a program many times for various sets of input data. The program generates a large volume of output, and the experimenter occasionally wants to save the data in a file. The following fragment shows one way this could be handled, where unit number 3 is assumed to be the user's terminal.

```
INTEGER TERM
PARAMETER (TERM = 3)
CHARACTER RESP * 1, STAT * 6
:
:
WRITE (TERM, ' DO YOU WANT TO SAVE THE OUTPUT FILE? (Y/N)'
READ (TERM, *) RESP
IF (RESP .EQ. 'Y') THEN
    STAT = 'KEEP'
ELSE
    STAT = 'DELETE'
ENDIF
OPEN (UNIT = 10, FILE = 'OUTFIL', ERR = 999)
:
:
CLOSE (UNIT = 10, STATUS = STAT)
:
:
```

This approach will save the experimenter the work of explicitly deleting unwanted files after each run.

10.3 SEQUENTIAL FILES

A typical sequential file in FORTRAN would be a file n records of the same length, written one after the other, and terminated by an end-of-file indicator:

| record 1 | record 2 | record 3 | $\cdots$ | record n | EOF |

This is simplistic since the physical representation of the file on a medium such as tape may be somewhat different. Other files may precede or follow it. Successive records may be combined into sequences of multiple records, called *physical records*, that are separated by gaps on the tape to speed up the transfer of data. The physical structure is transparent to the FORTRAN program, however; only the fact that the records are organized sequentially matters.

When the file is opened, it is positioned to just before the first record. Once a sequential file has been opened, READ and/or WRITE operations may be performed on it, although there are some restrictions that apply to using READ and WRITE on the same file, to be discussed below.

There are three additional operations that may be performed on an opened sequential file. They are all related to file positioning.

The *REWIND statement* repositions the file at its beginning, called the *initial point*. The next READ operation after a REWIND therefore applies to the first record in the file.

The *BACKSPACE statement* repositions the file at the beginning of the preceding record. Therefore a READ-BACKSPACE-READ sequence applied to the same file would read the same record twice.

The *ENDFILE statement* writes an end-of-file (EOF) record on a sequential output file. It is this record that activates the END indicator in a READ statement.

We define these statements collectively as follows.

REWIND, BACKSPACE, ENDFILE Statements

Examples:

```
REWIND 6
BACKSPACE (UNIT = 10, IOSTAT = BSTAT)
ENDFILE (20, ERR = 999)
```

Remarks:
1. Executable. The unit identifier is required. The file must be connected for sequential access.
2. If the file is already positioned at its beginning, the REWIND and BACKSPACE statements have no effect.
3. If the file is connected but does not exist,
   a. REWIND has no effect,
   b. BACKSPACE is prohibited, and
   c. ENDFILE creates the file.

The REWIND operation is useful for applications in which a sequential file is written, rewound, and read back for further processing.

The BACKSPACE operation is essentially a carryover from the days when most file processing was done with tape drives. It is most often used for an application that adds records to an existing external file. Since records can only be added at the end of a sequential file, the file must be read until the EOF is reached, and then a BACKSPACE operation can be issued. The file is then in the proper position to add more records. The operation is inefficient, and you should avoid it if possible.

Note that the use of the ENDFILE statement is a good programming practice prior to closing an output file. However, most systems will automatically write an EOF record when the output file is closed—either explicitly or upon program termination—or when it is rewound.

Consider the following application of sequential files. Imagine an entomologist who is keeping a master file of dragonfly data. After the researcher makes periodic field trips and records the findings on a floppy disk file using a portable computer, the data are added to the main computer's file, which contains the complete collection of measurements, dates, locations, codes for the various species, and so forth. Statistical programs are used to process the records, which are in no particular order, and therefore the records are simply added to the end of the file.

The program that follows simply creates a new master file with the name supplied by the user, or it opens the existing file and positions it for the addition of the new data. It then reads the data from the floppy disk and writes it to the master file. (We are making many assumptions here about the compatibility of the portable computer with the main computer, the accessibility of the disk file, and so forth.) The program uses the subroutine in Example 10.1 to open the file properly.

EXAMPLE 10.2

```
      PROGRAM DFLYWR
*****************************************************************
* AUTHOR:  A.M. ROBINSON    4/26/87
*
* THIS PROGRAM APPENDS DATA TO THE DRAGONFLY MASTER DATA FILE,
* CREATING IT FIRST IF NECESSARY.  THE MASTER FILE IS CONNECTED
* TO UNIT NUMBER 90.  NEW DATA ARE SUPPLIED ON UNIT NUMBER 50;
* IT IS ASSUMED THAT THIS CONNECTION IS MADE EXTERNAL TO THE
* PROGRAM.  IF ANY ERRORS ARE DETECTED IN ONE OF THESE RECORDS,
* THE RECORD IS SKIPPED.  USER MUST SUPPLY THE NAME OF THE
* MASTER FILE INTERACTIVELY.  THE DRAGONFLY RECORD IS 120 CHARAC-
* TERS LONG.
*
* MFILE,DFILE -- MASTER AND NEW DATA FILE UNIT NUMBERS, RESPEC-
*                TIVELY.
* MNAME -- NAME OF MASTER FILE
* MSTAT -- STATUS OF MASTER FILE (NEW OR OLD)
* DUMMY -- DUMMY RECORD USED TO SEARCH FOR EOF ON MFILE
* DNAME -- NAME OF NEW DATA FILE
* DFLDTA -- DRAGONFLY DATA RECORD
* GETFIL -- RETRIEVE FILE NAME AND STATUS;OPENS FILE (SUBROUTINE)
*****************************************************************
      INTEGER MFILE, DFILE
      CHARACTER MNAME * 8, MSTAT * 3, DUMMY * 1, DFLDTA * 120
      CHARACTER DNAME * 8, DSTAT * 3
      PARAMETER (MFILE = 90, DFILE = 50)
      CALL GETFIL (MFILE, MNAME, MSTAT)
      IF (MNAME .EQ. 'STOP') STOP
      IF (MSTAT .EQ. 'OLD') THEN
*
* FIND THE EOF
*
*         WHILE NOT EOF DO
10        CONTINUE
              READ (MFILE, 100, END = 20) DUMMY
100           FORMAT (A1)
              GOTO 10
20        CONTINUE
*         ENDWHILE
*
* BACKSPACE OVER THE EOF
*
          BACKSPACE (UNIT = MFILE)
      ENDIF
```

```
*
* COPY THE DATA TO THE MASTER FILE
*
      CALL GETFIL (DFILE, DNAME, DSTAT)
      IF (DNAME .EQ. 'STOP') STOP
*     WHILE NOT EOF ON PC-DISK FILE DO
30    CONTINUE
        READ (DFILE, FMT = 200, ERR = 30, END = 40) DFLDTA
200     FORMAT (A)
        WRITE (MFILE, 200) DFLDTA
        GOTO 30
40    CONTINUE
*     ENDWHILE
      ENDFILE (UNIT = MFILE)
      CLOSE (DFILE)
      CLOSE (MFILE)
      END
```

Note that a dummy record (DUMMY) is used to bypass records in searching for the EOF records. A minimal format specification, (A1), is used since no detail is required. Likewise, since no details are required in the actual data records—they are simply copied from one file to another—the simplest possible format specification, (A), is used. Simplifying the format usually speeds up processing.

10.4 DIRECT-ACCESS FILES

Sequential files are inappropriate for applications that access only a small percentage of the records in the file. A file of inventory items, for example, may be accessed once a week, say, in order to change the totals on hand for items received or consumed since the last update run. If a sequential file were used, the entire file would have to be read sequentially and rewritten to another file, even though only a small percentage of the records would be changed.

Direct-access files (sometimes called *random-access files*), however, enable specific records to be read or written with no restrictions on their order. They are identified by means of a record number that is established when the record is written and uniquely identifies the record.

Clearly, direct-access files must be stored on a direct-access medium, such as a disk. It would be inappropriate to define a direct-access file to be accessed on a tape drive. Furthermore, it is likely that the physical representation of a direct-access file will be different from that of a sequential file. You will probably not be able to enter data into a direct-access file via your text editor. Instead, such files are generally written by a program.

These are a few differences you must take into account in your file I/O statements when the file is of type DIRECT:

1. To open a direct-access file, you must use the ACCESS and RECL specifiers. Access must usually be specified as 'DIRECT'. For example, the statement

```
OPEN (UNIT = 50, FILE = 'DAFILE', STATUS = 'OLD', ERR = 999,
$     ACCESS = 'DIRECT', FORM = 'FORMATTED', RECL = 180)
```

   would open the file DAFILE as a formatted direct-access file with records of length 180.

   Some systems will allow a program to specify ACCESS = 'SEQUENTIAL' on a file created for direct access if it is to be read in sequence. This approach can improve processing speed.

2. To read or write to a direct-access file, you must include the REC specifier. Recall that this specifier represents the *record number* of the record, which uniquely identifies the record to be read or written and is used by FORTRAN to locate the record in the file without first reading or writing the previous records. Therefore the records can be read or written in any order. The statement

```
WRITE (10, 250, ERR = 1000, REC = 23) (X(I), I = 1, 5)
```

   would write (or rewrite) the 23rd record to the direct-access file connected to unit number 10. Usually this specifier will be a variable name, as in REC = RNUM. Note also that the record number, once established, cannot be changed. As this example illustrates, it is not included as one of the fields in the record.

3. None of the file-positioning statements—REWIND, BACKSPACE, and ENDFILE—apply to direct-access files. Also, the END specifier is not allowed.

4. The records in a direct-access file may not be read or written using list-directed I/O statement.

Consider the following application. A college chemistry laboratory maintains a large inventory of various chemicals and supplies. Inventory records are stored and updated in a computer inventory file. At the end of each week a department staff member updates the records in the file, decrementing the totals on hand corresponding to consumption during the past week and incrementing the totals for deliveries received. The following program only allows changes to existing records. Enhancing the program to include deletions of records and additions of new records is left as an exercise.

It is possible to use a sequential file for this application, which is a special case of updating a master file. The usual approach for updating tape-based master files is to place all of the *transactions* (i.e., the update records) in another file, in sequence, and to read all the records in both files, rewriting the master records to an output file, including any changes represented by the corresponding transactions. The old file might then be deleted and the new one renamed. Alternatively, some FORTRAN implementations allow you to read master records until you find the one that matches the transaction record, backspace, write an updated record over the old one, and then continue. However, this also requires the transactions to be sorted first, and many systems do not allow the rewriting of records in a sequential file. (The Standard has nothing to say about this.) Both approaches are inefficient unless a reasonable number of records are being updated; one rule of thumb is 20 percent or more.

Using a direct-access file for this purpose enables us to read and write only those records we wish to change. Furthermore, we can present the transactions in any order. This approach results in considerable savings in both execution time and complexity of the program.

For simplicity in this example, we will assume the following structure for the inventory record:

Field	Part #	Description	Type	Total on hand	Weight/unit	Vendor	Address
Format	I5	A30	I1	I4	F8.2	A25	A50

For our example the only fields of interest are the part number and the total on hand. We assume that the records were written to the file using the part number as the record number. The general problem of assigning an identifying record number to a record can be difficult. One must be able to retrieve the record later without having to provide an artificial identifier this way.

One solution is to save another file, an *index file* that contains records with two fields: an identifying field, such as a name, and the record number field:

SMYTHE P D	1739

To find a given record, then, you search the index file for the particular identifier and then use the corresponding record number to access the record in the direct-access file.

Another way is to apply some transformation to an identifying field(s) to produce a number that can be used as the record number. In our case we use the part number directly. This approach has the advantage of simplicity, but it suffers from the disadvantage of potentially wasting file space. Suppose the file contains 10,000 records. If records exist with part numbers 00010 and 99990, the file might require space for nearly 100,000 records (how they are stored is implementation-dependent), 90,000 of which are wasted space.

The program functions as follows: (1) it accepts a part number from the user, (2) reads the corresponding record, (3) asks for verification that the record is correct, (4) accepts an increment/decrement in the total on hand, (5) changes the total accordingly, and (6) rewrites the record. Note again that the record number, which is the same as the part number here, is not normally explicitly listed as one of the fields in the record. Here is the program.

EXAMPLE 10.3

```
      PROGRAM CINVUP
**********************************************************
* AUTHOR:  H.M. BIGGS   4/9/87
*
* THIS PROGRAM UPDATES THE TOTALS ON HAND FIELDS FOR CHEMISTRY
* LAB INVENTORY RECORDS SELECTED INTERACTIVELY BY THE USER.  IT
* IS ASSUMED THAT LIST-DIRECTED INPUT/OUTPUT ARE CONNECTED TO THE
* USER TERMINAL.  ENTRY OF A PART NUMBER EQUAL TO ZERO TERMI-
* NATES THE PROGRAM.  THE FILE CINVEN IS CONNECTED TO UNIT
* NUMBER 10.
*
* INVUNT, INVFIL, INVLEN -- UNIT, FILE NAME, AND RECORD LENGTH
*                           FOR FILE
* OPSTAT, CLSTAT -- OPEN, CLOSE IOSTAT INDICATORS, RESP.
* UPDATE -- UPDATE PART NO. TOTALS (SUBROUTINE)
**********************************************************
      INTEGER INVUNT, INVLEN, OPSTAT, CLSTAT
      CHARACTER INVFIL *(*)
      PARAMETER (INVUNT = 10, INVLEN = 123, INVFIL = 'CINVEN')
      WRITE(*,'('' THE CHEM LAB INVENTORY UPDATE PROCEDURE''/)')
*
* OPEN THE FILE
*
      OPEN (UNIT = INVUNT, FILE = INVFIL, STATUS = 'OLD',
     $    ACCESS = 'DIRECT', RECL = INVLEN, FORM = 'FORMATTED',
     $    IOSTAT = OPSTAT)
      IF (OPSTAT .NE. 0) THEN
          PRINT *, 'ERROR NO. ', OPSTAT,' OPENING FILE ', INVFIL
          PRINT *, 'PLEASE CORRECT THE PROBLEM BEFORE RUNNING'
          STOP
      ENDIF
*
* UPDATE THE FILE
*
      CALL UPDATE(INVUNT, INVFIL)
```

```
      *
      * CLOSE THE FILE
      *
            CLOSE (UNIT = INVUNT, IOSTAT = CLSTAT)
            PRINT *, 'CLOSING FILE STATUS IS ', CLSTAT
            END

            SUBROUTINE UPDATE(INVUNT, INVFIL)
      ****************************************************************
      * INTERACT WITH USER TO UPDATE THE CHEMISTRY INVENTORY FILE
      *
      * INVUNT, INVFIL -- FILE UNIT AND NAME, RESP.
      * RDSTAT -- READ IOSTAT INDICATOR
      * PARTNO -- PART NUMBER ENTERED BY USER (= TO SECOND NUMBER)
      * IPART, DESCR, TYPE, TOTAL, WTPU, VENDOR, VENADR -- FIELDS IN
      *                                        THE INVENTORY RECORD
      * TOTAL -- TOTAL ON HAND (PART OF INVENTORY RECORD)
      * ANS -- USER RESPONSE (Y/N) ON RECORD VERIFICATION
      *
      * REWRIT -- UPDATE THE TOTAL FIELD IN INVENTORY REC. (SUBROUTINE)
      ****************************************************************
            INTEGER INVUNT, RDSTAT, PARTNO, IPART, TYPE, TOTAL
            CHARACTER DESCR * 30, VENDOR * 25, VENADR * 50
            REAL WTPU
            CHARACTER ANS * 1
            CHARACTER INVFIL *(*), INVFMT *(*)
            PARAMETER (INVFMT = '(I5, A30, I1, I4, F8.2, A25, A50)')
            PRINT*,'ENTER PART NO. TO CHANGE ITS TOTAL (0 TO STOP): '
            READ *, PARTNO
      *
      * LOOP UNTIL SESSION FINISHED
      *
      *     WHILE PART NUMBER NOT 0 DO
      10    CONTINUE
            IF (PARTNO .NE. 0) THEN
               READ (UNIT = INVUNT, FMT = INVFMT,
           $   IOSTAT = RDSTAT, REC = PARTNO) IPART, DESCR, TYPE,
           $   TOTAL, WTPU, VENDOR, VENADR
               IF (RDSTAT .NE. 0) THEN
      *
      * ERROR READING FILE
      *
                  PRINT *
                  PRINT *,'ERROR NO. ',RDSTAT, ' FILE WITH PART NO. ',
           $      PARTNO
               ELSE
      *
      * VERIFY THAT RECORD IS CORRECT ONE
      *
```

```
            PRINT *
            PRINT *, 'THE RECORD YOU REQUESTED IS: '
            PRINT *,'PART NO.: ', IPART, ' DESCRIPTION: ', DESCR
            PRINT *, 'TOTAL ON HAND: ', TOTAL
            PRINT *, 'IS THIS CORRECT? (Y/N) '
            READ *, ANS
            IF (ANS .EQ. 'Y' .OR. ANS .EQ. 'y') THEN
*
* RECORD CORRECT -- UPDATE IT
*
               CALL REWRIT(INVUNT, INVFMT, INVFIL, IPART, DESCR,
     $               TYPE, TOTAL, WTPU, VENDOR, VENADR, PARTNO)
            ENDIF
         ENDIF
*
* GET THE NEXT PART NO.
*
         PRINT *
         PRINT *, 'ENTER PART NO. TO CHANGE TOTAL (0 TO STOP) '
         READ *, PARTNO
         GOTO 10
      ENDIF
*     ENDWHILE
      END

      SUBROUTINE REWRIT(INVUNT, INVFMT, INVFIL, IPART, DESCR,
     $                  TYPE, TOTAL, WTPU, VENDOR, VENADR,
     $                  PARTNO)
***********************************************************************
* CHANGE THE TOTAL FIELD AND REWRITE THE RECORD
*
* ARGUMENTS -- SEE SUBROUTINE UPDATE PROLOGUE
* WRSTAT -- WRITE IOSTAT INDICATOR
* CHGTOT -- CHANGE IN TOTAL ON HAND
***********************************************************************
      INTEGER INVUNT, PARTNO, IPART, TYPE, TOTAL, CHGTOT
      REAL WTPU
      CHARACTER DESCR *(*), VENDOR *(*), VENADR *(*)
      INTEGER WRSTAT
      CHARACTER INVFIL *(*), INVFMT *(*)
*
* RECORD ASSUMED TO BE CORRECT -- UPDATE IT
*
      PRINT *, 'ENTER CHANGE TO TOTAL ON HAND '
      PRINT *, '(-VALUE FOR DECREMENT) '
      READ *, CHGTOT
      TOTAL = TOTAL + CHGTOT
      IF (TOTAL .LT. 0) THEN
```

```
          PRINT *, 'NEW TOTAL IS NEGATIVE, RESET TO 0. '
          TOTAL = 0
      ENDIF
*
* REWRITE THE RECORD
*
      WRITE (UNIT = INVUNT, FMT = INVFMT,
     $      IOSTAT = WRSTAT, REC = PARTNO) IPART,
     $      DESCR, TYPE, TOTAL, WTPU, VENDOR, VENADR
      IF (WRSTAT .EQ. 0) THEN
          PRINT *, 'RECORD REWRITTEN WITH NEW TOTAL ', TOTAL
      ELSE
          PRINT *, 'ERROR NO ', WRSTAT, ' WRITING FILE ',
     $             'WITH PART NO. ', PARTNO
      ENDIF
      END
```

Note that we can easily modify the program to accommodate changes in the size of the records, fields, and so forth. Only the corresponding parameters would need to change. (Of course, the file would have to be rewritten.) We could also modify it to do unformatted I/O (see Section 10.5).

The program is well-structured, employing a single WHILE loop for the entry of data and rewriting of records. It is a standard WHILE loop structure with the first READ used to enter the loop and subsequent reading of part numbers placed at the end of the loop. The IOSTAT indicators are used for error handling.

10.5 UNFORMATTED FILES

When an input or output operation is executed on formatted data, the data must be converted from or to a sequence of characters before the data transfer can take place. For example, if the value of Y is 137.4, then execution of the statement

```
            WRITE (*, 100) Y
     100    FORMAT (' ', F7.2)
```

would include the operations necessary to convert Y from its internal, binary, floating-point representation into the character string _137.40 for display on the standard output unit.

This conversion is time-consuming, and it is really unnecessary if the data written to a file will only be read by another program. You can avoid costly conversion time in such cases by using *unformatted* READ and WRITE statements.

The structure of these statements is the same as for their formatted counterparts, except that the format identifier is omitted. For example, the statement

        WRITE (12, ERR = 1000) X, Y, Z, COUNT

would write an unformatted (i.e., not edited) record to unit number 12. If X, Y, and Z are reals, and COUNT is an integer, then X, Y, and Z would be written as single-precision, floating-point binary numbers, and COUNT would be written as a single binary integer. The actual representation is obviously system-dependent, and therefore this approach should not be used if portability to incompatible systems is a possibility. This same record could be read with a statement like

        READ (12) A, B, C, N

but A, B, and C should be of type REAL and N should be of type INTEGER.

Unformatted I/O should not be confused with list-directed I/O. List-directed I/O operations format the data automatically; in unformatted I/O, no formatting occurs.

You should be aware of the following rules if you are considering using unformatted I/O:

1. Exactly 1 record is read or written by an unformatted READ or WRITE operation. This rule implies rules 2 and 3.

2. On input the number of values required by the input list must be less than or equal to the number of values in the record. If there are fewer values in the list, the remaining values in the record are ignored.

3. On output to a file connected for direct access, the output list must not specify more values than can fit into a single record; if the output list does not fill the record, the remainder of the record is undefined.

4. On input, the type of each value in the record must agree with the type of the corresponding item in the input list.

5. If the file is connected for formatted I/O, unformatted data transfer is prohibited.

Clearly, unformatted I/O should only be used in connection with tapes, disks, or similar media.

The default FMT option for direct-access files is 'UNFORMATTED' since only a program can read or write the data anyway. It is a straightforward exercise to modify Example 10.3 to do unformatted READ and WRITE operations to the inventory file (Exercise 10.15).

10.6 INTERNAL FILES

As the term implies, *internal files* are memory-resident. An internal file is not really a file at all but a character variable, character substring, character array element, or character array that is used in place of a unit specifier in a formatted I/O statement. The values stored in these character units are read or written just as if they were stored in an external file.

Internal files are used primarily for converting data from one type to another. They also provide another way to implement run-time formats.

Let us consider some simple examples to clarify matters. Let the character variable CREAL be defined as

$$CREAL = {}'793.48'$$

Suppose we want to compute a real number, RVAL, equal to the numeric equivalent of CREAL. How can we do it?

One way would be to pick off the character digits one at a time from CREAL, convert them to their numeric equivalents using the ICHAR function, and combine the digits as factors times the corresponding powers of 10 in the final result. This approach is tedious (even more so for a number in E format, for example). An alternative is to write CREAL to a scratch file and then reread it with a numeric format. If there are many such values to convert, this approach has the disadvantage of being slow because of the I/O operations.

The same effect is obtained by treating CREAL as an internal file and reading RVAL as follows:

```
          READ (UNIT = CREAL, FMT = 100) RVAL
    100   FORMAT (F7.2)
```

Here the unit identifier is CREAL. The effect is the same as if the value of CREAL were read from a record in an external file using the edit descriptor F7.2.

This approach is more flexible than you might imagine at this point. Define the values of the character variables CREAL and CINT to be

```
          CREAL = '-3.9528E+04'
          CINT = '91325'
```

The problem is to assign the numeric equivalents to the real and integer variables RVAL and IVAL, respectively. We can do this with one READ statement, as follows:

```
          CREC = CREAL // '___' // CINT
          READ (UNIT = CREC, FMT = 200) RVAL, IVAL
    200   FORMAT (I5, 3X, E11.4)
```

where CREC is a character variable of the proper length.

The internal file is treated as a single record if it is a character variable, array element, or a substring name. Using a character array for the internal file allows us to read more than 1 record with a single READ since each array element is treated as a single record. For example, let CARRAY be defined by

```
CHARACTER CARRAY(100) * 3
```

and

```
CARRAY(1) = '__1', CARRAY(2) = '__2',..., CARRAY(100) = '100'
```

Then

```
INTEGER IARRAY(100)
:
READ (CARRAY, '(I3)') (IARRAY(I), I = 1,100)
```

would set

```
IARRAY(I) = I for I = 1, 2,..., 100.
```

Writing to an internal file is a similar process. The values of the output list items are converted to character strings and concatenated as the value of the character variable that is the unit specifier. The following sequence

```
REAL TEMP
CHARACTER * 12, CVAL
TEMP = -293.576
WRITE (CVAL, '(E12.5)') TEMP
```

results in

```
CVAL = '-0.29358E+02'
```

Define

```
CHARACTER CLIST(50) * 5
DO 10, I = 1, 50
   RLIST(I) = REAL(I) + 0.5
10    CONTINUE
```

Then

```
WRITE (CLIST, '(F5.1)'), (RLIST(I), I = 1, 50)
```

assigns

```
CLIST(1) = '__1.5'
CLIST(2) = '__2.5'
:
CLIST(3) = '_50.5'
```

Internal files may also be used to construct a format specification during execution time. It would be useful to be able to write a specification such as

FW.D

where W and D are integer variables that would enable the programmer to vary the precision dynamically. FORTRAN does not support this feature, but we can achieve the same effect with an internal file. Consider the following sequence.

```
      REAL X,Y
      INTEGER W, D
      CHARACTER FORM * 16
      W = 8
      D = 2
      WRITE (FORM, 10) W, D
10    FORMAT ('(1X,', '2(2X,F', I2, '.', I1, '))')
      .
      .
      .
      WRITE (*, FORM), X, Y
      .
      .
      .
```

The format specification is constructed by the first WRITE statement in the character variable FORM as

'(1X,2(2X,F_8.2))'

FORM, in turn, is used later as the format to print out X and Y.

Another use for internal files is to provide detailed error-checking in input data. Normally, if a character is assigned to an integer variable during a real operation, for example, the result will be a trap to the operating system, and the program will be aborted.

Now the IOSAT specifier could be used to trap such errors in the program, but it may be difficult to continue, based on the information available from IOSTAT. For example, if there were an error in the value assigned to A(3) in

READ (*, '(16I5)') (A(I), I = 1, 16)

it is likely that the variables A(4), A(5), . . . , A(16) would also not be assigned values, yet the record would have been read. Therefore, unless all of these values can be ignored, continued processing is not possible.

A better approach is first to read the record into a character array. No errors will occur since any byte can be read as a character. Then each array element can be read as an internal file using an IOSTAT specifier to do the error checking on the individual array elements. The following sequence illustrates this approach.

```
      INTEGER A(100), RSTAT, I
      CHARACTER CA(16) * 5
      READ (*, 100) (CA(I), I = 1, 16)
```

```
100      FORMAT (16A5)
         DO 10, I = 1, 16
            READ (CA(I), '(I5)', IOSTAT = RSTAT) A(I)
            IF (RSTAT .NE. 0) THEN
               {process the error here}
            ENDIF
10       CONTINUE
```

Error processing in the loop could entail printing an error message that includes the incorrect data and the number of the record containing it, replacement of the array element value with 0, say, and so forth. In this way a program can maintain complete control over error detection and handling.

Exercises

Section 10.2

1. Write OPEN statements to open the following files:
   *a. A sequential file of 80-character formatted records with the name 'HOPFIL', to be read from unit number 15.
   b. A sequential file whose name is stored in a variable called MFILE; blanks in numeric fields are to be ignored; the file is to be read from unit 50. The status of the OPEN step is to be reported in the variable MSTAT.
   *c. A direct-access file called 'RANDAT' to be created to hold unformatted records of length 450; it will be written to unit number 20. Error recovery begins at statement number 5000.
   d. A direct-access file called 'BROWNN' that contains formatted records of length 125 is to be read from unit number 25. The status of the OPEN step is to be assigned to the variable BSTAT.
   e. A sequential scratch file to be written as unit number 30.

2. Write a program to read a sequential file and write every third record to another sequential file.

Section 10.3

3. Suppose that a reel of magnetic tape contains a library of FORTRAN subprograms in the form

```
            $SUB1
             subprogram
            $DENFUN
             subprogram
               .
               .
               .
            $$
```

---

  *The solution to this exercise appears in Appendix D.

Write a program to read a subprogram name entered interactively by the user, locate the subprogram, read the program from the tape, and print it. Be sure to allow for the case where the file is not on the tape.

4. Design an experiment to test the relative efficiency of the Shell, selection, and binary-merge sorting algorithms that were discussed in previous chapters. Write an input file of 10,000 real numbers that are generated via a random number generator. Each of the sorting procedures should be run three times, reading 100, then 1000, and then 10,000 numbers from the file into arrays. The procedures should be modified to
   a. count the number of comparisons,
   b. count the number of interchanges (count three moves in the binary merges as one interchange), and
   c. use a FORTRAN library function that gives the current time to measure the actual sort time (call it once just before the sort begins and again after the sorting is complete).
   Draw a graph of the results.

5. Recall the Shell sort algorithm that was used to sort character strings in Chapter 8. One problem with this type of sorting procedure is that interchanges can be expensive if long records are sorted because of the amount of information that must be moved.

   Create a sequential file of formatted records of length, say, 80 characters and with 10 or so fields of various types, with the first field acting as a *key*—each record is identified by its unique key.

   Read the file into a set of linear arrays, one for each field. Then modify the sort procedure to use *pointers* (subscripted subscripts here) as follows:
   a. Initialize an integer array, POINT, so that POINT(I) = I.
   b. In the comparison of keys, compare

$$KEY(POINT(J)) \text{ to } KEY(POINT(J + NTPL))$$

   rather than comparing

$$KEY(J) \text{ to } KEY(J + NTPL)$$

   c. If an interchange is required, *swap the pointer values only.*
   d. To print out the records in order, use the pointer value as the subscript reference. For example, to print the KEY field in ascending order, print

$$KEY(POINT(I)) \text{ for } I = 1, \ldots, N$$

   where N is the number of records in the field.
   With this approach, none of the records have to be moved; only the

pointer values are swapped. The time savings can be significant for a large file of large records.

6. Write a program to delete selected records from a sequential file by reading the records, matching them against another file of transaction records—the ones to be deleted—and then writing those not deleted to an output file. For this process to work efficiently, both files should be sorted on the key—a field or set of fields that uniquely identifies each record.

*7. An application that appears occasionally in everyday applications is the *merging* of two files into a single file. Generate two sequential files sorted in ascending order on the same key. Then write a program to read the files and merge them into a third file: compare successive keys from each file, always writing the record with the smaller key to the output file. Be sure that the program works if the files have different numbers of records.

8. Generalize Exercise 7 to merge *n* sequential files.

9. Try an experiment in code breaking. Enter several paragraphs totalling at least 200 words into a file. Write one program to read the file, counting the total number of As, Bs, blank spaces, and so forth. This program should convert all lowercase letters to uppercase before counting. It should print a table of the percentages of use of each character.

　　Next write a second program to create a second file of text that is *encrypted* by means of a substitution cipher (recall Exercises 8.18 and 8.19).

　　Finally, write a third program that assigns characters to the encrypted text based solely on the percentages obtained in the first program. For example, if E has the highest percentage of use in the first program, then E should replace the character with the highest percentage in the encrypted text. Print out the result. How close is the result to the original text? You may have better results if you use text for the count and for the encryption steps from the same author. This problem could be used as a team project.

10. Write a program to read a file that contains a FORTRAN source program and produce a *cross-reference listing* of all of the variables and statement parts used in the program. Each element should be printed, along with all of the line numbers on which it appears, as in

```
BCOUNT   :   5   27   42   87
X        :   4   5   18
INTEGER  :   1   4   5
  :
  :
```

The list should be sorted. Be sure that the same line number does not appear more than once for each item, even though the item may appear more than once in a statement. You may assume that the items contain no embedded blanks and that they are separated from other items by a blank space or a special character.

11. Write a program to read a text file and print a table of all of the words used, together with a frequency count of the words. Print the list in alphabetical order.

Sections 10.4–10.5

12. Modify Example 10.3 to add new records and delete records no longer needed in the chemistry lab inventory file.

*13. Write a program to read and compare the records from two direct-access files. If the records are identical, write one of the files to an output file. If they are different, write both files to an error file, together with their record numbers.

14. Try an experiment to compare the efficiency of unformatted I/O versus formatted I/O. Write a program to write a direct-access file of formatted records. The records should have 10 fields of varying lengths and types. They could be read from a sequential file. Call a library function to measure the time required to write the file, but be sure you avoid including other computations in that value, such as the time to generate the records. Then modify the program to write unformatted records, and compare the two times.

15. Modify Example 10.3 to use unformatted READ and WRITE operations for the inventory file.

Section 10.6

16. Dates are often written in different forms. For example, December 25, 1987 could be written as

$$12 \ / \ 25 \ / \ 87$$

or as

$$25 \ DEC \ 87$$

Write a character-valued function that uses an internal file to convert a character-string argument, DATE, in the first form to one in the second form.

*17. Write a subprogram that converts a character-string argument representing a social security number in the form XXX–XX–XXXX to return three integer values.

18. Write a subprogram to convert a real number of the form XXXXX.XXXX to two integer values representing the whole and fractional parts of the number.

19. A 10-by-8 matrix of real numbers is to be printed, using the format specification (8(F7.2, 2X)). Write a subroutine to replace each of the values having an absolute value greater than 99,999 with a field of seven asterisks.

11 *Other Topics*

The previous chapters presented a complete set of standard FORTRAN 77 statements that you would need to write a well-structured, robust, transportable program. In this chapter we will cover three unrelated topics that may be important to you, depending on your particular involvement with FORTRAN.

In the first section we will complete the presentation of standard FORTRAN statements that should be avoided, where possible, in writing new programs. Most of these statements fall into a category that the proposed FORTRAN 8X standard refers to as *deprecated features*. They include language structures that are targeted for deletion from a future standard because they are considered outmoded (for the 8X standard and beyond) or because their use may result in a program with a poor structure. However, for someone faced with the task of maintaining or modifying an old program, it is essential to know how these statements work.

The second topic should be of interest to anyone who needs to write programs that execute efficiently. The best way to reduce the execution time of a program is to use an efficient algorithm. Given that, there are still additional techniques that you can use in your program to make it run faster without sacrificing clarity.

Finally, we will examine some extensions to FORTRAN that are used in today's *supercomputers*. Supercomputers are used by scientists and engineers to solve problems that are so large that they are considered intractable for minicomputers or even fairly large computer systems. A problem that might require days or weeks to solve on a "normal" computer, could be solved in hours or even minutes on a supercomputer. Examples of such problems include global weather modelling, nuclear reactor simulations, and supersonic aircraft design. One class of supercomputers, called *vector computers*, apply operations to all the elements of a vector, essentially *in parallel*, in order to speed up computation. These operations often require some extensions to standard FORTRAN.

11.1 OTHER LANGUAGE FEATURES OF FORTRAN 77

The document that describes the draft revision to the FORTRAN 77 standard, known as FORTRAN 8X, categorizes certain statements as *deprecated features* because other features in FORTRAN 77 or some new ones proposed for the next standard are more effective for reliable software production than earlier features. These features are slated for removal from the standard that is to follow the next one.

It is important to note, however, that these features are part of both the FORTRAN 77 Standard *and* the proposed 8X standard. Their presentation was deferred to this section because either (1) they are already obsolete as part of FORTRAN 77, or (2) they may be needed occasionally in a FORTRAN 77 program but will be replaced by some more effective construct if the proposed 8X standard is accepted. In the latter case most of the statements have already been described in an earlier chapter and will only be identified here as being one of the proposed deprecated features.

In general, you should try to avoid using these features. However, you may need some familiarity with them if you will be working with older FORTRAN programs that employ them. In this section we define these statements informally; formal syntax diagrams appear in Appendix C.

IMPLICIT Statement

The *IMPLICIT statement* is not a deprecated feature of the proposed FORTRAN 8X standard, but it is included here because of the modern trend toward explicitly typing all variables used in a program. If you follow this trend, you should not use the IMPLICIT statement.

Admittedly, the IMPLICIT statement is handy; it allows you to declare the types of whole collections of variables, parameters, arrays, and external functions according to the first letter in the name. Here are some examples:

1.   `IMPLICIT INTEGER (A, Q, X-Z)`

   declares that all variables beginning with the letters A, Q, X, Y, or Z are to be INTEGER variables.

2.   `IMPLICIT REAL (A-Z)`

   declares that *all* items in the program unit are to be of type REAL.

3.   `IMPLICIT CHARACTER * 12 (C)`

   declares that all items beginning with the letter C are to be of type CHARACTER with a length of 12.

4.   `IMPLICIT REAL (A-H, O-Z), INTEGER (I-N)`

   is equivalent to the default typing provided by FORTRAN.

5.   `IMPLICIT REAL * 8 (A-H, O-Z)`

   is a common way in many versions of FORTRAN (recall Chapter 6) to declare all the default REAL items in a program to be double precision.

The following are rules for using the IMPLICIT statement:

1. The IMPLICIT statements must precede all other declarations in the program unit except PARAMETER statements.
2. They apply only to the program unit in which they appear.
3. They do *not* change the type of any intrinsic functions.
4. Type specifications by an IMPLICIT statement may be overridden by the explicit typing of the item(s) in a type statement. Thus, in the sequence

```
IMPLICIT REAL (A-Z)
INTEGER HIGH, LOW, COUNT
```

HIGH, LOW, and COUNT are of type INTEGER.

The remaining statements discussed in this section are included among the deprecated features of the proposed 8X standard.

The *DIMENSION statement* is another declaration for specifying the sizes and shapes of arrays. Its form is

DIMENSION Statement

```
DIMENSION alist
```

where *alist* is a list of array declarators. Here is an example:

```
DIMENSION X(100), MAT(25, 50), BOX(-25:25)
```

The DIMENSION statement pervades the existing collection of FORTRAN programs. We have resisted using it in favor of the INTEGER, REAL, and other type declaration statements. The DIMENSION statement is less powerful because it does not explicitly specify the data types of the arrays.

The *EQUIVALENCE statement* is a nonexecutable declaration statement that allows two or more variable names or array element names to refer to the same memory location. It has the form

EQUIVALENCE Statement

$$\text{EQUIVALENCE } (n_1, n_2, \ldots n_k), (n_{k+1}, n_{k+2}, \ldots, n_J), \ldots$$

All of the names enclosed in a set of parentheses refer to the same element. For example, in

```
EQUIVALENCE (A, B(10), C), (LOW1, LOW2)
A = 1.0
LOW1 = 50
```

the variables A and C, and the array element B(10) all have the value 1.0; likewise, LOW1 and LOW2 are equal to 50 (assuming A, B, and C are of type REAL and that LOW1 and LOW2 are of type INTEGER). The statement should appear at the beginning of the program with the other declarations.

The original purpose of the EQUIVALENCE statement was to save memory space. The same block of memory could be used for two or more purposes. For example, suppose an array, RAWDAT, is used to store raw input data to be processed by some smoothing function. Later in the program RAWDAT is no longer required, but another array, OUTDAT, is needed to store data that will eventually be printed to a file. The statement

```
EQUIVALENCE (RAWDAT(1), OUTDAT(1))
```

allows the arrays to share storage, but with the added benefit that the array names reflect their use. Therefore if these arrays are specified by

```
REAL RAWDAT(1000), OUTDAT(1500)
```

then the total storage requirement is only 1500 words, since RAWDAT(I) coincides with OUTDAT(I) for I = 1, 2, . . . , 1000.

EQUIVALENCE statements have also been used to establish equivalence among variables of different types. For example, an array of complex numbers may have to be passed as a real array to a subroutine. This can be accomplished as shown in the following example:

```
REAL XY(100)
COMPLEX Z(50)
EQUIVALENCE (XY(1), Z(1))
```

Then XY(I) for I = 1, 3, 5, . . . , 99 represent the real parts of the elements of Z and XY(I) for I = 2, 4, 6, . . . , 100 represent the imaginary parts. The array Z could be manipulated directly in the main program, while XY could be passed as an argument to the subprogram.

EQUIVALENCE statements can be used to speed up execution of a program. Suppose a program must repeatedly zero out the elements of a large array, as in this example:

```
REAL A(50, 20, 100)
   .
   .
   .
DO 30, I = 1, 50
   DO 20, J = 1, 20
      DO 10, K = 1, 100
         A(I, J, K) = 0.0
10          CONTINUE
20       CONTINUE
30    CONTINUE
```

Recall that a storage-mapping function must be used during execution to locate each of the elements of the array. In this example about 20,000 multiplications and additions may be needed (depending on the compiler) for this purpose. To reduce the overhead, one can state the equivalence of the array A with a linear array and zero out the linear array instead, as follows.

```
      REAL A(50, 20, 100), ASUB(10000)
      EQUIVALENCE(A(1, 1, 1), ASUB(1))
          :
          :
      DO 10, I = 1, 10000
          ASUB(I) = 0.0
10        CONTINUE
```

This approach requires about 10,000 additions for the mapping over-head, a considerable savings.

The preceding examples represent valid uses of EQUIVALENCE statements, but they have sometimes been used to relate integers and reals, or integers and character variables; or they have been used in combination with variables in COMMON, in order to implement various programming tricks. The resulting programs are generally nontransportable, difficult to understand, and prone to errors. For these reasons we do not list all of the usage rules for these unusual applications.

Another use of the EQUIVALENCE statement is to provide alternate names for character substrings, as in the following example:

```
 CHARACTER LOCATN*43, STREET*20, CITY*10, STATE*2, ZIP*5
 EQUIVALENCE (LOCATN(1:1), STREET (1:1)), (LOCATN(23:23),
$            CITY(1:1)), (LOCATN(35:35), STATE(1:1)),
$            (LOCATN(39:39), ZIP(1:1))
```

Each of the character variables STREET, CITY, and so forth act as subfields of the LOCATN string as illustrated here:

```
  LOCATN = '4930 OAK GROVE DRIVE, PASADENA__, CA, 91109'
```

The same effect could be accomplished with assignment statements, although perhaps with some execution time penalty.

The author believes that you should avoid using the EQUIVALENCE statement if possible. Except for very unusual circumstances, you will not need it to solve a problem. Each of the above applications could be accomplished with assignment statements or with extra memory space. Furthermore, it is unlikely that you will be involved with programs requiring this kind of sophistication at your stage of FORTRAN development. Also, the next FORTRAN standard will render this statement obsolete by making more powerful features available.

The *ENTRY statement* enables execution of a subprogram to begin at a statement other than the first executable statement following the FUNCTION or SUBROUTINE statement. An application of this feature is, for example, in a subroutine that includes some initialization process that must take place the first time it is called but must be skipped on later calls.

ENTRY Statement

The ENTRY statement, which is nonexecutable, has the form

$$\text{ENTRY } ename (a_1\ a_2, \ldots, a_n)$$

where *ename* is the name of the entry point and the a_i are arguments that are analogous to the arguments in a FUNCTION or SUBROUTINE statement. A subprogram can contain more than one ENTRY statement, but they must have unique names. To begin execution of the subprogram at a given entry point, you call the subprogram using that entry point's name exactly the way you would call the subprogram.

The following example should make this clear. Let ROOT be a function subprogram that computes one of the roots of a quadratic equation $ax^2 + bx + c = 0$. The first time it is called, it reads the coefficients b and c before computing the root. The value of a is passed as an argument. (We assume here that the coefficients are such that the formula is valid.)

We define the function as follows:

```
REAL FUNCTION ROOT(A)
REAL A, B, C
READ *, B, C
ENTRY ROOT1(A)
ROOT = (-B + SQRT(B * B - 4.0 * A * C)) / (2.0 * A)
END
```

The following skeleton illustrates a calling sequence:

```
      .
      .
      .
YINIT = ROOT(ALOW)
      .
      .
A = A + REAL(I) * H
Y = ROOT1(A)
      .
      .
      .
```

This example doesn't really justify the existence of the ENTRY statement, since the same effect could be produced by reading the coefficients outside the function. However, more complex applications require GOTOs to jump around entry sequences, resulting in unstructured code. Also, the entry names are hidden within the sequence of statements that make up the body of the subprogram, which makes it difficult to understand the behavior of a particular subprogram call.

We can obtain the same effect by using an input argument that is used by a block IF structure to select the appropriate sequence, or sometimes by using separate subprograms. Furthermore, the proposed Standard includes a new feature, the *module*, that will make the ENTRY statement completely obsolete.

Alternate Return

The *alternate return* feature of FORTRAN is the inverse of the multiple entry feature. It enables a return from a *subroutine* (*not* a function) to statements other than the one immediately following the subroutine call. The argument list in the CALL statement must include the alternative statement numbers, preceded by an asterisk, as in

```
       CALL SUB(X, Y, *100, FLAG, *200, Z)
       PRINT *, X
          .
          .
100    PRINT *, Y
          .
          .
200    PRINT *, Z
          .
          .
```

The SUBROUTINE statement corresponding to such a call must have an asterisk as the dummy argument for the statement number, as in

```
       SUBROUTINE SUB(A, B, *, FLG, *, C)
```

The body of the subroutine definition must include a separate RETURN statement for each alternative, of the form

$$\text{RETURN } i$$

where i is an integer constant or variable whose value marks the relative position of the statement number in the argument list where the return is to be made. Corresponding to the above example, execution of

```
       RETURN 1
```

in SUB will cause a return to statement 100.

```
       RETURN 2
```

will return to statement 200. A RETURN without a number will return to the statement following the CALL.

As with other deprecated features, this one violates structured programming principles. A better approach is to use a return code in the argument list, together with an IF-block for selection, as in this sequence:

```
       CALL SUB (X, Y, Z, RETCOD)
       IF (RETCOD .EQ. 0) THEN
          PRINT *, X
             .
             .
       ELSE IF (RETCOD .EQ. 1) THEN
          PRINT *, Y
             .
             .
       ELSE
          PRINT *, Z
             .
             .
       ENDIF
```

Statement Function

The *statement function* is a feature that was introduced in the earliest versions of FORTRAN. It is called as a function subprogram is, but it is actually not a subprogram. It is defined by a single statement, and unlike a subprogram, it can be referenced *only* from the program unit in which it appears. In this sense it is like a user-defined function in Pascal.

The statement function definition, which must precede all executable statements and follow all other declarations in the program unit, has the form

$$fname\ (a_1, a_2, \ldots, a_n) = e$$

where *fname* is the function name, the a_i are the variables specifying the dummy arguments, and *e* is an expression that may include the dummy arguments. For example,

```
    FREQ (T,L) = 1.5 * SIN(T) - L * COS(T - 1.0)
```

defines the function FREQ as the expression on the right.

Calling a statement function is akin to calling a function subprogram, as in this example:

```
        YGA = FREQ(PI * MSEC, LEN) + 1.0
```

This is equivalent to defining YGA by the statement

```
YGA = 1.5 * SIN(PI * MSEC) - LEN * COS(PI * MSEC - 1.0) + 1.0
```

Essentially, the statement function saves the programmer from entering what may be a complex expression in several places in the program. Modification is easy since the expression must be changed only in the statement function definition.

However, statement functions are less flexible than function subprograms; they must be definable as a single expression, and they can be referenced only in the program unit that defines them. For these reasons they should be avoided in favor of function subprograms. The proposed new standard provides a more general construct, called an *internal function*, which will be a better choice than the statement function.

Arithmetic IF Statement

The *arithmetic IF statement* has the form

$$IF\ (e)\ s_1, s_2, s_3$$

where *e* is an arithmetic expression and the s_i are statement numbers. The statement works as follows:

Control transfers to
  s_1 if the value of *e* is *negative*
  s_2 if the value of *e* is *zero*
  s_3 if the value of *e* is *positive*

Two of the s_i could be the same.

For example,

```
        IF (A + B - 1) 50, 150, 100
```

is equivalent to

```
IF (A + B .LT. 1) GOTO 50
IF (A + B .EQ. 1) GOTO 150
GOTO 100
```

The use of the arithmetic IF statement is not recommended because it leads to poorly structured programs. It was included in early versions of FORTRAN to take advantage of the architecture of computers that were popular at the time. Use a block IF statement instead. The following two sequences are equivalent.

```
          IF (X - Y) 10, 20, 30        IF (X .LT. Y) THEN
10        DFLAG = -1                       DFLAG = -1
          GOTO 40                      ELSE IF (X .EQ. Y) THEN
20        DFLAG = 0                        DFLAG = 0
          GOTO 40                      ELSE
30        DFLAG = 1                        DFLAG = 1
40        CONTINUE                     ENDIF
```

The *computed GOTO statement* is a generalized GOTO statement that selects one of a set of statements to be executed, depending on the value of an integer expression. Its form is

Computed GOTO Statement

$$\text{GOTO } (s_1, s_2, \ldots, s_n), i$$

Where i is an integer expression and the s_i are statement numbers. If the value of i is k, then control transfers to statement number s_k. If the value of i is less than 1 or greater than n, the program continues with the next statement.

For example, in

```
GOTO (10, 20, 10, 40, 100), IVAL
```

control transfers to statement number 10 if IVAL equals 1 or 3, to 20 if IVAL is 2, to 40 if IVAL is 4, and to 100 if IVAL is 5. A block IF, ELSE_IF combination is much more effective from the standpoint of structure and clarity. These two sequences are equivalent:

```
          GOTO (50, 50, 60, 75), N    IF (N .LE. 2 .OR. N .GT. 4)THEN
50        X = X + 1.0                     X = X + 1.0
          XCOUNT = XCOUNT + 1            XCOUNT = XCOUNT + 1
          GOTO 90                      ELSE IF (N .EQ. 3) THEN
60        Y = Y + 1.0                     Y = Y + 1.0
          YCOUNT = YCOUNT + 1            YCOUNT = YCOUNT + 1
          GOTO 90                      ELSE
75        X = 0.0                         X = 0.0
          Y = 0.0                         Y = 0.0
90        CONTINUE                     ENDIF
```

Assigned GOTO Statement

The *assigned GOTO and ASSIGN statements* are used in combination to produce an effect similar to that of the computed GOTO statement. The structure of the former is

$$\text{GOTO } i, (s_1, s_2, \ldots, s_n)$$

where i is an integer variable and the s_k *are statement numbers.* The value of i *must* be one of the s_k in the list. Control transfers to statement s_k, where $i = s_k$.

The variable i is given a value only by means of an ASSIGN statement (an arithmetic assignment statement may not be used), which has the form

$$\text{ASSIGN } s \text{ to } i$$

where s is a statement number that appears in the assigned GOTO list, and i is the integer variable that is used there.

For example, if STMT is an integer variable in

```
ASSIGN 75 TO STMT
GOTO STMT, (20, 50, 80, 75, 100)
```

control will transfer to statement 75. ASSIGN is used to define STMT as 75 since that value represents a location in the program and not the integer value 75. Therefore STMT may not be modified anywhere in the program except by another ASSIGN statement. As in the case of the computed GOTO, the use of these statements should be avoided by the use instead of an IF-ELSE-IF block.

PAUSE Statement

The *PAUSE statement* has the form

$$\text{PAUSE}$$

or

$$\text{PAUSE } s$$

where s is an integer with five or fewer digits or a character string constant, as in

```
PAUSE 900
```

or

```
PAUSE 'INVERSION COMPLETED'
```

This statement temporarily halts execution, which can be resumed at the same point by some system-dependent means. The value of s is displayed on the user terminal or on the computer operator's console.

The statement was intended for program testing and debugging by programmers who had sole control of the computer. It is meaningless in a batch program in a multiuser system, and it has only limited usefulness now since most modern FORTRAN compilers provide much more powerful debugging operations. The same functionality can also be achieved by means of an appropriate PRINT and READ combination that awaits some input data.

Some of the statements and features described in previous chapters are included among the deprecated features in the proposed new standard, although they are still important for many applications under the current version of FORTRAN. When the next Standard is available most, if not all, of these features may be rendered obsolete. Therefore we close this section with Table 11.1, which lists these features for reference to alert you to the possibility of their eventual obsolescence.

TABLE 11.1 FORTRAN 77 Features Expected to Become Deprecated Features in FORTRAN 8X

Feature	Possible alternative
DOUBLE PRECISION	REAL variable precision to be explicitly specified, as in `REAL (PRECISION = 14) X` which imples that X is to have at least 14 digits of precision
COMMON and BLOCK DATA subprograms	Global data pools will be provided by MODULE program units.
DATA statements	To be replaced by a more general INITIAL specifier
Specific names for intrinsic function	Replace by generic names, e.g., replace IABS(INTV) by ABS(INTV) to compute the absolute value of the integer variable INTV. See Appendix B.
DO loop termination	END DO statements to be required for each DO loop.

11.2 IMPROVING PROGRAM EFFICIENCY

Computer time can be expensive. As of this writing one institution was charging approximately $800 per hour of CPU time (i.e., the time that the computer is actually executing your program instructions) on a Cray

2 supercomputer. Engineers and scientists, who may be repeatedly executing programs over extended periods of time in order to solve problems, must be concerned about these costs. Often funds are limited and partly dependent on outside grants.

Sometimes, too, the response time is critical. A program that requires 24 hours to predict the weather for the next day is of little use, except to verify the accuracy of the model.

Therefore the efficiency of a program is often of major concern. The choice of an algorithm is most important. Where one algorithm may require hours to produce a solution for a given problem, a more sophisticated algorithm may do it in a few minutes, representing a speedup by a factor of thousands or more.

Once the algorithm has been selected and the program design completed, there remain a number of techniques you can use to reduce the execution time of a program. They may yield modest improvements (5 to 20 percent) that can result in significant cost reductions over a long time period.

We should note that a number of these techniques will be implemented automatically by a good *optimizing compiler*. An optimizing compiler generally compiles very slowly in comparison with the standard compiler, but the resulting object code runs much faster. Therefore, if you are no longer making changes to a program, you should compile it once with an optimizing compiler, if available, and rerun the resulting object code without recompiling each time.

Before implementing any of these techniques, you may wish to first code and debug your design and run the program through a *profiling tool*, if you have one available. A profiling tool is a utility program that prints a listing of a source program showing percentages of computer time spent on each statement, loop, subprogram, and so forth. Then you can concentrate on improving the code that is taking up most of the time.

The results produced by such tools will help you to keep the following suggestions for improvement in proper perspective. It may, in fact, not be worth the costs of software development to save 10 CPU seconds per week. However, an inefficient program that requires days of CPU time, or one that must react immediately to external events (e.g., one that controls some of the functions of a modern jet aircraft) are good candidates for possible improvement.

The first technique we describe, which may be obvious to some readers, is to *remove unnecessary computations from loops*. Any statement whose value or condition does not depend on the elements that are changing with each repetition should not be there. Consider the following example:

```
      DO 20, I = 1, 1000
         SUM(I) = 0.0
         DO 10, J = 1, 1000
            SUM(I) = SUM(I) + REAL(K) * VEL * R(I) + TINC(J)
10          CONTINUE
20       CONTINUE
```

The product REAL(K) * VEL, although unchanging in both loops, is evaluated one million times! Similarly SUM(I) and R(I) do not depend on the inner loop and need not be there. An improvement is:

```
         KVEL = 1000.0 * REAL(K) * VEL
         DO 20, I = 1, 1000
            TEMSUM = 0.0
            DO 10, J = 1, 1000
               TEMSUM = TEMSUM + TINC(J)
10             CONTINUE
            SUM(I) = KVEL * R(I) + TEMSUM
20          CONTINUE
```

Careful examination will show that this sequence accomplishes precisely what the first one does, with less work. The disadvantage is a possible loss of clarity, and therefore such changes should be documented well.

Second, *remove common subexpressions*. Inefficiency is illustrated by the sequence

```
   X1 = (-B + SQRT(B * B - 4.0 * A * C)) / (2.0 * A)
   X2 = (-B - SQRT(B * B - 4.0 * A * C)) / (2.0 * A)
```

It is wasteful to repeat all this computation, especially if X1 and X2 are computed in a loop. This sequence can be rewritten as

```
      DENOM = 2.0 * A
      SQDESC = SQRT(B * B - 4.0 * A * C)
      X1 = (-B + SQDESC) / DENOM
      X2 = (-B - SQDESC) / DENOM
```

This results in five fewer arithmetic operations and one less function call (multiplied by the number of times these statements are executed in a loop). Again, there is a slight loss of clarity. Compilers are good at removing common subexpressions, but they become less effective as the separation between these subexpressions increases.

Another technique is to *nest DO loops with increasing range of the DO index*, if possible. Sometimes the order in which loops are nested does not affect the results, as in the following example (we are ignoring any changes in the accumulated roundoff error here):

```
            SUM = 0.0
            DO 10, I = 1, 100
                DO 20, J = 1, 20
                    DO 30, K = 1, 5
                        SUM = SUM + A(I, J, K)
    30              CONTINUE
    20          CONTINUE
    10      CONTINUE
```

Implicit in this sequence is the incrementing and testing of the loop indices. The number of increment and test operations for each index is given by:

  I: 100 times
  J: 2,000 times
  K: 10,000 times

In this case we can reorder the nesting sequence as follows:

```
            SUM = 0.0
            DO 30, K = 1, 5
                DO 20, J = 1, 20
                    DO 10, I = 1, 100
                        SUM = SUM + A(I, J, K)
    10              CONTINUE
    20          CONTINUE
    30      CONTINUE
```

The number of increment-test operations then becomes:

  I: 10,000 times
  J: 100 times
  K: 5 times

resulting in a substantial saving.

The number of loop increment-test operations can also be reduced by *"unrolling"* loops, if execution time is critical. This approach is illustrated by replacing

```
            DO 10, I = 1, 10000
                X(I) = 0.0
    10      CONTINUE
```

by

```
            DO 10, I = 1, 5000
                X(I) = 0.0
                X(I + 5000) = 0.0
    10      CONTINUE
```

This cuts the number of loop test-increment operations in half. Further unrolling is possible, as in

```
          DO 10, I = 1, 2500
             X(I) = 0.0
             X(I + 2500) = 0.0
             X(I + 5000) = 0.0
             X(I + 7500) = 0.0
    10       CONTINUE
```

However, as one extends the unrollings this way the benefits are marginal.

Another technique is to *replace a slow operation by a faster one*. For example, integer addition is usually faster than integer multiplication. Then the following sequence

```
          DO 10, I = 1, 10000
             IVAR = KPARM * I
                .
                .
                .
    10       CONTINUE
```

can be replaced by

```
          IVAR = 0
          DO 10, I = 1, 10000
             IVAR = IVAR + KPARM
                .
                .
                .
    10       CONTINUE
```

which, in effect, replaces 10,000 multiplications by 10,000 additions. However, you must be cautious with this approach on real numbers, because it is possible to significantly increase the roundoff error (recall the examples in Chapter 7).

Perhaps a more subtle technique is to *use one-dimensional arrays in place of arrays of higher dimension*, if clarity can be preserved. Recall that whenever an array element is referenced, its storage-mapping function must compute its relative location from the beginning of the array. The complexity, and corresponding time cost, increases with the number of subscripts.

If the array elements are accessed in a linear fashion, we can access a one-dimensional array that is *declared equivalent* (with the EQUIVA-LENCE statement) to the higher dimensional array. An example was given in Section 11.1. Another example is the following sequence, which stores random numbers in the array X (recall the IMSL routine RNUNF in Chapter 7).

```
          REAL X(20, 100, 200)
             .
             .
          DO 30 I = 1, 20
             DO 20 J = 1, 100
                DO 10 K = 1, 200
                   X(I, J, K) = RNUNF(DSEED)
    10          CONTINUE
```

```
20         CONTINUE
30       CONTINUE
```

This can be replaced by the following more efficient code:

```
REAL X(20, 100, 200), XX(400000)
EQUIVALENCE(X(1, 1, 1), XX(1))
   :
   :
*
* INITIALIZE MODEL SPACE TO RANDOM VALUES (X EQUIVALENCED TO XX)
*
      DO 10, I = 1, 400000
         XX(I) = RNUNF(DSEED)
10    CONTINUE
```

If this approach is used, it should be well-documented.

Use DATA statements to initialize arrays. Then initialization will take place at compile time. Thus, for example, replace

```
REAL A(5000)
   :
   :
DO 10, I = 1, 5000
   A(I) = 1.0
10    CONTINUE
```

by

```
DATA A / 5000 * 1.0 /
```

Clearly, however, if the array is to be reinitialized in a loop, then a **DATA** statement is inappropriate.

Input and output operations are generally very time-consuming. Implied DO loops, in particular, can be costly because FORTRAN compilers generally produce code that causes a subroutine call at execution time *for each item in the I/O list*. This includes those generated by an implied DO loop. Thus, for example, the execution of

```
INTEGER NAME(100)
   :
   :
READ (10, 100) (NAME(I), I = 1, 100)
```

would produce 100 subroutine calls.

One way to reduce this overhead is to use the *array name alone in place of an implied DO*, as in

```
INTEGER NAME (100)
   :
   :
READ (10, 100) NAME
```

which uses only one subroutine call. Obviously this approach has limited usefulness because of the fixed size requirement; the actual number of array elements used must match the array dimensions.

Another cost saver is to *use unformatted I/O* where appropriate. This saves the time for conversion between internal and external representations of the data. Unformatted I/O was covered in the previous chapter.

Calls to subprograms incur some cost overhead for each argument in the argument list. In general, the shorter the list, the more efficient the data transmission.

One way to reduce the size of the argument list is to *pass as many arguments as possible in COMMON*. For example, the subroutine

```
SUBROUTINE DOSOM (A, B, C, X, N)
DIMENSION X(N)
.
.
END
```

could be written as

```
SUBROUTINE DOSOM
COMMON / DOSUB / X(100), A, B, C
.
.
END
```

However, this approach leads to a rigid structure and suffers from the usual problems associated with the use of COMMON blocks. (Recall the discussion of COMMON in Chapter 7.)

These schemes should be sufficient for any "tuning" you might want to do at this stage. There are a number of other, more subtle, techniques that can be used to reduce execution time. However, in the author's opinion, most of them produce only modest improvements in performance with some accompanying undesirable side effects, such as loss of clarity and/or flexibility. This is also true for some of the techniques described above. If you are interested in pursuing this further, check the FORTRAN manual for your particular computer system. It may contain specific suggestions for improving the run time of a program, although you may risk making your program nontransportable. A good general text with many related ideas is *Writing Efficient Programs*, by Bentley.*

11.3 FORTRAN EXTENSIONS FOR SUPERCOMPUTERS

It is difficult to define a supercomputer in the context of this textbook. Improvements are being developed so frequently that a rigorous definition here will be out of date before the text is published. Generally,

*J. L. Bentley, *Writing Efficient Programs* (Englewood Cliffs, N.J.: Prentice-Hall, 1982).

supercomputers have very large memories ranging from 64 million to even a billion words. They are extremely fast, capable of computational bursts of hundreds of millions of floating-point operations per second. Examples of current supercomputers are the Cray 2, the CDC (Control Data Corporation) Cyber 205, and the Hitachi S810/20.

There are many different architectures for supercomputers. We will focus on FORTRAN for the so-called *vector computers*, which employ special high-speed processors capable of performing simultaneous operations on an entire array, or vector, of numbers. Many computational problems in the sciences and engineering involve operations on large matrices and vectors; thus, vector supercomputers are well-suited for such problems. Indeed, because these problems are so common, the proposed new FORTRAN standard contains numerous features to facilitate array computation. For example, it may be possible with the next FORTRAN standard to write expressions such as

$$A = B + X * SQRT(P)$$

where A, B, X, and P are arrays, with the proper shape. This will promote machine-independence for supercomputer programs.

As of this writing, however, programs written in FORTRAN for one supercomputer are not likely to be transportable to one from a different vendor. The bottom line is usually speed, and scientists and engineers will usually take advantage of the manufacturer's *extensions* to FORTRAN in order to gain execution speed.

This topic is much too broad to do justice to here. Our intent is simply to give you a sense of some of the issues you must be concerned with if you write FORTRAN programs on a supercomputer. The whole process is different. Even though a program may be completely designed, coded, and tested, you may spend weeks *tuning* the program, trying to take advantage of various machine dependencies in order to make it run faster.

A usual objective is to *vectorize* as many operations as possible. Essentially this means writing the segments of code—in particular the loops—so that the compiler can translate the code in ways that take full advantage of the vector features of the machine.

It happens that this is not an easy task, at least given the current status of the compilers. The compiler will produce vectorized code for a loop *only* if it is certain that the vectorized loop will produce the same final result as the nonvectorized (*scalar*) loop. Without certain restrictions on the loops, the compiler is not able to tell if the code will vectorize.

Let us consider the Cray FORTRAN compiler, CFT, as an example. Please note that the examples considered here are from a 1987 version of CFT, and it is likely that a number of improvements will eventually overcome these limitations.* Realize, however, that the problems described here are common to most vector supercomputers. .

Generally, only the inner DO loop of a nested set of loops will vectorize. For this reason loops are often nested, where possible, with the longer loop inside. In fact, many vector computer practitioners will create and operate on a vector of length N * N rather than using an N-by-N matrix in order to take advantage of this feature. The result is a single loop, rather than a nested pair. This technique, which is sometimes done automatically by the compiler, is called *loop collapsing*. For example, the sequence

```
      REAL A(10, 10), B(10, 10), C
      :
      :
      DO 20 I = 1, 10
         DO 10 J = 1, 10
            A(I, J,) = B(I, J) + C
10          CONTINUE
20       CONTINUE
```

can be collapsed to

```
      REAL A(100), B(100), C
      :
      :
      DO 10 IJ = 1, 100
         A(IJ) = B(IJ) + C
10       CONTINUE
```

if this makes sense in the context of the problem.

IF (WHILE) loops will not vectorize. In fact, any of the following constructs within a loop will usually inhibit vectorization:

1. I/O statements
2. Subroutine calls
3. Recursion (we will examine recursion in some detail shortly)
4. Complex IF statements
5. Many function references
6. Nonlinear indexing

With all of these impediments, you may wonder if vectorization is possible at all. It is, in fact, possible to vectorize much of the code in real applications; it just takes extra work on the part of the programmer. For example, complicated DO loops can be split up into a set of loops, some of which will vectorize. I/O sequences are usually grouped into their own loops.

---

*Reprinted by permission of Cray Research, Inc., publication SG-0115.

The following loops will not vectorize:

```
        DO 50 I = 2, 99
          DO 40 J = 2, 99
            DRK = A(I, J)
            BTEMP = B(I, J)
            CALL NEQT(DRK, BTEMP)
            DAT(I, J) = DRK
            B(I, J) = BTEMP
40        CONTINUE
50      CONTINUE
```

where NEQT is defined by

```
        SUBROUTINE NEQT(R, Y)
        COMMON GAM, V, W
        Y = (R / (V + W)) ** GAM
        R = R - Y
        END
```

One approach to this problem is to place the loops inside the subroutine, as in

```
        SUBROUTINE NEQT(R, Y)
        COMMON GAM, V, W
        REAL R(100, 100), Y(100, 100)
        DO 50 I = 2, 99
          DO 40 J = 2, 99
            Y(I, J) = (R(I, J) / (V + W)) ** GAM
40        CONTINUE
50      CONTINUE
```

In this case the J-loop will vectorize. An alternative solution is to expand the subroutine body in the loop. Then no subroutine call is required, and the inner loop will vectorize. Unfortunately this technique tends to nullify the modularity of a program.

Recursion can pose a real challenge to vectorization. The term *recursion*, as used by vector computer programmers, means something different than it does to Pascal or BASIC programmers, where it implies a function or procedure that calls itself. Here recursion means that the output from one pass through a loop is used as input to a computation on a subsequent pass. Cray defines recursion as two or more appearances of an array element in the same loop, where at least 1 of the elements appears to the left of an equal sign.

To see how recursion affects vectorization, realize that vectorization is essentially parallel computation on an *array* of values. Consider, for example,

```
            DO 50 I = 2, 3
               A(I - 1) = 7.0
               B(I) = A(I)
    50      CONTINUE
```

This loop is equivalent to the sequence

```
            A(1) = 7.0
            B(2) = A(2)
            A(2) = 7.0
            B(3) = A(3)
```

but vectorization would cause the sequence to be reordered to

```
            A(1) = 7.0
            A(2) = 7.0
            B(2) = A(2)
            B(3) = A(3)
```

This vectorized sequence most likely will produce different results.
    Consider the following example:

```
            X(1) = STRT
            DO 10 I = 2, 1000
               X(I) = X(I - 1) + 1.0
    10      CONTINUE
```

Here $X(1)$ is used to compute $X(2)$, $X(2)$ is used to compute $X(3)$,
and so forth. However, if this code were to be vectorized, *all* of the X
terms would be fetched at once, 1.0 would be added to each of them,
and only the first value would be known to be correct.
    Likewise, for

```
            DO 1 I = 1, 10
               A(I) = X(I)
               Y(I) = A(I + 1)
    1       CONTINUE
```

the scalar ordering would be different than the parallel ordering. However, in this case simply reordering the assignments in the loop will
produce a vectorizable loop:

```
            DO 1 I = 1, 10
               Y(I) = A(I + 1)
               A(I) = X(I)
    1       CONTINUE
```

This approach works here because in the scalar ordering of both loops,
the old value of $A(I + 1)$ is assigned to $Y(I)$ and then replaced by a new
value on the next iteration. Thus, although recursion is involved, the two
statements are actually *not dependent*. For examples like this one, it is

likely that the compiler will reorder the statements and produce a vectorized loop.

Similarly, the following loops are considered recursive, but with no dependency problems:

```
        DO 20 I = 1, 1000
            X(I) = X(I + 1) + 1
20          CONTINUE

        DO 30, I = 1, 1000
            A(I) = A(I) + X(I) + Y(I)
30          CONTINUE
```

In the DO 20 loop, no X value is reused after being computed, and therefore there is no feedback. In the DO 30 loop, no A value is reused after being generated; it is merely stored. Consequently, both loops will vectorize.

Alas, the use of additional variables in the subscript can also prevent a loop from being vectorized. For example,

```
        L = 10
        :
        DO 60 I = 1,5
            X(I) = X(I + L)
60          CONTINUE
```

does not vectorize because the compiler does not know that L is not negative since L is defined at run time. L is said to be an *ambiguous subscript*. However, the programmer can *force* such loops to vectorize by including a *compiler directive*, CDIR$, in the code that tells the compiler to do it, as follows:

```
        L = 10
        :
CDIR$ IVDEP
        DO 60 I = 1, 5
            X(I) = X(I + L)
60          CONTINUE
```

This time the loop will vectorize, but it is the programmer's responsibility to be sure it will produce the correct results (in this case, that L is nonnegative).

Sometimes a reordering of the loops will allow the inner loop to vectorize. The fundamental operation of a matrix product illustrates this technique. The usual way of coding the matrix product

$$C = A * B$$

is as follows:

```
      DO 30 I = 1, L
        DO 20 J = 1, M
          C(I, J) = 0.0
          DO 10, K = 1, N
            C(I, J) = C(I, J) + A(I, K) * B(K, J)
10          CONTINUE
20        CONTINUE
30      CONTINUE
```

Unfortunately the inner loop will not vectorize due to the recursion on C; imagine what would happen if all N steps of the K loop took place simultaneously.

However, we can rewrite the loops as follows:

```
      DO 30 I = 1, L
        DO 10 J = 1, M
          C(I, J) = 0.0
10        CONTINUE
        DO 20 K = 1, N
          DO 15 J = 1, M
            C(I, J) = C(I, J) + A(I, K) * B(K, J)
15          CONTINUE
20        CONTINUE
30      CONTINUE
```

Here the inner loop vectorizes completely, resulting in an execution speed of five to ten times that of the first sequence. In this case an entire row of C is incremented simultaneously; the operations are done in a different order, but both forms yield the same results, including round-off errors. The disadvantage is that most people do not recognize a matrix product in this form, although those who work on super-computers are used to it.

One relatively easy way to achieve vectorization is to use some of the library subroutines provided for this purpose. Where possible, simple loops that calculate a single scalar result can be replaced with a call to the appropriate optimized subroutine.

For example,

```
            SUM = 0.0
            DO 10 I = 1, 100
              SUM = SUM + A(I)
10          CONTINUE
```

is more efficiently written as

```
        SUM = SSUM(100, A(1), 1)
```

where SSUM is a library routine in the Cray series $SCILIB library. Likewise, the preceding matrix product sequence could be written as:

```
        CALL MXM(A, L, B, M, C, N)
```

A disadvantage of this approach is, of course, the loss of portability to other types of supercomputers. (However, the state of supercomputer programming is such that portability is not a practical issue—yet.)

The presence of one or more IF statements inside a loop also may inhibit automatic vectorization. However, techniques exist that allow the programmer to achieve vectorization in other ways, depending on the structure of the code. For example, some of the standard intrinsic functions or some of the special utility functions can be often used in place of IF statements to produce vectorization loops.

For example, the loop

```
        DO 10 I = INIT, TERM
          X(I) = A(I)
          IF (B(I) .GT. A(I)) X(I) = B(I)
10      CONTINUE
```

can be rewritten as

```
        DO 10, I = INIT, TERM
          X(I) = MAX(A(I), B(I))
10      CONTINUE
```

which will vectorize.

One utility function, CVMGT(A, B, L), is defined to be A if L is true and B otherwise. It can be used to *merge* the results of different vector operations, as in the next example:

```
        DO 50 I = 1, 1000
          IF (A(I) .LT. 0.0) THEN
              B(I) = A(I) + D(I)
          ELSE
              B(I) = A(I) * E(I)
          ENDIF
50      CONTINUE
```

This loop can be rewritten to vectorize as follows:

```
        DO 50 I = 1, 1000
          B(I) = CVMGT(A(I) + D(I), A(I) * E(I), A(I) .LT. 0.0)
50      CONTINUE
```

Actually, recent versions of the Cray CFT compiler will vectorize the first loop. However, more complex forms, such as nested IF-THEN blocks, will prevent automatic vectorization.

For example, the loop

```
        DO 10 I = 1, N
          IF (A(I) .GT. X) THEN
              A(I + 1) = B(I) + C
          ENDIF
10      CONTINUE
```

cannot vectorize since the elements of A appear in the IF condition and the assignment statement. Thus, as in preceding cases, the A values might be different in scalar and vector versions.

Nonlinear indexing also poses a problem for vectorization. Generally, for vectorization to take place, the array elements must be referenced in a linear order. Therefore the following loop will not vectorize:

```
        DO 10 I = 1, 1000
            J = INDX(I)
            X(I) = Y(J) * SIN(X(I)) / A
   10       CONTINUE
```

However, this loop can be rewritten as:

```
        DO 20 I = 1, 1000
            J = INDX(I)
            TEMP(I) = Y(J)
   20       CONTINUE
        DO 30 I = 1, 1000
            X(I) = TEMP(I) * SIN(X(I)) / A
   30       CONTINUE
```

Loop 20 doesn't vectorize, but loop 30 does, and if the computation is extensive enough, as in this example, there can be a significant time savings.

There also exists a library routine, GATHER, for collecting the data elements to be manipulated into successive array elements that we can subsequently reference in a vectorized DO loop. The preceding problems and corresponding techniques represent only a small sample of those encountered in such applications.

A number of the problems just described can now be handled automatically by some of the compilers currently in production. However, much of a programmer's work on such machines still involves a great deal of tuning and rewriting in order to achieve optimal results. These problems are common to all vector supercomputers. Furthermore, programming some of the other classes of supercomputers is even more complicated.

The intent here was to give you a sense of the additional considerations involved in writing real production programs for supercomputers. The process is not as tidy and well-structured as we would like it to be. Indeed, many of the style, structure, and modularity guidelines we have suggested are often violated in favor of vectorization. But don't give up. Continue to use the principles of good structure, modularity, and style that were put forth in earlier chapters. The compilers are continually being improved, and the next standard will certainly provide additional language features to help you out. FORTRAN is a powerful, evolving language that will be used by engineers, scientists, and mathematicians to solve computational problems for a long time to come.

APPENDIX A

Three Common Character Sets

A.1 ASCII

Left digit(s)	Right digit	0	1	2	3	4	5	6	7	8	9
3				blank	!	"	#	$	%	&	'
4		(	)	*	+	,	-	.	/	0	1
5		2	3	4	5	6	7	8	9	:	;
6		<	=	>	?	@	A	B	C	D	E
7		F	G	H	I	J	K	L	M	N	O
8		P	Q	R	S	T	U	V	W	X	Y
9		Z	[	\	]	^	_	`	a	b	c
10		d	e	f	g	h	i	j	k	l	m
11		n	o	p	q	r	s	t	u	v	w
12		x	y	z	{	|	}				

Codes 00 to 31 and 127 are control characters that are not printable. Code 32 is the blank.

A.2 EBCDIC

Left digit(s)	Right digit	0	1	2	3	4	5	6	7	8	9
6						blank					
7						¢	.	<	(	+	|
8		&									
9		!	$	*	)	;	¬	-	/		
10								^	,	%	_
11		>	?								
12			`	:	#	@	'	=	"		a
13		b	c	d	e	f	g	h	i		
14							j	k	l	m	n
15		o	p	q	r						
16			~	s	t	u	v	w	x	y	z
17									\	{	}
18		[	]								
19					A	B	C	D	E	F	G
20		H	I								J
21		K	L	M	N	O	P	Q	R		
22								S	T	U	V
23		W	X	Y	Z						
24		0	1	2	3	4	5	6	7	8	9

Codes 00 to 63 and 250 to 255 represent nonprintable control characters. Code 64 is the blank.

A.3 CDC Scientific

Left digit	Right digit	0	1	2	3	4	5	6	7	8	9
0		:	A	B	C	D	E	F	G	H	I
1		J	K	L	M	N	O	P	Q	R	S
2		T	U	V	W	X	Y	Z	0	1	2
3		3	4	5	6	7	8	9	+	−	*
4		/	(	)	$	=	blank	,	.	≡	[
5		]	%	≠	↦	∨	∧	↑	↓	<	>
6		≤	≥	¬	;						

Code 45 is the blank.

APPENDIX B

Table of Intrinsic Functions*

Intrinsic function	Definition	Number of arguments	Generic name	Specific name	Type of — Arg.	Func.
Type con-version	Convert to integer	1	INT	—	Int	Int
				INT	Real	Int
				IFIX	Real	Int
				IDINT	Dble	Int
				—	Cmplx	Int
	Convert to real	1	REAL	REAL	Int	Real
				FLOAT	Int	Real
				—	Real	Real
				SNGL	Dble	Real
				—	Cmplx	Real
	Convert to dble.	1	DBLE	—	Int	Dble
				—	Real	Dble
				—	Dble	Dble
				—	Cmplx	Dble
	Convert to complex	1 or 2	CMPLX	—	Int	Cmplx
				—	Real	Cmplx
				—	Dble	Cmplx
				—	Cmplx	Cmplx
	Convert to integer	1		ICHAR	Char	Int

*The symbol a represents the argument; a_i represents the ith argument. Also, a_r and a_i are the real and imaginary parts of a complex argument.

Intrinsic function	Definition	Number of arguments	Generic name	Specific name	Type of Arg.	Type of Func.
	Convert to character	1		CHAR	Int	Char
Truncation	$\text{Int}(a)$	1	AINT	AINT	Real	Real
				DINT	Dble	Dble
Nearest whole #	$\text{Int}(a + .5)$ if $a \geq 0$ $\text{Int}(a - .5)$ if $a < 0$	1	ANINT	ANINT	Real	Real
				DNINT	Dble	Dble
Nearest integer	$\text{Int}(a + .5)$ if $a \geq 0$ $\text{Int}(a - .5)$ if $a < 0$	1	NINT	NINT	Real	Int
				IDNINT	Dble	Int
Absolute value	$\|a\|$	1	ABS	IABS	Int	Int
				ABS	Real	Real
				DABS	Dble	Dble
	$(a_r{}^2 - a_i{}^2)^{1/2}$			CABS	Cmplx	Real
Remaindering	$a_1 - \text{int}(a_1/a_2) * a_2$	2	MOD	MOD	Int	Int
				AMOD	Real	Real
				DMOD	Dble	Dble
Transfer of sign	$\|a_1\|$ if $a_2 \geq 0$ $-\|a_1\|$ if $a_2 < 0$	2	SIGN	ISIGN	Int	Int
				SIGN	Real	Real
				DSIGN	Dble	Dble
Positive diff	$a_1 - a_2$ if $a_1 > a_2$ 0 if $a_1 \leq a_2$	2	DIM	IDIM	Int	Int
				DIM	Real	Real
				DDIM	Dble	Dble
Dble Prec product	$a_1 * a_2$	2		DPROD	Real	Dble
Choosing largest value	$\max(a_1, a_2, \dots)$	≥ 2	MAX	MAX0	Int	Int
				AMAX1	Real	Real
				DMAX1	Dble	Dble
				AMAX0	Int	Real
				MAX1	Real	Int
Choosing smallest value	$\min(a_1, a_2, \dots)$	≥ 2	MIN	MIN0	Int	Int
				AMIN1	Real	Real
				DMIN1	Dble	Dble
				AMIN0	Int	Real
				MIN1	Real	Int
Length	Length of char entity	1		LEN	Char	Int
Index of a substrg	Location of substring a_2 in string a_1	2		INDEX	Char	Int
Imaginary part of cmplx arg	a_i	1		AIMAG	Cmplx	Real
Conjugate of cmplx arg	$(a_r, -a_i)$	1		CONJG	Cmplx	Cmplx

Intrinsic function	Definition	Number of arguments	Generic name	Specific name	Type of Arg.	Type of Func.
Square root	$(a)^{1/2}$	1	SQRT	SQRT	Real	Real
				DSQRT	Dble	Dble
				CSQRT	Cmplx	Cmplx
Exponential	$e ** a$	1	EXP	EXP	Real	Real
				DEXP	Dble	Dble
				CEXP	Cmplx	Cmplx
Natural logarithm	$\log(a)$	1	LOG	ALOG	Real	Real
				DLOG	Dble	Dble
				CLOG	Cmplx	Cmplx
Common logarithm	$\log 10(a)$	1	LOG10	ALOG10	Real	Real
				DLOG10	Dble	Dble
Sine	$\sin(a)$	1	SIN	SIN	Real	Real
				DSIN	Dble	Dble
				CSIN	Cmplx	Cmplx
Cosine	$\cos(a)$	1	COS	COS	Real	Real
				DCOS	Dble	Dble
				CCOS	Cmplx	Cmplx
Tangent	$\tan(a)$	1	TAN	TAN	Real	Real
				DTAN	Dble	Dble
Arcsine	$\arcsin(a)$	1	ASIN	ASIN	Real	Real
				DASIN	Dble	Dble
Arccosine	$\arccos(a)$	1	ACOS	ACOS	Real	Real
				DCOS	Dble	Dble
Arctangent	$\arctan(a)$	1	ATAN	ATAN	Real	Real
				DTAN	Dble	Dble
	$\arctan(a_1/a_2)$	2	ATAN2	ATAN2	Real	Real
				DATAN2	Dble	Dble
Hyperbolic sine	$\sinh(a)$	1	SINH	SINH	Real	Real
				DSINH	Dble	Dble
Hyperbolic cosine	$\cosh(a)$	1	COSH	COSH	Real	Real
				DCOSH	Dble	Dble
Hyperbolic tangent	$\tanh(a)$	1	TANH	TANH	Real	Real
				DTANH	Dble	Dble
Lexically > or =	$a_1 \geq a_2$	2		LGE	Char	Char
Lexically >	$a_1 > a_2$	2		LGT	Char	Char
Lexically < or =	$a_1 \leq a_2$	2		LLE	Char	Char
Lexically <	$a_1 < a_2$	2		LLT	Char	Char

APPENDIX C

Syntax of the FORTRAN Language*

The charts in this appendix are duplicated in appropriate places throughout the book.

arithmetic assignment statement

arithmetic expression

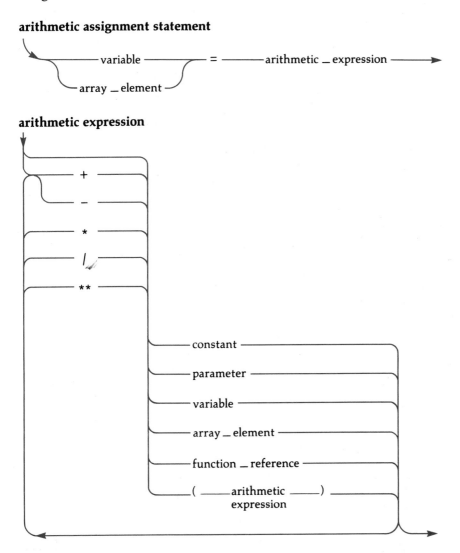

* Syntax charts are reproduced with permission from American National Standards Institute publication ANSI X3.9-1978, copyright 1978 by the American National Standards Institute. Copies of this standard may be purchased from the American National Standards Institute at 1430 Broadway, New York, NY 10018.

array declarator (restricted)

array declarator

array element (restricted)

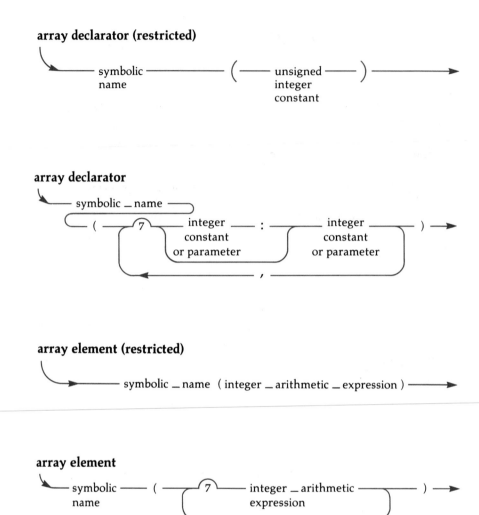

array element

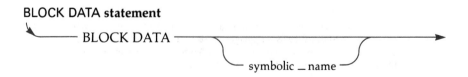

BACKSPACE statement: See REWIND statement.

BLOCK DATA statement

CALL statement

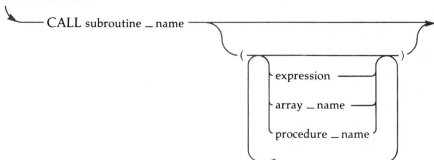

character expression

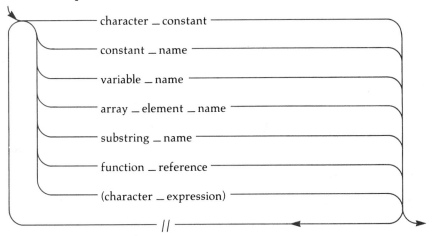

CHARACTER statement

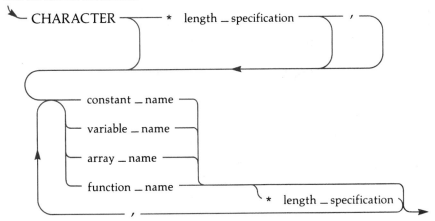

CLOSE statement

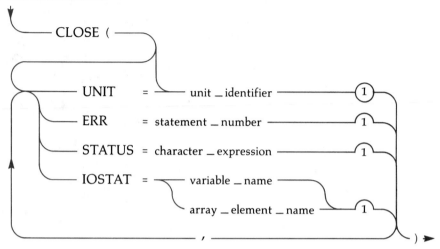

COMMON statement

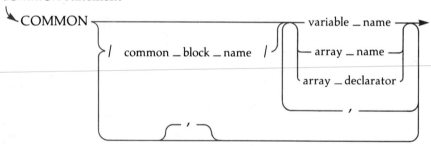

complex constant

COMPLEX statement

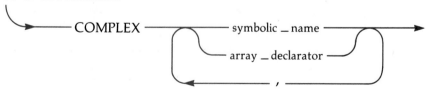

control information list

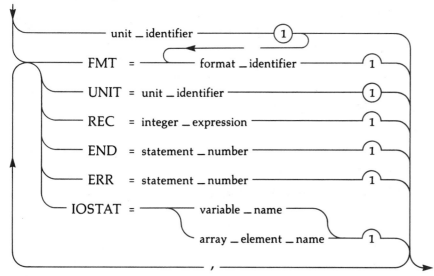

digit

DO statement

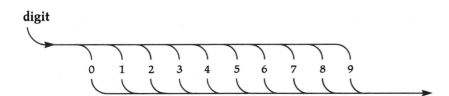

double precision constant

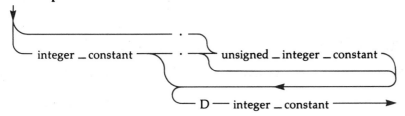

DOUBLE PRECISION statement

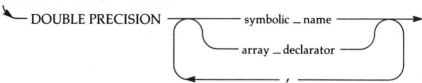

ENDFILE statement: See REWIND statement.

EXTERNAL statement

FORMAT statement

function reference

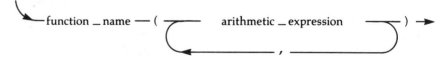

FUNCTION statement

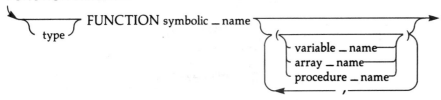

GOTO statement

block IF structures

1. IF (logical expression) THEN

    $\left[\begin{array}{l} \text{block of 1 or more statements—} \\ \text{executed only if logical expression is } \textit{true} \end{array}\right]$

    ENDIF

2. IF (logical expression) THEN

    $\left[\begin{array}{l} \text{block of 0 or more statements—} \\ \text{executed only if logical expression is } \textit{true} \end{array}\right]$

    ELSE

    $\left[\begin{array}{l} \text{block of 0 or more statements—} \\ \text{executed only if logical expression is } \textit{false} \end{array}\right]$

    ENDIF

3. IF (logical expression 1) THEN

    $\left[\begin{array}{l} \text{block of 0 or more statements—} \\ \text{executed only if logical expression 1 is } \textit{true} \end{array}\right]$

    $\left\{\begin{array}{l} \text{ELSE IF (logical expression 2) THEN} \\ \left[\begin{array}{l} \text{block of 0 or more statements—} \\ \text{executed only if logical expression 2 is } \textit{true} \\ \text{and logical expression 1 is } \textit{false} \end{array}\right] \\ \vdots \end{array}\right.$

    ELSE

    $\left[\begin{array}{l} \text{block of 0 or more statements—} \\ \text{executed only if } \textit{all} \text{ of the above logical} \\ \text{expressions are } \textit{false} \end{array}\right]$

    ENDIF

implied DO list

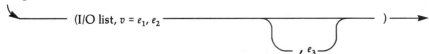

integer constant

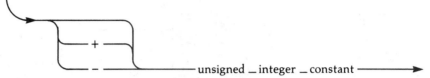

INTEGER statement

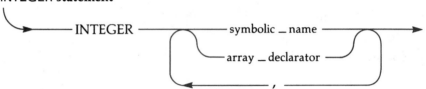

INTRINSIC statement

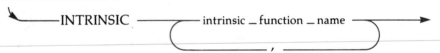

length — specification

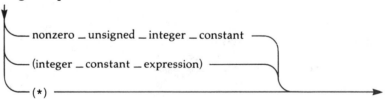

logical assignment statement

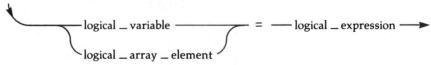

logical expression

logical IF statement

LOGICAL statement

OPEN statement

PARAMETER statement

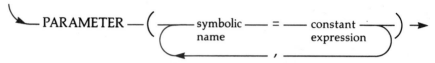

PRINT statement (general): See WRITE statement.

PRINT statement (list-directed)

PROGRAM statement

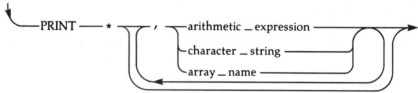

READ statement

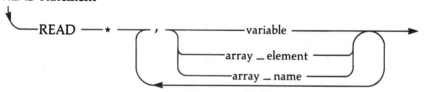

READ statement (general): See WRITE statement.

READ statement (revised)

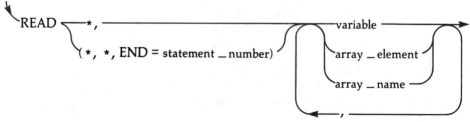

real constant

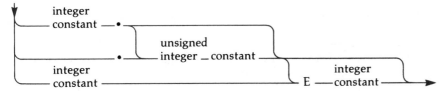

REAL statement

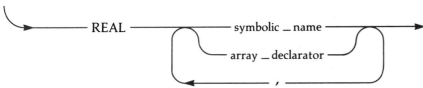

relation

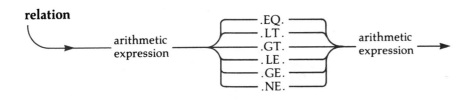

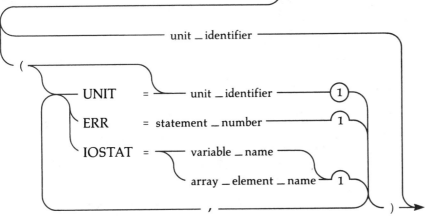

SAVE statement

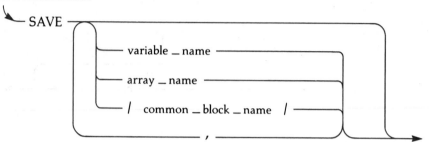

SUBROUTINE statement

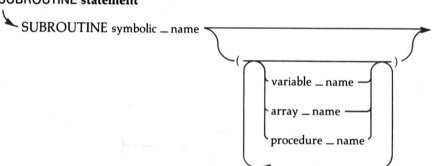

substring name

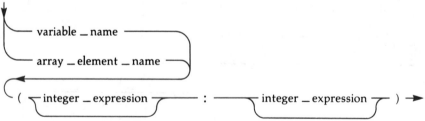

symbolic name

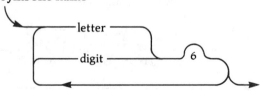

unsigned integer constant

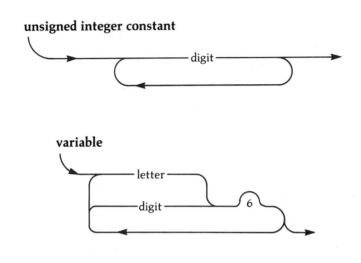

variable

WRITE statement → WRITE

READ statement → READ

PRINT statement → PRINT

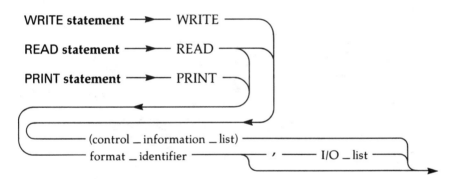

(control – information – list)

format – identifier

I/O – list

APPENDIX D

Answers to Starred Exercises

Chapter 1

5. A comment statement is characterized by a letter C or an asterisk (*) in column 1.

6. a. `INTEGER ALPHA, BETA`

   c. `PRINT *, PROD, QUOT`   (same line)

      `PRINT *, PROD`   (different lines)

      `PRINT *, QUOT`

   e. `REAL DEL(1000)`

   g. `STCNT = 1`   (assuming STCNT is declared to be an integer)

7. c. `IF (THRESH .GE. EPS) Y = EPS * (X1 - X2)`

   e. `IF (B .NE. 0.0) PRINT *, A / B`

f. IF (ABS (X — Y) .LT. EPS * 0.01) THEN
        X = 0.0
        Y = 0.0
     ENDIF

(ABS is an *intrinsic function* that is used here to take the absolute value of X − Y. See Chapter 2.)

8. a.   XSUM = 0.0
          DO 10 I = 1, 50
             READ *, X
             XSUM = XSUM + X
   10   CONTINUE
   c.   DO 20 I = 1, 100
             XMT(I) = 0.0
   20   CONTINUE

9. This program reads a list of 1,000 or fewer integers, computes the sums of all the numbers (A) and the negative values (N), and prints the sums.

12. The program halts with the error message,

"MAXIMUM NO. OF VALUES EXCEEDED"

19. The initial value of N will always be zero since it is used as a counter to accumulate the sum. Since it will never be changed and since the initial value would not be clarified in any way by the use of a symbolic name, a parameter is not necessary here.

21. Define an additional parameter MINST = 100.0. Insert after line 35:

IF (VALUE .LE. MINST) THEN

and insert after line 41:

ENDIF

Chapter 2
  1. a. Valid
     d. Invalid (strictly speaking, although many compilers will accept lowercase letters)
     e. Valid
     f. Valid (but not recommended)
     i. Valid (spaces are ignored)
  2. a. 0.7193E + 0   **d.** −0.1E−7   **f.** 0.3E−6
  4. The symbolic constant LIM should be defined before it is used as the dimension of the array CAL.
  6. b. 11.0 (real), 11 (integer)
     d. 0.0 (real), 0 (integer)
     g. 4.0 (real), 4 (integer)

  h. −0.015625 (real), 0 (integer)
  l. 0.666667 (real), 0 (integer)
  n. 1.75 (real), 1 (integer)

7. b. Not equivalent. For I = 1, J = 2, and X = 6.0, the original assignment yields Y = 3.0, while Y = 0.0 for (b).
  d. Equivalent. I would be converted to real before the division takes place.

9. c. Valid (if A is an array)
  g. Invalid (missing right parenthesis)
  i. Invalid (EPSILON is too long)

11. b. `T = 0.5 * B * H`
  d. `Z = X / (A + X / B)`
  g. `A = P * (1.0 + R / K) ** (K * N)`
  k. `T = N / ((N - A) * (N - B))`
  m. `X = SQRT((C * T) ** 2 - Y ** 2 - Z ** 2)`
    (for example)
  r. `Q = LOG10(ABS(SEC(X) + TAN(X)))`
  n. `F = X * ATAN(X / A) + B / 2.0 * LOG(X * X + B * B)`

12. a. $a + b/c + d$
  c. $x^y \cdot c^d + 1$

13. b.
```
INTEGER SIZE
PARAMETER (SIZE = 300)
REAL SCORE(SIZE), DIFF(300)
```
  d.
```
PRINT *, A,B,C
PRINT *
PRINT *, 'SUM = ', X(1)
PRINT *, 'ERROR SUM = ', X(2)
```

17.
```
      PROGRAM TRIANGLE
***************************************************
* COMPUTE OPPOSITE SIDE AND AREA OF TRIANGLE
* GIVEN TWO SIDES AND ANGLE.
* NON--INTERACTIVE INPUT.
* PI = 3.1415926
* ANGLE -- GIVEN ANGLE IN DEGREES (INPUT)
* B, C, -- TWO SIDES ADJACENT TO ANGLE (INPUT)
* A -- SIDE OPPOSITE ANGLE (OUTPUT)
* AREA -- AREA OF TRIANGLE (OUTPUT)
***************************************************
      PARAMETER (PI = 3.1415926)
      REAL A, B, C, ANGLE, AREA
      READ *, ANGLE
      READ *, B, C
      A = SQRT(B*B + C*C - 2.0 * B * C * COS(ANGLE*PI/180.0))
      AREA = 0.5 * B * C * SIN(ANGLE * PI / 180.0))
```

```
          PRINT * 'COMPUTE THIRD SIDE AND AREA OF A TRIANGLE :'
          PRINT *, 'FOR SIDES B, C, = '; B, C
          PRINT *, 'AND ANGLE A (IN DEGREES) = ', ANGLE
          PRINT *, 'SIDE A = ', A
          PRINT *, 'AREA OF TRIANGLE = ', AREA
          END
```

22.
```
          PROGRAM SINAPX
     ***********************************************************
     * THIS PROGRAM CONPUTES AN APPROXIMATION TO SIN(X), WHERE X
     * IS AN INPUT VALUE, USING 1ST 4 TERMS OF TAYLOR SERIES.
     * X - THE ARGUMENT (INPUT)
     * SINX - APPROX. TO SIN(X)
     ***********************************************************
          REAL X, SINX
          READ *, X
          SINX = X - X**3 / 6.0 + X**5 / 120.0 - X**7 / 5040.0
          PRINT *, 'FOR X = ', X
          PRINT *,'THE 4--TERM TAYLOR SERIES APPROX. TO SIN(X): '
     $         , SINX
          PRINT *,'THE INTRINSIC FUNCTION VALUE FOR SIN(X): ',
     $           SIN(X)
          PRINT *, 'THE DIFFERENCE: ', SIN(X) - SINX
          END
```

Chapter 3

1. **a.** Invalid; A .GT. 0.0 .AND. (B .EQ. 2.0 .OR. C .GT. A)
    d. Valid
    g. Valid
    i. Invalid; P .OR. (.NOT. Q)   **l.** Valid

3. **a.** X .LT. Y .AND. Y .LT. Z
    d. (X .LE. (A+B)) .AND. (Y .LE. (A+B))

4. **a.** IF (ABS(FX) .GE. EPS .AND. N .LT. NMAX) N = N + 1
    c.
```
    IF (MYGRAD .GE. 90) THEN
        GRADE(1) = GRADE(1) + 1
    ELSE IF (MYGRADE .GE. 80) THEN
        GRADE(2) = GRADE(2) + 1
    ELSE IF (MYGRADE .GE. 70) THEN
        GRADE(3) = GRADE(3) + 1
    ELSE
        GRADE(4) = GRADE(4) + 1
    ENDIF
```

5. **a.**
```
        I = 1
        ODDSUM = 0.0
        EVNSUM = 0.0
    *   WHILE (NOT END OF ARRAY) DO
```

```
10      CONTINUE
        IF (I .LE. K) THEN
            IF (MOD(NUM(I), 2) .EQ. 0) THEN
                EVNSUM = EVNSUM + NUM(I)
            ELSE
                ODDSUM = ODDSUM + NUM(I)
            ENDIF
            I = I + 1
            GOTO 10
        ENDIF
*       ENDWHILE
d.      I = 1
        LARGE = SAMPL(1)
        SMALL = SAMPL(1)
        DIFF = 0.0
*       WHILE (MORE ARRAY VALUES AND VALID RANGE) DO
10      CONTINUE
        IF (I .LE. N .AND. DIFF .LE. MAXDIF) THEN
            IF (ABS(SAMPL(I)-CRIT) .LE. EPS) PRINT*, SAMPL(I)
            IF (SAMPL(I) .GT. LARGE) THEN
                LARGE = SAMPL(I)
            ELSE IF (SAMPL(I) .LT. SMALL) THEN
                SMALL = SAMPL(I)
            ENDIF
            IF (LARGE - SMALL .GT. DIFF) DIFF = LARGE - SMALL
            I = I + 1
            GOTO 10
        ENDIF
*       ENDWHILE


8.      PROGRAM POLYN
***************************************************************
* THIS PROGRAM COMPARES THE EVALUATION OF A POLYNOMIAL BY
* THE STANDARD REPRESENTATION AND BY HORNER'S METHOD. THE
* DEGREE AND THE COEFFICIENTS OF THE POLYNOMIAL ARE READ IN.
* THE POLYNOMIAL IS LIMITED TO DEGREES 25 OR LESS; IT DOES
* NOT AVOID COMPUTING VALUES OUTSIDE THE RANGE OF MACHINE-
* REPRESENTABLE NUMBERS.
*
* P -- POLYNOMIAL
* X -- POINT WHERE P IS EVALUATED
* XPOW - CURRENT X-TERM IN STANDARD REPRESENTATION OF P
* A -- ARRAY OF COEFFICIENTS OF P
* N -- DEGREE OF P + 1
* NMAX -- LIMIT ON N
* MCOUNT, ACOUNT -- COUNT OF NO. OF MULT. AND ADD.
* MACHHI, MACHLO -- LARGEST, SMALLEST REP. OF REALS IN
*                   THIS MACHINE
***************************************************************
```

```
      INTEGER N, MCOUNT, ACOUNT
      PARAMETER (NMAX = 26)
      REAL A(NMAX), X, XPOW, P, MACHHI, MACHLO
      PARAMETER (MACHHI = 1.E37, MACHLO = 1.E-37)
*
* INITIALIZE P
*
      READ *, N
      IF (N .GT. NMAX) THEN
         PRINT *, 'N IS TOO LARGE ', 'N = ', N
         STOP
      ENDIF
      DO 10 I = 1, N
         READ *, A(I)
10    CONTINUE
      READ *, X
*
* EVALUATE P IN STANDARD FORM
*
      P = A(1)
      XPOW = X
      DO 20 I = 2, N
         P = P + A(I) * XPOW
         XPOW = XPOW * X
         IF(ABS(XPOW) .GT. MACHHI / 10.0 .OR. ABS(XPOW) .LT.
     $         MACHLO * 10.0 .OR. ABS(P) .GT. MACHHI / 10.0
     $         .OR. ABS(P) .LT. MACHLO * 10.0) THEN
            PRINT *,'COMPUTED VALUE TOO CLOSE TO MACHINE LIM'
            PRINT *,'CHOOSE SMALLER/LARGER X AND/OR SMALLER N'
            STOP
         ENDIF
20    CONTINUE
      MCOUNT = 2 * (N - 1)
      ACOUNT = N - 1
      PRINT * , 'FOR X = ', X, ' P = ', P
      PRINT * , 'FOR STANDARD REPRESENTATION OF P '
      PRINT * , 'THE NO. OF MULTIPLICATIONS IS: ', MCOUNT
      PRINT * , 'THE NO. OF ADDITIONS IS: ', ACOUNT
*
* HORNER'S METHOD FOR P
*
      P = X * A(N)
      DO 30 I = N - 1, 2, -1
         P = X * (A(I) + P)
30    CONTINUE
      P = P + A(1)
      MCOUNT = N - 1
      ACOUNT = N - 1
      PRINT * , 'FOR X = ', X, 'P = ', P
```

```
      PRINT * , 'USING HORNER SCHEME FOR P'
      PRINT * , 'THE NO. OF MULTIPLICATIONS IS: ', MCOUNT
      PRINT *,  'THE NO. OF ADDITIONS IS: ', ACOUNT
      END
```

10. a.
```
      PROGRAM TABFUN
      *****************************************************************
      * TABULATES THE FUNCTION 1/3 * LOG((1+COS X)/(1-COS X)) ON THE
      * GIVEN INTERVAL.  INTERVAL LIMITS AND STEPSIZE ARE PARAMETERS.
      *****************************************************************
      REAL LOW, HIGH, STEP, Y, X, X0
      INTEGER STEPNO
      PARAMETER (LOW = 0.5, HIGH = 1.5, STEP = 0.1)
      X0 = LOW
      STEPNO = 0
      PRINT *, 'TABLE OF 1/3 * LOG((1+COS X)/(1-COS X)) VALUES'
      PRINT *
      PRINT *, ' X ', ' Y '
      X = X0
*     WHILE STILL IN INTERVAL DO
10    CONTINUE
      IF (X .LE. HIGH) THEN
         Y = 1.0 / 3.0 * LOG((1.0 + COS(X)) / (1.0 - COS(X)))
         PRINT *, X, Y
         STEPNO = STEPNO + 1
         X = X0 + REAL(STEPNO) * STEP
         GOTO 10
      ENDIF
*     ENDWHILE
      END
```

Chapter 4

2. This program prints the middle value of the three numbers A, B, and
C. A structured version is the following:

```
PROGRAM MIDDLE
REAL A, B, C
READ *, A, B, C
IF ((B .GE. A .AND. A .GE. C) .OR. (C .GE. A .AND.
$    A .GE. B)) PRINT*, A
 IF ((A .GE. B .AND. B .GE. C) .OR. (C .GE. B .AND.
$    B .GE. A)) PRINT *, B
 IF ((A .GE. C .AND. C .GE. B) .OR. (B .GE. C .AND.
$    C .GE. A)) PRINT *, C
 END
```

4. The algorithm works even if $A > B$. If $A = B$, it will print the error
message that F has the same sign at the end points.

7.
```
        PROGRAM FIB2
***************************************************************
* COMPUTES FIBONACCI SEQUENCES THREE DIFFERENT WAYS.
* INTFN2, INTFN1, INTFN -- SUCCESSIVE TERMS IN INTEGER SEQUENCE
* RLF2, RLF1, RLFN -- SUCCESSIVE TERMS IN REAL SEQUENCE
* FNDRCT -- NTH TERM IN SEQUENCE USING DIRECT FORMULA
* SQRT5 -- SQUARE ROOT OF 5
***************************************************************
        INTEGER INTFN, INTFN1, INTFN2, N
        REAL RLFN, RLFN1, RLFN2, SQRT5, FNDRCT
        SQRT5 = SQRT(5.0)
        RLFN2 = 0.0
        RLFN1 = 1.0
        INTF2 = 0
        INTF1 = 1
        PRINT *, 'N', 'DIRECT', 'REAL, 'INTEGER'
        PRINT *, 0, 0.0, 0.0, 0
        PRINT *, 1, 1.0, 1.0, 1
        DO 10 N = 2, 50
           INTFN = INTFN1 + INTFN2
           RLFN = RLFN1 + RLFN2
           FNDRCT=((0.5 * (1.0 + SQRT5)) ** N - (0.5 *
     $           (1.0 - SQRT5)) ** N) / SQRT5
           PRINT *, N, FNDRCT, RLFN, INTFN
           INTFN2 = INTFN1
           INTFN1 = INTFN
           RLFN2 = RLFN1
           RLFN1 = RLFN
10      CONTINUE
        END
```

The integer sequence will *overflow* (the high-order bits used to represent the number are lost), when the terms in the sequence become too large to represent as an integer in the computer. After that point the numbers in the sequence will be meaningless.

10.
```
        REAL FUNCTION COSINE(X, N)
***************************************************************
* COMPUTES AN APPROXIMATION TO THE TAYLOR SERIES FOR THE
* COSINE FUNCTION.  THE FUNCTION DOES NO ERROR CHECKING.
*
* N - THE EXPONENT OF THE LAST TERM TO BE USED (INPUT)
* X - THE ARGUMENT (INPUT)
* I - THE LOOP INDEX
* SUM - SUM OF THE TERMS IN THE SERIES
* TERM - THE CURRENT TERM TO BE ADDED
***************************************************************
        INTEGER N, I
        REAL SUM, TERM, X
        I = 0
```

```
          SUM = 0.0
          TERM = 1.0
*         WHILE (TERMS REMAIN TO BE ADDED) DO
10        CONTINUE
          IF (I .LE. N) THEN
              SUM = SUM + TERM
              TERM = -TERM * (X * X) / REAL ((I + 1) * (I + 2))
              I = I + 2
              GOTO 10
          ENDIF
          COSINE = SUM
          END
```

12.   PROGRAM GEOM2

```
      ***************************************************************
      * AUTHOR: A.B. AUTHOR  6/14/88
      *
      * THIS PROGRAM COMPUTES VOLUMES, SURFACE AREAS, AND SO FORTH
      * OF VARIOUS GEOMETRICAL OBJECTS, BASED ON INPUT FROM THE
      * USER.  THE PROGRAM DOES NO ERROR CHECKING.
      *
      * CHOICE -- MENU ITEM NUMBER (INPUT)
      * VOLSPH -- COMPUTES VOLUME OF SPHERE (FUNCTION)
      * ARASPH -- COMPUTES SURFACE AREA OF SPHERE (FUNCTION)
      * VOLCYL -- COMPUTES VOLUME OF CYLINDER (FUNCTION)
      * ARACYL -- COMPUTES SURFACE AREA OF CYLINDER (FUNCTION)
      * TAREA  -- AREA OF A TRIANGLE (FUNCTION)
      * RADIUS -- RADIUS OF SPHERE OR BASE OF CYLINDER
      * HEIGHT -- HEIGHT OF CYLINDER
      * A, B, C -- SIDES OF TRIANGLE (INPUT)
      ***************************************************************

          INTEGER CHOICE
          REAL A, B, C, RADIUS, HEIGHT, VOLSPH, ARASPH
          REAL VOLCYL, ARASPH, TAREA
*         REPEAT
10        CONTINUE
              PRINT *, 'ENTER   1 TO COMPUTE VOLUME OF SPHERE'
              PRINT *, '        2 TO COMPUTE AREA OF SPHERE'
              PRINT *, '        3 TO COMPUTE VOLUME OF CYLINDER'
              PRINT *, '        4 TO COMPUTE AREA OF CYLINDER'
              PRINT *, '        5 TO COMPUTE AREA OF TRIANGLE'
              PRINT *, '        6 TO EXIT'
              PRINT *
              READ *, CHOICE
              PRINT *
              IF (CHOICE .EQ. 1) THEN
                  PRINT *, 'ENTER THE RADIUS OF THE SPHERE: '
                  READ *, RADIUS
                  PRINT *, 'VOLUME OF THE SPHERE IS: ',VOLSPH(RADIUS)
```

```
              ELSE IF (CHOICE .EQ. 2) THEN
                 PRINT *, 'ENTER THE RADIUS OF THE SPHERE: '
                 READ *, RADIUS
                 PRINT *, 'AREA OF THE SPHERE IS: ', ARASPH(RADIUS)
              ELSE IF (CHOICE .EQ. 3) THEN
                 PRINT*,'ENTER RADIUS OF THE BASE OF THE CYLINDER:'
                 READ *, RADIUS
                 PRINT *, 'ENTER THE HEIGHT OF THE CYLINDER: '
                 READ *, HEIGHT
                 PRINT *, 'VOLUME OF THE CYLINDER IS: ',
     $                    VOLCYL(RADIUS, HEIGHT)
              ELSE IF (CHOICE .EQ. 4) THEN
                 PRINT*,'ENTER RADIUS OF THE BASE OF THE CYLINDER:'
                 READ *, RADIUS
                 PRINT *, 'ENTER THE HEIGHT OF THE CYLINDER: '
                 READ *, HEIGHT
                 PRINT *, 'AREA OF THE CYLINDER IS: ',
     $                    ARACYL(RADIUS, HEIGHT)
               ELSE IF (CHOICE .EQ. 5) THEN
                  PRINT*,'ENTER LENGTHS OF THREE SIDES OF TRIANGLE:'
                  READ *, A, B, C
                  PRINT *, 'THE AREA OF THE TRIANGLE IS: '
                  PRINT *, TAREA(A, B, C)
           ENDIF
           PRINT *
           IF (CHOICE .NE. 6) GOTO 10
     *     UNTIL (CHOOSE TO STOP)
           END

           REAL FUNCTION VOLSPH (RADIUS)
           REAL PI, RADIUS
           PARAMETER (PI = 3.1415926)
           VOLSPH = 4.0 / 3.0 * PI * RADIUS ** 3
           END

           REAL FUNCTION ARASPH (RADIUS)
           REAL PI, RADIUS
           PARAMETER (PI = 3.1415926)
           ARASPH = 4.0 * PI * RADIUS * RADIUS
           END

           REAL FUNCTION VOLCYL (RADIUS, HEIGHT)
           REAL PI, HEIGHT, RADIUS
           PARAMETER (PI = 3,1415926)
           VOLCYL = ÞI * RADIUS * RADIUS * HEIGHT
           END

           REAL FUNCTION ARACYL (RADIUS, HEIGHT)
           REAL PI, HEIGHT, RADIUS
```

```
          PARAMETER (PI = 3.1415926)
          ARACYL = 2.0 * PI * RADIUS * (RADIUS + HEIGHT)
          END

          REAL FUNCTION TAREA (X, Y, Z)
          REAL X, Y, Z, S
          S = 0.5 * (X + Y + Z)
          TAREA = SQRT (S * (S - X) * (S - Y) * (S - Z))
          END
```

15.
```
          PROGRAM PIVALS
     ****************************************************************
     * THIS PROGRAM COMPUTES AND PRINTS A TABLE OF APPROXIMATIONS
     * TO PI USING TWO DIFFERENT SERIES CALCULATIONS FOR N, THE
     * NUMBER OF TERMS, RUNNING FROM 1 TO 10.
     *
     * NTRMS -- MAX NO. OF TERMS (PARAMETER)
     * N -- CURRENT TERM
     * PI945 -- FUNCTION TO COMPUTE PI USING SERIES IN EX. 2.16.
     *          (FUNCTION)
     * PI8 -- FUNCTION TO COMPUTE PI USING SERIES IN EX. 4.15.
     *        (FUNCTION)
     * PI1, PI2 -- TEMPORARY VALUES FOR PI945 AND PI8, RESP.
     ****************************************************************
          INTEGER N, NTRMS
          REAL PI1, PI2, PI, PI945, PI8
          PARAMETER (NTRMS = 10, PI = 3.14159265)
          PRINT *, 'N', 'PI 945', 'ERROR 945', 'PI8', 'ERROR I8'
          N = 1
     *    WHILE TABLE INCOMPLETE DO
10        CONTINUE
          IF (N .LE. NTRMS) THEN
              PI1 = PI945(N)
              PI2 = PI8(N)
              PRINT *, N, PI1, PI - PI1, PI2, PI - PI2
              N = N + 1
              GOTO 10
          ENDIF
     *    ENDWHILE
          END


          REAL FUNCTION PI945(NTRMS)
     ****************************************************************
     * COMPUTES APPROX. TO PI USING FORMULA IN EX. 2.16
     *
     * NTRMS -- NO. OF TERMS
     * N -- NUMBER OF CURRENT TERMS
     * SUM -- SUM OF TERMS
     ****************************************************************
```

```
          INTEGER N, NTRMS
          REAL SUM
          N = 1
          SUM = 1.0
*         WHILE SUM INCOMPLETE DO
10        CONTINUE
          IF (N .LT. NTRMS) THEN
             N = N + 1
             SUM = SUM + 1.0 / REAL(N) ** 6
             GOTO 10
          ENDIF
*         ENDWHILE
          PI945 = (945.0 * SUM) ** (1.0 / 6.0)
          END


          REAL FUNCTION PI8 (NTRMS)
*****************************************************************
* COMPUTES APPROX. TO PI USING FORMULA IN EX. 4.15.
*
* NTRMS -- NO. OF TERMS
* N -- NUMBER OF CURRENT TERMS
* SUM -- SUM OF ALL TERMS
* PSUM -- SUM OF ALL BUT FIRST TERM
*****************************************************************

          INTEGER N, NTERMS
          REAL SUM, PSUM
          N = 1
          PSUM = 0.0
          SUM = 8.0
*         WHILE SUM INCOMPLETE DO
10        CONTINUE
          IF (N .LT. NTRMS) THEN
             N = N + 1
             PSUM = PSUM + 1.0 / (REAL(2 * N - 3) ** 2
     $            * REAL(2 * N - 1) ** 2)
             GOTO 10
          ENDIF
*         ENDWHILE
          SUM = SUM + 16.0 * PSUM
          PI8 = SQRT(SUM)
          END

18.       PROGRAM BSORT
*****************************************************************
* SORTS AN ARRAY OF N REAL NUMBERS INTO ASCENDING ORDER
* USING THE BUBBLE SORT ALGORITHM.  READING AND PRINTING IS
* FROM THE STANDARD INPUT/OUTPUT UNITS.
*
```

```
* A -- THE ARRAY OF NUMBERS
* N -- THE TOTAL NUMBER OF VALUES
* SORTED -- LOGICAL VARIABLE USED TO EXIT FROM LOOP WHEN LIST
*            IS IN ORDER
* MAXN -- DIMENSION OF A  (PARAMETER)
* TEMP -- TEMPORARY VALUE USED TO SWAP ARRAY ELEMENTS
* LAST -- POSITION OF NEXT LARGEST ELEMENT IN THE ARRAY
* I -- LOOP INDEX
****************************************************************

      LOGICAL SORTED
      INTEGER N, MAXN, LAST
      REAL TEMP
      PARAMETER (MAXN = 100)
      REAL A(MAXN)


*
* GET THE DATA AND PRINT IT
*
      PRINT *, 'THE ORIGINAL ARRAY: '
      N = 1
*     WHILE DATA REMAINS DO
10    CONTINUE
         READ (*,*, END = 20) A(N)
         PRINT *, A(N)
         N = N + 1
         IF (N.LE. MAXN) GOTO 10
20    CONTINUE
*     ENDWHILE
      PRINT *
      N = N - 1
*
* SORT THE ARRAY
*
      LAST = N
      SORTED = .FALSE.
*     WHILE ARRAY NOT SORTED DO
30    CONTINUE
      IF (.NOT. SORTED) THEN
         SORTED = .TRUE.
         I = 1
         LAST = LAST - 1
*        WHILE HAVE NOT SCANNED TO LAST ELEMENT DO
40       CONTINUE
         IF (I .LE. LAST) THEN
            IF (A(I) .GT. A(I + 1)) THEN
               TEMP = A(I)
               A(I) = A(I + 1)
```

```
                A(I + 1) = TEMP
                SORTED = .FALSE.
             ENDIF
             I = I + 1
             GOTO 40
          ENDIF
*         ENDWHILE
          GOTO 30
       ENDIF
*    ENDWHILE
*
*  PRINT THE SORTED ARRAY
*
       PRINT *, 'THE SORTED ARRAY IS: '
       I = 1
*     WHILE I <= N DO
50     CONTINUE
       IF (I .LE. N) THEN
          PRINT *, A(I)
          I = I + 1
          GOTO 50
       ENDIF
       END
```

19. **a.**

```
       PROGRAM CAREA
*****************************************************************
* COMPUTES APPROXIMATIONS TO THE AREA UNDER A CURVE
* USING THE RECTANGULAR RULE.
*
* NDIV - TOTAL NO. OF RUNS (SUBDIVISIONS)
* N - CURRENT NO. OF SUBINTERVALS
* I - POINTER TO NO. OF SUBDIVISIONS
* LEND, REND -- LEFT AND RIGHT ENDPOINTS (PARAMETERS)
* AREA -- THE APPROXIMATE AREA
* INTGRL -- RETURNS APPROXIMATE AREA (FUNCTION)
*****************************************************************

       INTEGER N, I, NDIV
       REAL AREA, LEND, REND, INTGRL
       PARAMETER (NDIV = 3)
       INTEGER SDIV(NDIV)
       PARAMETER (LEND = 0.0, REND = 3.1415926)
       I = 1
       READ *, SDIV(1), SDIV(2), SDIV(3)
*     WHILE SUBDIVISION REMAINS DO
10     CONTINUE
       IF (I .LE. NDIV) THEN
          N = SDIV(I)
          AREA = INTGRL (N, LEND, REND)
```

```
          PRINT *, 'THE APPROX TO THE INTEGRAL OF THE FUNCTION'
          PRINT *, 'WITH LEFT AND RIGHT ENDPOINTS:', LEND, REND
          PRINT *, 'AND NO. OF SUBDIVISIONS: ', N
          PRINT *, 'IS: ', AREA
          PRINT *
          I = I + 1
          GOTO 10
       ENDIF
*      ENDWHILE
       END

       REAL FUNCTION INTGRL (N, LEFT, RIGHT)
*****************************************************************
* COMPUTES INTEGRAL OF THE FUNCTION FUN USING
* RECTANGULAR RULE
*
* N -- NO. OF SUBINTERVALS
* LEFT, RIGHT -- LEFT AND RIGHT ENDPTS
* H -- STEPSIZE
* STEP -- CURRENT STEP
* SUM -- SUM OF THE RECTANGULAR AREAS
*****************************************************************

       REAL LEFT, RIGHT, H, FUN, SUM
       INTEGER N, STEP
       STEP = 0
       SUM = 0.0
       H = (LEFT - RIGHT) / REAL(N)
*      WHILE THERE ARE POINTS TO ADD DO
10     CONTINUE
       IF (STEP .LT. N) THEN
          SUM = SUM + H * FUN (LEFT + H * REAL(STEP))
          STEP = STEP + 1
          GOTO 10
       ENDIF
*      ENDWHILE
       INTGRL = SUM
       END

       REAL FUNCTION FUN(X)
*****************************************************************
* FUNCTION TO BE INTEGRATED
*****************************************************************
       REAL X
       FUN = SIN(X)
       END
```

Chapter 5

1. **a.** DO 10 P = 1, 100, 3
   c. DO 10 CNTDN = 10, 0, -1
   e. DO 10 INCR = 0.0, 5.001, 0.01
      (The choice of 5.001 here ensures that roundoff error will not
      prevent the last pass through the loop from taking place.)
   g. DO 10 MIL = -2 * N, 0, 2

2. **a.** 7; 22
   c. 33; 9.6 (in the absence of roundoff error)
   e. 0; 10
   g. 5; M + 3

3. **a.** 0

4. **a.** I = 11, J = 10, K = 6, L = 5, N = 50

5. **a.**
```
         K = 0
*        WHILE K <= N+1 DO
10       CONTINUE
         IF (K .LE. N + 1) THEN
             IF (K .NE. L) THEN
                 SUM = SUM + REAL(K ** 3) / REAL(K + 1)
             ENDIF
             K = K + 1
             GOTO 10
         ENDIF
*        ENDWHILE
```

7.
```
              :
              :
         SUMI3 = 0
         DO 10 I = 1, 9
             SUMI3 = SUMI3 + I ** 3
10       CONTINUE
         DO 20 I = 11, 30
             SUMI3 = SUMI3 + I ** 3
20       CONTINUE
```

9.
```
              :
              :
         SUM = 0
         DO 10 I = 0, N - 1
             DO 20 J = 0, N
                 SUM = SUM + (1 + I * J)
20           CONTINUE
10       CONTINUE
              :
              :
```

13.
```
         PI = 3.1415926
         XSUM = 0.0
         KEL = -276.0
```

```
          RAD = PI / 180.0
          SQ2 = SQRT(2.0)
          DO 200 IT = 0, 100
             T = REAL(IT) * 0.1
             ABS1MT = ABS(1.0 - T ** 3)
             T3PKEL = T ** 3 + KEL
             YPROD = 1.0
             VOLMAX = MAX(INT((VN - V0 + 0.2) / 0.2), 0)
             DO 100 IVOL = 1, VOLMAX
                VOL = V0 + 0.2 * REAL(IVOL - 1)
                XSUM = XSUM + T3PKEL * COS(VOL * RAD)
                YPROD = YPROD * ABS1MT
                FTV = XSUM - T * YPROD
                PRINT *, T, VOL, FTV
  100        CONTINUE
             PRINT *, YPROD
  200     CONTINUE
```

18.
```
                 .
                 .
                 .
          DPROD = 0.0
          DO 10 I = 1, N
             DPROD = DPROD + X(I) * Y(I)
   10     CONTINUE
                 .
                 .
                 .
```

22.
```
          DO 30 I = 1, N
             DO 20 J = 1, N
                SUM = 0.0
                DO 10 K = 1, N
                   SUM = SUM + A(I, K) * B(K, J)
   10           CONTINUE
                C(I, J) = SUM
   20        CONTINUE
   30     CONTINUE
```

24.
```
          PROGRAM PBBEET
   *****************************************************************
   * COMPUTES COEFFICIENTS IN EQUATION RELATING INFECTED
   * TREES TO ALTITUDE BY LINEAR LEAST SQUARES.   DATA
   * IS READ FROM THE STANDARD INPUT UNIT.
   *
   * B, M -- COEFFICIENTS TO BE COMPUTED
   * SUMA, SUMAS2, SUMAT, SUMT -- SUMS FOR LEAST SQ.
   * N -- NUMBER OF ALTITUDE MEASURMENTS
   * A -- ARRAY OF ALTITUDES
   * T -- ARRAY OF NUMBER OF INFECTED TREES
   * I -- LOOP INDEX
   *****************************************************************
```

```
        INTEGER N, I
        REAL A(30), T(30), SUMA, SUMASQ, SUMAT, SUMT, B, M
        READ *, N
        DO 10 I = 1, N
           READ *, A(I), T(I)
10      CONTINUE
        SUMA = 0.0
        SUMASQ = 0.0
        SUMAT = 0.0
        SUMT = 0.0
*
* COMPUTE THE LEAST - SQUARE SUMS
*
        DO 20 I = 1, N
           SUMA = SUMA + A(I)
           SUMASQ = SUMASQ + A(I) ** 2
           SUMAT = SUMAT + A(I) * T(I)
           SUMT = SUMT + T(I)
20      CONTINUE
*
* COMPUTE THE COEFFICIENTS (HAVING SOLVED THE SYSTEM
*                             OF EQS.)
*
        M = (REAL(N) * SUMAT - SUMT * SUMA) /
    $      (REAL(N) * SUMASQ - SUMA * SUMA)
        B = (SUMAT - SUMASQ * M) / SUMA
        PRINT *, 'THE LEAST-SQUARES COEFF. FOR THE DATA:'
        PRINT *, 'B = ', B, ' M = ', M
        END
```

25. a. `PRINT *, (X(I), Y(I), I = 0, M)`
   c. `PRINT *, ((A(I) + J, J = 0, 3), I = 0, 3)`

26. a. `PRINT *, (A(I,K), K = 1, N)`

28. a.
```
        DO 10, K = 1, N, 2
           READ *, (A(K, J), J = 1, N, 2)
           READ *, (A(K + 1, J), J = 2, N + 1, 2)
10      CONTINUE
```

(This assumes that N is odd and that there are N + 1 rows.)

29.
```
        PROGRAM HISTGM
***************************************************************
* COMPUTE AND PRINT A HISTOGRAM REPRESENTING THE
* RELATIVE FREQUENCIES OF INTEGER INPUT DATA READ FROM
* THE STANDARD INPUT UNIT.  RANGE OF VALUES IS
* ASSUMED TO BE 0 - 20.  IF THE LIST-DIRECTED SPACING IS
* BAD, YOU WILL HAVE TO USE FORMATTED PRINT (CHAPTER 9).
* IT IS ALSO ASSUMED THAT EACH BAR WILL FIT ON THE PAGE.
```

```
*
* MIN, MAX -- MINIMUM AND MAXIMUM VALUES OF INPUT DATA
* N -- NUMBER OF INPUT VALUES
* NUM -- CURRENT INPUT VALUE
* FREQ -- ARRAY OF FREQUENCIES
* I, K -- LOOP INDICES
****************************************************************

      INTEGER MIN, MAX, N, NUM, I, K
      PARAMETER (MIN = 0, MAX = 20)
      INTEGER FREQ (MIN:MAX)
*
* INITIALIZE FREQUENCY ARRAY
*
      DO 10 I = MIN, MAX
         FREQ(I) = 0
10    CONTINUE
*
* READ VALUES, ACCUMULATE FREQUENCIES
*
      READ *, N
      DO 20 I = 1, N
         READ *, NUM
         FREQ(NUM) = FREQ(NUM) + 1
20    CONTINUE
*
* PRINT HISTOGRAM
*
      DO 30 I = MAX, MIN, -1
         PRINT *, I, '!', ('*', K = 1, FREQ(I)), FREQ(I)
30    CONTINUE
      PRINT *, ('_', I = 1, 75)
      END
```

31. a. `INTEGER FREQ(1000)`
`DATA FREQ /1000 * 0/`

Chapter 6

1. a. 103   **c.** 63
2. a. 147; 67   **c.** 77; 2F
3. a. 111 000 111 ; 445; 1C7
  c. 110 000 000 000; 3072; C00
4. a. 1010 0000 0101; 2565; 5005
  c. 10 000 010 010 000; 8336; 20220
5. a. 1100011; 143; 63
  c. 1000000; 100; 40
6. a. 11000110   **c.** 10000010

7. **a.** 0.875   **c.** 0.61875

8. **a.** 0.7   **b.** 0.E

9. **a.** 0.111 000 010; 0.87890625
   c. 0.110 001 010; 0.76953125

10. **a.** 0.1010 1110; 0.67343750
    c. 0.1111 0000 1000; 0.959375

11. **a.** 0.111 111 010 111 . . . ; 0.7727 . . . ; 0.FD7 . . .
    c. 0.000 111 000 110 . . . ; 0.0706 . . . ; 0.1C6 . . .

12. **a.** 0.17224×10^4 **c.** 0.58294×10^{-3}

13. **a.** 0.173×10^4 **c.** 0.650×10^{-4}

16. **a.** $x \ll 1$; rewrite as $-x^2$
    c. $x \approx y \pm 2n\pi$; rewrite as $2 \sin([x - y]/2) \cos([x + y]/2)$

19.
```
        PROGRAM EVHCOS
  **************************************************************
  * PROGRAM TO COMPARE COSH WITH ITS DEFINITION USING
  * EXP(X).  PRINT BOTH VALUES AND DIFFERENCES FOR
  * X RANGING FROM -10 TO 10 IN STEPS OF .1.
  *
  * X - ARGUMENT, H - STEP, XMIN - STARTING VALUE
  * COSHA -- COSH(X) USING EXP FORMULA
  * COSHX -- INTRINSIC FUNCTION VALUE
  * DIFF -- DIFFERENCE
  * I -- LOOP INDEX
  **************************************************************
        REAL X, COSHX, COSHA, DIFF, H, XMIN
        INTEGER I
        XMIN = 10.0
        H = 0.1
        PRINT *, 'X', 'COSH (EXP)', 'COSH(X)', 'DIFFERENCE'
        DO 10 I = 0, 200
           X = XMIN + REAL(I) * H
           COSHA = 0.5 * (EXP(X) + EXP(-X))
           COSHX = COSH(X)
           DIFF = COSHA - COSHX
           PRINT *, X, COSHA, COSHX, DIFF
  10    CONTINUE
        END
```

22. Since $e^x - e^{-x} = (1 + x + \dfrac{x^2}{2!} + \cdots) - (1 - x + \dfrac{x^2}{2!} - \cdots)$

$$= 2x + 2\frac{x^3}{3!} + \cdots = 2(x + \frac{x^3}{3!} + \cdots),$$

the following procedure computes SINHX to approximately six decimal place accuracy.

```
          PROGRAM SINHP
          INTEGER N
          REAL SINH, X, EXPNEW, TERM
          PARAMETER (EPS = 0.5E-6)
          READ *, X
          TERM = X
          EXPNEW = TERM
          N = 1
  *       WHILE RELATIVE DIFFERENCE > EPS DO
  10      IF (ABS(TERM / EXPNEW) .GT. EPS) THEN
              N = N + 2
              TERM = TERM * (X * X / REAL(N * (N-1)))
              EXPNEW = EXPNEW + TERM
              GOTO 10
          ENDIF
  *       ENDWHILE
          SINH = EXPNEW
          PRINT *, 'FOR A VALUE OF: ', X
          PRINT *, 'SINH IS: ', SINH
          END
```

25. This approach yields no round off error in the value of the node.

29. The result should be zero, if your computer is capable of representing an exponent as large as 50, since the values of 812 and 511 are too small to be represented relative to 10^{50} and 10^{35} and are therefore "shifted out" during addition.

30.
```
          PROGRAM ETEST
          REAL NFAC, EM1, TERM, X, ESUM, RN1, RN2
          INTEGER N, TIMES
          PARAMETER (EM1 = 1.71828183)
          X = 1.0
          DO 20 TIMES = 1, 2
             NFAC = 1.0
             TERM = 1.0
             RN2 = EM1
             ESUM = 1.0
             DO 10 N = 1, 10 * TIMES
                 NFAC = NFAC * REAL(N)
                 TERM = TERM * (X / REAL(N))
                 ESUM = ESUM + TERM
                 RN1 = EXP(X) - ESUM
                 RN2 = REAL(N) * RN2 - X ** N
                 PRINT *, N, RN1 / NFAC, RN2 / NFAC
  10         CONTINUE
             PRINT *
  20      CONTINUE
          END
```

Chapter 7

1. a.
```
        REAL FUNCTION LOGFUN (X)
        REAL X
        LOGFUN = 1.0 / 3.0 * LOG((1.0 + COS(X)) / (1.0 - COS(X)))
        END
```

2.
```
        REAL FUNCTION INPROD (VECA, VECB, N)
        REAL VECA, VECB
        INTEGER N, I
        INPROD = 0.0
        DO 10 I = 1, N
            INPROD = INPROD + VECA(I) * VECB(I)
10      CONTINUE
        END
```

3. If the function passes very close to (i.e., within FTOL) but does not cross the axis, the program will assume, incorrectly, that there is a root at that point.

6.
```
        DOUBLE PRECISION FUNCTION TRACE (A, N, NMAX)
        DOUBLE PRECISION A(NMAX, NMAX)
        INTEGER N, NMAX, I
        TRACE = 0.0
        DO 10 I = 1, N
            TRACE = TRACE + A(I, I)
10      CONTINUE
        END
```

12.
```
        SUBROUTINE EXCHG (VECA, VECB, N)
        REAL VECA, VECB, TEMP
        INTEGER N, I
        DO 10 I = 1, N
           TEMP = VECA(I)
           VECA(I) = VECB(I)
           VECB(I) = TEMP
10      CONTINUE
        END
```

17. a.
```
        PROGRAM TRAPINT
        REAL A, B, TRAP, FUN, INTGRL
        INTEGER N
        READ *, A, B
        READ *, N
        INTGRL = TRAP(FUN, A, B, N)
        PRINT *, "FOR THE INTERVAL ', A, B
        PRINT *, 'USING ', N, ' NODES'
        PRINT *, 'THE INTEGRAL IS: ', INTGRL
        END
```

```
      REAL FUNCTION TRAP (FUNC, A, B, N)
      REAL A, B, FUNC, H, SUM
      INTEGER N, I
      SUM = 0.0
      H = (B - A) / REAL(N)
      DO 10 I = 1, N - 1
         SUM = SUM + FUNC(A + REAL(I) * H)
10    CONTINUE
      SUM = SUM + 0.5 * (FUNC(A) + FUNC(B))
      TRAP = H * SUM
      END

      REAL FUNCTION FUN(X)
      REAL X
      FUN = EXP(X)
      END
```

18. a. Replace the function FUN by

```
      REAL FUNCTION FUN (X, N)
      REAL X
      FUN = EXP(X) * COS(REAL(N) * X)
      END
```

and replace the calls to include the given values of N.

21.
```
      PROGRAM APRXFN
*****************************************************************
* APPROXIMATES FUNCTION F AT VARIOUS POINTS X USING
* LINEAR INTERPOLATION.  INTERPOLATED VALUES ARE READ FROM
* THE STANDARD INPUT UNIT.
*
* F -- ARRAY OF KNOWN FUNCTION VALUES
* NODE -- ARRAY OF POINTS WHERE F IS KNOWN
* Y -- INTERPOLATED FUNCTION VALUE
* N -- NO. OF POINTS WHERE F IS KNOWN
* NMAX -- DIMENSION OF F, NODE
* READND -- SUBROUTINE TO INITIALIZE F AND NODE
* INTERP -- FUNCTION THAT RETURNS INTERPOLATED VALUE
*****************************************************************
      INTEGER N, NMAX
      PARAMETER (NMAX = 100)
      REAL F(NMAX), NODE(NMAX)
      REAL X, Y, INTERP
      CALL READND(NODE, F, N)
*     WHILE NOT EOF DO
10    CONTINUE
         READ (*, *, END = 20) X
```

```
                          Y = INTERP(NODE, F, N, X)
                          PRINT *, 'AT X = ', X, 'F(X) = ', Y
                          GOTO 10
        *            ENDWHILE
        20           CONTINUE
                     END


                     SUBROUTINE READND (X, F, N)
                     INTEGER N, I
                     REAL X(N), F(N)
                     DO 10 I = 1, N
                          READ *, X(I), F(I)
        10           CONTINUE
                     END


                     REAL FUNCTION INTERP (NODE, F, N, X)
        *
        * ASSUMES THAT X >= NODE(1) AND X <= NODE(N)
        *
                     INTEGER N, I
                     REAL NODE(N), F(N), X
                     I = 1
        *            WHILE X NOT IN (NODE(I), NODE (I+1)) DO
        10           CONTINUE
                     IF (X .GT. NODE(I+1)) THEN
                          I = I + 1
                          GOTO 10
                     ENDIF
        *            ENDWHILE
                     INTERP = F(I + 1) * (X - NODE(I)) - F(I) *
        $                 (X - NODE(I + 1))
                     INTERP = INTERP / (NODE(I + 1) - NODE(I))
                     END
```

23. It does not check because the algorithm works even if the values of A and B are interchanged.

26. a.
```
        REAL FUNCTION INPROD
        REAL VECA(100), VECB(100)
        INTEGER N, I
        COMMON /VECTOR/ VECA, VECB, N
        INPROD = 0.0
        DO 10 I = 1, N
             INPROD = INPROD + VECA(I) * VECB(I)
10      CONTINUE
        END
```

28. b. Suppose A is dimensioned as

```
        REAL A(L1:U1, L2:U2)
```

Then

$$loc(A[I, J]) = loc(A[L1, L2]) +$$
$$(U1 - L1 + 1) * (J - L2) + (I - L1)$$

30. 1   7   1   2

Chapter 8
1. **a.** `CHARACTER * 20, INVTYP, INVPRT, CORPL`
   c. `CHARACTER *(*), PTITL`
   `PARAMETER (PTITL = 'HYDROSTATIC PRESSURE')`

2. **a.** `'SULPH'`

4. **a.** False in all cases
   d. True for EBCDIC and ASCII; false for CDC Scientific
   f. True for ASCII; false for EBCDIC and CDC Scientific
   i. False for ASCII and EBCDIC; true for CDC Scientific

9. **a.** `'STATIC_'`
   c. Undefined—the last assignment is invalid

10. **a.** `'REENGINE'`
    c. `'REENIGNE'`
    e. `'NEER____'`

11. **a.** A   a
       B   b
          ⋮
       Z   z
    c. 30   21   `IS A REAL`

13. Replace the DO 10 loop by the following:

```
        IF(TEXT(1:1) .NE. '*' .AND. TEXT(1:1) .NE. 'C'
     $     .AND. TEXT(1:1) .NE. 'c') THEN
           DO 10 I = 1, LEN(TEXT)
              L = INDEX(TEXT(I:I), ALPHLC)
              IF (L .GT. 0) THEN
                 OUTLIN(I:I) = ALPHUC(L:L)
              ELSE
                 OUTLIN(I:I) = TEXT(I:I)
              ENDIF
10         CONTINUE
        ELSE
           OUTLIN = TEXT
        ENDIF
```

```
19.         PROGRAM SHCIPH
      *****************************************************************
      * THIS PROGRAM ENCIPHERS A MESSAGE IN UPPER CASE LETTERS
      * USING A SHIFT CIPHER AND ALSO PRINTS THE DECIPHERED MESSAGE
      * FOR VERIFICATION
      *
      * SHIFT -- NUMBER OF CHARACTERS SHIFTED IN THE CIPHER SEQUENCE
      *          CHANGE IT TO CHANGE THE CIPHER. SHIFT MUST BE <= 27
      * INSTR -- ONE LINE OF THE INPUT DATA
      * OUTSTR -- ONE LINE OF THE OUTPUT DATA
      * CISEQ -- THE CIPHER SEQUENCE
      * I, K -- INDICES
      *****************************************************************
            INTEGER SHIFT, I, K
            CHARACTER * 80, INSTR, OUTSTR
            CHARACTER * 27, CISEQ
            PARAMETER (SHIFT = 6)
            CISEQ = 'ABCDEFGHIJKLMNOPQRSTUVWXYZ '
      *     WHILE SOURCE DATA REMAINS DO
      10    CONTINUE
            READ (*, *, END = 40) INSTR
               PRINT *, 'THE ORIGINAL STRING:'
               PRINT *, INSTR
      *
      * ENCIPHER THE STRING
      *
               DO 20 I = 1, LEN(INSTR)
                  K = MOD(INDEX(INSTR(I:I), CISEQ) + SHIFT,
           $              LEN(CISEQ))
                  OUTSTR(I:I) = CISEQ(K:K)
      20       CONTINUE
            PRINT *
            PRINT *, 'THE ENCIPHERED STRING:'
            PRINT *, OUTSTR
      *
      * REVERSE THE PROCESS
      *
               DO 30 I = 1, LEN(OUTSTR)
                  K = MOD(INDEX(OUTSTR(I:I), CISEQ) + LEN(CISEQ)
           $                 - SHIFT + 1, LEN(CISEQ))
                  INSTR(I:I) = CISEQ(K:K)
      30       CONTINUE
            PRINT *
            PRINT *, 'THE DECIPHERED STRING:'
            PRINT'*, INSTR
            GOTO 10
      40    CONTINUE
      *     ENDWHILE
            END
```

Chapter 9

1. a. `READ (UNIT = 6, FMT = 400, END = 900, ERR = 1000) A, B, C`

2. a. `__12345___-28_____9.24`

4. a. `_-973.8257`   **e.** `-973.825700`   **c.** `-973.`

5. a. `-0.500E+01`   **c.** `_0.527E-04`   **e.** `_0.790E+07`

7.
```
       PRINT 100, PARTNO, DESC, PRICE, WT, QTY, TOTPR, TOTWT
100    FORMAT(1X, 4X, I5, 2X, A22, 1X, F6.2, 2X, F6.3, 1X,
     $        I3, 2X, F9.2, 1X, F9.3)
```

10. a. `ABCDEFG ... Z`

11. a. `____9237____9237___9237`

   c. `SUPER MAN WOMAN MAN`

13. a. A = 79356.0, B = −2053.0, C = 812.8793

   c. A = 7.935, B = −20.53, C = 812.8793

14. a. A = 3026.15 and B = 288.3

   c. X = 30261.0, P = 2883.0, I = 2883, and J = 8830

15. a. I = 781, N = −294, and K = 503

   c. X = 7810.0, N = 45, and L = .TRUE.

16.
```
       READ(*,*,100) NAME, ADDR, CITY, STATE, ZIP, PHONE,
     $               YIORG, INTAR, SIAM, IEEE
100    FORMAT (A20, A25, A13, 1X, A2, A5, 3X, A10, I2,
     $        1X, A3, L1, L1)
```

18. a. `FORMAT(3I3)`

   c. `FORMAT(2(I3, F7.1), 2(E12.2, 2X))`

21. a. I = 107, J = 35, M = 882, N = 41

   c. I = 10, J = 73, X = 52.8, K = 88, L = 41, M = 90, N = 60

23. a.
```
       READ 200, P, Q, T, A, B, V, I, J, CH
200    FORMAT(2(F5.0, 2X), I4 / F3.0, 2X, F6.1, 3X, 2I2, A4)
```

24. a. This routine uses the TRUNC function given in Section 8.3.

```
          INTEGER LLINE, REND, TRUNC, LMARGN, I
          PARAMETER (LLINE = 80)
          CHARACTER * 80, STRING, BSTR, TEMP, OUTSTR
          CHARACTER * 1, BLANK
          PARAMETER (BLANK = ' ')
          READ 100, STRING
100       FORMAT(A)
          REND = TRUNC(STRING)
          LMARGN = (LLIN - REND) / 2
          BSTR = ''
          DO 10 I = 1, LMARGN
             TEMP = BSTR // BLANK
             BSTR = TEMP
```

```
10      CONTINUE
        OUTSTR = BSTR // STRING(1:REND)
        END
```

Chapter 10

1. a. OPEN (UNIT = 15, FILE = 'HOPFIL')

   c.
```
        OPEN (UNIT = 20, FILE = 'RANDAT', ACCESS = 'DIRECT',
     $              RECL = 450, IOSTAT = STAT)
        IF (STAT .NE. 0) GOTO 5000
```

7.
```
        PROGRAM FMERGE
***************************************************************
* THIS PROGRAM MERGES TWO SEQUENTIAL, SORTED FILES INTO A
* THIRD.  IT ASSUMES THE RECORDS ARE 80 CHARACTERS LONG AND
* HAVE AN INTEGER KEY IN COLUMNS 1-5.
*
* FILE1, FILE2 -- INPUT FILES
* OUTFIL -- OUTPUT FILE
* KEY1, KEY2 -- KEYS FOR FILES FILE1 AND FILE2
* REST1, REST2 -- REMAINING PART OF EACH RECORD
* F1READ, F2READ -- LOGICAL FLAGS -- TRUE IF A RECORD HAS BEEN
*                        READ BUT NOT WRITTEN
***************************************************************
        INTEGER KEY1, KEY2
        CHARACTER * 75, REST1, REST2
        LOGICAL F1READ, F2READ
        OPEN (10, FILE = 'FILE1')
        OPEN (20, FILE = 'FILE2')
        OPEN (30, FILE = 'OUTFIL')
        F1READ = .FALSE.
        F2READ = .FALSE.
*
* MERGE THE TWO FILES
*
*       WHILE NOT EOF (OF EITHER FILE) DO
10      CONTINUE
            IF (.NOT. F1READ) THEN
                READ (10, 100, END = 200) KEY1, REST1
100             FORMAT (I5, A)
                F1READ = .TRUE.
            ENDIF
            IF (.NOT. F2READ) THEN
                READ (20, 100, END = 200) KEY2, REST2
                F2READ = .TRUE.
            ENDIF
            IF (KEY1 .LE. KEY2) THEN
                WRITE (30, 100) KEY1, REST1
                F1READ = .FALSE.
```

```
              ELSE
                  WRITE (30, 100) KEY2, REST2
                  F2READ = .FALSE.
              ENDIF
              GOTO 10
*         ENDWHILE
200       CONTINUE
          IF (F1READ) THEN
*
* COPY REMAINDER OF FILE1
*
*             WHILE NOT EOF ON FILE1 DO
30            CONTINUE
                  WRITE (30, 100) KEY1, REST1
                  READ (10, 100, END = 300) KEY1, REST1
                  GOTO 30
*             ENDWHILE
          ELSE
*
* COPY REMAINDER OF FILE2
*
*             WHILE NOT EOF ON FILE2 DO
40            CONTINUE
                  WRITE (30, 100) KEY2, REST2
                  READ (20, 100, END = 300) KEY2, REST2
                  GOTO 40
*             ENDWHILE
          ENDIF
300       CONTINUE
          END
```

13.
```
          PROGRAM COMFIL
    ************************************************************
    * THIS PROGRAM COMPARES RECORDS FROM TWO DIRECT ACCESS FILES
    * AND WRITES ONE OF THEM TO A THIRD FILE IF THEY ARE
    * IDENTICAL, AND BOTH TO AN 'ERROR' FILE IF THEY ARE NOT.
    *
    * IT IS ASSUMED THAT BOTH FILES ARE OF THE SAME LENGTH,
    * AND THAT THE RECORDS ARE CHARACTER STRINGS OF THE SAME
    * LENGTH AS THE RECORD.
    *
    * RECNO -- RECORD NUMBER
    * RECLEN -- RECORD LENGTH
    * FILE1, FILE2, OUTFIL, ERRFIL -- INPUT FILES (2), OUTPUT
    *                                 FILE, ERROR FILE, RESP.
    ************************************************************
          INTEGER RECNO, RECLEN
          CHARACTER * 120, REC1, REC2
```

```
          PARAMETER (RECLEN = 120)
          RECNO = 1
          OPEN (UNIT = 15, FILE = 'FILE1', ACCESS = 'SEQUENTIAL',
     $        RECL = RECLEN, STATUS = 'OLD')
          OPEN (UNIT = 16, FILE = 'FILE2', ACCESS =
     $        'DIRECT', RECL = RECLEN, STATUS = 'OLD')
          OPEN (UNIT = 17, FILE = 'OUTFIL', ACCESS =
     $        'DIRECT', RECL = RECLEN, STATUS = 'NEW')
          OPEN (UNIT = 18, FILE = 'ERRFIL', ACCESS =
     $        'SEQUENTIAL', STATUS = 'NEW')
*         WHILE NOT EOF DO
10        CONTINUE
             READ (15, END = 20) REC1
             READ (16, REC = RECNO) REC2
             IF (REC1 .EQ. REC2) THEN
                WRITE (17, REC = RECNO) REC1
             ELSE
                WRITE (18, 100) RECNO, REC1
                WRITE (18, 100) RECNO, REC2
100             FORMAT (I5, 1X, A)
             ENDIF
             RECNO = RECNO + 1
             GOTO 10
*         ENDWHILE
20        CONTINUE
          CLOSE (15)
          CLOSE (16)
          CLOSE (17)
          CLOSE (18)
          END


17.       SUBROUTINE CVTSSN (SSN, SSN1, SSN2, SSN3)
*****************************************************************
* THIS ROUTINE CONVERTS A SOCIAL SECURITY NUMBER
* IN THE FORM OF A CHARACTER STRING 'XXX-XX-XXXX' TO
* THREE INTEGERS REPRESENTING THE THREE PARTS.
*
* SSN - THE ORIGINAL STRING
* SSN1, SSN2, SSN3 - THE THREE INTEGER PARTS OF SSN
*****************************************************************
          CHARACTER * 11 SSN
          INTEGER SSN1, SSN2, SSN3
          READ (UNIT = SSN, FMT = 100) SSN1, SSN2, SSN3
100       FORMAT (I3, 1X, I2, 1X, I4)
          RETURN
          END
```

Index